# The Presidency of
# GEORGE W.
# BUSH

AMERICAN PRESIDENCY SERIES

*Clifford S. Griffin, Donald R. McCoy, and Homer E. Socolofsky, Founding Editors*

*George Washington*, Forrest McDonald
*John Adams*, Ralph Adams Brown
*Thomas Jefferson*, Forrest McDonald
*James Madison*, Robert Allen Rutland
*James Monroe*, Noble E. Cunningham, Jr.
*John Quincy Adams*, Mary W. M. Hargreaves
*Andrew Jackson*, Donald B. Cole
*Martin Van Buren*, Major L. Wilson
*William Henry Harrison & John Tyler*, Norma Lois Peterson
*James K. Polk*, Paul H. Bergeron
*Zachary Taylor & Millard Fillmore*, Elbert B. Smith
*Franklin Pierce*, Larry Gara
*James Buchanan*, Elbert B. Smith
*Abraham Lincoln*, Phillip Shaw Paludan
*Andrew Johnson*, Albert Castel
*Ulysses S. Grant*, Charles W. Calhoun
*Rutherford B. Hayes*, Ari Hoogenboom
*James A. Garfield & Chester A. Arthur*, Justus D. Doenecke
*Grover Cleveland*, Richard E. Welch, Jr.
*Benjamin Harrison*, Homer B. Socolofsky & Allan B. Spetter
*William McKinley*, Lewis L. Gould
*William Howard Taft*, Lewis L. Gould
*Theodore Roosevelt*, Second Edition, Lewis L. Gould
*Woodrow Wilson*, Kendrick A. Clements
*Warren G. Harding*, Eugene P. Trani & David L. Wilson
*Calvin Coolidge*, Robert H. Ferrell
*Herbert C. Hoover*, Martin L. Fausold
*Franklin Delano Roosevelt*, George McJimsey
*Harry S. Truman*, Donald R. McCoy
*Dwight D. Eisenhower*, Second Edition, Chester J. Pach, Jr., & Elmo Richardson
*John F. Kennedy*, Second Edition, James N. Giglio
*Lyndon B. Johnson*, Vaughn Davis Bornet
*Richard Nixon*, Melvin Small
*Gerald R. Ford*, John Robert Greene
*James Earl Carter, Jr.*, Second Edition, Burton I. Kaufman & Scott Kaufman
*George H. W. Bush*, Second Edition, Revised, John Robert Greene
*George W. Bush*, John Robert Greene

The Presidency of
# GEORGE W.
# BUSH

*John Robert Greene*

UNIVERSITY PRESS OF KANSAS

Published by the University Press of Kansas (Lawrence, Kansas 66045),
which was organized by the Kansas Board of Regents and is operated and funded
by Emporia State University, Fort Hays State University, Kansas State University,
Pittsburg State University, the University of Kansas, and Wichita State University.

Library of Congress Cataloging-in-Publication Data

Names: Greene, John Robert, 1955– author.
Title: The presidency of George W. Bush / John Robert Greene.
Description: Lawrence, Kansas : University Press of Kansas, 2021. | Series:
American presidency series | Includes bibliographical references and
index.
Identifiers: LCCN 2021012544
ISBN 9780700632688 (cloth)
ISBN 9780700632695 (ebook)
Subjects: LCSH: Bush, George W. (George Walker), 1946– | Presidents—
United States—Biography. | United States—Politics and government—2001–2009.
| United States—Foreign relations—2001–2009. | United States—
Economic policy—2001–2009.
Classification: LCC E903 .G74 2021 | DDC 973.931092 [B]—dc23
LC record available at https://lccn.loc.gov/2021012544.

British Library Cataloguing-in-Publication Data is available.

Printed in the United States of America

10 9 8 7 6 5 4 3 2 1

The paper used in this publication is acid free and meets the minimum
requirements of the American National Standard for Permanence of Paper
for Printed Library Materials Z39.48-1992.

For Oliver William Greene

# CONTENTS

*Photo gallery follows page 156.*

# FOREWORD

The aim of the American Presidency Series is to present historians and the general reading public with interesting, scholarly assessments of the various presidential administrations. These interpretive surveys are intended to cover the broad ground between biographies, specialized monographs, and journalistic accounts. As such, each will be a comprehensive work which will draw upon original sources and pertinent secondary literature, yet leave room for the author's own analysis and interpretation.

Volumes in the series will present the data essential to understanding the administration under consideration. Particularly, each book will treat the then current problems facing the United States and its people and how the president and his associates felt about, thought about, and worked to cope with these problems. Attention will be given to how the office developed and operated during the president's tenure. Equally important will be consideration of the vital relationships between the president, his staff, the executive officers, Congress, foreign representatives, the judiciary, state officials, the public, political parties, the press, and influential private citizens. The series will also be concerned with how this unique American institution—the presidency—was viewed by the presidents, and with what results.

All this will be set, insofar as possible, in the context not only of contemporary politics but also of economics, international relations, law, morals, public administration, religion, and thought. Such a broad approach is necessary to understanding, for a presidential administration is more than the elected and appointed officers composing it, since its work so often reflects the major problems, anxieties, and glories of the nation. In short, the authors in this series will strive to recount and evaluate the record of each administration and to identify its distinctiveness and relationships to the past, its own time, and the future.

*The General Editors*

# PREFACE

Life lessons come at you at the strangest times. One afternoon in early September 1978, I attended my first class as a doctoral candidate. The professor, a well-published gentleman who specialized in early colonial history, sized up the five students, each of whom had declared their field of interest in modern American political history. After some opening pleasantries, he looked at us and softly growled, "Nothing that happened after 1776 is history. It's all just current events." Hyperbolic instructional melodrama, to be sure—but there is a grain of truth to the observation. While there has long been a healthy debate over how far removed a professional historian has to be from a person or an event before they can properly draw a judgment, there can be little doubt that works of "instant history"—like those books, articles, press accounts, and internet observations written, for example, while a president is in office—do not have the proper distance from their subject to be classified as solid historical analysis.

But a decade would seem to offer a reasonable space of time, after which preliminary judgments might be more balanced. It has now been thirteen years since the end of the presidency of George W. Bush, who served from 20 January 2001 to 20 January 2009. It has also been eight years since the George W. Bush Presidential Library opened to scholars in 2013. The records of the Bush administration, as well as other archives around the country, are slowly being made available for professional scrutiny. They can now provide a welcomed addition to the preliminary literature on the Bush administration and can only add to our understanding of the most tumultuous presidency of the modern period.

When one mentions the name of the forty-third president of the United States, the first thing that comes into most people's minds is a grotesque visual, one that is firmly stamped in the minds of anyone who was of age on 11 September 2001—that of two commercial airliners exploding, as they rammed the World Trade Center in New York City. The attacks of 9/11 and the resulting War on Terror are, indeed, the defining events of the administration of the second Bush, and these pages will utilize newly available documents to explore the result of those events. But unlike much of the earlier literature on the topic, this book will not judge the Bush presidency based solely on its handling of the War on Terror. As is the goal of this series—one in which I have been privileged to publish two other volumes—the goal of this book is to provide the reader with a detailed overview, and an analysis of, the whole of the presidency of George W. Bush. Along with national security issues, other topics—domestic policies, economic policies, social welfare policies—are covered here. My judgments on that presidency have been informed not just by the existing literature but also by newly available archival material, housed primarily at the Bush Library but also in several other repositories—the first scholarly work on the second Bush to be so sourced.

I hope that in writing this book, I have utilized time and distance to my advantage as a scholar. Having worked on this project for more than eight years, I have had time not only to collect much new information but to digest it and process my conclusions. The reader will find that this led to my disagreeing with the hyperbolic conclusions of much of the early literature on the Bush presidency. In addition, I hope that having the luxury of historical distance and a wider array of sources will allow for more measured, balanced, and—one would hope—accurate conclusions, so that the reader might better understand the pivotal importance of this first American presidency of the twenty-first century.

Working toward these goals for the better part of eight years, one naturally incurs many debts. I must first express my gratitude for the valuable contributions made by the authors and scholars who have already studied the Bush administration. I have offered my analysis of these works in the bibliographical essay.

I am also grateful to have had the opportunity to utilize the documents housed at the George W. Bush Presidential Library, many of which are utilized in this volume for the first time. The staff at the Bush Library made the many research trips a pleasure—I thank library director Brig.

Gen. Patrick X. Mordente and Allen Almodovar, Virginia Butler, Malisa Culpepper, Rachel Friend, Tally Fugate, Shirley Kolling, Elizabeth Lanier, Eric McCrory, Sarah Quick, Paul Santa Cruz, Jill Zawacki, and Brandon Zogg. I also am appreciative of the willingness of many researchers to submit Freedom of Information Act (FOIA) requests for material in the Bush Presidential Records—their efforts led to the opening of new material that all scholars, including myself, can utilize.

Other archives and archivists were as quick to assist me in this project: Edith A. Sandler at the Library of Congress; university archivist Dan Linke, April Armstrong, and Crista Cleeton at the Seeley G. Mudd Manuscripts Library, Princeton University; Mary Finch at the George H. W. Bush Presidential Library; and Tonia J. Wood, senior reference archivist at the Texas State Library and Archives Commission.

I cannot thank enough those who agreed to be interviewed for this work. They include Ambassador L. Paul Bremer III, Andrew J. Card Jr., B. Alexander "Sandy" Kress, Jay Lefkowitz, Vice Admiral John M. McConnell, John McLaughlin, Terry Nelson, Karl Rove, Frances Townsend, and Tevi Troy. All interviews were recorded; all recordings will be donated to the George W. Bush Presidential Library.

Two programs deserve the thanks of all modern historians. Since 1982, the Hofstra University Cultural Center, in conjunction with the Departments of History and Political Science of that institution, has put on a series of conferences dealing with the modern American presidency. Scholars, administration alumni, and often the president himself get together for a series of valuable discussion sessions. On 24–26 March 2015, Hofstra put on a conference dealing with the presidency of George W. Bush. Recordings of selected conference sessions are available at https://www.hofstra.edu/community/culctr/gwb/gwb-video.html. The second is the Miller Center at the University of Virginia, which houses one of the nation's premier oral history programs on the American presidency. At the time of this writing, the Miller Center has released forty-six of these interviews dealing with the presidency of George W. Bush. They can be found at https://millercenter.org/the-presidency/presidential-oral-histories/george-w-bush.

I have been fortunate—and, given the demographics of academia, somewhat unique—to have worked at only one institution for the first forty-two years of my career. I have many friends at Cazenovia College, and many of them helped me with this work. I particularly want to thank President Ronald Chesbrough, vice president for academic affairs Sharon

Dettmer, administrative assistant Rebekah Beckwith, and division chair Stewart Weisman for their consistent support of this project. My thanks to the staff at my home library, the Terry Library at Cazenovia College's Witherill Learning Center: director Heather Whalen Smith and Judy Azzoto, Lauren Michel, and Sarah O'Neill. My computer only works because of my friends in Information and Computer Technologies: director David Palmer and Bryant Beers, Sue Bock, Michael Cameron, Kelly Cresswell, Will Gordon, Duane Heishman, Genevieve Phillips, and Lee Tietje. Several talented undergraduates also contributed to this work. Robert Foster's research and writing on the election of 2000 were particularly useful, and I thank Kyle Durkee and Abby House for their assistance in transcribing several recorded interviews, as well as Alexandra Maassmann for research assistance.

This will be my sixth book with the University Press of Kansas. I owe any success I have had as a published author to my good friend emeritus director Fred Woodward, who encouraged this project from its inception in 2015, as he has each of my books with UPK. Upon Fred's retirement, support for my work did not waver. Chuck Myers listened to my concerns with a quiet, sympathetic ear as the book began to evolve. Acquisitions editor David Congdon was equally supportive (and illustrated the maxim of patience being a virtue as my work blew through several deadlines). Susan Ecklund again improved my prose with a great copyedit; Kelly Chrisman Jacques again turned my prose into a book; Karl Janssen again designed a wonderful cover; and Mike Kehoe again saw to it that the world knew about this book. Together they create a supportive environment for an author—I am proud to be a UPK author.

The Cazenovia College Faculty Development Fund was instrumental in helping me obtain the photos found in this volume. I am also grateful to the George W. Bush Presidential Library and Museum, the George H. W. Bush Presidential Library and Museum, and Reuters Pictures for their permission to use these photos. I am also indebted to Erin Greb Cartography for creating the maps found in this volume.

I came to better understand George W. Bush by traveling to Texas, both to utilize the Bush Library and to interview many of those close to him and his administration. Those several months of trips would not have been possible without the consistent hospitality of the Kibby and Usrey families (thanks to whom I went to my first—and probably last—professional rodeo).

Several people read portions of this manuscript and gave me their unvarnished view of my shortcomings. I particularly want to thank the two anonymous readers for the University Press of Kansas; their forthright and thoughtful comments helped to shape the manuscript into a better book. I also wish to thank Sherrie and Ken Kubiak, both of whom commented on the early chapters of this work. While I have always thought it a bit redundant for an author to announce that "all judgments and mistakes in this book are mine and mine alone," let it be said anyway.

Ultimate thanks must go to my family, who after four decades understand the commitment of time and attention that is necessary to write a book. I cannot thank Patty, T.J., Kate, Chris, Jenny, and Mary Rose enough, and it is to Oliver that this book is dedicated.

*Chittenango, New York*
*2021*

The Presidency of
GEORGE W.
BUSH

# 1

★ ★ ★ ★ ★

# GEORGIE

George Herbert Walker Bush—the second of two sons, future president of the United States, and future father of a president of the United States—was born in Milton, Massachusetts, on 12 June 1924. He attended the tony Greenwich Country Day School and boarded at the Phillips Academy, an all-boys prep school twenty miles north of Boston that all Ivy League hopefuls referred to by its location—Andover. The president of his graduating class and assured of a place in his father's investment banking business, Bush took another path. Profoundly affected, as were many young men of his generation, by the Japanese attack on Pearl Harbor on 7 December 1941, he lost no time in finding his way into the ensuing conflict. Deferring his acceptance to Yale University, Bush enlisted in the navy on 12 June 1942—his eighteenth birthday. He trained to become a fighter pilot; when he earned his wings, he was the youngest pilot in the navy. On 2 September 1944, after flying forty-nine successful missions, Bush and his two-man crew came under enemy fire near Chichi Jima, an island some 150 miles north of Iwo Jima. His crew perished, but Bush parachuted into the shark-infested Pacific Ocean. There he drifted for half an hour until the crew of the USS *Finback*, a submarine patrolling the waters, rescued him.[1]

Although he had fulfilled his term of service, Bush never considered leaving the navy until the war was over. Immediately following his ordeal, he returned to his squadron and served for three more months of combat

1

missions. He then took a leave of absence, returned home on 6 June 1945 to marry his sweetheart, Barbara Pierce, and made plans to return to the Pacific. However, the events of early August 1945 made his reenlistment moot. At war's end, he had flown fifty-eight missions, accrued 1,228 hours of flying time, and earned the Distinguished Flying Cross.[2]

Bush joined the largest group of returning veterans in our nation's history—close to 15.7 million strong—that became known as the "G.I. Bulge." All were looking to reenter society and make a better life for themselves than they, children of depression and war, had previously known. Many wanted to enter the workforce forthwith. A surprising number—close to 7.8 million by 1947—wanted to go to college. The Servicemen's Readjustment Act of 1944, better known as the G.I. Bill, allowed them to do so. While he was not in need of government funds to further his education, Bush lost little time in joining his mates in the classroom, finally accepting Yale's offer to matriculate in the fall of 1945. There, he played baseball, made Phi Beta Kappa, and pledged the supersecret Skull and Bones society. He and Barbara also began a family. On 6 July 1946—the first year of the postwar baby boom—their first son was born. George Walker Bush was named for his father and his great-grandfather; despite the predilection of the press in later life to call him "Junior," he wasn't one (when writing a biography of his father in 2014, he asked his mother why he hadn't been named George H. W. Bush Jr.; she quipped, "Son, most forms don't have room for five names").[3]

The Bush family lived in New Haven for another two years; Bush graduated from Yale with a degree in economics in June 1948. Rejecting offers of certain comfort and security in various parts of the family business in the Northeast, Bush chose instead to cast his lot with thousands of other adventurous and ambitious young men and women who flocked to Texas to try their hand in the booming oil industry. In the summer of 1948, the Bushes moved to Odessa, Texas, a blue-collar town of about thirty thousand people that stank of oil and gas fumes but that promised a quick payoff—62,249,000 barrels of oil were extracted from Odessa in 1948 alone. Bush began his work for Dresser Industries as a clerk. His living conditions were Spartan, to say the least—the Bushes rented a small duplex and shared a bathroom with a mother and daughter who worked as prostitutes.[4]

The Bushes were not in Odessa long. For a year, starting in April 1949, Bush worked for Dresser at four different cities in California. But in April 1950 he and his family (now larger, with the addition of daughter Pauline

Robinson—"Robin"—born in December 1949) returned to Texas. Midland was located some twenty-three miles northwest of Odessa and midway (thus the name) between El Paso and Fort Worth. There, Bush formed the Bush-Overby Oil Development Company, which morphed into Zapata Petroleum in 1952. Bush was now part of the golden age of oil exploration in Midland. By 1950, 215 oil companies had offices in the town, whose population would skyrocket from 21,713 in 1950 to 62,625 in 1960. It existed for oil, serving as the hub of the oil boom centered in Texas's Permian Basin, which chugged out close to 20 percent of all oil used by Americans in the 1950s. Less of a blue-collar town than Odessa, Midland was home to the managers, geologists, and oil company executives—thus the saying, "Raise hell in Odessa; raise a family in Midland." The terrain surrounding the city was flat and unforgiving, often seared by drought. The nearest town (excepting Odessa) was a two-hour drive away, and the work offered no real security—oil wells either came in or failed, and failure was a harsh master. But Bush had a safety net that most wildcatters did not—a family of means who came to his aid often. Thus, Bush never really shed his eastern roots. He was a true hybrid—in Texas-speak, a "transplant"—born of northeastern privilege and a Texas wildcatter by choice. This would harden into a duality of personality that biographer Herbert S. Parmet labeled that of a "Lone Star Yankee."[5]

Little George, as he was known to his family, or, as his father referred to him in his correspondence with friends, "Georgie," was no transplant. He was a Texan through and through. He was four years old when the family moved to Midland, and the experience in West Texas would be the first great sculptor of the boy. For the younger Bush, his early life in Midland was, in his later words, "comfortable, carefree . . . [and] idyllic." While the town is Sahara-like in its climate and oil-obsessed in its attitude, Bush nevertheless waxed poetic about its beauty in the first volume of his memoirs: "When you step outside in Midland, Texas, your horizons suddenly expand. The sky is huge. The land is flat, with not even the hint of a hill to limit the view. The air is clean and bright. The impression is one of the sky as a huge canopy that seems to stretch forever." Yet Midland's beauty formed only a part of Bush's memory. He also remembered that Midland offered him the security blanket of growing up in a small town. Bush remembered a setting where he could ride his bike downtown to see a movie; where the children walked to school; where the entire town spent Friday nights cheering on the high school football team; and where all the mothers stayed home and were there for their children at the end of the day. To Bush, his home was "a small town with small town values. . . . No one locked their doors. . . . It was a happy childhood."[6]

The younger Bush would also come to see his formative experience in Midland as being the great separator between himself and his father. Whenever anyone asked about the differences between him and his father, he would habitually reply with the same line: "I went to Sam Houston Elementary school in Midland, Texas, and he went to Greenwich Country Day School in Connecticut." From an early age, the son was completely without his father's patrician manners. Where the father was often smooth and erudite, the son was just as often rough-hewn and crude. Indeed, Georgie was a born troublemaker who was described by his father as follows in a letter to a friend: "Georgie has grown to be a near-man, talks dirty once in a while and occasionally swears, aged 4½. He lives in his cowboy boots." One biographer believes that this was all an act—that the younger Bush became adept at assuming the persona of a good ol' boy. But there is little evidence of this. Indeed, most observers agreed that young George was more like his often irreverent and blunt mother than he was his reserved father. But father and son did share one passion. Renouncing the Texas fixation with football, the son adopted his father's love of baseball. Georgie was a Little League catcher (his father was, for a time, his team's coach). He collected baseball cards, read the sports columns, and memorized player stats. His favorite player was Willie Mays.[7]

They also shared in a traumatic family loss. In spring 1953, Georgie's sister Robin was diagnosed with an advanced case of leukemia. Her parents decided to treat the three-year-old child at Memorial Sloan Kettering Cancer Center in New York City, hoping to lessen her agony and save her life. Neither happened. Barbara stayed with the child, Bush commuted to New York on weekends, and seven-and-a-half-year-old George—who had not been told about his sister's condition—stayed back in Midland with neighbors and a family nurse (as did his baby brother John Ellis, or "Jeb," who had been born some two months before Robin received her diagnosis). After seven excruciating months (twenty-eight-year-old Barbara's hair turned white during the ordeal), Robin died at Sloan Kettering on 11 October 1953. A picture of her two brothers hung above her hospital bed.[8]

Georgie learned of his sister's passing almost by accident, when he ran out of his elementary school to meet his parent's car, thinking he saw his sister in the back seat, only to be told she had died. His mother justified keeping her son in the dark by telling herself that "we thought he was too young to know." Nevertheless, he was devastated both by the news and by his parents' secrecy—repeating over and over to them, "Why didn't you tell me?" As he would later remember, "Those minutes remain the starkest memory of my childhood."[9]

The family mourned in stoic silence. The elder Bush threw himself into his work. But Barbara grieved through her eldest son. Suffering from periodic bouts of depression, she overwhelmed Georgie with the time and attention she felt she had been denying him, to the point that, as he remembered later, "She kind of smothered me, then realized it was the wrong thing to do." He would later recall that "after seven months of staying strong, . . . [she] cratered." One day, Barbara found her son and told him she needed to go to the doctor; on the way, she told him that she had just had a miscarriage. To add to the shock, she showed her son the fetus, which she had saved in a jar to take to the hospital. But despite such terrible grief, the Bush family did, indeed, grow; Neil was born in 1955; Marvin, in 1956; and finally Dorothy ("Doro"), in 1959.[10]

As the Bush family boomed, so too did Texas oil. And the future of the oil business was in offshore drilling. In 1958 Zapata Oil split in half; the following year, Bush took his half to Houston. Bush enrolled his eldest son at Houston's Kinkaid School, a private, coed school. In 1998, as his son prepared his own run for the presidency, the senior Bush tried to make stories about his son's adolescent life disappear by writing to *Time* magazine columnist Hugh Sidey that all the stories about his Georgie's misspent youth were "pure nuts." They weren't. The teenage Bush developed into a full-bore hellion. He took to sneaking a smoke and killed his sister's goldfish by pouring vodka into the fishbowl. He greeted an elderly parishioner at a church picnic with the decidedly casual, "Hiya little lady, lookin' sexy!" He was involved in two car wrecks, then he borrowed his father's car, put it into reverse, and accidentally ripped off the door. Any reader with children will instantly empathize with young Bush's exasperated father, who in a letter to his own father-in-law wrote, "Georgie aggravates the hell out of me at times (I am sure I do the same to him), but then at times I am so proud of him I could die."[11]

In the fall of 1961, after completing the ninth grade at Kinkaid, the fifteen-year-old Bush followed in his father's footsteps and was enrolled at Andover. It was not Georgie's choice—he saw it as a banishment ("I liked Kinkaid, but the decision had been made. Andover was a family tradition.

I was going"). Once he got there, the teenage Texan was lost. He knew that he did not fit in; he felt, in his own description, "isolated." For a growing boy, Andover presented yet another problem—"there were no women."[12]

Georgie was soon acting out again. Andover's motto—*Non Sibi*, "Not for Self"—meant little to the hell-raising Texas teen. He flaunted his disobedience of the school's dress code, choosing instead to wear jeans, sneakers, and an army jacket. Even his choice of extracurricular activity was one that befitted an extrovert—as head cheerleader, he once performed in a skit as a girl in a sweater while mocking the opposing team. His nickname was well-earned: "The Lip." But Andover also brought out a more reflective side of the teen. He intervened on behalf of a classmate thought to be gay and who was being bullied by the other boys by throwing down the challenge, demanding, "Why don't you try walking in his shoes and seeing how it feels?" As Bush later recalled, when, at the age of eighteen, he graduated from Andover in the spring of 1964, the feeling he had was "like ridding myself of a straitjacket."[13]

While his son was suffering at Andover, the elder Bush began his political career. In 1964, Bush ran for the US Senate seat then held by Ralph Yarborough. That summer, Georgie joined his father on the retail campaign, driving with him on the Texas backroads from town to town. He also did research at his father's campaign headquarters. Four months before the election, Georgie left his father's campaign to begin his freshman year at Yale University. He had originally chosen the school because he could room with his close friend from Fort Worth, Clay Johnson, who had also attended Andover. Despite his rather average high school grades, the young legacy had no trouble getting in—when asked on his admissions form to list relatives who had attended Yale, Bush provided a list that ran two pages.[14]

It was Andover redux. Once again, the young Texan was isolated; once again, he distinguished himself not by his performance as a history major but by acting out. Bush pledged, and would eventually become president of, the hell-raisers of Delta Kappa Epsilon, the "Dekes." He and his fraternity brothers engaged in sophomoric hijinks. They stole a Christmas wreath from a hotel and escaped being charged with disorderly conduct only because they apologized. After coming home drunk from a party in his freshman year, Bush shouted to a friend, "Let's rock and roll! You rock, and I'll roll!" He then dropped to the ground and proceeded to roll toward home. After tearing down the goalposts after a game at Princeton (inspired, as he later remembered, by "more than a little booze"), Bush was shown the door by the local constabulary and told that he was no longer welcome in that town. The hijinks could also be more serious. In 1967 the Dekes branded forty pledges by searing the Greek letter delta into their skin with a hot coat hanger. When asked about the incident by the *Yale Daily News*, brother Bush dismissed the concern, claiming that the branding had caused "only a cigarette burn."[15]

In the fall of 1964, Lyndon Johnson not only won his own term as president by a landslide but also piloted the Democratic ship to victory in most races. This included the Senate race in Texas, where the senior Bush lost to Yarborough. Georgie took his father's defeat hard. To get him some help in working his way through the loss, Bush's father suggested to his son that he visit Yale's chaplain, William Sloane Coffin. On its face, the advice made sense. The senior Bush counted Coffin as a friend—they had attended Andover and Yale together, and Bush had sponsored Coffin for Skull and Bones. But Coffin had evolved beyond the strictures of Yale conservatism. When the junior Bush went to see him, Coffin snapped: "I knew your father, and your father lost to the better man." Both Bushes were furious with Coffin; the younger Bush blamed Yale. He would long keep his antipathy for his alma mater. When contacted by Clay Johnson in 1993 and asked for a donation, Bush acidly replied, "I want to give nothing." Moreover, the incident soured him on academia in general; he would later remember that Coffin's "self-righteous attitude was a foretaste of the vitriol that would emanate from many college professors during my presidency."[16]

But, for now, Bush was a Yale man. His summers were filled with various jobs—a messenger at Baker, Botts, Shepherd and Coates (the law firm of family friend James A. Baker III); a salesman at Sears and Roebuck; a ranch hand in Arizona; and a roughneck at a drilling company. They were also punctuated with romance. In his junior year, Bush became engaged to Caroline Wolfman, who attended Rice University in Houston. By the following year, however, the romance, doomed by distance, fell apart.[17]

About those years, Georgie would remember, with some amount of understatement, that "it was a confusing and disturbing time." Over the course of Bush's four years, Yale had changed from a largely conservative environ of the privileged to a hotbed of antiwar sentiment and protest. As he approached the end of his tenure in New Haven, Bush faced the question that hounded many young men of the Vietnam generation—what to do about military service. Bush remembered emphatically: "I knew I would serve. Leaving the country to avoid the draft was not an option for me; I was too conservative and too traditional." One of Bush's friends put a decidedly less lofty spin on Bush's reasoning, telling a biographer that Bush decided to serve so as not to disrupt his father's political career.[18]

Regardless of his reasoning, Bush decided not to wait to be drafted, but to be proactive. He thought that "flying planes would be an exciting way to serve." But Bush did not volunteer for service in the US Air Force. Rather, he joined the Texas Air National Guard. The story of both Bush's acceptance and his service in the Guard is decidedly muddy. Let us begin with the tale that Bush tells through his memoirs. Bush remembered that after telling his parents of his interest in flying, his father, who had been elected to Congress in 1966, contacted family friend and prominent Houston business executive Sidney Adger. As Bush later remembered it, it was Adger who recommended that he join the Guard. Following up on Adger's advice, in January 1968 Bush took his pilot aptitude test at Westover Air Force Base in Chicopee, Massachusetts. Armed with his test scores, on 27 May 1968, several weeks before his graduation from Yale, he presented himself at Ellington Air Force Base in Houston, where he met Col. William "Buck" Staudt and requested permission to join the Texas Air National Guard. That same day, Bush took the oath as a second lieutenant—twelve days before he was to formally lose his student draft deferment.[19]

However, this is not the complete story of Bush's acceptance into the National Guard. His scores on the aptitude test were borderline at best—his 25 percent total was defined by the Guard as "barely passing." Thus, the question becomes how Bush, with such middling scores, was bumped ahead of other young men who had done better on their entrance exams and was accepted into a branch of the military that all but guaranteed he would not see action in Vietnam. Ben Barnes, a Democrat who was then serving as the youngest Speaker of the Texas House in that state's history, offers an answer to that question. Barnes remembered that from his position, he had been able to help "a couple of dozen young men—boys from political families, some from wealthy families, and even a few Dallas Cowboys football players—avoid service in Vietnam by pulling strings to get them into the National Guard." Knowing of this, Adger contacted Barnes and asked for a favor—his help in getting the marginally qualified George W. Bush into the Texas Air National Guard. According to Barnes, the reason for the request was simple: "If I could help Bush jump ahead in line, it would ensure he wouldn't get sent to Vietnam." Barnes made it clear that neither the senior nor the junior Bush contacted him directly; he further contended that he did not know if Adger had spoken to the senior Bush. But regardless, Barnes was inclined to grant the favor. Indeed, even though he was a Democrat, Barnes remembered it as being "a simple political favor of the kind that might one day pay back a dividend or two. And I'm embarrassed to say that I really didn't think anything more of it than that." Barnes recalled that after meeting with Adger, he called Gen. James Rose of the Texas Air National Guard and recommended that young Bush be given a place. He was in.[20]

In June 1968 Bush graduated from Yale. The next month, he began his six-week basic training at Lackland Air Force Base in San Antonio. Just before he finished basic, however, he asked for and was granted a leave of absence to work on the Florida Senate race of Edward Gurney. Following Gurney's victory, Bush began thirteen months of flight training at Moody Air Force Base in Valdosta, Georgia. Bush genuinely enjoyed flying. He learned the ropes on a Cessna T-41 Mescalero trainer, advancing to a T-38 Talon trainer to complete his preparation. In December 1969, Bush graduated from flight school. His father, then mulling over a second run at the Senate, was the keynote speaker at the graduation and proudly pinned wings on his son. Bush was then assigned to the 147th Reconnaissance Wing at Ellington Air Force Base, where he learned to fly the F-102A Delta Dagger Interceptor. Although Bush fulfilled his active-duty commitment to the Guard in June 1970, he continued flying F-102s at Ellington on weekends and also flew out of the 187th Fighter Wing of the Alabama National Guard from late 1972 to early 1973. [21]

In the spring of 1972, Jimmy Allison, a Bush family friend from Midland who had managed the senior Bush's 1964 and 1966 campaigns for the House, arranged for the younger Bush to serve as the political director for the Alabama Senate campaign of Winton Blount, then serving as Nixon's postmaster general. So that Bush could work closely with the campaign, a transfer was effectuated. Bush was allowed to move to Montgomery, Alabama, with the condition that he was to continue his Guard commitment there. Bush remembered in the second volume of his memoirs that he had informed his commanders that he was going to miss "several meetings during the campaign." Miss them, he did; however, Bush could not keep Blount from losing big to incumbent John Sparkman.[22]

On 21 November 1974, Bush received an honorable discharge. But this would not be the end of the story of Bush's service in the National Guard.

As Bush progressed through his Guard commitment, his father's career progressed at an accelerated rate. In 1970, at the request of the Nixon White House, Bush gave up his safe congressional seat and ran for the US Senate from Texas. His son had finished his active-duty commitment to the Guard, and that summer he joined his father's campaign. While living in Houston and flying out of Ellington on the weekends, young Bush made stump speeches for his father, often appearing in his leather flight jacket. However, his father lost to moderate Democrat Lloyd Bentsen. Bush's consolation prize from Nixon was the ambassadorship to the United Nations, a position he took over in early 1971.[23]

Bush enjoyed his time on his father's congressional and Senate campaigns, as well as his time with the Gurney and Blount campaigns, but there were few career opportunities for sons of ambassadors who had volunteered for local campaigns. He flailed around for almost two years. He applied to the law school at the University of Texas, but his application was denied. He worked at a Houston agribusiness company. He also worked at an unpaid position at a Houston antipoverty program, the Professional United Leadership League (PULL), founded by a former Houston Oilers football player. Working at PULL was a challenge, as Bush was exposed to a level of poverty that he had never experienced. He remembered playing in a pickup basketball game, where one of the players fell after taking a shot, and a gun tumbled out of his pocket; he also remembered buying a pair of shoes for a boy who showed up to the center one day with bare feet because he could not afford shoes. Bush indeed had some success working with these troubled teens—a colleague remembered that "he was the first white boy the kids really loved." He talked of going to South Africa to challenge apartheid (an early indication, perhaps, of the important status that Africa would have in Bush's heart and in his administration) and even thought about running for the Texas State Senate in 1972, ultimately deciding against it.[24]

But nothing stuck. He continued to drift, and alcohol continued to fuel many of his adventures. One such exploit took place over Christmas break in 1972, when, after obliterating a neighbor's garbage can with the family car after a night of revelry, the twenty-six-year-old Bush almost came to blows with his father, who was now serving as the chairman of the Republican National Committee and had become the chief public defender of the embattled Richard Nixon. Legend has it that the drunken son accosted his father with the slurred challenge, "You want to go mano a mano right here?"[25]

Bush then surprised his parents—as his father surprised his own parents by moving to Odessa in 1945—by announcing that he had been accepted to the graduate program of the Harvard Business School. The stereotype of the school neatly fit the quip made by Bush's cab driver as he arrived in Boston in the spring of 1973: "Here you are at the West Point of capitalism." But the school was still housed at Harvard, where under 8 percent of the student body was registered a Republican, and where there had long been a tradition of political activism. Thus, Harvard was an even odder fit for Bush than Yale had been. While his classmates cheered every moment of Nixon's Watergate-related agony, Bush carried his Texas conservatism with pride. He wore his cowboy boots to class, frequented a country-and-western bar, and spit tobacco into a cup while listening to a lecture. A former girlfriend told a biographer that while other students were "drinking Chivas regal, he was drinking Wild Turkey. They were smoking Benson and Hedges [cigarettes] and he was dipping Copenhagen [chewing tobacco], and while they were going to the opera, he would listen to [country music star] Johnny Rodriguez."[26]

When the twenty-eight-year-old Bush graduated from Harvard in the fall of 1975 with his MBA degree, he made no effort to land a Wall Street job and instead moved back to Midland. As he remembered, it was an easy decision to make: "West Texas was in my blood." But there was a less romantic reason. Thanks to the 1973 Arab oil embargo and the resulting energy crisis, American oil had become an even more prized commodity (the price of oil rose 800 percent from 1973 to 1981). Texas in general and Midland and the Permian Basin, in particular, were experiencing another oil boom—Laura Bush remembered that from 1974 to 1981, Midland's bank deposits rose from $385 million to almost $2 billion. Indeed, Midland in the 1980s was the richest town in America, having the highest per capita income in the country.[27]

Once back in Midland and knowing only that he "wanted to be my own boss," Bush became a landman—the one person responsible for researching subterranean rights to unpumped oil and evaluating the land's availability for leasing. He was unusually well-suited for this job—he had both formal business training and experience in the fields, and his personality was tailor-made for both tasks. Soon, Bush learned to trade mineral and royalty interests and began to invest small sums into drilling ventures.[28]

His father, then serving as the American envoy to the People's Republic of China, was pleased, writing in his diary that his eldest was "starting out on what I hope will be a challenging new life for him. He is able. If he gets his teeth into something semi-permanent or permanent, he will do just fine." But the new job did not bring instant maturity. Usually beer-fueled and living in an apartment that his friend Joe O'Neill called a "toxic waste dump," Bush was part of a posse that included O'Neill, Charles Younger, and Donald Evans—all of whom wanted a piece of the West Texas oil boom. One story that Bush told with some gusto in his second memoir was about the night that he and Younger got drunk, went to a Willie Nelson concert, and jumped up on the stage. As they left the arena, a bottle of beer that they were smuggling out of the concert dropped on the floor and exploded, sending the two delinquents running for cover. Georgie and his friends dubbed themselves the Greyhounds, since they ran like the dogs at the track.[29]

Things came to a head in September 1976. While vacationing at the family retreat in Kennebunkport, Maine, Georgie went out drinking with friends, including professional tennis player John Newcombe. On his way home, he was stopped by police, who asked him to step out of his car and instructed him to walk a straight line. This he could not do. Bush was charged with driving under the influence, a charge to which he pled guilty. The twenty-nine-year-old Bush paid a $150 fine and lost his right to drive in the state of Maine.[30]

The young man whose friends had taken to calling "Dubya" or the "Bombastic Bushkin" was clearly not ready to settle down. However, he had never lost his interest in politics, and a pathway soon presented itself. On 6 July 1977—Bush's thirty-first birthday—Democrat George Mahon announced that he was not going to run for reelection from the Texas Nineteenth Congressional District. Mahon had served that district for twenty-two terms, making him at that point the nation's longest-serving congressman. The district encompassed Midland and nearby Lubbock and was strongly Democratic. However, Bush was optimistic about his chances, choosing to interpret the presidential vote of the district—it had gone Republican for the last twenty-five years—as evidence that a Republican could at least keep the congressional race close. Moreover, Bush was fueled by a growing distaste for governmental regulation. Two pieces of legislation—the Natural Gas Policy Act and the Fuel Use Act, both of which would be passed in 1978, and both of which controlled prices on domestic natural gas—infuriated virtually every oilman, including Bush. Writing in 1999, Bush argued that these pieces of legislation were proof that "Washington had substituted its judgement for the marketplace. . . . [It] was a move toward European-style socialism." Two weeks after Mahon announced his retirement, Bush announced that he planned to run for the vacated seat. He would run as an economic conservative, preaching the virtues of a lightly regulated oil economy, condemning the federal government, and virtually ignoring social issues, with one exception—he would often mention that the Social Security system was broken and could not be sustained unless it was amended to allow for individuals to invest their payroll tax in accounts of their own choosing. The elder Bush wrote a friend that he was "tickled pink" that his son was running.[31]

Ten days after he declared his candidacy, at a barbecue hosted by O'Neill (who was also serving as the treasurer of Bush's congressional race), Bush was introduced to Laura Welch, the daughter of a Midland home developer and a homemaker who kept the books for her husband's business. A graduate of Southern Methodist University with a bachelor's degree in education, Welch spent time as a second-grade teacher before returning to school and earning a master's degree in library science from the University of Texas. At the time she met Bush, she was working as a librarian in Houston; she had come to Midland to visit her parents. The couple's paths had come close to crossing before that day. While growing up, they had lived ten blocks away from each other in Midland, and they had attended the same junior high school. They had even lived in the same Houston apartment building—all without ever meeting.[32]

It was a perfect case of the time-worn cliché that opposites attract. The quiet, demure Laura found herself quite taken with Bushkin; the younger Bush found himself quite taken with the reserved librarian. More to the point, he was smitten, remembering that his instant reaction was that she was "gorgeous . . . intelligent and dignified, with a warm and easy laugh." Laura remembered it with a more practical air, recalling that "we were not looking for someone to date but for someone with whom to share life, for the rest of our lives. We both wanted children. We were ready to build an enduring future." It was the virtual definition of a whirlwind romance—they were married four months later, on 5 November 1977. It was a small affair, with no ushers, bridesmaids, or groomsmen.[33]

The young couple was immediately thrust into a political campaign. After coming in second in a three-way Republican primary race, Bush had ended up in a runoff against former sportscaster and Odessa mayor Jim Reese. Reese, who had run against George Mahon two years earlier and had polled 46 percent of the vote, turned out to be a formidable opponent. He believed it was his turn, and that the young landman from Midland was an overly ambitious usurper. Moreover, Reese had some formidable out-of-town-support. Ronald Reagan, who was gearing up for a run for the presidency in 1980 and seeing the elder Bush in his rearview mirror as a potential opponent, took a swipe at Bush by taking a swipe at his son. Despite a plea from the elder Bush to sit the race out, a Reagan political action committee gave Reese $3,000, and Reagan himself endorsed Reese in a campaign ad (as the younger Bush later remembered, "Dad wasn't particularly pleased about that"). Moreover, Reese painted the younger Bush as a carpetbagger. Calling him "Junior," Reese condemned Bush for being born not in Texas but in Connecticut. His father had warned him that this would happen—in a July 1977 letter to his son, Bush suggested "that you establish very fast that you are your own man." The younger Bush countered Reese's jabs with self-effacing humor: "No, I wasn't born in Texas, because I wanted to be close to my mother that day." He was also a surprisingly indefatigable campaigner. Bush outlasted Reese: he lost every district save for the city of Midland, but he won Midland so decisively (4,427 to 1,287) that he won the primary.[34]

However, it was a still a Democratic district. Allan Shivers, former governor of Texas and Bush family friend, was blunt when the young candidate asked for his advice on the general election. Shivers responded, "Son, you can't win. This district is just made for Kent Hance. It's rural, conservative, and Democrat, and he's a rural conservative Democrat." Moreover, Hance, a Democratic state senator from Lubbock, was a fast learner. Quick to conclude from the closeness of the Republican primary that Bush's greatest liability in West Texas was his last name, Hance lost no time in picking up where Reese had left off. With an air of contempt, he told one audience, "I don't think he's ever been in the back of a pool hall in Dimmitt, Texas" (a charge that, given Bush's wild oat–sowing, one would not have been surprised to find out was untrue) and told others, "We don't need someone from the Northeast telling us what the problems are." Hance even attacked Bush for being rich, accusing him through a surrogate of using his "vast sums of money" to pay to provide free beer at a Bush rally at Texas Tech University.[35]

There was an irony to this—of all the Bush siblings, the eldest son was the most Texan. Regardless, unlike he had done in the primary, Bush did not mount an adequate defense against Hance's charges of being his father's son. In a tactic that smacked of desperation, Bush took to displaying his birth certificate at speeches, so as to verify that his full name was different from his father's. Exasperated, he sighed and asked, "Would you like me to run as Sam Smith? I can't abandon my background." Bush lost by sixty-six hundred votes—roughly 6 percent of the total votes cast. He had learned what he later characterized as "an important lesson. When someone attacks your integrity, you have to respond. . . . If someone attacks me, I will never again fail to fight back."[36]

Defeated for the Congress, and with the energy business soaring as a result of swelling oil prices, Bush threw himself into the care and feeding of Arbusto (Spanish for Bush) Energy, a holding company he had formed to advance his mineral and royalty rights. As a result, he played but a small role in his father's 1980 campaigns. While the elder Bush ran for the Republican nomination for the presidency, his eldest son worked the phones from Midland, talked to his Texas friends, and did a limited amount of surrogate speaking at home and in Iowa. He was not consulted by his father regarding Reagan's eventual offer of the vice presidency—indeed, the younger Bush learned of his father's choice while at dinner in New York City, where he was raising money for Arbusto.[37]

The younger Bush did not attend many Washington events during the first term of his father's vice presidency. Indeed, he had new responsibilities—not only to his growing oil company but also to a growing family. At first, he and Laura had tried to adopt. But no sooner were they approved for adoption than they found out that Laura was pregnant. However, the pregnancy took a scary turn; Laura was diagnosed with preeclampsia and was confined to her bed for the last weeks of the pregnancy. Fortunately, on 25 November 1981 Laura gave birth to healthy twin girls, named after their grandmothers—Jenna and Barbara.[38]

But soon after the birth of the twins, Midland had cratered into what locals called "bust mode." By 1982 Texas the oil boom had dried up—the price of oil dropped from about thirty-five dollars per barrel to an astonishing nine dollars. In Midland, banks were closing; fragments of the oil business were moving out of town. Arbusto was a small part of the problem—despite Bush's prodigious efforts to capitalize his company, during its first five years only half of its wells produced petroleum. Some Midland wags began to call the firm "Ar-bust-oh." As a result, in 1984 Bush merged Arbusto with Spectrum 7, a Cincinnati oil drilling operation owned by Bill DeWitt Jr.—whose father had been owner of major-league baseball's St. Louis Browns and Cincinnati Reds—and his partner Mercer Reynolds.

The merger doubled Bush's operation. Bush served as Spectrum's CEO; DeWitt and others in the Cincinnati group raised money for the company while staying in Cincinnati.[39]

The turbulence in the oil business may have played a role in pushing the younger Bush back into politics. By 1985 the elder Bush had begun to plan his second run for the presidency. Recognizing his own limitations, he brought on Lee Atwater as his campaign manager. Born in Atlanta in 1951, Atwater was younger than most political consultants. However, Atwater was no political lightweight. He had interned in the office of Sen. Strom Thurmond (R-SC), and between 1974 and 1978, he had worked in or directed twenty-eight winning campaigns and had worked both in Reagan's presidential campaign and in the Reagan White House. Bush needed to give his campaign a jolt of energy, and Atwater, a born clown and troublemaker whose background and temperament remind one very closely of George W. Bush, was the perfect choice.[40]

However, the Bushes had long been wary of outsiders coming too close to the family business. In the spring of 1985, Atwater had a frank and forthright meeting with the two eldest Bush sons at Camp David. Young George got right to the point, asking, "How do we know we can trust you?" Caught off guard, Atwater asked for clarification; Jeb provided it—"If someone throws a grenade at our dad, we expect you to jump on it." Thinking quickly, the cagy Atwater decided to bring his inquisitors inside the tent. He quipped that one of them should move to Washington, join the campaign, and keep an eye on things. Jeb, who had set down roots in Miami, took a pass and chose instead to work for his father in Florida. George, however, decided to take Atwater up on his offer.[41]

Atwater's proposal came at a particularly opportune time for the younger Bush, as things in the oil industry were getting worse by the day. In early 1986, oil prices nose-dived (Bush remembered the price going from twenty-six to ten dollars per barrel). Indeed, Spectrum 7 had lost money in the two previous quarters. As he would later tell a biographer, "I wanted to get out of Midland." Bush sold Spectrum 7 to the Dallas-based Harken Energy Corporation. Harken picked up Spectrum's sizable debt and gave young Bush two thousand shares of stock, originally worth $312,000, and an annual salary of $120,000—all for the privilege of doing business with the son of a man who might become president. The elder Bush could not have been happier, as he confided to his diary: "I think George Bush coming up here will be very helpful and I think he will be a good insight to me." Early in 1988, young Bush and his family headed for Washington.[42]

Prior to his move, Bush reevaluated his personal life. In the spring of 1984, he heard Arthur Blessitt, a traveling evangelist known for carrying a large wooden cross into every nation of the world, ministering on the radio. Something in Blessitt's message connected with Bush; the minister was visiting Midland, and the two men briefly met. Then, in the summer of 1985, Bush met Rev. Billy Graham, who was visiting Kennebunkport. While out walking, they talked about what it would take for a man like the younger Bush to give his life to Jesus Christ. The two men swam together in the Atlantic Ocean; later, Graham offered to send the young Bush a Bible. According to Bush, Graham "planted a seed in my heart and I began to change." When he returned to Midland, Bush began to read his new Bible regularly and joined a Bible study group.[43]

Bush also began to reevaluate his drinking habits. As Laura remembered in her memoir, "It was the fact of turning forty; [that] none of the Bush children ever wanted to do anything to embarrass their dad . . . [and] it was also having talked with Billy Graham." It was also one epic night of debauchery. On 28 July 1986, after a joint fortieth birthday celebration with friends in Colorado Springs, Bush emerged with an epic hangover and a quiet lecture from his wife ("Can you remember the last day you didn't have a drink?"). That day, he swore off alcohol and by all accounts stayed true to that promise. There was no rehab, no meetings—just a promise kept.[44]

This change marked the end of the shallow, prepubescent "Georgie." Bush remembered that "quitting drinking made me more focused and more disciplined." Laura recalled that he exercised more, and that reading "became a pleasure for him again." Bush had finally become an adult, just in time for his father's presidential campaign.[45]

Those within the campaign who derisively dubbed George W. Bush "Junior" when he moved into the Washington office of Bush for President in 1986 severely undersold the young man's political experience. By any measure, he was no political novice. He had shadowed his father on each of his congressional and senatorial campaigns, worked closely with the candidate on two other statewide campaigns (Gurney's and Blount's), and run his own congressional campaign. The younger Bush quickly took responsibility for reining in the manic Atwater, chastising him, for example, when he posed for a photo accompanying an *Esquire* article with his pants dropped to his ankles, wearing red boxer shorts, and saluting at the camera. He also took on the role of campaign consigliere. When rumors appeared in several news outlets of a possible adulterous relationship between his father and his secretary, Jennifer Fitzgerald, Atwater asked the younger Bush what should be done. The younger Bush took it upon himself to speak to Howard Fineman of *Newsweek*—"The answer to the Big A question is N-O." When *Newsweek* ran a cover story that claimed that the taciturn vice president was "Fighting the Wimp Factor," his son went ballistic; he accused reporter Margaret Warner of effecting a "political ambush" and told her, "You ought to quit if that's the kind of journalistic integrity you have."[46]

Once his father won the nomination (it was his eldest son who announced in New Orleans the votes of Texas that gave his father the nomination), he spent the better part of the fall campaign in small towns—"off markets"—speaking to large crowds for the first time. After his election, Bush put his son in charge of the "Scrub Team"—a group that vetted potential administration appointees and rejected those whose loyalty to the Bush family was in question.[47]

Just prior to his father's electoral victory, Bush received a call from Bill DeWitt, who told him that the Texas Rangers major-league baseball team that made its home just outside of Dallas was on the market. Bush was immediately interested. As it had with his father, his love of baseball, and his knowledge of the intricacies of the game, ran deep (Laura remembered in her memoir that her husband could recite from memory the lineups of many of the great teams of the 1950s). Owning the team would also fill a gaping hole in his résumé. As one friend told him, "George, everybody likes you, but . . . you just haven't done shit. You're a Bush and that's all." As Bush pithily remembered it, he "pursued the purchase like a pit bull on the pant leg of opportunity." Bush had seed money—his Harken stock had appreciated to $606,000. But it was hardly enough to buy a professional team outright. Therefore, Bush partnered with DeWitt, and together they put together a thirty-nine-member investment team. In April 1989 Bush and his group bought 86 percent of the Texas Rangers for $75 million—they would soon own the team in its entirety.[48]

Bush served as the team's comanaging general partner, earning $200,000 per year. This job was perfect. It mixed his love of baseball with both his academic and his practical business training. He reveled in being one of the boys, signing baseball cards and attending every game, sitting not in a skybox but in the stands. But his real coming-out party was the building of the Ballpark in Arlington—a state-of-the-art, 49,166-seat facility, built for $191 million. Bush led the effort to convince voters to pass a referendum approving the public financing of 70 percent of the project in January 1991. The *New York Times* called the Rangers' new home, completed in April 1994, "the house that Bush built." By 1996, the Rangers produced the highest profits in major-league baseball, and young Bush had realized a personal return of $14.9 million.[49]

While Bush was experiencing his first real taste of business success, his father's administration was in serious trouble. Immediately following the 3 March 1991 end of the Persian Gulf War—a war that saw the successful expelling of Iraqi occupier Saddam Hussein from Kuwait and the skyrocketing of Bush's approval ratings—the rest of the year saw a downward spiral. On March 3 Lee Atwater died of a brain tumor, thus denying Bush the counsel of his sagest political adviser. In June, the administration nearly botched the Supreme Court confirmation of Clarence Thomas, a nominee whose sketchy past only served to widen the chasm that existed between Bush, Blacks, and women. The summer brought a coup against Mikhail Gorbachev and the final fall of the Soviet Union—as well as further criticism of Bush by conservatives who felt that he stood by Gorbachev too long—and an economy that had spiraled into recession. By the end of the year, Bush's numbers were in free fall, and his reelection chances in serious jeopardy. As Bush pollster Bob Teeter summed things up in March 1992: "The situation is about as bad as it could be."[50]

Once again, as he had done in 1988, the elder Bush brought his son to Washington. This time, in the words of the junior Bush, he was there to "analyze how to improve the functioning of the White House and to make recommendations about how to structure the 1992 campaign." Bush began his work by interviewing all members of the senior and campaign staff. After the interviews, Bush told his father that the White House staff needed a shake-up, and that Chief of Staff John Sununu would have to go. Unable to bring himself to fire Sununu, the president sent his son to break the ice. The younger Bush remembered, "I merely told John he should go see the President, have a heart-to-heart discussion, and give him the opportunity to make a change if the President so desired. I don't know what transpired after that." But this was not the end of the younger Bush's recommendations. He lobbied unsuccessfully for the dismissal of Vice President Dan Quayle, suggesting that his father replace Quayle with his secretary of defense, Dick Cheney. He lobbied more successfully for moving Jim Baker from State to the campaign, but by the time Baker agreed, it was too late. Bush lost to a combination blitzkrieg from Bill Clinton and Texas billionaire and longtime Bush adversary H. Ross Perot. It was his eldest son who, on election night, delivered the bad news to the candidate.[51]

There would be no serious discussion of a political comeback for George H. W. Bush. His son, however, could now begin his own political career in earnest. Indeed, Bush later admitted that "had dad won in 1992, I doubt I would have run for office in 1994, and I almost certainly would not have become president." Now freed from his role as his father's fixer and riding high on the financial success of the Texas Rangers, George W. Bush was ready to make his move.[52]

# 2

★ ★ ★ ★ ★

# GOVERNOR BUSH

Make it he did, and against an old Bush family enemy. At the 1988 Democratic National Convention, the effervescent Ann Richards, then serving as Texas state treasurer but with her eye on the statehouse, made a national name for herself when, in her folksiest drawl, she sneered at the audience and threw shade at Bush the elder: "He can't help it. He was born with a silver foot in his mouth." In 1990, she captured the governorship of Texas, thanks largely to the bigotry of her opponent, Clayton Williams, whose Neanderthal-like comments—that bad weather "is a little like rape. As long as it's inevitable, just relax and enjoy it," and that going to prostitutes was the only way to get "serviced" in the 1950s—sunk him at the polls. As governor, Richards was a national celebrity, but her policies were far from universally popular in Texas. Her support of a state lottery and expensive programs like a massive prison construction project, as well as a tax hike to help fund that venture, earned her the enmity of the state's conservatives. But it was a controversial school funding proposition called the "Robin Hood" plan, which would have redistributed tax revenues from wealthier to poorer school districts, that angered conservatives most. Richards fought hard for the proposal, but in a special election held on 1 May 1993, it sank to defeat by 63 percent. Bush remembered that that election night was "the night I first thought I might run for governor."[1]

The timing was certainly right. The political map of Texas had changed quite markedly since Bush had last run for office in 1978. The suburbs of Dallas and Fort Worth (most notably those in Collin and Denton Counties) and the suburbs of Houston (most notably those in Williamson County) had turned Republican. One of the first to see the whole of the political landscape in the early 1990s, and one of the first to see the possibility of a statewide victory for George W. Bush, was Karl Rove. Rove was born in Denver, Colorado, and in 1950 moved with his family first to Nevada, then to a suburb of Salt Lake City. While in high school, Rove excelled in debate. In 1969 he entered the University of Utah, but the following year saw his family torn apart: first his father left, and then his mother abandoned her children, telling Karl that he would now have to fend for himself.[2]

Despite his family tragedies, Rove soon found his calling. He parlayed an internship into his first real job in politics—organizing college students to help in the campaign of Illinois senator Ralph Smith. Smith lost, but Rove still went to Washington—to help reorganize the College Republicans, a part of the Republican National Committee. He dropped out of the university, took the job, and in June 1971 became that organization's executive director, a position he held for two years. In 1973, Rove ran for the national chairmanship of the College Republicans. The election was so close that it was left to the then chairman of the Republican National Committee, George H. W. Bush, to proclaim Rove the victor. Once in office, Rove asked a new friend, the chairman of the South Carolina Young Republicans, Lee Atwater, to serve as his executive director. While chairman, Rove first met George W. Bush—the elder Bush asked Rove to locate his son and give him the keys to the family car.[3]

But Rove would not stay a batman for long. In 1974 he helped in a Nebraska congressional race; in 1975 he became the finance director for the Virginia Republican Party. While in Virginia, Rove mastered the techniques of direct mail. In 1977 he took a job as legislative aide to a senior Republican in the Texas House, and in 1979, Rove was one of Jim Baker's first hires to a political action committee that was set up to help fund Bush's upcoming presidential campaign. Following the 1980 campaign that elected Bush vice president, Rove's reward was a place in the administration of William Clements, the new governor of Texas. In October 1981, Rove left Clements to start his own direct mail operation, Rove + Company, which consulted nationally on campaigns for governor, senator, and Congress. His clients included Missouri's John Ashcroft, Utah's Orrin Hatch, and, in 1988 and 1992, the presidential campaigns of George H. W. Bush.[4]

After the May 1993 special election, Bush and Rove began to put together a campaign for the governorship. Houston lawyer Vance McMahan was brought on as director of policy. And Margaret LaMontagne of the Texas Association of School Books was made political director. Karen Hughes, a former television reporter, public relations executive, and executive director of the Texas Republican Party, became the campaign's communications director. The final add was Joe Allbaugh, who had served as chief of staff for Oklahoma governor Henry Bellmon and as that state's deputy transportation commissioner, and who came on as campaign manager.[5]

Bush announced his candidacy for governor on 8 November 1993. His strategy—largely the brainchild of Rove and Hughes and privately called by the staff the "campaign of joy"—was deceptively simple: Bush was to stick to his talking points, not go rogue, and never let anyone see his temper outbursts—in other words, he couldn't let Richards get under his skin. A newly calm, cool, and collected Bush worked the state like a veteran, concentrating on four issues: the need for education reform, reform of the juvenile justice system, welfare reform, and tort litigation reform.[6]

Bush was particularly single-minded on the issue of education reform. A true and sincere champion of local control of education issues, he promised that he would lead the fight to transfer control of public schools away from the state, and over to the local school districts. This position was immensely popular with Texas conservatives, and Bush made it a part of every stump speech. Richards was frustrated at her inability to derail Bush on the issue; later, she would sigh: "You know, if you said to George, 'What time is it?' he would say, 'We must teach our children to read.'"[7]

But policy and philosophy were only part of the story in 1994. Had Richards not lent Bush a helping hand, the outcome might well have been different. Rove predicted that Richards, who had benefited from Williams's crass comments in 1990, would try to goad Bush into saying something just as stupid. She tried, and the strategy backfired. She told reporters that the governorship was "not a job where the federal government gives you the job training funds so you can learn as you go. You can't be shaving one morning and look at yourself in the mirror and think, 'I'm so pretty I'll run for Governor.'" Despite Richards's attempt to bait him in their only debate (the night of the debate, she found herself in an elevator with Bush and growled, "This is going to be rough on you, boy"), Bush kept his composure and emerged unscathed. She publicly called Bush a "jerk," and she semipublicly referred to him as "Shrub." A more mature Bush did not respond in kind.[8]

23

Nor did he let mistakes become disasters. On 1 September, while on a photo op hunting trip, Bush bagged what he thought was a dove, but turned out to be a killdeer—a bird protected by Texas law, but nonetheless dead and in Bush's hunting bag. Rather than rush to cover up the blunder, Bush immediately found a judge, admitted his crime, and paid the fine; then he found a reporter and confessed his sin with a sparkling bit of self-effacement ("Thank goodness it was not deer season: I might have shot a cow"). Even when he found himself at the same church rally as former Democratic congresswoman Barbara Jordan—a heroine of Watergate and icon of American liberalism who had just then endorsed Richards from the pulpit—Bush came out smelling like a rose. He stated: "I am humbled and honored to follow the great Barbara Jordan. She is the epitome of a soldier for what is right. I just happen to disagree with her choice for governor." Even the endorsement of Richards by Bush family antagonist Ross Perot did not phase Bush, who responded: "She can have Ross Perot, and I'll take [Texas Rangers star pitcher] Nolan Ryan and Barbara Bush." By the end of the campaign, it was the young challenger who looked more statesmanlike than his incumbent opponent.[9]

In November 1994, while his brother went down to defeat in the Florida gubernatorial election, George W. Bush was elected the forty-sixth governor of Texas, taking 53.5 percent of the vote—the largest margin of victory for any Texas gubernatorial candidate in the past two decades. Bush the younger did not gloat. Bush the elder, however, did. He told his friend Hugh Sidey, a columnist for *Time* magazine, "I must say, I felt a certain sense of joy. . . . We showed [Richards] what she could do with that silver foot, where she could stick that now."[10]

On the morning of his son's inauguration as governor, the elder Bush gave him his most prized personal possession—a set of gold cufflinks that his father, Prescott, had given him in 1942 when he earned his aviator's wings. But his overflowing emotions did not allow him to personally give them to his son. Instead, he put them in an envelope which he had Barbara deliver. The accompanying note showed a father's pride:

> These cufflinks are my most treasured possession. . . . I want you to have them now; for, in a sense, though you won your Air Force wings flying those jets, you are again "getting your wings" as you take the oath of office as our Governor. . . . You have given us more than we ever could have deserved. You have sacrificed for us. You have given us your unwavering loyalty and devotion. Now it is our turn. We love you. Devotedly, Dad.

The son responded with a note of his own: "I am where I am because of you. You should always know this." His mother, however, was her usual caustic self, remembering that "that day, I took [George and Laura] off my worry list."[11]

Few people who knew the blustery, boozing George W. Bush only a few years earlier would have thought him capable of the subtlety necessary to guide a state. But Bush had learned much. His time as his father's staff herdsman had taught him the value of a collegial approach that allowed his staff equal and frequent access to the boss. Bush would write that Joe Allbaugh, now Bush's executive assistant, was "the first among equals," who, while not blocking access to any of the senior staff, nevertheless saw to it that the office ran smoothly. McMahan reprised his campaign role as director of policy, as did Hughes as communications director. LaMontagne became Bush's chief education policy adviser. They were joined by Clay Johnson, who served as appointments director in charge of overseeing selections to state boards and agencies, and Alberto Gonzales, a Houston lawyer who served as Bush's general counsel until he was named Texas secretary of state in 1997 and then named to fill a vacancy in the Texas Supreme Court in 1999. By all accounts Bush's senior staff worked remarkably well together ("I gave them a piece of advice: 'Always return each other's phone calls first'"). All would eventually follow him into the White House.[12]

Bush also understood his own strengths. Like his father, he was a master at forming interpersonal relationships. He also showed a trait that eludes many a mature politician—an ability, as well as a desire, to reach out to the other side of the aisle and govern as a true bipartisan. One example was Bush's convincing Democratic state representative Elton Bonner to resign his safe seat in the Texas House of Representatives to come to work for the Bush administration as state insurance commissioner. Another was Bush's outreach to the members of the Texas Supreme Court. By the end of his first two months as governor, Bush had met with all but 6 of the 181 state legislators.[13]

But the biggest and best example of Bush's personal bipartisanship was his bromance with the two leaders of the Texas state legislature. Democrat Bob Bullock, the independently elected lieutenant governor who led the Texas Senate, was a bigger-than-life old-school pol whose personality reminds one of the famously vulgar Lyndon Johnson. Rove later wrote that Bullock had "a Ph.D. in abuse." But Bullock's power and influence were indisputable. Bush reached out to the crass, obscene, and brilliant Bullock during the campaign. After the election, he continued to work with Bullock, until an unlikely but powerful bond was formed. Bush also reached out to another key Democrat, Pete Laney, the speaker of the Texas House of Representatives. A cotton farmer and used-car dealer from West Texas, Laney famously told Bush, "Governor, we're not going to let you fail." When the legislature was in session, Bush had a weekly breakfast with Bullock and Laney. Bullock was all bluster; Laney was more circumspect; Bush remembered that he listened a lot. Journalist and professional Bush irritant Molly Ivins sniffed that the governor "got along just fine by doing pretty much what Bullock told him to"—cute, but not true. The observation of Sandy Kress, another Democrat recommended to Bush by Rove who would become influential in Bush's plans for education reform, is closer to the mark when describing Bush's relationship with Bullock and Laney: "It was bipartisan plus . . . they got a lot of things done."[14]

Having formed several unexpected bipartisan alliances, Bush went to work on each of his campaign promises. First up was tort reform—bringing an end to what many saw as a spate of frivolous lawsuits and disproportionate punitive damages. Bullock convened a working group of legislators and supported Bush in his desire to have McMahan included as a member. On the issue of punitive damages, Bullock suggested a cap of any amount lower than two times the actual damages plus $1 million. Bush made it clear that he could not live with such a high cap, and Bullock ultimately agreed to $750,000—a figure higher than Bush wanted but one that all sides could live with.[15]

But it was education reform that won for Bush a national profile. The issue was close to his heart: as he wrote to conservative activist Phyllis Schlafly, who advocated the teaching of phonics, "We both agree. . . . Obviously the current teaching methods must change, and our teachers must be trained to teach a system that works. Reading can be taught." In 1996 Bush introduced what he called his "Reading Initiative"—legislation that would direct $29 million of Texas's federal allotment of education funding to new programs designed to strengthen the teaching of reading. It would also appropriate $35 million to create special reading academies. The second part of Bush's education package was the first reboot of the Texas Education Code in almost fifty years. The Ratliff-Sadler Bill created a system that offered more choice for parents and educators—if they didn't like where their child was going to school, they could set up a charter school, send the child to a different public school, or form a home-rule education district separate from state control. Then came reform of the state curriculum. The old curriculum was known as the Texas Essential Knowledge and Skills Plan. Bush ordered a complete overhaul of this massive program: "I wanted a clear, straight-forward outline of high academic standards for Texas schools." With Bush showing himself once again to be skilled at attracting broad-based support for a program, his overhaul of education in Texas was passed by the legislature. The press dubbed it the "Texas Miracle."[16]

Bush had long believed that one step toward welfare reform was to have government assist community service organizations, including organizations that had ties to churches. He also believed that those organizations should be on an equal footing with secular programs when competing for government monies. In 1996 Bush formed the Task Force on Faith-Based Programs. "Our goal," he announced, "is to identify ways that Texas can create an environment where faith-based organizations will flourish and meet the needs of people in crisis with focused and effective aid." The report of the task force—"Faith in Action"—was released in December 1996. It concluded that government must become the "enabler" of faith-based groups and that the state must give those groups direct aid—both financially and cooperatively. Bush then signed an executive order that encouraged state agencies to use the 1996 "charitable choice" provision of the federal welfare reform law (a portion of President Clinton's welfare reform package) that allowed government agencies to partner with faith-based organizations to distribute social services.[17]

On several issues, Bush looked decidedly progressive. In 1996, the Federal Appeals Court for the Fifth Circuit banned the affirmative action program in which the University of Texas had reserved a certain number of spots in its freshman class for minority students. Rather than quietly accept the decision of the court, Bush pushed the legislature to craft a law that required all state-funded colleges and universities in Texas to accept *any* student who graduated in the top 10 percent of their high school. Bush also refused to stand with his party's right wing on the volatile issue of immigration. California governor Pete Wilson strongly supported a referendum that denied state benefits to illegal aliens; Bush publicly opposed such a measure.[18]

On the issue of tax reform, Bush tried to pass progressive changes, but his efforts were less successful. Bush had campaigned on the need for both an across-the-board tax cut and a comprehensive reform of the Texas tax code. But his initial proposals met with resistance from the legislature. To force the issue, eight days after the 1996 presidential election, Bush seized control of a state budget surplus, calling it a "down payment" on a plan to reduce school property taxes. Bush had no constitutional power to authorize such tax relief. Moreover, the surplus itself was questionable as it was based only on preliminary numbers from the office of the comptroller. Bush got the $1 billion cut that he wanted, but his tactics kept him from getting the sweeping reform plan that he had wanted. In his 1999 memoirs, Bush wrote that the defeat had taught him two things: first, "it's hard to win votes for massive reform unless there is a crisis"; second, "Texans appreciated bold leadership. I had earned political capital by spending it."[19]

In several areas, however, Bush was far from progressive. One such issue was the right of indigent defendants to counsel, a right guaranteed to all citizens by the Supreme Court in *Gideon v. Wainwright*,[20] but one that, in the eyes of many, had been hamstrung in Texas by political considerations. State law provided for judges to appoint counsel for defendants, sometimes the very judge who was hearing their case. Besides the very real possibility of conflict of interest, reformers argued that the system allowed for the rewarding of lawyers who had contributed to the judge's past campaigns. In June 1999, both houses of the state legislature unanimously approved a bill that stripped judges of this authority, giving that power to commissioner's courts that could set up public defender's offices and contract with outside agencies. The judges were apoplectic in their opposition, and Bush sided with them. He vetoed the bill, arguing in his veto message that "while well intentioned . . . the bill inappropriately takes appointment authority away from judges." The veto made national headlines; the Committee of the State Bar of Texas cried that "the state of Texas is a national embarrassment in the area of indigent legal services." But Bush stood firm.[21]

A second area was that of Bush's rock-ribbed support for the death penalty. Since 1974, Texas had executed 464 inmates—by far the most in the nation. There were 152 executions during Bush's two terms in office; only once did he grant clemency. The most famous instance of Bush and the death penalty was that of Karla Faye Tucker, who was found guilty of helping commit a gruesome set of murders in 1983 (she and her then boyfriend beat one man with a hammer and finished him off with a pickax; they then turned the pickax on a second victim, a woman, and hacked her to death). Since she freely admitted that she was aware of her actions at the moment of the crime (to the point of experiencing sexual enjoyment with each swing of the pickax), Tucker received the death penalty.[22]

While in jail awaiting execution (her partner died in prison of liver failure before the decision of the court could be carried out), Tucker converted to Christianity and began to lobby for a commutation of her sentence to life imprisonment so that she could use the rest of her life to minister to other inmates. Petite, pretty, and articulate, Tucker cut a sympathetic figure. The fact that a woman had not been executed in the United States since 1984, and in Texas since 1863, also worked in her favor. Nevertheless, the Texas Board of Pardons and Paroles voted unanimously against clemency, and the Supreme Court denied a request to halt her execution.

Soon, Bush was receiving letters calling for him to commute Tucker's sentence to life imprisonment. He heard from correspondents as diverse at Pat Robertson, Bianca Jagger, and Pope John Paul II. Several observers charged Bush with hypocrisy—how could he support the death penalty, and at the same time support a pro-life stand against abortion? (Bush: "To me, it's the difference between innocence and guilt.") Aided by the counsel of Alberto Gonzales, who visited Tucker in prison, Bush came to believe that even though Tucker had changed while in prison, the fact that she had admitted to her crime left him no choice. He refused to commute Tucker's sentence. The decision of the court was carried out on 3 February 1998 at the Texas State Penitentiary at Huntsville.[23]

The case of Henry Lee Lucas was not nearly as cut-and-dried as that of Tucker. Lucas, who had been arrested in 1983 for the 1979 murder of a young woman (her body had been left by the side of the road naked, save for a pair of orange socks), confessed to the crime to police; his taped confession won him the death penalty. However, following his sentencing, Lucas tried to recant his confession. While prosecutors had established that he had committed several other crimes, doubts soon surfaced as to whether Lucas could have committed what the press had dubbed the "Orange Socks Murder" (the victim could not be identified). Moreover, it came to light that Lucas had confessed to many murders that he never could have committed. It was this doubt that led the Board of Pardons and Paroles to recommend the commutation of his sentence to life imprisonment. After consulting with his advisers and finding that, as he remembered, "this case would never have a smoking gun," Bush agreed with his commission, and on 27 June 1998, he commuted Lucas's sentence to life imprisonment.[24]

In his memoirs, Bush does not speak of the years 1996–1998 as a time when he was thinking about the presidency. Karl Rove is not nearly as reticent. Rove makes it clear that "for the next two years, I was constantly plotting, planning, and scheming about electing Bush president." Rove was a close student of the career of William McKinley. As such, he borrowed McKinley's famous "Front Porch Campaign" as a tactic for testing the waters for Bush. Rove spent much of 1998 bringing potential donors and voters to Bush. Small groups traveled to Austin., where they ate lunch with Bush, then listened to a brief speech from the governor. The meetings got him good press, and they were far more efficient than having Bush travel to meet them in their home state.[25]

Bush also worked to buttress his foreign policy bona fides. In 1998 he traveled to Israel, a trip sponsored by the Republican Jewish Coalition, where he first met Ariel Sharon, then in the cabinet of prime minister Benjamin Netanyahu, the leader of the right-wing Likud Party. Sharon gave Bush a tour of Israel from his helicopter. As they flew over the country, Sharon said things like "I fought there" and "I built that settlement." Bush remembered being "struck by Israel's vulnerability in a hostile neighborhood." On his return, his father noted that "President [Ezer] Weizman and P[rime] M[inister] Netanyahu volunteered that you had made a very favorable impression in Israel. President [Hosni] Mubarak of Egypt said essentially the same thing. All with whom I spoke hoped that you will run."[26]

Bush also sought the blessing of the disciples of Ronald Reagan. On 22 April 1998, accompanied by Laura, Karl Rove, Don Evans, and his California fundraiser, Brad Freeman, Bush made a pilgrimage to the home of George Shultz on the campus of Stanford University. As Reagan's secretary of state, Shultz had come to symbolize for many conservatives what they felt to be the successes of the Reagan foreign policy. There, Bush met with a group that included economists Michael Boskin, John Taylor, and John Cogan; Reagan's domestic policy chief, Martin Anderson; former US district judge and Shultz aide Abraham Sofaer; and Stanford University provost Condoleezza Rice. All except for Rice had ties to the Reagan administration. Bush surprised the group with both the seriousness of his intent, his impressive grasp of foreign affairs, and his willingness to learn about matters as arcane—but important to the group—as the International Monetary Fund. They were also impressed—and surprised—by his willingness to take on an issue that the Democrats had called their own since 1935: that of Social Security reform. Following the presentation and discussion, Shultz quietly told Rove that Bush was "presidential timber," and that he would help Bush if he decided to run. He then cornered Bush and promised his support. Bush continued his full-court press. In July 1998, he invited several members of the Shultz group to Austin for a second meeting. Here, he told them that he was considering a run for the presidency and he wanted their help.[27]

But, first, Bush had to be reelected governor, and it was Rove's task was to ensure that Bush won the 1998 election in a landslide, thus impressing the nation with his electoral prowess. Rove also worked to ensure that Bush won big in the Hispanic community—a key electoral bloc for national Republicans—and that he demonstrated his fundraising prowess by raising money from sources from all around the nation. Also, the Bush camp worked hard to defuse the criticism that if he became president, he would be leaving the administration of Texas in the hands of the Democrats. To this end, Bob Bullock supported Bush for a second term. In Bullock's stead, the Bush campaign worked hard to secure the election of Republican Rick Perry as lieutenant governor.[28]

The Democratic candidate for governor, land commissioner Garry Mauro, tried to use the Lucas commutation against Bush, calling him soft on crime. It didn't take, as the public had not forgotten Bush's decision in the Tucker case. For his part, Bush made education reform—particularly a proposal to end "social promotion" (the practice of promoting a child to the next grade level whether or not the promotion was justified by their grades)—and his tax cut proposal the cornerstones of his campaign. Sources are in dispute as to how much money Mauro had—one source says $3.5 million; another says he had less than $2 million. It didn't matter one way or the other. Bush had between $20 and $24 million. Bush also left little to chance—an in-house dust-busting effort, which gathered information on Bush for use in parrying any Mauro thrust, was headed up by Harriet Miers, a Dallas lawyer and former member of the Dallas City Council.[29]

The issue was never in doubt. In November 1998, Bush was reelected governor with 69 percent of the vote—the first governor elected to consecutive four-year terms in the history of the state. As important was the wide swath of his victory. Bush won 49 percent of the Latino vote, 27 percent of the African American vote, 65 percent of women, and 70 percent of those who listed themselves as an independent. In his victory speech, Bush described himself as a "compassionate conservative" no fewer than five times. It would not be the last time that that phrase would be used.[30] Two hours before he was to be sworn in for his second term, Bush attended a prayer service at the First Methodist Church in downtown Austin that, as he later recalled, "reached out and grabbed me, and changed my life." Pastor Mark Craig indeed put on a spellbinder. He challenged each attendee to "use or lose" 86,400—the number of seconds in a day; he told of his visit to Yellowstone Park and the Old Faithful geyser and observed that "people are starved for faithfulness." But the line that stuck with the younger Bush was Craig's observation that "people are starved for leadership." Bush's mother later told her son that Craig "was talking to you;" Bush believed it to be so. In his first memoir, written to accompany the next phase of his political life, Bush credited Craig and his sermon with having "prodded me out of my comfortable life as Governor of Texas and toward a national campaign." Bush had decided to run. He told his family. The response of his daughters: "Dad, you're going to lose. You're not as cool as you think you are." The response of his brother Marvin: "Are you nuts?"[31]

And so began the campaign for the presidency.

# 3

★ ★ ★ ★ ★

# ELECTING A PRESIDENT

It took Bush only a matter of weeks after his second inauguration to make the first significant move toward the structure of a presidential campaign. Bush made Joe Allbaugh his campaign manager and asked Karen Hughes and Karl Rove to reprise their roles as his communications manager and his chief political strategist, respectively. Bush now had his three closest advisers in Texas as his three closest advisers on his presidential campaign staff. They were given equal status and paid the same salary—even though no member of the "Iron Triangle" had ever worked inside the federal government or served on a national campaign.[1]

Perhaps to make up for this deficiency in insider experience, in February 1999 Bush named Joshua Bolten his campaign's policy director. Bolten earned his BA from Princeton University (1976) and his JD from Stanford Law School (1980). He had clerked at the US District Court in San Francisco, worked in private practice, served as an executive assistant to the Kissinger Commission on Central America, and taught international trade law at the Yale Law School. From 1985 to 1988 he served as counsel to the Senate Finance Committee, and from 1989 to 1991 he served in the first Bush administration as the counsel to the US trade representative and as a deputy for legislative affairs. In 1999 he was working for Goldman Sachs as that company's legal director. Bolten's policy pedigree was accompanied by an offbeat sense of humor, plebian interests—he was an avid bowler and a motorcycle enthusiast—and a quieter demeanor than that of the often-boisterous team of Texans.[2]

Bush was confident in his views toward domestic, economic, and social policies. The ideas he advocated in the presidential campaign were remarkably consistent with the views he had advocated as governor. However, when these views hit the national stage, many analysts—some of whom were closely observing Bush for the first time—were surprised to find that the governor of Texas might, in domestic affairs at least, be a different kind of Republican than they had become accustomed to.

No one was surprised when Bush made a tax cut the central focus of his domestic package. But many arched an eyebrow when Bush promised that those cuts would "double the child tax credit and reduce the lowest tax bracket for the working poor." And everyone was caught off guard when he advocated rerouting a portion of federal tax revenue directly to churches and charitable organizations. Bush's faith-based plan called for the spending of $8 billion per year to help stimulate private and religious charities.[3]

Along with this, Bush quietly dropped the demand of many in his party to do away with the Department of Education and kept his Texas education package—based on the rerouting of federal tax dollars to those schools that showed improvement as indicated on standardized tests. On 5 October 1999, in a speech to the Manhattan Institute, a conservative think tank, Bush rolled out his education proposals, replete with campaign buzzwords: "Our nation has a moral duty to ensure that no child is left behind."[4]

Even more so than with faith-based grants and education reform policies, both of which Bush had made his own in Texas, observers were stunned when he made Social Security reform—the "third rail" of American politics that no one dared touch—a central feature of his presidential campaign. Moreover, Bush was calling for reforms to the system that had been championed by Democrats. A document that accompanied a May 2000 speech at Rancho Cucamonga, California, laid out Bush's views on the issue:

- Modernization must not change existing benefits for retirees or near-retirees.
- The Social Security surplus must be locked away only for Social Security.

- Social Security payroll taxes must not be increased.
- The government must not invest Social Security funds in the stock market.
- Modernization must preserve the disability and survivor's components.
- Modernization must include individually controlled, voluntary personal retirement accounts, which will augment the Social Security net.[5]

Bush believed that his domestic package would help bring the nation out of era that had, as he phrased it in a July 1999 speech in Indianapolis, produced a "society of addiction and abandonment and stolen childhood." But unlike many in his party, Bush did not advocate having the federal government do as little as possible and letting the free market correct any social imbalances. He rejected the "destructive" view that government should have "no higher goal . . . than leave us alone." Rather, as he proclaimed in the same speech, "In every instance where my administration sees a responsibility to help people, we will look first to faith-based organizations, charities, and community groups" and then turn to the federal government, particularly for those "things that government should be doing—like Medicare for poor children. Government can't be replaced by charities—but it can welcome them as partners, not resent them as rivals."[6]

Liberals had long branded the party of Ronald Reagan, the senior Bush, and Bob Dole as a collection of doddering old Scrooges, who advocated programs that would aid big business and glut the military, all paid for with slashing cutbacks to federal programs for the poor, for children, for women, and for workers of all stripes. The younger Bush sought to change that perception by offering a new direction for the Republican Party. Influenced by the works of philosopher Michael Novak as well as conservative writer and University of Texas professor Marvin Olasky, Bush's vision was that of a more caring Republican Party—one no less fiscally conservative, but one that recognized its responsibility to the less fortunate of the nation's citizenry. He even had a name for his vision. As Bush put it, "I like to joke that a compassionate conservative is a conservative with a smile, not a conservative with a frown. Some who would agree with a conservative philosophy have been turned off by a strident tone. I have set a different tone."[7]

Bush's primary opponents panned his idea and loudly disparaged what they felt to be the banality of the phrase "compassionate conservative." Sen. Lamar Alexander (R-TN) called it "weasel words"; former vice president Dan Quayle called it "silly and insulting;" billionaire publisher Steve Forbes called it "mealy-mouthed rhetoric." Even comic Robin Williams weighed in, quipping that phrase was "an odd combination—like 'A Volvo with a Gun Rack.'"[8]

Regardless, compassionate conservatism represented a significant break with the Republicanism of the recent past. It was also good politics. A survey done by the University of Michigan found that while 80 percent of all Republicans called themselves "conservatives," when asked about the "most important problems" facing the country those same conservatives listed education, social welfare, and medical care most often. Second, this view appealed to the moderates who Bill Clinton had won to his side with his "New Democrat" beliefs, and who had abandoned Dole in 1996. *Washington Post* reporter Dan Balz seemed admiring when he noted that Bush had shown a "shadow of Clintonism" with compassionate conservatism and had essentially "stolen a page from President Clinton's political playbook." This view also helped Bush's standing in the evangelical community, a group that was suspicious of the governor because of the moderate social positions held by his father. To them, in the words of political observer E. J. Dionne, when he spoke of compassionate conservatism, Bush "seemed to be proposing God, not government."[9]

But such a strategy came with decided risks for Bush. It particularly put him at risk of losing support of those in his party who saw compassionate conservatism as a potential spending boondoggle and as evidence that Bush was, to put it charitably, too soft. On 25 January 1999, C-SPAN's Brian Lamb interviewed Bush at his office in Austin. In his first question, Lamb asked Bush to explain a line from his second inaugural address—that he was hoping for "prosperity with a moral and spiritual center." Bush jumped on the question as the opportunity to tell the story of his visit to the juvenile detention facility at Marlin, Texas, where a boy asked him, "What do you think of me?" Bush recounted to Lamb how he felt about the boy's question: "It was a question that was so profound and so right." Bush felt that it meant "Is there a role for me in society?"[10]

That was too much for conservative columnist George Will to bear. Will, who had been a critic of Bush's father (and whose wife was the campaign manager for one of Bush's primary opponents, Elizabeth Dole), denounced Bush for using "the emotive language of today's therapeutic ethos." Translation: Bush was weak. But in case Will's high-flown language missed its mark (Bush's softness "testifies to the ubiquity of the culture of

emotional vulnerability"), he gave Bush the highest insult that any conservative Republican could give to another Republican who wanted to be
known as a conservative: he called Bush "Clintonesque."[11]

While Bush was confident in his views on domestic affairs, he had much
to learn about foreign and national security affairs. His tutor, one of the
Stanford academics who had been present at Bush's journey to the seat of
Reaganism, would become Bush's closest adviser as president.

Condoleezza Rice was born in Birmingham, Alabama, in 1954; her
family moved to Denver after the Birmingham church bombing of 1963.
Originally, Rice wanted to be a concert pianist, a dream she carried with
her when she enrolled at the University of Denver at the age of fifteen
(she had skipped the first and seventh grades). During her junior year,
however, she took a political science class with Josef Korbel, a Czech immigrant, who ignited a passion in Rice for the study of the Soviet Union.
Following her graduation from Denver (at age nineteen), Rice took only
one year to complete her master's degree at the University of Notre Dame.
She then returned to the University of Denver, where once again under
Korbel's tutelage she completed her doctorate. Rice took a professorate at
Stanford University but left that position in 1989 when she began a stint
on George H. W. Bush's National Security Council (NSC), first as director
then as senior director of Soviet and East European affairs. She left the
NSC in 1991 and returned to her faculty position at Stanford. In 1993 she
became the first African American, first female, and youngest provost in
Stanford's history. While serving in that position, she assisted her former
boss on the NSC, Brent Scowcroft, who included her in memory-jogging
sessions as he and Bush prepared to write their joint memoir. Scowcroft
worked tirelessly to keep her name in front of the Bush family whenever
the discussion turned to foreign policy advice for the younger Bush.[12]

Scowcroft's machinations worked. In August 1998, four months after
the Stanford meeting, the senior Bush set up a meeting at Kennebunkport
between Rice and his son. The weekend featured informal conversations
on foreign policy and baseball (like Bush, Rice was a sports fanatic) conducted over joint fishing trips and workouts on the exercise equipment.
The two hit it off, to the point where he told her that if his reelection bid
in Texas was decisive, he would probably run for the presidency. Rice remembered being impressed, noting that he knew more about Mexico than
she did.[13]

Rice brought the viewpoint of the Republican realists to Bush's policy table. Realism was evidenced in the statecraft of leaders as diverse as Richard Nixon, Henry Kissinger, Brent Scowcroft, and George H. W. Bush. The Realists argued that foreign policy revolved around the goals of state actors whose actions stemmed from a logical desire to acquire as much power for their nation as possible. Since realists assume that every nation is acting in the same manner, national security, then, was based on a balance of power, where the art of diplomacy was the art of the deal. A true realist did not allow either ideological constraints or moral beliefs to get in the way of achieving that balance, because to achieve that balance—even if it meant visiting the Soviet Union and the People's Republic of China in 1973, playing North Vietnam off against the PRC in 1974, looking the other way to the carnage at Tiananmen Square in 1989, or allowing Saddam Hussein to stay in power in 1991. All were all concessions that were worth making for the common good. Often described, with some fairness, as a Machiavellian outlook, realism gives a little to get a lot of stability, and the realist does not let moral or ideological beliefs get in the way of that balance.[14]

However, a group of thinkers who called themselves neoconservatives wanted to bring moral considerations and ideological definitions back into the world of international diplomacy. Neoconservatives largely, but not exclusively, began their political gestation as Democrats. However, they came to loathe what they saw as the leftward, pacifistic drift of their party in the 1960s and 1970s. While many neocons left the Democratic party, many others felt just as uncomfortable with Republican realism. To a neocon, the ideals of democracy are not only worth preserving but also worth imposing on other nations—whether or not that other nation *wanted* to live in democracy seemed to be of little interest to a neocon. Neocons would rather fight a Communist than deal with a Communist, and preserving a balance was not uppermost on their minds. Thus, while neocons cheered, and played a part in, Ronald Reagan's adventurism in Latin America, they stewed and ultimately booed George H. W. Bush's refusal, for example, to hold the PRC accountable for Tiananmen, and for his decision to maintain the balance of power in the Middle East by not going to Baghdad to overthrow Saddam Hussein at the end of the Persian Gulf War. Moral judgments, then, played an important part in how neocons saw the world. For them, state actors needed to be held accountable for their actions, because some things were simply, and always, wrong.[15]

No one represented the neoconservative mindset as well as did Paul Wolfowitz. Wolfowitz attended Cornell, where he took a degree in mathematics, and the University of Chicago, where he earned a PhD in political science and economics in 1972. During the Carter administration he served in the Pentagon, and during the Reagan presidency he served in the State Department and as ambassador to Indonesia. In the administration of the first Bush, Wolfowitz served under Secretary of Defense Dick Cheney as undersecretary of defense for policy. However, the 1991 decision not to pursue the overthrow of Saddam Hussein, a leader whose sadistic transgressions were well known, enraged Wolfowitz. More than any other issue, neocon writing in the 1990s obsessed over Iraq, as neocons searched for a champion who would help to right this wrong. In 1997, Wolfowitz and Zalmay Khalilzad, then the director of the Strategy, Doctrine, and Force Structure at the RAND Corporation, wrote an article for the *Weekly Standard* calling for the "liberation of Iraq from its tyranny." As Scowcroft, Shultz, and the senior Bush had brought Rice to the younger Bush's campaign team, it was Dick Cheney who brought Wolfowitz.[16]

As we will see, George W. Bush disagreed with his father over the decision not to try to overthrow Saddam. But in 2000, Bush was not yet president. He wisely included both Realists and neocons on his campaign team in a very high-profile advisory capacity. Counting themselves, Rice and Wolfowitz put together a team of eight advisers who represented the two strains of Republican thought on foreign policy (Cheney was not an official member of the group). Representing the Realists was Richard Armitage, who had been instrumental in the evacuation of US troops and personnel from Saigon in 1975 and had served in the Defense Departments of both the Reagan administration and the first Bush administration; Stephen Hadley, who had worked for Cheney as assistant secretary of defense for international security policy; Robert Zoellick, who had served in the first Bush's Department of State as undersecretary for economic and agricultural affairs, served as deputy chief of staff, and from 1990 to 1993 took the lead on the process of reunification in Germany; and Robert Blackwill, who worked with Rice in the Bush NSC. Richard Perle and Dov Zakheim, both of whom had worked in the Pentagon during the Reagan administration, represented the neoconservative strain.

Absent from the group were several key Realist advisers from his father's administration—most notably former secretary of state James A. Baker III and former national security adviser Brent Scowcroft—an omission that was not missed by the press. Also missing from Bush's team was Colin Powell, a decorated veteran of the Vietnam War who had served as Reagan's national security adviser. On the recommendation of Cheney, he was chosen as the first African American to serve as the chairman of the Joint Chiefs of Staff, a position he held until 1993. Following the first Persian Gulf War, Powell shot to the top of the list of presidential contenders, a perch he held throughout the Clinton presidency. In 1996 Powell seriously looked at a run but decided against it, citing family obligations. While not a Vulcan, Powell's views were represented at their meetings by Armitage, who was one of his closest aides.[17]

This was a group of new Republican Wise Men—and, in a significant area of departure, women. They met with Bush in Austin for the first time on 24 February 1999. Bush told the group, which Rice had named the "Vulcans" (so named for a statue in Rice's hometown of Birmingham), "I need your help . . . not to become president. I will take care of that. But I need your help to be a good president."[18]

On Saturday, 12 June 1999, Bush flew to Iowa on board a chartered plane wittily named *Great Expectations* (the candidate himself got on the microphone to tell the press who had joined the trip to "please stow your expectations securely in your overhead bin as they may shift during the trip and could fall and hurt someone—especially me"). In Cedar Rapids, Bush finally announced what everyone already knew. In a brief, almost offhand remark, he declared, "I'm running for President of the United States. There's no turning back. And I intend to be the next president of the United States." It was his father's seventy-fifth birthday. The day after his announcement, the younger Bush traveled to the family retreat in Kennebunkport. As he met with the press, his father, who was standing by his side, smiled as he claimed, "He doesn't need a voice from the past. . . . I had my turn. I got some things right. Maybe I messed some things up. But it's his turn now in the family. . . . He doesn't need advice from me."[19]

The comment from the senior Bush brought one of the key issues of his son's campaign into clear relief. Always hanging over the campaign—as it would be, for some, throughout the younger Bush's administration—was the question of the father's influence. It was, to say the least, a delicate situation. If Bush was to be successful in including all wings of the party in his campaign, he would have to use his father subtly, so as to not anger those in his party—particularly evangelicals, social conservatives, economic conservatives upset about the tax increase, and neoconservatives—many of whom had come to distrust the policies of his father. As a result, Bush's campaign staff soon found out that they were not to trade on either the name or the influence of Bush's father. As one example, when Ron Kaufman, who had served as the senior Bush's political director, sent out an unsolicited mailing asking for a donation to the son's campaign, Karl Rove made it clear to Kaufman that such unapproved intrusions were neither sanctioned nor desired.[20]

Bush moved to distance himself from his father with the November 1999 publication of his first memoir, *A Charge to Keep*. We will soon see that what was left out of the book was as important as what was put in the book. But careful readers were quick to notice the significant amount of space Bush spent in subtle criticisms of his father. Bush began the section on his father's political legacy by repeating his oft-used quote from his gubernatorial campaigns—"I went to Sam Houston Elementary School, and he went to Greenwich Country Day"—thus implicitly touting himself as a true Texan and not a member of the eastern elite. Then, after professing his love and admiration for his father and mother, he laid out some specific critiques of his father's performance, both as a campaigner and as a chief executive. First, he expressed what he felt to be the chief reason for his father's 1992 loss: "I respect his humility and try to emulate it in my private life. In the public arena, though, if you don't define and promote yourself, someone else will define you. In 1992, Bill Clinton and Ross Perot and Pat Buchanan defined him, and he lost in a long and miserable year." He then moved to separate himself from what he felt to be a significant political and policy blunder, when he wrote of the "death of a thousand cuts in politics. . . . One cut was self-inflicted, by my dad's famous statement: 'Read my lips. No new taxes.' . . . Breaking his pledge cost him credibility and weakened his base." This made it clear to the party's conservative base that the younger Bush would keep his word on tax cuts. He then criticized his father's managerial style: "I learned you must give your senior advisors direct access to the boss, or they become frustrated and disillusioned." And he finished his examination of his father with what was, perhaps, the most damning criticism: "I learned voters are interested in what you have done, but they are more interested in what you will do next."[21]

All this being said, Bush was nonetheless not above quietly taking his father's help when it came to fundraising. Bush decided to pass on accepting federal matching funds; thus, his campaign for the nomination would not be bound by spending limits. The campaign did this, according to Bush pollster Matthew Dowd, because it assumed that billionaire publisher Steve Forbes, who would be one of Bush's opponents in the Republican primaries, would be their most formidable adversary. Despite

Bush's innate cockiness—he told his cousin that there were not many times in life when the only thing that would be standing between him and the Republican nomination for the presidency was Steve Forbes—the campaign didn't want to get to the end of the primary season, be out of money, and have to deal with Forbes's deep pockets. The senior Bush saw to it that the financial playing field was somewhat leveled. He made it clear to donors in the family Rolodex that he wanted them to wait before committing to a candidate. As a result, Bush's opponents in the early primaries found that there was little money to be had. On only the second day of the formal campaign, Bush announced that it had raised $35.5 million that quarter—twice as much as Al Gore had raised, six times the amount raised by Bush's nearest Republican competitor, and $7 million more than all his competitors, combined, had raised in the first quarter of the year. When the amounts were announced, an audible gasp was heard from the reporters in the room.[22]

Bush made his first major address as a candidate on foreign affairs on 23 September 1999, in a speech delivered at The Citadel. In it, he sharply differentiated himself from what he saw to be the adventurism of the Clinton administration when he pointed out that while he did not sanction a "retreat from the world," he nevertheless argued that "sending our military on vague, aimless and endless deployments is the swift solvent of morale." In the same speech, Bush made a promise that, while virtually ignored in the moment, would become one of the most ironic of his political career: "I will put a high priority on detecting and responding to terrorism on our soil. The federal government must take this threat seriously."[23]

On 14 August, Bush won the first test of the electoral season, winning the Iowa straw poll with 31 percent of the vote, to Steve Forbes's 21 percent, former secretary of labor Elizabeth Dole's 14 percent, and former secretary of education Lamar Alexander's 6 percent. The straw poll was a beauty contest that earned no one any delegates. Nevertheless, both Dole and Alexander dropped out of the race. More important, the victory cemented Bush as the front-runner in the eyes of the media. By the end of the summer, expectations for Bush were almost stratospheric. In response, the number of media requests for interviews was, by any measure, staggering.

Bush almost wilted under the pressure. His slips of the tongue were too many to be ignored. Malapropisms such as his calling Greeks "Grecians," calling Kosovars "Kosovians," quipping that "you can't take the high horse and claim the low road," and stating, "I know how hard it is for you to put food on your family"—were seen as proof that Bush was a lightweight. Episodes like Bush being asked during a television interview in Boston to name the leaders of Chechnya, Taiwan, Pakistan, and India—something he could not do on the spot—fed this narrative. Rice knew that the interview had exposed weaknesses both in Bush's knowledge base and in his team's preparation. She told him, "We've got to step it up," to which he replied, "I know."[24]

The Iowa caucuses, featuring a byzantine voting system that came first on the political calendar, had a history of being unforgiving to front-runners. No one knew that better than Bush—in 1980 his father had upset the front-runner Ronald Reagan, and in 1988 Bob Dole beat his father. To win in Iowa, the younger Bush would have to convince his party's elders both that he had the gravitas to lead in foreign policy and that compassionate conservatism was a path worth following. In that vein, Bush stayed on point with a tenacity that surprised only those who had not seen his discipline in his two campaigns for governor. Two issues were key. On the subject of taxes, Bush made it clear that he would not, as his father had, reverse himself on his promise of a tax cut—in a January 2000 debate at the University of New Hampshire, Bush proclaimed, "This is not only 'no new taxes.' This is tax cuts so help me God."[25]

Secondly, and most important, Bush cemented his link to his party's evangelical wing, a key constituency both in Iowa and nationwide. Bush's father had, to his electoral disappointment, distanced himself from the religious Right. But the religious Right had been watching its influence wane in the Clinton years, and in 2000, candidates who were strong supporters of the Christian Right and had good name recognition—Pat Buchanan, Dan Quayle, and John Ashcroft—had fallen by the wayside before Iowans had cast one ballot.

That left Bush, whose conversion story was known to all (the title of his campaign biography, *A Charge to Keep*, was taken from a well-known Methodist hymn). Indeed, Bush spoke fluent evangelical. Since his 1998 reelection victory, Bush had personally spoken to several leading televangelists, telling them, "I believe God wants me to be president." At a 15 December 1999 debate in Des Moines, he answered a generally innocuous question from a local anchor—"What political philosopher or thinker do you most identify with?"—with "Christ, because he changed my heart." When pressed by the moderator to expand upon how his life was changed, Bush responded: "Well, if they don't know, it's going to be hard to explain.

When you turn your heart and your life over to Christ, when you accept Christ as the savior, it changes your heart. It changes your life. It happened to me." Many were dumbfounded by the answer; his own father told him, "Don't worry son, I don't think the Jesus answer will hurt you very much." Searching for a candidate, the religious Right was willing to forgive Bush his parentage. His answer in the debate was exactly what it needed to hear; it was further evidence that, unlike his father, Bush was one of them.[26]

Bush's plan to reroute federal monies to churches in a new faith-based war on poverty both impressed and delighted evangelicals. But two issues formed the bedrock of evangelical politics. Bush was crystal clear on one, and more opaque on the second. On the issue of abortion, Bush was unabashedly pro-life. His stand on the issue was well stated in a response to a July 1999 letter from Gary Bauer, the head of the Family Research Council and himself running in the Iowa caucuses, and his wife, Susan. In his letter, Bush articulated his views on abortion—views that were consistent with his statements on the campaign trail. He emphasized, "I want to reduce the number of abortions in Texas." He noted that he had supported a bill that year that required parental notification before an abortion could be performed on a minor and also supported policies to encourage adoption and waiting periods to allow the mother a period of time to consider alternatives to abortions. He told the Bauers that he opposed partial-birth abortions, as well as using taxpayer dollars to fund abortions. He concluded his letter: "The future of our society depends on the strength of our families. I hope you and others in your community will join me in speaking out in favor of life and for a return to individual responsibility and accountability."[27]

But on the issue of gay rights, Bush fumbled for a clear answer. During a 22 November 1999 appearance on NBC's *Meet the Press*, Bush told host Tim Russert that he would not meet with the Log Cabin Republicans—a group representing gay and lesbian Republicans—even though John McCain had already done so. Bush argued that such a meeting "creates a huge political scene. . . . I am someone who is a uniter, not a divider. I don't believe in group thought, pitting one group against one another." Unconvinced, Russert followed up: "But you're against gay marriage?" Bush answered, "I am against gay marriage because I believe that marriage is for men and women." Russert bored in: "What about gay adoption?" Bush: "I don't support gay adoption either because I believe that society ought to aim for the ideal, and the ideal is for a man and a woman to adopt children."[28]

On 24 January 2000, Bush won the Iowa caucuses with 40.99 percent of the vote, winning ten of the state's twenty-five delegates. Forbes (30.24 and eight delegates, despite the endorsement of the state's largest, and most conservative, newspaper) was badly hurt; and neither former ambassador Alan Keyes (14.24 percent and four delegates) nor Gary Bauer (8.53 percent for one delegate) showed any appreciable strength and would no longer be a factor in the race. The press narrative was now both simple and true—the race for the Republican nomination was now between Bush and a candidate who barely visited the state but walked away with 5 percent of the vote and one delegate.

John S. McCain III was born into the navy. After attending some twenty different schools due to his father's constant relocation as a naval officer, McCain graduated from the US Naval Academy in 1956. He then attended the National War College for two years and became a navy pilot. In 1967 he volunteered for combat duty in Vietnam. On 26 October 1967, McCain's bomber was shot down over Hanoi; he broke both of his arms and one of his legs in the crash. The North Vietnamese captured McCain and moved him through several prison camps, where he was repeatedly beaten and tortured. In December 1969 McCain was brought to Hoa Loa prison—known to the prisoners as the Hanoi Hilton.

McCain's autobiography, *Faith of My Fathers: A Family Memoir* (1999) shares the gruesome details of his captivity and imprisonment at Hoa Loa. After his captors discovered that he was the son of a US Navy admiral, he was offered an early release. McCain refused and instead continued the grueling regimen of torture and interrogation with the other prisoners. On 14 March 1973, immediately following the cease-fire agreement, McCain and his fellow prisoners were released. Initially, McCain returned to his first love, serving as a flight instructor for the navy. Then, in 1977, he moved to Washington to serve as the navy's liaison with the US Senate. Bitten by the political bug, in 1981 McCain moved to Arizona, and in 1982 he was elected to the first of two terms in the House of Representatives. McCain built and nurtured a reputation as a nonconformist—most notably when he broke with the Reagan administration on its plan to keep a marine contingent active in Lebanon. In 1986 McCain was elected to the Senate for the first of six consecutive terms. There, he broke with party

regulars in his support of gay rights, gun regulations, and campaign finance reform. He also earned the support of many neoconservatives, who
embraced him when he supported Clinton's military intervention against
Slobodan Milošević in Kosovo.[29]

In 2000 McCain wrote off Iowa and went all in in New Hampshire. He
employed his tour bus—dubbed the "Straight Talk Express"—as a traveling press conference. The candidate made himself available to reporters around the clock, with no real filter. Frustrated with trying to break
through the veneer of the highly scripted Bush campaign, the press adopted McCain as its own and presented him as the antidote to politics as
usual. As a result, the media became, in the words of one reporter who
covered his campaign, "McCain's base."[30]

As Bush remembered it, "McCain, a member of Congress since 1983,
had managed to define himself as an outsider and me as an insider." McCain
didn't have to work very hard at it—Bush *was*, as Alberto Gonzales put
it in his memoir, "the ultimate insider." He had worked two presidential
campaigns at close range and had been an informal adviser in his father's
White House. But that wasn't why Bush was flailing in New Hampshire.
Rove later admitted that the Bush campaign paid less attention to New
Hampshire than it should have, choosing instead to begin its planning for
the general election campaign even before it had left Iowa.[31]

Missing the fact that McCain's candor was co-opting press coverage,
Bush threw only a weak counterpunch. He rechristened his campaign airplane *Air Access*, but he gave the press corps no more access than before—
they derisively dubbed the Bush plane "the Stalag." Bush seemed to be
above it all; indeed, his campaign skipped a debate with the other five
Republicans in the race so that Bush could attend a ceremony honoring
Laura Bush as an outstanding alumna of Southern Methodist University.
His advertisements were bland, featuring him and Laura sitting on a couch
in Crawford talking straight to a camera. Bush was also inadvertently hurt
by his father, who, during a campaign trip to New Hampshire, praised
"this boy, this son of ours." The comment tasted of both elitism and con-
descension and played into the hands of those who felt that Bush's only
real preparation for the presidency was that his father had been president.
Rove put the situation succinctly: "We let Bush be seen as if he felt entitled
to the nomination."[32]

On 1 February 2000, Bush lost big. New Hampshire Republicans gave
him only 30.36 percent of the vote and five delegates, to McCain's 48.53
percent of the vote and ten delegates. Forbes won only 12.66 percent and

two delegates. Celebrating with McCain were reporters who were, in the words of one who followed the campaign, "thoroughly embedded" with the McCain campaign. An ecstatic McCain shouted, "Someone yell 'Timber!'"—as if he had just chopped down a sturdy oak.[33]

Out of practice with losing, Bush told Rove to call McCain with his concession. An aide intercepted Rove's call, angrily telling him that staffers do not concede in a presidential campaign. But the damage had been done. Bush soon called McCain personally, but the ninety-second conversation was little more than perfunctory. Bush was more gracious with his own stunned staff, telling them, "This is my fault, not yours." This was a seminal moment for the Bush team. Each of them remembers the moment in their own way, but all remember it with a tone of reverence and awe. To them, it showed that their candidate cared more about them than he did about winning.[34]

But he had, nevertheless, lost. Once again, Laura Bush had to give her husband a dose of castor oil. The candidate's wife sternly lectured him after his defeat, noting that he had "gotten away from his core message of changing Washington," and that he had better not let himself "get defined again."[35]

Bush's 8 February victory in Delaware—which gave him the same number of delegates that McCain had won in New Hampshire—was important to the Bush campaign because it made it feel that it could win a primary even after the defeat in New Hampshire. But both campaigns were looking past Delaware and on to the first test in the South, the 19 February primary in South Carolina. Two weeks before the New Hampshire primary, Bush had led McCain in South Carolina by twenty-four points. Now, one week after his loss in New Hampshire, he trailed McCain in South Carolina by eight points. Unquestionably, as Bush privately admitted to Rove, if he lost in South Carolina, his candidacy was over.[36]

Following Laura's advice, in South Carolina the Bush campaign attempted to seize the title of reformer away from McCain—Bush's new campaign slogan was "Bush: A Reformer with Results." New advertisements highlighted Bush's reforms in Texas and stated that McCain's claim to being a reformer was baseless because he had not actually passed any reform legislation. Bush also changed his campaign style, discarding his lengthy set speeches in favor of short stump speeches, often delivered in shirtsleeves on a stage while answering questions from the audience.[37]

Bush also charged after the state's evangelical vote. The day after the

New Hampshire primary, Bush delivered a speech at Bob Jones University, a Greenville, South Carolina, school that had lost its tax-exempt status for refusing to admit Black students; although that policy had been changed in 1971, the institution still forbade interracial marriage and dating. Following the speech, the press excoriated Bush and held McCain up as a paragon of virtue because he had not chosen to speak there. But the South Carolina Republican base could now draw the conclusion—without any help from Bush, who did not address the issue either directly or indirectly—that Bush agreed with the school's policies.[38]

Bush also launched an attack on McCain's character that turned into a negative campaign of astonishing brashness. In a speech delivered the day after the Bob Jones event, at an event honoring South Carolina Medal of Honor recipients, Bush was introduced by Thomas Burch, the chairman of the National Vietnam and Gulf War Veterans Committee. In that introduction, Burch stunned the audience by launching a full-frontal attack on McCain: "He has never, ever sponsored or cosponsored a piece of Veteran's legislation that means anything to Vietnam or Gulf War veterans. . . . He had the power to help the veterans. But he came home, forgot us." Bush not only shook Burch's hand at the end of the introduction but, when asked to condemn Burch, coldly replied, "He's entitled to his own opinion." This event drew an angry, bipartisan response: Democrats Max Cleland, John Kerry, and Bob Kerrey and Republican Chuck Hagel—all members of the Senate, and all Vietnam veterans—signed a letter that protested Bush's actions and defended McCain's honor.[39]

But this was just the beginning. McCain's family and his integrity were savagely attacked, and the tracks of the attackers led directly to Bob Jones University. Jones himself wrote an article for a conservative magazine in which he claimed that McCain—a "liberal-even-Marxist" politician—had divorced his first wife and married a "rich, attractive, and well-connected . . . twenty-five-year-old former cheerleader" who was "addicted to barbiturates."[40] Richard Hand, a Bob Jones University professor, wrote an email that claimed that Bush had led a life of "partying, playing, drinking, and womanizing," and that McCain "chose to sire children without marriage," including a nonwhite child. In an irony of epic proportions, the claim that McCain had a nonwhite child was actually true—he and his second wife, Cindy, had adopted a Bengali baby from Mother Teresa's orphanage in Bangladesh. But the hint that McCain had fathered a mixed-race child out of wedlock had thrown more red meat to the conservative base.[41]

As important, Bush had gotten under McCain's skin, and the Arizonan's reaction was ineffective. He ran a response ad that compared Bush to Clinton ("Do we really want another politician in the White House America can't trust?") and an ad claiming that Bush's ad "twists the truth like Clinton." More than a little disingenuously, Bush felt that in comparing him to Clinton, McCain's ad "crossed a line." Bush responded with an ad of his own, which featured him talking straight to the camera: "When John McCain compared me to Bill Clinton and said I was untrustworthy, that's over the line. Disagree with me, fine. But do not challenge my integrity." Bush pollster Matthew Dowd remembered that immediately after the ad aired, Bush's numbers began to rise. McCain was now completely on the defensive. He announced that he was personally ordering an end to any negative ads his campaign might still be running, and he demanded that Bush pledge to do the same. Bush responded with undisguised contempt: "That's an old Washington trick. . . . He runs ads for eighteen days defining me for something I'm not, then all of a sudden says, 'Okay, let's all quit.' I'm going to make sure people understand exactly what I believe, exactly where I stand."[42]

The bad blood spilled onto the stage at a debate held on 16 February. McCain claimed that he had stopped all his own negative ads. Bush quickly produced a leaflet, found only the day before on a car windshield, which attacked Bush on Social Security. McCain claimed that he was not responsible for the ad, to which Bush replied, "Well, it says 'Paid for by John McCain'" a line that elicited howls of laughter from the audience. After the debate, Bush put his arm around his adversary and began to tell him that his team had nothing to do with Hand's email; McCain snarled, "Don't give me that shit. And get your hands off me."[43]

Bush's negative campaign worked. Rove remembered that before the controversy over the ads erupted, McCain had been up by eight points, and that when it was over, Bush was up by five—a lead he never relinquished. Helping to seal the deal was a last-minute CBS story claiming that McCain had flown thirty-five times on private jets from thirteen different companies—all for free. On 19 February, Bush trounced McCain, 53.39 percent and thirty-four delegates, to 41.87 percent and only three delegates.[44]

McCain was badly bloodied, but he continued to fight on. In heavily Catholic Michigan, he ran a campaign as negative as Bush's had been in South Carolina, using robocalls which claimed that Bush believed that the pope was "the antichrist" and that Catholicism was a "satanic cult." As it had done for Bush in South Carolina, McCain's negative campaign—along with the fact that independents and Democrats were allowed to vote in the primary—helped him win on 22 February in Michigan, scoring 50.97 percent and fifty-two delegates to Bush's 43.05 percent and only six delegates.[45]

But Michigan only prolonged McCain's agony. Bush won in Washington (a state with an independent streak that many thought McCain would do well in) with 48.26 percent of the vote, in Virginia with 52.79 percent, and in North Dakota with 75.72; Bush had won a total 77 delegates to McCain's 9. Then, on 7 March—"Super Tuesday"—Bush won nine of thirteen primaries, winning 485 delegates to McCain's 88. It was over.

Bush and McCain met on 9 May 2000 to bury the hatchet. At that meeting, Bush claimed that he regretted not denouncing Tom Burch for his introduction-attack on McCain; all McCain said was "thank you." When McCain met the press after the meeting, a reporter observed that while he had praised his party's presumptive nominee, he had not once used the word "endorse" in his statement. A visibly angry McCain looked straight ahead and grumbled, "I endorse Governor Bush. I endorse Governor Bush. I endorse Governor Bush. I endorse Governor Bush. I endorse Governor Bush. I endorse Governor Bush." What had now become a blood feud would keep McCain from ever being considered as Bush's running mate.[46]

Much like George W. Bush, Albert A. Gore Jr. took his time finding his true calling in politics. Gore was born in Washington, DC, in 1948. Although he spent some time on the family farm in Carthage, Tennessee, Gore was largely raised inside the Beltway. His father, a US senator from Tennessee, moved his family to be with him in Washington, and they lived in the Fairfax Hotel on Embassy Row. After graduating from prep school and from Harvard University, where he took a bachelor's degree in government in 1969, the younger Gore enlisted in the army. He stayed stateside for almost a year, working for an army newspaper. In January 1971, he was sent to Vietnam as a field reporter for *Stars and Stripes*; he was discharged in May 1971. Gore attended the Vanderbilt University School of Religion for one year, at the same time that he worked at the *Nashville Tennessean* as an investigative reporter. Changing his focus, he took a leave of absence from the *Tennessean* and then attended Vanderbilt's School of Law from 1974 to 1976. He ended his law school tenure to run for the House of Representatives from Tennessee's Fourth Congressional District, a seat that had been held by his father. Gore served three successive terms in the

House, carving out a niche for himself as an expert in arms control issues. In 1984 he won election to the US Senate, in 1988 he ran unsuccessfully for the Democratic nomination for the presidency, and in 1990 he was re-elected to the Senate. In a surprise move, in July 1992 Bill Clinton asked Gore—who far surpassed Clinton in Washington experience—to be his running mate. As vice president for both of Clinton's terms, Gore spear-headed initiatives to curb governmental waste and began to carve out a name for himself in environmental issues.

On the one hand, Gore held some good cards, most notably a strong economy. In 1992, with a campaign slogan that proclaimed, "It's the Economy, Stupid," Clinton had promised that he would fix the recession that plagued the elder Bush's last year in office. In large measure, Clinton's administration delivered on this promise. Between 1993 and 1997, ten million new jobs were created; between 1997 and 2000, eight million more were added. By April 2000, unemployment dropped to 4 percent. During Clinton's time in office, household income rose by 13 percent, the gross domestic product (GDP) increased by some $2.5 trillion, and close $1.5 trillion in capital moved through the New York markets daily. Few noticed that the market boom was based on excessive speculation in technological companies—the "dot-coms." Even fewer seemed to notice that Congress fed that boom by removing a safety net that dated back to the Great Depression. In 1999 the Gramm-Leach-Bliley Act overturned the Glass-Steagall Act of 1932, which had prohibited commercial banks from taking part in the investment business. This opened the door for mergers of gigantic proportions, and by the end of the 1990s investment banks fueled a tremendous glut in internet stocks. But even when the tech bubble burst in 2000, leading to a sharp recession that lasted into 2001 in which some $5 trillion in investments and two million jobs were lost, there was little panic in the financial sectors. At least partly because of the booming economy, Clinton had survived impeachment intact, and his job approval numbers were higher than ever. Stuart Stevens, a Bush campaign consultant, jokingly suggested that Bush's campaign slogan should be "Times Have Never Been Better—Vote for Change."[47]

But Gore was also tied to the greatest liability of the Clinton administration—the president himself. If George Bush had to separate himself from his father, Al Gore had to find a way to separate himself from Bill Clinton. What was often missed was that along with Clinton's high job approval rating went historically low personal favorability ratings. Regardless of his own personal behavior, which all believed to be above reproach, Gore could be expected to be tied to Clinton's poor choices. This led to an internal debate within the Gore campaign that was never fully resolved—how best to use Clinton on the campaign trail. Gore decided not to use him, and Clinton was relegated to the sidelines. The president understood: he said that it was fine for Gore to call his affair with Monica Lewinsky "inexcusable" ("Al, if I thought it would help in the campaign, I would let you flog me at noon right on the doorstep of the *Washington Post*").[48]

Gore's reputation for being somewhat cold in public, particularly when paired against the effusive glad-hander he served as vice president, would also be a liability. Carter Eskew, one of Gore's closest advisers, called Gore a "techno-populist. In other words, he can sit down and talk to you for four hours about the human genome, but at the end of it will be, 'and we've got to make sure these insurance companies don't screw people with this information.'" Reporter Anthony Lewis wrote to himself (in typed notes): "Gore: All trees, no forest. No melody. But Bush is disturbing."[49]

Gore had also left himself open to charges of flip-flopping on the issues with an eye toward the direction of the political winds. The most notable example of this occurred earlier that year, on one of the most contentious issues of the day. Elizabeth Rodriguez, her boyfriend, and her son Elian González attempted to flee Cuba with twelve others in a small motorboat. During the passage, Rodriguez drowned. When the refugees finally made it to Florida, the Immigration and Naturalization Service (INS) placed Elian with relatives in Miami. Represented pro bono by future Supreme Court justice Brett Kavanaugh, the relatives requested that the boy receive asylum in the United States. But Elian's father, Juan Miguel González, was still in Cuba, and he demanded Elian's return. In June 2000 the US district court ruled that only Elian's father could petition for asylum, and Attorney General Janet Reno ordered that the boy be returned to Cuba. In a scene as surreal as it was terrifying, federal agents in body armor swooped down on the apartment where Elian was staying, brandished their weapons, and seized the screaming child.[50]

In a public statement made on 30 March, Gore had initially voiced his support in favor of legislation that would give the boy permanent residence status in the United States. But after the court's decision and Reno's actions, Gore changed his mind and supported Elian's deportation. As Bush media adviser Matthew Dowd remembered it, "It reinforced the perception that Gore would do things for political reasons, not for the right reason." Cuban Americans were furious with Gore. They would not forget.[51]

In the Democratic primaries, Gore benefited from having only one adversary. New Jersey Senator Bill Bradley's campaign never gained traction, and in Iowa Gore succeeded in painting him as an out-of-touch easterner. Bradley lost in Iowa and then in New Hampshire; he dropped out of the race on 9 March. Gore's choice of vice president was both shrewd and effective. Joseph Lieberman, senator from Connecticut, was one of Clinton's most vocal critics—in a February 1999 statement he had called Clinton's behavior "embarrassing for all of us as Americans." Having Lieberman on the ticket gave the Gore campaign badly needed distance from the White House. Lieberman's position as the first Jewish candidate on a major party ticket added to the novelty of the moment and guaranteed positive opening press coverage.[52]

Lieberman's choice all but ensured that Gore would make up ground following the Democratic Convention, held in Los Angeles from 14 to 17 August. But he gained a point or two by momentarily shedding his reputation for stiffness and passionately kissing his wife, Tipper, on the convention platform in full view of the cameras. Following the convention, Gore went from being eleven points behind Bush to being one point ahead. At the annual meeting of the American Political Science Association, seven scholars announced that it was a mathematical certainty that Gore would win the general election.[53]

Bush had seen firsthand the shoddy vetting of Dan Quayle by his father's campaign in 1988.[54] He had also seen the attempts that Quayle's staff had made to position him as his father's heir apparent; this was but one of the reasons he had participated in the unsuccessful attempt to get Quayle thrown off the ticket in 1992. Bush had resolved that there would be a process that would show to the world how serious he was about finding a running mate with both the needed experience to be president and, in the buzzword of the moment, "gravitas" within the Washington establishment. There was, indeed, a vetting process. But in the end, it didn't account for much. From the start, Bush knew exactly who he wanted.[55]

Born in Lincoln, Nebraska, in 1941, Richard Bruce Cheney had attended Yale University and Wyoming's Caspar College before receiving his BA (1965) and MA (1966) from the University of Wyoming. Following a congressional fellowship, in 1969 Cheney became a special assistant to

Donald Rumsfeld, then the director of the Office of Economic Opportunity. Cheney worked in several staff positions in the Nixon White House, and when Rumsfeld became Gerald Ford's chief of staff in 1974, Cheney became his deputy. When Rumsfeld moved to Defense in 1974, Cheney was promoted to serve as Ford's chief of staff, a position he held to the end of the Ford presidency. In 1978, Cheney was elected to the House of Representatives as the at-large congressman from Wyoming, where he served for the next eleven years. A consistent supporter of Reagan-era defense increases, Cheney served on the House Intelligence Committee and served as the ranking Republican member of the committee that investigated the Iran-Contra scandal. Cheney rose steadily through the leadership ranks, reaching the position of minority whip—the second-ranking Republican in the House.

Cheney was one of those rare birds who, after being elected to Congress, did not argue loud and often in favor of the congressional prerogative. He watched with growing concern as Congress, suddenly interested after Vietnam and Watergate in reinvigorating its oversight role, put significant checks on the executive branch, and he found such measures as the War Powers Act (1973) to be both dangerous and unconstitutional. In 1988, in the wake of the Iran-Contra scandal, Congress was considering a bill that would have required the president to give Congress forty-eight hours' notice before the beginning of any covert operation. In an op-ed for the *Wall Street Journal*, Cheney was unsparing in his criticism of the measure: "On the scale of risks, there is more reason to be concerned about depriving the president of his ability to act than about Congress's alleged inability to respond."[56]

In 1989, following the aborted nomination of John Tower, George H. W. Bush chose Cheney as his secretary of defense. The only serious questions at his confirmation hearings centered on the state of his health—since 1978, Cheney had had three heart attacks and quadruple bypass surgery. Nevertheless, he was unanimously confirmed by the Senate. Cheney was an integral part of Bush's national security team, distinguishing himself in the prosecution of the first Persian Gulf War (1990–1991). After Bush's defeat in 1992, Cheney became a senior fellow at the American Enterprise Institute. In 1995 he seriously considered a run for the presidency but finally dismissed the idea, claiming, as he told Colin Powell, that "the business of raising money had become distasteful." Later that year, Cheney was named chief executive officer of the Halliburton Company, a Dallas-based energy company. Popular with the neoconservatives, Cheney had nonetheless maintained cordial relations with the senior Bush (who advised his son that Cheney would make a good vice president. Although he was not close to the junior Bush, and certainly not originally part of the inner campaign circle, both his contacts and his advice were appreciated.[57]

George W. Bush wanted Dick Cheney as his running mate. Cheney brought a world of insider experience to the ticket that, despite his own involvement in his father's campaigns and administration, the governor of Texas lacked. Equally important was that Bush liked the fact that Cheney had no further political ambitions—a vice president who wasn't running for president was a novelty in recent political history and would be an asset to Bush receiving unvarnished advice from his second-in-command.[58]

In November 1999 Bush asked Cheney to chair his campaign. Pleading a busy schedule at Halliburton, Cheney turned him down. Bush sent Allbaugh back to Dallas to ask Cheney if he would he consider making himself available as a possible running mate. Cheney turned Allbaugh down flat. He noted the poor imagery presented by Bush running with another oilman; his three heart attacks; and the fact that he would carry no appreciable electoral votes with him (Cheney: "If you need me on the ticket to carry Wyoming, you have bigger problems") and that he was happy at Halliburton. Cheney might well have added that his thirty-year-old daughter, Mary, who had come out to her parents as gay in high school, was certain to be used as a fulcrum to force Cheney into a discussion about gay rights—a discussion that Bush hoped to avoid as long as possible. He also might have added that there was a constitutional issue that could prevent the match—the Constitution made it clear that two residents of the same state could not together receive electoral votes.[59]

Regrouping, Bush asked Cheney to spearhead the search for his running mate. Cheney immediately agreed, largely because he felt it was a "definable" task that would be over by convention time. On 24 April, while campaigning in Dayton, Ohio, Bush announced that Cheney would be spearheading his vice presidential selection process—in so doing, Bush also announced that this choice would not exclude Cheney from being considered as Bush's running mate. Thus, the process that would ultimately lead to Cheney was now controlled by Cheney. This led many to conclude that Cheney somehow rigged the process, offering Bush candidates for the position who were ultimately unacceptable or, in the words of one Cheney friend, would ultimately "light themselves on fire." Naturally, Cheney disagreed with such characterizations of the process, telling his authorized biographer that "a lot of people don't believe it, but I really did not enter into the effort with the notion that somehow I was going to get the job."[60]

Cheney set up a vetting team that included his daughter Elizabeth; his son-in-law Phil Perry; and David Addington, a lawyer who had served as Cheney's special assistant when the latter was secretary of defense. Together they developed a questionnaire of almost two hundred questions, organized under seventy-nine headings, that dealt with every aspect of the potential candidate's life—both professional and personal. After filling out the form, Tennessee Senator Bill Frist quipped: "Dick Cheney knows more about me than my mother, father, and wife." Two of the most recognizable names—the two who would bring the instant star power to the ticket—were quickly excluded. McCain was eliminated without much discussion. The media hyped Colin Powell, but Powell made it clear that he didn't want the job, and he didn't want to be asked.[61]

With the biggest names out of the picture for sundry reasons, the list of candidates that Cheney ultimately presented to Bush—all thoroughly vetted, with a level of detail that Rove wittily dubbed "the political equivalent of a proctology exam"—was hardly a list of stellar superstars. The list included three present governors: John Engler of Michigan, Frank Keating of Oklahoma, and Tom Ridge of Pennsylvania; three senators: Frist, Chuck Hagel of Nebraska, and John Kyl of Arizona; Representative John Kasich of Ohio, former senator John Danforth of Missouri, and former governor and senior Bush cabinet member Lamar Alexander of Tennessee. The list included nine names, but, as Bush was later to write, "in my mind, there was always a tenth."[62]

It seemed that Bush was the only one on his team who wanted Cheney. Hughes told Bush that she favored Ridge. Rove and Bolten both favored Danforth, and Bush himself admitted to being "intrigued" by the former minister, Missouri senator, and staunch defender of Clarence Thomas. Indeed, Bush wrote later, "I thought seriously about offering the job to Danforth, but I found myself returning again and again to Dick Cheney."[63]

Just before the Fourth of July, Bush met with Cheney at his ranch. The convention was but four weeks away, and so far, Bush, who was clearly enthralled with none of the candidates with which he had been presented, had held no formal interviews for the position. During a lunch attended by Bush, Laura, Karen Hughes, and a family friend, Bush stunned the room by responding to Laura's question about the vice presidential search with either "The man I really want to be vice president is here at the table" (Hughes's recollection) or "Dick, you are the perfect running mate" (Bush's recollection). Following lunch, Bush took Cheney outside to the porch. As Cheney remembered it, Bush looked at him, and said either "You know, Dick, you're the solution to my problem" (Cheney's recollection) or "Dick, I've made up my mind." (Bush's recollection). Cheney protested: he reminded Bush of his three heart attacks and that his daughter was gay, making it clear on the latter point that "if you have a problem with this, I'm not your man." Bush remembers telling Cheney that he "could not care less about Mary's orientation" and asking him to consider what was now clearly a bona fide offer.[64]

Cheney immediately began to consider it. Several days after the meeting with Bush, he contacted Dave Lesar, the chief operating officer of Halliburton, and informed him that there was a good chance that Bush would choose him as a running mate and that Lesar should be ready to take over the reins of the company. Cheney also called a meeting of Halliburton's board of directors, giving them essentially the same news. Cheney also agreed to have a health examination, the results of which were sent to Dr. Benton Cooley, a Houston cardiologist. On 12 July, Bush called Cheney to tell him that Cooley had given him a clean bill of health.[65]

On 15 July, Cheney met with Bush and his team in Austin to discuss the pros and cons of a Cheney candidacy. Perhaps in an attempt to defuse the resistance of his staff, Bush turned to Rove and asked him point-blank, "Tell me why you think I shouldn't pick Dick Cheney." Rove listed all the reasons that Cheney himself had initially given when Bush first asked him to run and added one more that was sure to hit home: that asking Cheney would look like the son needed the help of his father's advisers both to get elected and to make his own administration work. Cheney did not disagree with Rove's assessment; indeed, he came prepared to add another negative to Rove's list: "Look, I'm conservative." Bush responded: "We know that." Cheney parried: "No, I'm *really* conservative." Bush was unfazed by the discussion. Nothing said by Rove or by Cheney had changed his mind; Bush still wanted Cheney.[66]

Then the campaign concocted an elaborate ruse to throw the media off the scent. On 18 July, Cheney flew to St. Louis, picked up John Danforth and his wife, and escorted them to Chicago, where he met with Bush in a hotel room to discuss matters both personal and political. More than a chat and less than a formal interview, the meeting had the desired effect—news of it leaked almost immediately (with some help from Rove, who reportedly told a Bush aide who had been suspected of being a leaker that the choice was definitely Danforth). This gave Cheney just enough cover and time to fly to Wyoming on 21 July and fill out the paperwork required to register to vote in that state's upcoming primaries. Now the presumptive presidential and vice presidential nominees were registered to vote in different states, thus avoiding a constitutional commotion.[67]

Clearly, an offer had been made, and tacitly accepted, several weeks before Bush made what he remembered as the "formal offer," which came at 6:22 a.m. on 25 July, after Bush was done with his morning exercises. Cheney accepted and remembered telling his wife, "Honey, let's sell the house. I quit my job. We're going back into politics." The formal announcement was made in Austin that day. Cheney had not submitted himself to his own vetting procedure—he had not filled out a copy of his own questionnaire, and no independent source had seen or consulted his tax, financial, or medical records.[68]

The Republican National Convention, held in Philadelphia from 31 July to 3 August, was run by Andrew H. "Andy" Card Jr. Born in Brockton, Massachusetts, Card attended the US Merchant Marine Academy and in 1971 received his BS from the University of South Carolina in engineering. Card worked as a structural design engineer until 1975, when he won election to the Massachusetts House of Representatives, where he served until 1982. Card chaired George H. W. Bush's 1980 presidential campaign in Massachusetts, then managed Bush's 1988 campaign in New Hampshire. When Bush chose New Hampshire governor John Sununu as his first chief of staff, Sununu brought Card along as his assistant. Card served in that role under both Sununu and his successor, Samuel Skinner, and in 1992 Bush named Card as Skinner's successor as secretary of transportation. After chairing the transition to the Clinton administration, Card returned to corporate America; in 2000 he was the chief lobbyist for General Motors. After doing some fundraising for the younger Bush, Card was put in charge of the convention.

Card remembered that he wanted to "change the way the convention [was] organized," remembering that his view was that "George Bush needed to be introduced to the American people . . . and so I wanted the convention not to be as much of a coronation as it usually is. . . . I wanted the whole convention to be a miniseries on George W. Bush." A key part of this was defusing any show of discord on the floor that would distract from the message. Toward this end, Card convinced McCain to speak, as well as Colin Powell.[69]

Bush's acceptance address, delivered on 3 August, had been written by Michael Gerson, a former senior policy adviser for the conservative Heritage Foundation and senior political editor for *U.S. News & World Report*, now serving as one of Bush's speechwriters. The speech was an attempt to turn Gore's advantages against him. Instead of glossing over the economic prosperity, Bush accused Clinton and Gore of allowing the nation to coast on its laurels: "For eight years, the Clinton/Gore administration has coasted through prosperity. And the path of least resistance is always downhill. But America's way is the rising road. . . . My generation tested limits—and our country, in some ways, is better for it. . . . At times, we lost our way. But we are coming home." Bush rhetorically closed the door on Clinton's tenure: "Our current president embodied the potential of a generation. So many talents. So much charm. Such great skill. But, in the end, to what end? So much promise, to no great purpose. . . . This administration had its moment. They had their chance. They have not led; we will." Then, Bush looked straight at American evangelicals and once again made it clear that he was one of them: "I believe in a God who calls us, not to judge our neighbors, but to love them. I believe in grace, because I have seen it; in peace, because I have felt it; in forgiveness, because I have needed it." It was a less than subtle tip of the strategy: Bush would position himself as a humble sinner squaring off against an administration of liars and cheats. He would beat Gore by running against Clinton. The speech was well received and played a large part in Bush's erasing Gore's lead. Bush got a convention bump of about six points. The race was now a dead heat.[70]

Within days of his nomination, Bush received his first classified briefing from the CIA in Crawford. Deputy CIA director John McLaughlin dryly told the candidate: "Governor Bush, if you are elected president, there will be a major terrorist attack during your time in office." McLaughlin remembered Bush's response: "He absorbed it and was interested and took it on board."[71]

The Bush campaign had begun to plan its fall strategy during the primary campaign. Rove understood that if Bush carried only those states carried by Dole in 1996, and then was able to win back those states that had been traditionally Republican prior to that year—a list on which Rove included Florida—Bush would still need about 20 electoral votes to reach the magic number of 270. This meant winning Pennsylvania—23 electoral votes, but hardly a sure thing—or, in Rove's mind, "some combination of Iowa (7), Wisconsin (11) and Michigan (18)." For Rove, "that was too risky a strategy." He therefore enlarged the list of target states to include the traditionally Democratic bastions of Tennessee (Gore's home state), Arkansas (Clinton's), and—the biggest surprise of all—West Virginia, which Republican had not won since 1984, and Dole had lost by fourteen points. Indeed, Rove later remembered with a laugh that the campaign in West Virginia was "fun . . . because it was out of the box."[72]

But the early days of the campaign were disastrous for Bush. On 31 August, Cheney delivered a speech designed to introduce the campaign's school bonds program, but the audience was mistakenly a group of Fort Lauderdale third graders (Cheney gamely made the speech anyway). Then, on 4 September in Naperville, Illinois, when Bush and Cheney were accepting the welcome of the crowd, a nearby live microphone picked up their exchange to each other: Bush: "There's Adam Clymer, major league asshole from the *New York Times*." Cheney: "Oh yeah, he is. Big time." Later, Bush told the press: "I regret that a private comment I made to the vice-presidential candidate made it to the public airwaves." But neither man apologized to Clymer. Both were roundly criticized in the press (if nothing else, the episode earned for Cheney a new nickname within the campaign: "Big Time.") Also, on 12 September, the *New York Times* revealed that in one frame of a Bush ad denouncing "Bureaucrats," the spot showed the word "RATS" in big white letters—an attempt to use subliminal advertising to manipulate the audience. (Rove: "Our defense was the truth—we thought it was an accident.") Thanks to these gaffes, Gore sneaked ahead of Bush and led the race by about five points in mid-September.[73]

Then things started to change. First, Bush picked up the support of Colin Powell. With it came the support of many previously uncommitted Republican moderates, as well as hopes that the Republicans might make a tiny dent in the Black vote. Then, in a decision that caught the Gore campaign completely off guard, the Bush campaign ran several contrast ads that showed its position on Social Security and Medicare reform and attacked Gore's. Bush promised to work for partial privatization of the programs, and to establish a Social Security reform commission.[74]

Gore also helped Bush with his penchant for stretching the truth. In the space of one week's campaigning in Florida, Gore claimed that his mother-in-law paid almost three times as much for the same arthritis medicine given to his sick dog—a claim disproved by the *Boston Globe*. Then he told an audience of Teamsters that he remembered his mother singing him to sleep to the strains of the song "Look for the Union Label." This too was quickly disproved—the jingle had been introduced in a television ad in 1975, when Gore was twenty-seven years old. Then Gore announced that he was in favor of Clinton's decision to release thirty million barrels of oil from the nation's reserves to help calm rising oil prices—it took the Bush campaign a nanosecond to remind the voters that less than one year before, Gore had publicly opposed such a move. Immediately into Bush's stock speech went the line: "He'll say or do anything to be president." Gore's lead began to shrink. As the campaigns readied themselves for the debates, Gore held a four-point lead.[75]

All gaffes aside, no one in the Bush camp had deluded themselves into thinking that a debate against Al Gore would be a cakewalk. He had gained experience in the vice presidential debates of 1992 and 1996, and in a November 1993 CNN debate over the North American Free Trade Agreement, Gore had wiped the floor with Ross Perot. On the Republican side, Bush simply had no comparable experience with debating—it would be the expert against the novice. Indeed, as they readied themselves for the first debate, to be held at the University of Massachusetts in Amherst on 3 October, the Bush team made a rookie mistake. Not wanting Bush to face the protesters who were sure to surround a Boston hotel, Rove had him stay in West Virginia the night before the debate, but the food and service there were terrible, and Bush spent a restless night listening to the racket of train whistles and barge horns.[76]

The next day, an exhausted Bush arrived for the debate. After shaking hands with Gore, Bush removed his wristwatch, so as not to duplicate the mistake made by his father in 1992, when during a town hall debate with Clinton and Perot, the older Bush looked at his watch with a bored, "I'd-rather-be-anywhere-but-here" look that hurt him in the polls. He needn't have worried, for Gore handed him a victory. First, Gore once again dissembled, claiming that he had visited Texas to check on government reaction to wildfires with James Lee Witt, director of the Federal Emergency Management Agency (FEMA), when he had not. But more damaging was Gore's body language. When Bush was speaking, the network feed caught Gore's reactions—audible sighs and rolling eyes made him seem petulant and impatient. In Card's memory, Bush was "not that good, but good enough." But the debate produced a line that would be thrown in Bush's face many times after 2003: accusing Gore of supporting "nation building," Bush opined: "I would be very careful about using our troops as nation builders. I believe the role of the military is to fight and win war. . . . I don't want to try to put our troops in all places at all times. I don't want to be the world's policeman."[77]

The vice presidential debate, held at Centre College, Danville, Kentucky, on 5 October, showed a Dick Cheney who was quite quick on the draw. Cheney and Lieberman were seated opposite each other at a table, and the discussion was markedly civil. But Cheney got in a few zingers. Lieberman spent a moment talking about how much better the country was since Clinton had taken over. Then he looked at Cheney and, clearly intending to draw attention to Cheney's wealth, quipped: "And I'm pleased to see, Dick, from the newspapers, that you're better off than you were eight years ago, too." The audience laughed, but Cheney's response was quick and received even more laughter: "And I can tell you, Joe, that the government had absolutely nothing to do with it." Lieberman pushed the issue, pointing to his wife in the audience and quipping, "I can see my wife, and I think she's thinking, 'Gee, I wish he would go out into the private sector.'" Cheney pounced: "Well, I'm going to try to help you do that, Joe." The audience roared with laughter. The debate resulted in a slight bump in the polls for the Republican ticket—a bounce that rarely happens after vice presidential debates.[78]

The second presidential debate, held on 11 October in Winston-Salem, North Carolina, focused on foreign policy, which was billed as Gore's strength. The debate was scored by most as a draw; Rove remembered that it was distinguished only by Gore agreeing with much of what Bush said, and his wearing so much pancake makeup that, on the air, he looked orange.[79]

The third and final debate almost didn't happen. The day before the debate, Missouri governor Mel Carnahan, who was running against John Ashcroft for a Senate seat, was killed in a plane crash. Card remembered that both sides discussed whether or not to call off the debate, but the decision was made to go ahead. Held on 17 October at Washington University in St. Louis, the town hall–style debate led to one of the iconic moments of the campaign. During debate prep, Ohio congressman Rob Portman had stood in for Gore. Portman remembered that during both his last senatorial debate, as well as in a debate against Bradley—both of which were held using town hall formats—Gore had gotten out of his seat, walked across the stage, and stood within touching distance of his opponent. When Portman did precisely that to Bush, the candidate got visibly angry and argued vociferously that Gore would never do such a thing. Portman countered that Gore could be counted on to use that attempt to rattle his opponent, because he had done it before. Portman was right. Following the first question, Gore walked across the stage, moving deliberately into Bush's space—a violation of the previously negotiated debate rules. Refusing to take the bait, Bush did not miss a beat. He looked briefly at Gore, gave him what he accurately described as "a look of amused disdain," and continued his answer without comment. His debate performance gave Bush a significant bounce: Rove remembered that Gallup now had Bush up by ten points. It looked as if it was now Bush's election to lose.[80]

On Thursday, 2 November—five days before the election—Bush campaign spokesman Dan Bartlett called Karen Hughes with some particularly unwelcome news. Bartlett had been informed that a local Fox reporter in New Hampshire had asked a Bush staffer if Bush had ever been arrested for driving under the influence.[81]

The campaign had already been through one automobile-related crisis. In May, the press had unearthed a 1963 Midland arrest report that attested that Laura Bush (then Laura Welch, age seventeen) had run a stop sign, leading to an accident that killed a friend of hers driving in another car. But this story had not been hidden—indeed, all Midland knew about it—and in the heady days before the convention, the story had a short shelf life.

Reporters had also been on the trail of cocaine use by Bush in the past. But those reports were never fully corroborated and were largely defused by Bush giving the story the back of his hand: "When I was young and irresponsible, I was young and irresponsible." But Bush's DUI was different. It was verifiable: Allbaugh, Hughes, Bartlett, Rove, and Gonzales all knew about it.[82]

Most important, Bush knew about it and had missed at least two opportunities to get out in front of the DUI story before his campaign began. The first came in 1996, when then governor Bush appeared for jury duty (ironically, for a case that dealt with drunk driving). Bush was excused from jury service because he might have to decide as governor whether or not to pardon the defendant. On his way out of the courthouse, a reporter asked Bush point blank "Have you ever been arrested for DUI?" Bush offered a nonanswer: "I do not have a perfect record as a youth. When I was young, I did a lot of foolish things. But I will tell you this, I urge people not to drink and drive." The story disappeared. But the second opportunity came in 1999, when he wrote his campaign biography *A Charge to Keep*; Bush decided to leave the DUI out of the book.[83]

Bush would later write, "If I had it to do over, I would have come clean about the DUI that day at the courthouse." Rove agreed in a 2018 interview, admitting that "we should have found a moment in the spring, when it wouldn't have caused us damage." Bush's argument for not doing so was his belief that he needed to protect his daughters from learning of his arrest ("I didn't want them to say, 'Daddy did it and he turned out okay, so we can too'"). Regardless, it was the wrong political decision. Had Bush admitted to the offense at either time, or had he included the story in *A Charge to Keep*, there would have been no news to announce in October 2000. But now, there was.[84]

After Hughes gave Bush the news, they agreed that the only way to deal with the situation was with an immediate admission from both the campaign and the candidate. Hughes began her statement with "Twenty-four years ago." In Milwaukee at the time, Bush faced the press: "It's an accurate story. I'm not proud of that. I've often times said that years ago I made some mistakes; I occasionally drank too much. I did on that night. I was pulled over. I admitted to the policeman that I had been drinking. I paid the fine. I regretted that it happened. I learned my lesson." Bush's explanation did little to help the situation. As Rove so pithily put it: "We had made a big issue of Gore's credibility and now we had a problem with Bush's."[85]

Overnight, the race closed to a dead heat. Prior to the revelation, Bush had been up by five points in Maine; the day after the revelation, Gore was up by four points, and he would eventually win the state by five points. According to Bush's own polling, Florida was now too close to call. Bush now had his own character problem, with little time left to repair the damage. He did his best to mitigate the harm. The Sunday before the election, he swung through Florida and had breakfast with Billy Graham, who then met the media and gave Bush his endorsement. As it was, however, the DUI report had tightened the race into a knot. On 6 November, the day before the election, it was a statistical tie in the popular vote, and in the electoral college, eighteen swing states were so close that either candidate could win them.[86]

And then, as Andy Card later recalled, "Election Day came and never left."[87]

# 4

★ ★ ★ ★ ★

# NAMING A PRESIDENT

At 7:00 p.m. eastern standard time (EST) on Tuesday, 7 November 2000, most of Florida's polls closed. However, districts in the state's heavily Republican western panhandle, many of which lay in the central time zone—one hour behind the rest of the state—were still open. By 7:40, Gore was in the lead in the state. At 7:49 EST, even though voters in the panhandle were still voting, NBC called Florida for Gore. Thirty-one seconds later, after comparing the precinct votes in the balance of the state to precinct votes in Kentucky, which had also closed, CBS also called the state for Gore—ten minutes before the polls closed in the panhandle. Karl Rove later mused about the gravity of the situation—the chairman of the Bush campaign in California called him to tell him that having learned the Florida result, people were starting to leave their place in line at the polls, believing the election to be over, and volunteers at the party's phone banks were beginning to leave. The chairman's message to Rove—"We're coming apart." The Gore camp was euphoric.[1]

It wouldn't last. According to Kathleen Frankovic, director of surveys and producer for CBS News, it soon became clear that CBS had made several mistakes in its Florida count. Its statistical computation had been based on a comparison between Bush's 2000 presidential vote and Jeb Bush's 1998 gubernatorial vote, when a comparison between Gore's 2000 vote and Clinton's vote in 1996 would have been more accurate. Also, the survey sampling for the exit polls had been taken too early in the day, and too few precincts were used as a sample in those polls. Finally, the report of vote totals from Duval County had vastly overestimated Gore's overall vote totals. As the network became aware of its mistakes, its estimators began to see that Bush held a lead in the state. At 9:54 p.m. CBS did what to that point in election coverage had been unthinkable—retracted its announcement and listed Florida as too close to call. The other networks quickly followed suit. Florida was back in play.[2]

Over the next four hours, Bush's lead continued to grow, although the returns were conflicting. By 2:00 a.m. EST, the Bush lead in Florida had, by CBS's new assessment, grown to 29,000 votes; by 2:09 his lead was 51,000; but by 2:16, after a correction in the Volusia County report, Bush was up by only 30,000. The state of Florida had counted 97 percent of its vote. Even though Bush was losing ground, Fox News called Florida for Bush at 2:16 a.m.; one minute later, CBS called Florida—and the election—for Bush.[3]

At his suite in the Lowes Hotel in Nashville, Tennessee, Gore believed he had just lost one of the closest presidential elections in American history. He wanted to call Bush, concede as graciously as possible, and then go to Nashville's War Memorial Plaza and thank his supporters. Gore got Bush's phone number from a staffer; the perfunctory call took less than two minutes (Bush remembered that Gore said, "We sure gave them a cliff-hanger"). Gore and his family then left the hotel to make the short drive to the plaza. No one on Gore's team had thought to double-check the vote in Florida; they simply took the word of the television networks.[4]

But a Gore vote watcher, Michael Whouley, had taken notice of the fact that Bush's lead in Florida was rapidly shrinking. Whouley was also under the impression that Florida law mandated an automatic machine recount if election results were closer than a margin of one half of 1 percent. If all this was true, Gore was on his way to concede an election that, given time, he might still win. Whouley jumped into action. Through a roundabout method that involved bypassing cell phones through the White House switchboard, Whouley finally contacted Bill Daley, Gore's campaign chairman. Riding in the car behind Gore, Daley was able to phone Michael Morehouse, who was riding several cars behind Daley. Morehouse ran through a phalanx of supporters and Secret Service agents, catching up to Gore as the vice president and his wife were going to step onstage at the War Memorial. Out of breath, Morehouse explained the situation to Gore. Gore then called Bob Butterworth, the Florida attorney general and Gore's campaign chair in the state, and asked if he was positive that an automatic machine recount was mandated by law. Butterworth told him he was sure. With that news, Gore decided not to concede. Without addressing his supporters, he hurried back to his hotel room.[5]

Once there, Gore learned that the race in Florida had now shrunk to a statistical tie—Bush was still ahead, but by only two thousand votes. At 2:30 a.m., Gore placed a second call to Bush: "Circumstances have changed drastically since I first called you. The state of Florida is now too close to call." Suddenly sensing why Gore had called, Bush had to say it aloud: "Are you saying what I think you're saying? Let me make sure I understand. You're calling to retract that concession?" He was. Gore seemed surprised that Bush was angry—"You don't have to get snippy" (Bush: "I don't know about snippy, but I was hot"). Then the conversation turned juvenile, with Bush protesting, "My little brother says it's over." Gore shot back: "I don't think that is something that your little brother gets to decide." An impasse having been reached, Bush icily told Gore, "Do what you have to do," and hung up the phone. A few minutes later, Daley met with the cheering crowd at the War Memorial and crowed, "Our campaign continues."[6]

Many of those around Bush wanted him to simply declare victory, but heeding the advice of Jeb, who worried that the vote was becoming too close, Bush did not. The instincts of the Bush brothers were on the mark. By morning, Bush's lead had dropped to a mere 1,784 votes.[7]

Given the closeness of the results, Florida law did indeed mandate an immediate machine recount. But it soon became clear that a simple recount of the votes would be impossible. The biggest problem was the "butterfly ballot" in populous—and Democratic-laden—Palm Beach County. There were so many candidates for president in 2000 that it was impossible to fit all their names onto the front of one ballot without shrinking the font size so small that it was virtually unreadable, particularly by the large number of senior citizens who voted in Palm Beach. The county supervisor of elections, Theresa LePore, attempted to solve this by creating a ballot that used both sides of the page, arranging the candidates into two columns, facing each other. The punch-card ballot then had arrows that led from the candidate's name to the perforation that needed to be punched in order to vote for that candidate. Unfortunately, the arrows did not lead from the candidate's name *directly* to the perforation—even a cursory examination of the ballot showed that the layout could easily take the voter from the name of their choice to the perforation directly *above* the one needed to vote for that choice. Thus, many voters claimed that although they wanted to vote for Gore, their reading of the ballot took them to a perforation that actually cast a ballot for independent candidate Pat Buchanan. A Florida talk show host told her listeners: "I got scared I voted for Pat Buchannan. I almost said, 'I think I voted for a Nazi.'" Even Buchanan said later that he didn't believe he had won 3,407 votes in Palm Beach County.[8]

There were other problems. Charges were quickly leveled that "over-voting"—where the machine registered that the voter had voted for more than one candidate for the same office—had occurred statewide. In counties that had solved the ballot problem by shrinking the font rather than placing the candidate's names into columns, there was a different problem, that of "undervoting," in which the machine registered *no* choice for president. This was because in several counties—even those where there was no issue in reading the names of the candidates on the ballots—many voters did not fully punch out the perforation that signified their vote or, in many cases, did not (or could not) not punch it at all. These perforations, known as "chads," quickly became the symbol of what was fast becoming an electoral nightmare; if you didn't punch through your chad, or punched only a part of it and left the rest of it "hanging" from the ballot, the machine could not record your vote. Subsequent investigation showed that many of the machines were poorly maintained, to the point where the rubber backing on which the ballot rested resisted attempts to punch a stylus cleanly through the ballot. And in some of them, the backup of chads left behind from decades of punch-card elections clogged the machinery to the point where it was nearly impossible for some voters to punch their ballot clearly through. It soon became clear that the majority of the problems using dated and poorly maintained punch-card voting took place in poor and ethnic neighborhoods, which might have been expected to give their majorities to Gore, but either hadn't, or the result had been closer than expected. As Whouley understated, "It's a problem. It's a big fucking problem."[9]

To help the campaigns oversee the recount, as well as work their way through the labyrinth of problems in Florida, both sides called in big guns. Gore brought in Warren Christopher, who had served in the Johnson and Carter administrations, chaired the commission that investigated the 1992 beating of Rodney King in Los Angeles, and most recently had served as Clinton's secretary of state. His deputy was Ron Klain, a Washington lawyer who had been Christopher's principal deputy during the transition from the Bush to the Clinton White House, then served as associate White House counsel and chief of staff to Al Gore and had most recently run the Gore campaign's communication center.[10]

Bush also turned to a former secretary of state. Despite the fact that Bush had not included James A. Baker III, his father's secretary of state and a Bush family intimate, on his foreign policy team, Baker had cooperated with the younger Bush's fundraising efforts. On election night, he was in the Cheney family suite in Austin, waiting out the returns. When the election went into overtime, campaign chairman Don Evans suggested that Baker would be the perfect choice to go to Florida and oversee the next step. Bush agreed. The next day, Baker and his wife were driving home from the Houston airport when, according to Baker, Evans called to ask if he would agree to represent Bush in Florida; the answer was an immediate yes. Bush then called Baker to confirm the deal. After calling Christopher and visiting Bush at the Governor's Mansion in Austin, Baker flew to Tallahassee and, upon arriving, immediately met with the Bush team on the ground. After being briefed, Baker reportedly turned to Joe Allbaugh and said, "We're heading to the Supreme Court. . . . It's the only way this can end."[11]

One of the key themes in Jeffrey Toobin's prescient study of the election, *Too Close to Call*, was the difference in temperament between Christopher and Baker—a difference that would manifest itself in how each man ran his operation. Toobin observed that Baker was a relentless politico who would pull no punches in order to win. Conversely, he observed that Christopher was cautious and more interested in a solution that would preserve the sanctity of the electoral system than he was with winning for his candidate. For his part, Baker agreed with this assessment, observing in his memoir that "the biggest difference between Chris and me was that he had not been a political animal in the same sense I had." Baker certainly moved fast, and moved heavy. Utilizing his contacts in the Florida legal establishment, the Bush team scared off any law firm that even sounded like it might give Gore aid and comfort. This tactic left Gore starved for assistance—while the Bush team worked out of a suite of offices at the George H. W. Bush Republican Center, the Gore team worked out of a shopping center storefront and several hotel rooms.[12]

The first legal hurdle was the mandatory machine recount, which began on 8 November and was mandated by law to be completed by the close of business the following day. The counties received very little guidance on how to conduct the recount. Indeed, eighteen counties, containing some 1.8 million votes, never actually recounted their ballots—a fact that was not disclosed to either public or press. Everyone expected that the machine recount would confirm the results as reported on election night— that Bush held a razor-thin lead. But at the end of the first day of what was best an incomplete recount, Bush was ahead by only 327 votes. Baker was worried: "I began to think Bush-Cheney might fall behind . . . but we never did." The first Florida recount was over.[13]

The two sides settled in for a conflict of unknown duration. Baker began each day with a conference call with Bush and Cheney; normally, he would speak with Bush several additional times during the course of the day. For Baker and the rest of the Bush team on the ground in Florida, the postrecount strategy was simple. First and foremost was to state as often as possible that despite the closeness of the recount, Bush had nonetheless won the state of Florida. As Baker later argued, "George W. Bush and Dick Cheney had more votes. They had more votes on election day, more votes when the dispute ended thirty-six days later, and more votes every day in between. . . . The purpose of my going to Florida was to preserve the Bush-Cheney victory, not to take it away from the other side." Second was for Bush to play the public role of a president-elect. Bush told reporters, "I understand that there are still votes to be counted, but I am in the process of planning, in a responsible way, a potential administration . . . so that should the verdict that has been announced be confirmed, we'll be ready . . . to assume office and be prepared to lead."[14]

Third, the Bush team resolved to stand firmly in the way of any further recounts. By Florida law, a candidate had seventy-two hours from the closing of the polls to request manual recounts—the hand tallying of each ballot—in any or all of Florida's sixty-seven counties. Assuming correctly that Gore would avail himself of this opportunity following the machine recount, Baker took steps early on to bring suit in federal court to stop any such recounts. This was far from a unilaterally supported plan in Camp Bush; many felt that it would degrade a Bush presidency to sue for its status in court. This was the view of former Missouri senator John Danforth, who Baker contacted and asked to be Bush's lead attorney in federal court, should they decide to sue to stop a Gore-initiated hand recount. From his Mexican vacation spot, Danforth told Don Evans that while he would consider the offer, "Candidates don't sue. You could ruin Governor Bush's career. He's only fifty-four years old, and the decision to file a court case like this one would be a black mark that follows him forever. And it would destroy the reputation of everyone involved on the Bush side." Baker, however, would have none of it. The next phone call from Evans began with an icy "It sounds like your heart isn't in it." He then coolly told Danforth to enjoy his vacation. Baker then called Theodore Olson, former assistant attorney general in the Reagan administration and presently in a white-shoe Washington law firm, who agreed to represent Bush in federal court, should it be deemed necessary. But few thought it would be necessary. Indeed, one observer was adamant: when her son protested that the case was going to go to the Supreme Court, Sandra Day O'Connor sniffed, "Don't be ridiculous."[15]

Finally, Baker pushed hard to have Florida secretary of state Katherine Harris certify the election results with lightning speed, before Gore had an opportunity to catch up. A former beauty queen, former intern in the office of Florida governor Lawton Chiles, and a Republican fundraiser, Harris won the office in 1998 and served as one of eight cochairs of Bush's Florida campaign in 2000—indeed, she had traveled to New Hampshire to campaign for him. Later observers have stereotyped Harris as a lightweight who became easily distracted by suddenly being thrust before the television cameras. But as an elected official, she was destined to play a key role in the unfolding melodrama. The secretary of state wielded little power—indeed, Floridians had voted to make the office an appointive one after Harris's term was up in 2004. But one of Harris's constitutional duties was to oversee the election process in Florida (or, rather, her director of the Division of Elections, Clay Roberts, did it for her), and only she could certify the vote totals and formally end the election in Florida.[16]

To make sure that Harris stayed on task, Baker brought in J. M. "Mac" Stipanovich, a Republican lobbyist, to sit by her side. Stipanovich was there to make sure that Harris knew her lines for the press and that she scrupulously kept to the exact letter of the law when it came to deadlines. To Stipanovich, this meant, as he told Harris, that she was expected to "bring this election in for a landing." Harris announced that her office would follow the letter of Florida law, which stated that county canvassing boards were required to submit their certified votes within seven days of the election. This meant 14 November, a date that all agreed would be impossible to meet while conducting a hand recount. But Harris would not yield. Even though a state circuit court gave her some leeway to accept late ballots, Harris announced that she was sticking to the 14 November deadline, and she made it clear that her office would accept no late ballots. According to Harris, she was not acting according to her druthers; instead, Florida law left her no choice. Only a natural disaster, which she interpreted as being an event "such as Hurricane Andrew," would allow her to grant an extension.[17]

But Baker left nothing to chance. Should Harris cave to the pressure to extend the deadline, the Bush forces had another legally imposed deadline that they could utilize. Federal law[18] mandated that the state had until 12 December—the "safe harbor" deadline—to complete its judicial and administrative methods for settling the election. Once they were completed by that date, they were considered "conclusive, and shall [thus] govern in the counting of the electoral votes provided in the Constitution." Even this did not exhaust Baker's options. The Republican-controlled Florida legislature might be persuaded to invoke Article II, Section 1 of the federal Constitution ("Each State shall appoint, in such manner as the Legislature thereof may direct, a number of Electors") and actually bypass the electoral process altogether by appointing its own slate of electors—ones who would most likely support Bush. And Baker was not above ordering or supporting direct action in the streets: protests that would engage the media, inflame the situation, and thus slow down the hand recount.

The fundamental fact that drove Gore's strategy throughout the days of the Florida recounts was the fact that he, not Bush, was behind, even if only by a few hundred votes. It was always Gore, not Bush, who had to find the votes to make up the difference. While concession was an option, it was never seriously considered by the Gore team. Bush's lead was simply too small, Gore could not stomach conceding, and he believed that he could develop a strategy to find the few votes he needed to put himself into the lead. To do that, Gore had to keep the campaign going for Florida's votes and find a way to stop Harris from certifying the election. A hand recount of all the ballots might do that; so might a court challenge. But Gore was very aware that any strategy that extended the campaign past the end of the state-mandated recount would brand him in many quarters as a poor loser, and this was a role that Gore was loath to play.

The Gore campaign soon settled upon the strategy of demanding a statewide hand recount of all the ballots. Added to the fact that another recount would elongate the election, this strategy was driven by the fact that the Florida court had left the door open in its interpretation of what actually constituted a valid ballot in a manner that could favor Gore. In 1975, while it was vague regarding the specifics, the Florida Supreme Court had declared that no vote "shall be declared invalid or void if there is a clear indication of the intent of the voter."[19] Thus, a reasonable path for Gore to take was to demand a hand recount and have each ballot examined not for a punctured chad alone but also for evidence of the intent of the voter. Indeed, Gore made it clear that the mere counting of the vote totals would not be enough. To ensure a fair electoral tally in Florida, Gore argued, any recount would have to take into account whether or not the voter had actually intended to vote for a candidate and had been somehow stopped from doing so by faulty technology, poor construction of the ballot, or improper maintenance of the machines. If any of these things happened, according to Gore, that vote should nonetheless count—even if the ballot had been deemed invalid in the machine recount. How the Gore team might do this, they had yet to ascertain. But it was clear that it would take time.

Many analysts of the election have noted the irony inherent in these strategies. The Republicans, who usually railed against governmental activism and federal superiority over the states, were now attacking the rights of Florida to govern its own elections. The Democrats, on the other hand, usually preached the virtues of federal superiority over the states, but now they were demanding a strict adherence to Florida law and no meddling in the issue by the federal courts. At the time, however, none of this mattered to the troops in Florida. This was not a civics lesson; this was hand-to-hand combat for every ballot. As Ron Klain sputtered in a telephone conversation with Gore several days into the process: "Sir, you have to understand, this is Guatemala."[20]

After deciding to fight for hand recounts, the Gore team made two mistakes. The first—neglecting to immediately develop a plan to counter a possible Bush lawsuit to stop any hand recounts (indeed, the evidence suggests that the Gore team wasn't even considering the possibility of a Bush lawsuit at this time)—would be seen in the fullness of time. The second was more immediate. A spirited debate arose in the Gore camp over whether to ask all sixty-seven counties to recount their votes by hand, as was Gore's right, or to ask only a select few counties to undergo a manual recount. For those who argued in favor of recounting every vote in the state, the logic was obvious—more recounting, more possibility of finding votes, and more time off the clock. Christopher and Daley, however, led the charge against the whole-state strategy. They argued that overseeing a hand recount in the entire state would strain the campaign's resources. There was also the very real possibility that after all that work, some of the counties would refuse to run a hand recount. A whole-state strategy also ran the risk of turning public opinion against Gore by making him look like he was asking for a complete do-over in Florida after the election was over and the votes had been machine recounted. Moreover, limiting its request to only a few counties allowed the Gore team to pick counties that had been, at least in the recent past, reliably Democratic. Christopher and Daley proposed requesting hand recounts in only two counties, Palm Beach and Volusia, the two counties whose irregularities had started the ball rolling on election night. Eventually, Gore added Broward and Miami-Dade Counties, where reports of machine malfunctions and other problems led him to conclude that he might gain votes there. In the recent past, all four counties had been reliably Democratic. On 9 November, Gore asked for hand recounts in those four counties.[21]

It was a foolish decision. Baker neatly summarized the fallout: "Gore's decision to seek manual recounts in four heavily Democratic counties rather than all sixty-seven counties was a big mistake. It undermined his otherwise effective public relations slogan—'count every vote'—and gave us the moral high ground on that issue." It also spurred Olson to float a possible theory on which to base a lawsuit. Because Gore's recounts excluded the ballots of sixty-three Florida counties, the ballots in those counties were being treated with less legal respect than were those in the four counties where a potential hand recount could happen. Thus, Olson argued, Gore's hand recounts were a violation of the Equal Protection Clause of the Fourteenth Amendment of the Constitution of the United States, which specifies that no state shall "deny to any person within its jurisdiction the equal protection of the laws."[22]

On 11 November, the hand recount began in the four counties named by Gore in his challenge (through a series of advisory opinions from her Division of Elections, Harris attempted to stop the counties from agreeing to hand recounts, but to no avail). All eyes were initially on populous Palm Beach County, whose canvassing would, according to Florida law, begin the process. By any telling, the process was a nightmare. There was no consensus on how the canvassers would be able to learn the "intent of the voter." Some canvassers advocated the use of what was called the "Partial Separation Rule," last used in Palm Beach in 1990, which mandated that only a "chad that is hanging or partially punched may be counted as a vote." Others argued for the "Three Corner Rule," which required that a chad had to be completely detached on at least three of its four corners in order for the ballot to be counted. Others promoted the "Sunshine Rule," which said that if any amount of light shone through the chad—no matter how faint—the ballot was legitimate. Still others contended that if the chad was merely indented, the ballot counted—light or no light. After much time-consuming debate, Palm Beach County stepped away from its 1990 precedent and went instead with the "Sunshine Rule," but stipulated that any ballots that were challenged by either camp would be set aside and considered after the recount was complete.[23]

It was a recipe for a painfully slow process. By the afternoon of 11 November, only half of one precinct had been counted, Gore had made only slight gains, and the Bush team had stepped up the pace of its protests. The chair of the canvassing board, Judge Charles Burton, then changed the ground rules. He announced that the recount would now be conducted under the 1990 rules—the "Partial Separation" mandate. This did little to speed up the process. By 11:05 p.m., only 1 percent of the Palm Beach County vote had been hand recounted. After a full day of wrangling over the rules, then changing them midstream, Gore had gained thirty-three new votes to Bush's fourteen new votes—a net Gore gain of nineteen votes. The board immediately considered whether or not it should expand the recount beyond the 1 percent of the voters already completed. After contentious debate, the board voted 2–1 (with Burton in the minority) to expand the recount to include all 500,000 Palm Beach ballots.[24]

The situation in the other three counties was equally slow. Broward County adopted a generous two-corner rule, conducted its hand recount in four hours, and Gore gained 4 votes out of 3,893 cast in the county. However, the Gore forces protested the outcome, and the canvassing board agreed to meet the next day to consider those objections. The Miami-Dade canvassing board did not even meet until 14 November—Harris's date for certification. The county recounted only 1 percent of the ballots and allowed some dimpled chads, and at the end Gore had gained only 6 new votes. Only in Volusia County, which had used an optical scan ballot, did the recount go smoothly. Harris's 5:00 p.m. deadline on November 12 had arrived. Only one of the three counties had completed their recount, and the others weren't even close to being done.[25]

Thus began the tortured trip into the courts. On 11 November, as soon as the Palm Beach hand recount was done for the day, the Bush team filed a motion in the US Southern District Court of Florida, charging that hand recounts were inherently flawed. Olson argued for Bush that the recounts violated the Equal Protection Clause; Harvard constitutional law scholar Lawrence Tribe argued for Gore that a federal court had no right to insert itself in the middle of a state's election. On 13 November, the court dismissed Bush's complaint, as the judge—a Clinton appointee—ruled that jurisdiction for such complaints lay in the state courts.[26] Advantage Gore.

The Gore team had also headed to the courtroom. On 9 November, Gore had filed suit in the Second Circuit Court in Tallahassee demanding an extension to Harris's deadline. Palm Beach County joined the suit; Bush and Gore joined the suit as well. The Republicans argued that Harris had no choice under Florida law—she was bound to enforce the deadline. The Democrats argued that Harris's decision was merely a cover for her desire to ensure a Republican victory. On 14 November—the day after Gore's win in the Southern District Court and the day of the deadline—the Second Circuit handed down its verdict. Speaking for the court, Judge Terry Lewis ruled that the deadline was sacrosanct—all tallies had to be submitted to the office of the secretary of state by 5:00 p.m. that day. However, Lewis added that this did not prevent canvassing boards from filing revised returns at a later date, but Harris was under no legal obligation to receive those returns.[27] Advantage—unclear.

Lewis's opinion gave Harris the opportunity to be magnanimous and to extend the deadline without abrogating the deadline. It was an opportunity that she, with Stipanovich's prodding, refused to take. To virtually no one's surprise, seven hours after the deadline passed, Harris announced that by her reading of the decision, the law did not permit her to accept any revised returns. Just as predictably, the Democrats went ballistic. They demanded a new hearing from Lewis's court, where they moved that Harris had moved too quickly and precipitously—seven hours had not been enough time for her to thoughtfully review their requests.[28]

The decision of the Southern District Court remanding the issue to the state courts, as well as Lewis's tortured opinion, opened the door for the Florida Supreme Court to enter the fray. Here, team Gore would be at a decided advantage. After a period in the 1970s in which four of the seven justices of the Florida Supreme Court were being investigated for corruption, the voters passed a referendum in 1976 that gave the governor the unilateral power to appoint the members of that court. A string of three Democratic governors had solidified the Florida Supreme Court in 2000 as a Democratic stronghold—a Democratic governor had appointed all seven of its members. Thus, it came as no surprise when, on 16 November, the Florida Supreme Court ruled that the manual recounts could proceed.

However, this decision did not stop Judge Lewis from ruling the very next day that Harris could certify the election without the inclusion of the hand recounts that the Florida Supreme Court had just mandated. Three days later, on 20 November, the Florida Supreme Court, clearly frustrated with both Harris and Lewis, stepped in once more and issued a stay order, enjoining Harris from certifying the election until the court had the opportunity to hear oral arguments. Team Gore was ecstatic. It had told the vice president that even with the Democratic disposition of the court, it would never issue a stay. Now, the court had not only granted a stay but Gore had not even had to ask for it. Moreover, the hand recounts continued in Palm Beach, Miami-Dade, and Broward Counties, and Gore had closed the gap to fewer than 1,000 votes.[29]

On 20 November, the Florida Supreme Court heard oral arguments in *Palm Beach County Canvassing Board v. Harris*. It was as close to a done deal as could be expected. Even before the oral arguments began, Bush lawyer Benjamin Ginsberg was slipped a note from a contact inside the court that said the case had already been decided, that Gore would be the unanimous victor, and that a draft opinion had already been written. Indeed, during oral argument, the justices all but announced that they would order the hand recount to continue. The next day, the court announced its unanimous decision in favor of Gore. The hand recount was legal, the votes that had been won in that recount had to be added to the total, and the deadline for the certification of the total vote had been extended—the canvassing boards now had until 5:00 p.m. on Sunday, 26 November, to report the amended results. If the office was not open on Sunday, the deadline was the next day, Monday, 27 November. The hand recount now had five more days.[30]

From his ranch in Crawford, Bush bristled, charging that the Florida court "rewrote the law . . . it changed the rules and did so after the election was over."[31] Baker's reaction contained a thinly veiled threat: "One should not be surprised if the Florida legislature seeks to affirm the original rules."[32] Translation: the Florida state legislature could simply bypass all the legal wrangling of the past four weeks, invoke its Article II powers, and order its electors to vote for Bush.

But that was a tremendous gamble. As he would later remember, "The only way to deal with the Florida Supreme Court . . . was to go over its head." On 22 November the Bush team filed for a writ of certiorari before the Supreme Court of the United States, asking it to reverse the decision of the Florida Supreme Court. The move was not a knee-jerk reaction by the Bush team to the Florida Supreme Court decision. Baker had long argued that the case would ultimately end up before the US Supreme Court, as had Olson, and as had a young appellate lawyer from the firm of Hogan and Hartson who had lent his services to the Bush team in Florida—John G. Roberts. The Bush team argued that the Florida Supreme Court had violated a federal statute by changing the deadline for certification, that it had violated Article II of the US Constitution, which gave state legislatures the power to control how its electors were chosen, and that the lack of standards in the recount violated the Equal Protection Clause of the Fourteenth Amendment.[33]

On 22 November, the hand recount resumed. At Miami's Clark Center, where the recount was underway, the tension was profound. Outside the hall, Gore's flip-flop on Elian Gonzáles, discussed in the previous chapter, was coming home to roost.

The closeness of the race in Miami, a city that until that point had been reliably Democratic, was a direct result of the fallout over the Elian issue. The Cuban exile community of Miami—well organized and spurred on by Spanish-language radio stations, particularly the powerful Radio Mambi—was virulently anti-Gore. To exploit the explosiveness of the situation, Baker called in Roger Stone, a veteran of Republican presidential campaigns and reputed dirty trickster. On 22 November, hundreds of protesters, many shouting, "Remember Elian!" and waving anti-Gore posters, surrounded the building. The protesters were not just Cubans—Republican congressional staffers and campaign aides flew into Miami to join the fray. At the site, Stone was seen communicating on a walkie-talkie.[34]

Inside the Clark Center, the canvassing board, which had started its work on the eighteenth floor, agreed to move up to the nineteenth floor, where there would be more room to work. Several hundred spectators had gathered inside the building to watch the recount. As the board moved to the elevators, some fifty of the demonstrators followed them, cramming themselves onto the elevators. When the board finally reached the tabulation room, the demonstrators learned that they would not be allowed inside. Livid, they began to shout: "Let us in!" "They're stealing the election!" "We want to see the votes!" When Democratic party chair Joe Geller tried to get one of his questions answered by leaving the room to obtain a sample ballot, the demonstrators exploded with rage. Shouting, "He stole a ballot," they surrounded him as he fought his way to the elevator and made his way downstairs, where it took armed policemen to separate Geller from what had become a mob that clearly threatened his safety.

The rest of the demonstrators stayed upstairs and kept the commissioners trapped in their office. Congressman John Sweeney of New York, who had flown in with some of the demonstrators, was shouting, "Shut it down!" The commission, clearly fearing for its safety, stopped the recount. The "Brooks Brothers Riot"—so dubbed by the press because of the upscale clothing that the demonstrators wore—had worked.[35]

As the various recounts sputtered forward, the campaigns turned their sights on another trove of ballots that also might have been mishandled. Realizing that absentee ballots—largely military ballots posted from overseas—would favor the Republicans, Democrats had been arguing for the rejection of any absentee ballot that did not meet the letter of the law, such as having a valid postmark or being posted by the required date as prescribed by law. Vice presidential candidate Joe Lieberman appeared on *Meet the Press* on 18 November, and all expected him to say this same thing. However, Lieberman sent a jolt into the Gore campaign when he said that "the vice president and I would never authorize, and would not tolerate, a campaign that was aimed specifically at invalidating absentee ballots from members of our armed services." Going even further, Lieberman said, "I would give the benefit of the doubt to ballots coming in from military personnel generally."[36]

Seizing the moment, in a reversal of their earlier argument, it was now the Republicans' turn to argue for an expanded interpretation of voter intent. In an attempt to get as many of the absentee ballots as possible accepted as legitimate, Republican tabulators ignored all errors in the submission of those ballots. This led to what came to be known as Bush's "Thanksgiving stuffing"; in the hours before the 26 November deadline, 123 votes from absentee ballots were added to Bush's total.[37]

Historically, the US Supreme Court had largely followed the maxim of Justice Felix Frankfurter: "Courts ought not to enter the political thicket." Many disaffected Gore supporters would later argue that in 2000, the Republican-leaning court of Chief Justice William Rehnquist accepted the case that would become known as *Bush v. Gore* because from the start it had wanted to help Bush win the election. Deliberating as it does in complete secrecy, it is difficult to ascertain the intent of any one justice. But in this case, there is some evidence as to intent of one of them—the swing vote of Sandra Day O'Connor. The only member of the court who had served in electoral politics (as the Republican majority leader of the

Arizona legislature), in 2000 O'Connor had strong feelings about the two presidential candidates. On the night that Gore accepted his party's nomination, O'Connor and her husband started to watch his acceptance speech. John O'Connor would later write in his diary, "SOC couldn't stand it and went to bed." The campaign did not change her mind. *Newsweek*'s Michael Isikoff later reported that on election night, O'Connor and her husband were attending a party at the home of Mary Ann Stoessel, widow of the former deputy secretary of state. Recognizing that she was entertaining a house full of political junkies, Stoessel had put televisions in each room of the house to facilitate the viewing of the returns. When Florida was initially called for Gore, O'Connor did not bother trying to conceal her feelings: "This is terrible. That means it's over." She then walked away in disgust.[38]

On 24 November, the Supreme Court met to consider Baker's petition for certiorari. After reading the Republican petition—and without waiting for the Democrats to respond—the justices voted. The votes of four justices was necessary to grant cert; five—Rehnquist, O'Connor, Antonin Scalia, Anthony Kennedy, and Clarence Thomas—were in favor. Baker had been right—the Supreme Court was going to hear the case. Moreover, it had granted Baker an expedited writ—it would hear oral arguments on 1 December.[39]

On Sunday, 26 November at 5:00 p.m., Katherine Harris announced the modified returns and certified the results of the 2000 presidential election in Florida. George W. Bush had won 2,912,790 votes; Al Gore had won 2,912,253 votes. According to the Florida secretary of state, Bush had won the state of Florida by 537 votes. All recounts stopped. It was one day before the deadline imposed by the Florida Supreme Court—since Harris's office was closed on Sunday, the court had given her until the following day to announce her decision. However, Harris opted to certify the election as soon as she legally could.

From the steps of the Texas state capitol, Bush spoke to the nation: "The election was close but tonight, after a count, a recount, and yet another recount, Secretary Cheney and I are honored to have won the state of Florida, which gives us the needed electoral votes to win the election." Bush then spoke directly to Gore: "I respectfully ask [Gore] to reconsider" any further legal challenges, because "that is not the best route for America." Bush then announced that he had chosen Andy Card as his chief of staff (a decision that already been made several weeks earlier) and had appointed Cheney to head a formal transition team.[40]

One can almost hear Baker sighing when he recounted in his memoir that, "unfortunately, Vice President Gore did not accept the certified results and concede." But by this point, no one really believed that Harris's certification would end the matter. Gore immediately filed suit to contest the certification in the Leon County Circuit Court, charging that Harris's numbers were inaccurate. Jeffrey Toobin pulls no punches when describing presiding Judge N. Sanders Sauls, saying he had "reputation for knee-jerk conservatism . . . petty . . . inept . . . vindictive." A Democrat simply called Sauls a "redneck." Thus, Bush was guaranteed a victory in Sauls's court, but Gore had a broader plan. To be heard before the Democrat-laden Florida Supreme Court, a case first had to be heard before the circuit court. So from the point of view of the Gore team, what was needed was a fast trial and a quick decision in Sauls's courtroom, so that the case could be expeditiously appealed to the Florida Supreme Court, which could then rule with enough time to count the ballots before the 15 December "safe harbor" deadline. On 2 December the case *Albert Gore Jr. v. Katherine Harris* was heard before Sauls.[41]

On 1 December, the day before Sauls began to hear testimony, the US Supreme Court heard oral arguments in *George W. Bush v. the Palm Beach County Canvassing Board*, dealing with the decision of the Florida Supreme Court to extend the certification deadline. Once again, Ted Olson and Lawrence Tribe squared off against each other. Those who expected a Webster-like erudition of great constitutional principles would be disappointed. Indeed, the justices seemed confused as to why they had even taken the case. O'Connor noted, "If it were purely a matter of state law, I suppose we normally would leave it alone, where the state supreme court found it, and so you probably have to persuade us there's some issue of federal law here." Justice Kennedy agreed: "We're looking for a federal issue." But the conservatives on the court were angry at the way the Florida Supreme Court had rewritten electoral law; according to Toobin, O'Connor was particularly incensed that in that process, the Florida Supremes were helping Gore.[42]

On 4 December, the contestants heard both from Sauls and from the US Supreme Court. While Sauls admitted that "the record shows voter error, and/or less than total accuracy," he nonetheless ruled that there was no "reasonable probability that the statewide election result would be different" if all had gone according to plan.[43] No one was surprised at Sauls's ruling—indeed, the Gore team delivered its notice of appeal to the First District Court before Sauls was even done reading his decision from the bench. That district court certified the appeal and sent the case to the Florida Supreme Court, where oral arguments were scheduled for 7 December.[44]

The same day, The US Supreme Court handed down a per curiam (unsigned) decision in *Bush v. Palm Beach Canvassing Board*. Professing confusion and declaring that "there was considerable uncertainty as to the precise grounds" for the 21 November decision of the Florida Supreme Court, the Court nevertheless vacated the Florida court's decision and remanded the case to that court, requiring it to clarify its opinion.[45]

If the Florida Supreme Court was chastened by the ruling that it review its decision, it didn't show. It was, after all, still a Democratic court. On 8 December, in a 4–3 vote, the Florida court announced its decision in *Gore v. Harris*. It not only gave Gore the expected win—the recounting of the votes was to resume—but also gave him more than he had asked for. Along with ordering the Circuit Court of Leon County to tabulate by hand 9,000 ballots in Miami-Dade County, and ordering the inclusion into the certified vote totals of 215 Gore votes from Palm Beach County and 168 Gore votes from Miami-Dade, the court ordered a recount in all Florida counties where "undervotes" had not been subject to previous hand recounts. While Bush's team in Washington was frantically drafting a request to the US Supreme Court to stay the recount, the tide had turned. Gore now clearly had the upper hand.[46]

The case went back to Judge Sauls's courtroom, where Sauls now recused himself. Judge Terry Lewis heard arguments from both sides and then gave a legal shape to the upcoming recount. It was to begin at 8:00 the following morning. Lewis's circuit court would count the Miami-Dade undervotes. The outstanding disputed ballots would be counted by the appropriate county canvassing board under the administration of the court. Both parties could observe, but there would be no objections—the parties could only record their ballot protests and bring them to court at an unspecified date. Most important, the standard for a valid ballot was to be one that showed the "clear intent of the voter," based on the "totality of the ballot." The recounts got underway on time. There was remarkably little drama, and all parties seemed to believe that they could complete the recount by Judge Lewis's deadline.[47]

In its 8 December consideration of Baker's request for a stay of this recount, tempers boiled over at the US Supreme Court. Scalia was so angry at the Florida Supreme Court that he wanted to reverse its decision without hearing oral argument. It seemed that the conservatives on the Court would follow Scalia's lead, but Justice John Paul Stevens appealed directly to Rehnquist to call a conference for the following day. Stevens remembered that at that conference there was an "almost complete absence of any discussion of the merits of the case." Scalia continued to argue for immediate reversal, an argument that was favored by Rehnquist and Thomas. O'Connor and Kennedy both wanted to hear arguments but were in favor of a stay. Stevens, David Souter, Ruth Bader Ginsberg, and Steven Breyer were in angry dissent.[48]

At 2:40 p.m. on Saturday, 9 December, the Court tersely announced that it had granted the Bush team's request for a stay of the recounts. Four justices—Stevens, Souter, Ginsberg, and Breyer—issued written dissents. This not only was an unusual step but also hinted as to the odds. If one inferred that the other five justices were in favor of the stay order, then one could also infer that the Court would split 5–4 in favor of ending the recounts. But one thing was certain: once again, the recounts were stopped. The Court would hear oral arguments on 11 December, in the case now renamed as *Bush v. Gore*, and that decision would determine the fate of the recounts. The final act of this electoral melodrama was about to begin.

*Bush v. Gore* took the Court into previously uncharted legal territory. It had to rule on a major constitutional issue—that of the proper role between the state judiciary and those rules that governed federal elections, rules that many felt (and Olson was sure to argue) were sacrosanct, protected by Article II, Section 1, clause 2 of the federal Constitution. In his briefs, Olson argued that the Florida Supreme Court had erred by changing the rules of the election after Election Day. This led him to argue that this error violated both the Equal Protection Clause and the Due Process Clause of the Fourteenth Amendment—if Florida could change the rules after the election was over and, in effect, add votes to the total after Election Day, the votes of those who voted on time did not receive the "equal protection" of the courts. This argument had never been used in a federal case involving election issues. But the concept of using the Fourteenth Amendment in this manner actually had a deep-rooted background in American legal history. Throughout the Gilded Age and into the early part of the twentieth century, conservative courts had used the Due Process Clause for a purpose for which it was clearly not intended—to argue that owners could run their businesses—and treat their workers—in any heavy-handed way they saw fit. Denying them this right by, say, mandating that their employees work only an eight-hour day or placing an age limit on child labor, cut into the profits of a business and gave no remedy to the businessman. They argued, and the courts generally agreed, that this denied them their right to due process.[49]

The Gore brief began by stating that there was no federal law that could stop the Florida Supreme Court from interpreting a law of its own legislature—in this case, any of the various Florida laws that controlled its elections. As for the federal judiciary, Gore argued that the Supreme Court should not have taken the case; granting cert had run "an impermissible risk of tainting the result of the election in Florida—and thereby the nation." Gore charged that Bush's reading of Article II was wrong, in that it would deny the state appellate courts their constitutional rights to rule on issues of state law. As to the equal protection argument, Gore was simply dismissive—the law had not been changed, and the Florida Supreme Court had been "quite insistent that the counting of ballots must be governed by a *single* uniform standard: the intent of the voter must control." There was, to Gore, no unequal protection of the laws here.[50]

The Court heard oral arguments on 11 December. Olson once again represented Bush, but Gore had switched lawyers. Instead of Tribe (who he felt had delivered a listless argument on 1 December),[51] Gore went with David Boies, a veteran trial lawyer who had just finished representing the Department of Justice in a lawsuit against Microsoft. Reasonably certain that he already had five votes strongly leaning in his direction, Olson only had to stay out of trouble, which he did. The justices pressed him on what would be a fair standard, questions that Olson effectively ducked. The Court also gave a hint as to what it was thinking—when Olson tried to press his argument that Florida could not change its electoral laws after the election was over, Justice Kennedy interrupted him: "I thought your point was that the process is being conducted in violation of the equal protection clause, because it's standardless." Following Olson, Joe Klock, who represented Katherine Harris, faced the judges. Extremely nervous, Klock inadvertently supplied one of the few moments of levity in the proceedings. While being pressed by Stevens on the issue of fair standards,

Klock replied, "Well, Justice Brennan, the difficulty is that under . . ." The room broke out in laughter—Justice William Brennan had died in 1997. Klock tried to continue by answering a question from Justice David Souter, but he only prolonged his agony: "No Justice Breyer, what I am saying is that . . ." Already livid at the direction that the court was taking, Souter did not see the humor in the situation: "I'm Justice Souter. You've got to cut that out." Boies went last, his famous eccentricity on display by wearing tennis shoes with his suit. Regardless, he did not distinguish himself, answering Souter's questions on standards with "Well, I think that's a very hard question." In rebuttal, Ginsberg pointedly asked Olson: "How can you have one standard when there are so many varieties of ballots?" Olson did not have enough time to answer the question, which had become, for at least four of the justices, the key to the case.[52]

Following the arguments, Gore optimistically told an adviser: "They are not going to rule against me. They are going to rule in my favor." But he was wrong. The oral arguments had swayed no minds one way or the other. Stevens remembered that at the conference immediately following the oral argument, there was no discussion of the equal protection issue at all.[53] In fact, Stevens had begun work on his dissent before oral arguments were even heard.[54]

The decision in *Bush v. Gore*[55] came down on 12 December at 9:45 p.m. While the decision was per curiam, a reading of the concurrences and the dissents leads one to conclude that it was the expected 5–4 decision. After summarizing the complex trail of adjudication that had led to this moment, the majority opinion concentrated on the claim that the recount had violated the Equal Protection Clause and the Due Process Clause of the Fourteenth Amendment. "Having once granted the right to vote on equal terms, the State may not, by later arbitrary and disparate treatment, value one person's vote over that of another." The Court then found that Florida's recount procedures proceeded with an "absence of specific standards to ensure its equal application. The formation of uniform rules to determine intent based on these recurring circumstances is practicable, and we conclude, necessary." Thus, "the want of those rules here has led to unequal evaluation of ballots in various respects." It then specified its concerns by referring to the problem of the overvotes:

> The citizen whose ballot was not read by a machine because he has failed
> to vote for a candidate in a way readable by a machine may still have

his vote counted in a manual recount; on the other hand, the citizen who marks two candidates in a way discernable by the machine will not have the same opportunity to have his vote count, even if a manual examination of the ballot would reveal the requisite indicia of intent. Furthermore, the citizen who marks two candidates, only one of which is discernable by the machine, will have his vote counted even though it should have been tread as an invalid ballot. The State Supreme Court's inclusion of vote counts based on these variant standards exemplifies concerns with the remedial processes that were under way.

But this was not all. The majority also believed that the recount process itself was flawed. The Florida Supreme Court "did not specify who would recount the ballots. The county canvassing boards were forced to pull together ad hoc teams made up of judges from various Circuits who had no previous training in handling and interpreting ballots. Furthermore, while others were allowed to observe, they were prohibited from objecting during the recount." To the majority, this all served to create a recount process "inconsistent with the minimum procedures necessary to protect the fundamental right of each voter." Thus, "It is obvious that the recount cannot be conducted in compliance with the requirements of equal protection and due process without substantial additional work."

In a point of no small irony, conservatives—long champions of states' rights—were now arguing in the majority opinion for an unprecedented federal role in an election in one state. Rehnquist made that point even clearer in a lengthy concurring opinion, which argued in addition to the points made in the majority opinion that the Florida Supreme Court had overstepped when it created a recount with a deadline that superseded the deadline created by the state legislature. On the other hand, the liberals on the Court—long the champions of federal power and authority—now argued that the State of Florida had been unfairly treated by the majority, and that it should be given the opportunity, once again, to fix the mess. Stevens wrote a dissent that Ginsberg and Souter joined, arguing that the case should not have been heard by the Supreme Court in the first place ("If we assume—as I do—that the members of that court and the judges who would have carried out its mandate are impartial, its decision does not even raise a colorable federal question"), and as a result the case should have been remanded to the Florida Supreme Court for decision. Souter, who was so distraught over the affair that he considered resigning from the Court in protest, wrote his own dissent—joined by Breyer, Stevens, and Ginsberg—that argued not only that there was no federal question in the case but that a remand was realistically possible: "Unlike the majority, I see no warrant for this Court to assume that Florida could not possibly comply with this requirement before the date set for the meeting of the electors, December 18." Ginsberg was particularly disturbed by the outcome, having used the Equal Protection Clause to revolutionary effect in the 1970s in a series of cases attacking gender discrimination. Yet, in her dissent, joined by Stevens, and in part by Souter and Breyer, Ginsberg concentrated on the issue of federalism: "I might join the Chief Justice were it my commission to interpret Florida law." In the opening sentence of his dissent—joined in part by Stevens, Ginsberg, and Souter—Breyer could not have been blunter: "The Court was wrong to take this case. It was wrong to grant a stay. It should now vacate that stay and permit the Florida Supreme Court to decide whether the recount should continue." He went on: "I fear that in order to bring this agonizingly long election process to a definitive conclusion, we have not adequately attended to that necessary 'check upon our own exercise of power,' 'our own sense of self-restraint.'" It was left to Stevens to argue that the previous month's events had done real and lasting damage to the nation: "Although we may never know with complete certainty the identity of the winner of this year's Presidential election, the identity of the loser is perfectly clear. It is the Nation's confidence in the judge as an impartial guardian of the rule of law."[56]

For many who wished the decision had gone otherwise and believed that the fix was in, the most infuriating part of the majority opinion was its statement that the case could not be used as a precedent ("our consideration is limited to the present circumstances")—without saying why. But the immediate impact of the majority opinion was clear. The decision of the Florida Supreme Court was reversed. The Court had ordered an end to the Florida recount. This decision would give a 271–266 majority to Bush (270 electoral votes needed to win), thus electing him the forty-third president of the United States. The presidential election of 2000 was over.

Ron Klain read the opinion as soon as it was released and immediately understood its impact, mumbling, "I think we're kind of hosed here." It was left to Boies to break the news to both Gore and Lieberman on a conference call: "It may have been wrong [of the Court] to shoot us, but we're still dead."[57]

When the opinion came down, Bush was in bed reading, with the television coverage of the decision on in the background. The first phone call came from Rove, who greeted him with a jovial "Congratulations, Mr. President!" Bush immediately called Baker in Florida, who greeted him with "Congratulations, Mr. President-elect." Baker then spoke to Cheney, who quipped, "Only under your leadership could we have gone from a lead of 1,800 votes to a lead of 150 votes." Bush later observed, "I probably became the first person to learn he had won the presidency while lying in bed watching TV."[58]

Speaking to the nation from the Old Executive Office Building in Washington, Al Gore was stoic as he conceded defeat. He even reached for a little levity—"Just moments ago I spoke with George W. Bush and congratulated him on becoming the 43rd president of the United States. And I promised him that I wouldn't call him back this time." Some forty minutes later, the president-elect spoke to the nation from the House chamber in the Texas State capitol in Austin. Noting that "our country has been through a long and trying period," Bush was gracious to Gore, noting his "distinguished record," thanking him "for a call that I know it was difficult to make," and saying he was grateful that "we can resolve our electoral differences in a peaceful way." Then Bush called for national unity: "Tonight, I chose to speak from the chamber of the Texas House of Representatives because it has been a home to bipartisan co-operation. Here, in a place where Democrats have the majority, Republicans and Democrats have worked together to do what is right for the people we represent." He closed with: "I will be guided by President Jefferson's sense of purpose: to stand for principle, to be reasonable in manner, and, above all, to do great good for the cause of freedom and harmony."[59]

It was, to that point in time, the closest presidential election in American history. Al Gore defeated George W. Bush in the popular vote by only 540,520 votes, or a minuscule 0.51 percent. And yet Gore had received the second-highest popular vote total in American history (second only to Ronald Reagan's 1984 triumph), winning 50,996,582 votes (48.4 percent of the total popular vote) to George W. Bush's 50,056,062 votes (47.9 percent of the total). When on 18 December 2000 the Electoral College cast its votes, it gave George W. Bush 271 electoral votes and Al Gore 266 electoral votes, with one Gore elector abstaining.[60]

Thanks in part to its having a candidate at the top of the ticket who won a majority of the nation's votes, the Democratic Party also made significant gains across the board. In the House of Representatives, Democrats gained one seat (the Independents also gained a seat)—the new House would have 221 Republicans, 212 Democrats, and 2 Independents. In the Senate, the Democrats gained four seats, thus taking the Senate to a 50–50 tie (leaving Vice President Cheney to cast the deciding vote in case of a tie). Gubernatorial elections showed a one-house change in favor of the Democrats.

The biggest reason for both Gore's strong showing and that of his party was the outstanding job that the Democrats did with voter turnout—as Republican adviser Matthew Dowd later conceded, "The Democratic base was up over what you'd normally see." Gore/Lieberman 2000 outpolled Clinton/Gore 1996 among African Americans, organized labor, and those who made more than $100,000 per year. The ticket had won more votes than any other Democratic campaign in the nation's history, an impressive fact when there was a third-party candidate, Ralph Nader of the Green Party, running on Gore's left. The three main reasons that people voted for Gore—in almost equal measure—were his promise to protect Social Security, his promise to add a prescription drug benefit for seniors, and his promise to invest in education, including more teachers and smaller class sizes.[61] The DUI had also taken its toll. As Dowd observed, because of that revelation, "Late deciders, who normally go with challengers, broke toward the Vice President."[62]

There were two main reasons people voted for Bush—again, in almost equal measure. First was his promise to restore honor and dignity to the White House; second was his promise to restore America's military readiness. But it can be argued that the key to Bush's electoral strength—which was, after all, comparable to Gore's—was his support from evangelical Christians. To be sure, that support was stronger before the DUI than after—the turnout of white evangelicals dropped six points below the turnout for Dole in 1996. And yet those evangelicals who voted in 2000 stuck by Bush. He won 63 percent of the vote from those who attended church more than weekly, 57 percent from those who attended weekly, and 46 percent among those who attended monthly. Had that support dropped more precipitously, the gap between Bush and Gore might have been wider. Rove would make it his top political priority to increase those numbers for 2004.[63]

The closeness of the election, Gore's majority in the popular vote, the arguments over the legitimacy of the Florida recounts, and the decision of the court in *Bush v. Gore* led many to argue that Bush had somehow stolen the election, or that the Court had stolen it for him. Of this, the historian must say two things. First of all, before, during, and after all the varied recounts in Florida, Bush never trailed. Second, the only real evidence that we have of any Supreme Court justice being pro-Gore is in the case of O'Connor, and even given that evidence, there is no direct cause-and-effect evidence between her dislike for Bush and her vote in *Bush v. Gore*. As for her eight other colleagues, there is no evidence whatsoever to either suggest or prove that their vote in *Bush v. Gore* was politically motivated.

George W. Bush had now been named the forty-third president of the United States. And he had only thirty-two days to put together his administration.

# 5

# TRANSITION

Bush was not without some experience in the realm of presidential transitions. He had learned from the experiences of his father—both the transition from the Reagan to the Bush administration in 1988–1989 and that from the Bush to the Clinton administration in 1992–1993 caused bad blood on both sides. Most important, Bush had learned to plan early. The Bush transition began its work long before the general election was over and continued its work throughout the period of the recounts—despite there being doubt as to the outcome. Had the Bush team not begun its transition to power long before 18 December 2000, it could easily have entered an abbreviated transition period with too little time left to fill key positions. As it happened, the Bush transition did a good job. It moved quickly, key appointments were made in a timely fashion, there were few problems with major announced appointments, and on 20 January 2001 Bush was in a better position to "hit the ground running" than his father had been in 1989 or Clinton had been in 1993.

The 2000 transition began with the 1994 appointment of Clay Johnson to oversee appointments to state boards and commissions as Governor Bush's appointments director. Johnson's role, discussed in chapter 2, trained him in the intricacies of political hiring—by 1999, he was advising Bush on the filling of more than four thousand state positions. When Joe

CHAPTER 5

Allbaugh was named campaign manager, Johnson took over as Governor Bush's chief of staff. He was also given the portfolio of "thinking about" who would populate a potential Bush presidency. Johnson spoke to influential members of the Reagan administration and the first Bush administration, as well as with scholars of presidential transitions. He also went to Wyoming in August and conveyed Bush's desire to Dick Cheney that he become the director of the formal Bush transition team, on which Johnson would continue to play a role.[1]

The period of the Florida recount may well have been a blessing in disguise for Bush. It gave him the opportunity to conduct the first weeks of the transition—what political scientist John P. Burke calls the "quiet transition"—out of the glare of the media spotlight. While the focus was on the recounts, Bush had more time to think carefully about his staffing decisions.[2] It also, as noted in the previous chapter, gave Bush the opportunity to use the transition to show that he was in command of the situation even during the recount. As noted, on 26 November, as soon as Katherine Harris had certified the election, Bush immediately announced that Cheney was heading his transition team and Andy Card had been appointed chief of staff.

Despite its fast start, the Bush transition was not without its challenges. Most notably, the General Services Administration (GSA), arguing that despite Harris's certification the election was not yet over, refused to release its $5.3 million in federal funds to Bush to set up a transition office. The Bush team argued that the Clinton administration was playing politics and keeping it from funds that would aid in a legitimate transition, but the GSA would not budge. Nevertheless, on 29 November, Bush announced the creation of the Bush-Cheney Presidential Transition Foundation, Inc. It was paid for with private funds, and it operated out of Cheney's home in McLean, Virginia, and from leased office space. It was here that the Bush team, led by Johnson and directed by Cheney, continued the work of staffing the administration. The team continued its work even through a moment that seemed to highlight the precariousness of the entire situation. On the morning of 23 November, Cheney suffered his fourth heart attack. He underwent a cardiac catheterization, which resulted in the insertion of a stent in the affected artery. He spoke to the press the next day, was back home a few days later, and was soon back at the work of the transition. Once *Bush v. Gore* was decided, the GSA freed up the money and gave Cheney the keys to the office space, and a formal transition office was opened.[3]

Regarding how he wanted his White House staff to function, Bush knew exactly what he *didn't* want. He had seen the management of a White House up close, and what he didn't want was a White House that had been run like his father's, where, in Bush's memory, Chief of Staff John Sununu "denied [staffers] access to the Oval Office and limited the flow of information to Dad." Instead, he wanted a staff structure that was "tight enough to ensure an orderly flow of information, but flexible enough that I could receive advice from a variety of sources." To gain this balance, he would need an experienced Washington hand as his chief of staff. Thus, rather than turning to Joe Allbaugh, the third member of the "Iron Triangle" and Bush's chief of staff through the Texas days, Bush appointed Andy Card, who had been Sununu's deputy, as his chief of staff (Allbaugh was made director of the Federal Emergency Management Agency).[4]

Bush remembered that it was Card's experience (he had served under every chief of staff in both the Reagan and the first Bush White House) as well as his personal characteristics—Bush cited "perceptive, humble, loyal, and hardworking"—that led to Bush asking Card to take the position. Card accepted, but with one proviso—that Bush keep him apprised of any decision that he made when Card was not in the room. Card was both respected and well liked by the majority of his staff. Like the elder Bush, Card was a ubiquitous user of handwritten notes, the majority of which concluded with the same closing line: "Keep in Touch." In emails at least, the staff referred to Card as "Chief." Card named two deputy chiefs of staff: Josh Bolten was named deputy chief of staff for policy, and Joseph Hagin, Bush's deputy campaign manager, was named deputy chief of staff for White House operations.[5]

When asked later if he saw himself as the gatekeeper who controlled access to the president, Card replied: "You know, if you are the sole gatekeeper, you never leave the gate, and if you never leave the gate, you can't do your job." This perfectly matched Bush's preferences. He later remembered that he wanted his White House to have "a structure that was tight enough to ensure an orderly flow of information, but flexible enough that I could receive advice from a variety of sources." The most important of those sources, as Bush readily admitted in his memoir, was his "Texas political family," a group that he wanted to have "regular access to me." With Allbaugh eased aside, the remaining two members of the Iron Triangle were named to key positions in the White House inner circle. On the recommendation of Card, Karen Hughes was named counselor to the president (Hughes remembered that Card told her he had taken the title and modeled the job after the role of Edward Meese in the first Reagan administration). The job combined an advisory role with the role of communications director. Journalist Ron Suskind would later gush that Hughes was "the most powerful woman in America"—a point that observers of Condoleezza Rice might well contest. Nevertheless, she vied with Rice for the title of Bush's closest confidant; media consultant Mark McKinnon remembered that at Blair House on the day before the inauguration, Bush pointed at Hughes and said, "I don't want any important decision made without her in the room." Her deputy would be another Austin alum, former campaign spokesman Dan Bartlett.[6]

Originally, Karl Rove joined the administration as Bush's senior political adviser. But, unlike Hughes, who also carried the portfolio of director of communications, Rove's appointment left him with nothing else to do except give the president advice. This did not sit well with Card, who wanted every staff member to have a line responsibility. Therefore, Card created the Office of Strategic Initiatives and made Rove its director. This new group was charged with long-range planning, and its meetings became known as "strategery sessions"—so christened in honor of a *Saturday Night Live* skit that portrayed a confused Bush, played by comedian Will Ferrell, mangling the word "strategy" during a staff meeting.[7]

Also brought into the administration from Austin were Clay Johnson as head of the White House Personnel Office; Alberto Gonzales as White House counsel; Margaret LaMontagne as head of the Domestic Policy Council; Albert Hawkins as secretary to the cabinet; Harriet Miers as staff secretary; and Scott Everts as AIDS czar, whose appointment as an openly gay man disturbed many evangelicals. Bush's first press secretary was Ari Fleischer, who had served as deputy press secretary for the reelection campaign of Bush's father and had worked for Hughes during the 2000 campaign. His deputy would be Scott McClellan, the former chief of staff to a Texas state senator who had served as Bush's traveling press secretary during the 2000 campaign. Michael Gerson ran the speechwriting office. He brought in Matthew Scully, a former reporter for the *Washington Times*, editor of the *National Review*, and speechwriter for Dan Quayle; John McConnell, a graduate of Yale who had written for Quayle and Bob Dole; Peter Wehner, a libertarian and former aide to William Bennett; and David Frum, formerly of the *Weekly Standard*, as speechwriters.

Although she did not serve on Bush's gubernatorial staff, Condoleezza Rice had become so indispensable to Bush that her appointment as Bush's national security adviser surprised no one. For his part, Bush remembered that he decided to appoint Rice in 1999 during a walk over rough terrain at the Crawford ranch, when Rice was pontificating about the nuances of Yugoslav politics and neither the governor nor Mrs. Bush could keep up with her pace. While the national security adviser did not usually have cabinet-level rank, and Rice was no exception, Bush made it clear that he wanted her to attend every cabinet meeting, as it was important to him that she be an "equal partner of the senior team in the White House." This may have been because, despite her wide-ranging academic expertise, unlike most of her colleagues on the National Security Council she had never held a senior-level position in the executive branch. By some reports, Rice's lack of experience concerned Cheney, who managed the appointment of his former aide and former Vulcan Steve Hadley as Rice's deputy.[8]

Bush recalled that his first cabinet appointment "was easy." The appointment of Colin Powell as secretary of state was formally announced on 16 December at an elementary school in Crawford, as soon as the result of *Bush v. Gore* was declared. Bush would later gush, "I believed that Colin could be the second coming of George Marshall, a soldier turned statesman." But when Powell was introduced as America's first African American secretary of state designate, it was tempting to jump to the conclusion that it was Powell who was really in charge. It was the statuesque Powell who gave a wide-ranging monologue on the direction of American foreign policy; it was Powell, not the president, who made a policy statement when asked about the missile defense program (he forcefully declared, "We are going to go forward)." Bush stood by, silent and seemingly nonplussed. But others would later claim that Cheney was furious at Powell's performance. As his deputy, Powell chose former Vulcan Richard Armitage, about whom Powell would later affirm, "Rich had my total trust and I had his." At the strong suggestion of Cheney, Powell also chose John Bolton, a neoconservative who had served in the elder Bush's State Department, as his undersecretary of state for arms control and international security.[9]

Bush's first choice at Defense was Frederick Smith, the founder of Federal Express, who according to Bush refused the offer for health reasons. His second choice was Dan Coats, but the conservative former senator from Indiana gave what Card later remembered to be a "disappointing" interview. There is even evidence to believe that Bush considered Cheney for secretary of defense—an arrangement that was not precluded by the Constitution—but if this idea was indeed considered, it was just as quickly dropped. Bush's third choice at Defense was a surprise to many. While Donald Rumsfeld was a close friend of Cheney, he was hardly a Bush family favorite. Born in Chicago and trained in political science at Princeton University, Rumsfeld served in the navy from 1954 to 1957 and in the Navy Reserve from 1957 until 1975, when he was named Gerald Ford's secretary of defense. In the interim, Rumsfeld was a staff assistant on Capitol Hill, a member of the House of Representatives from the Illinois Thirteenth District from 1962 to 1969, the director of the Office of Economic Opportunity and the Economic Stabilization Program and the US ambassador to NATO under Nixon. In 1974, he spearheaded the transition from the Nixon to the Ford presidency and was named as Ford's chief of staff. In that position, he brought along his protégé, Dick Cheney, as his deputy. There had long been rumors that Rumsfeld had pushed the senior Bush into the CIA in order to remove him as a potential rival for the vice presidency in 1976. In 1975 Ford chose Rumsfeld as the youngest secretary of defense in the nation's history. Rumsfeld served until the end of the Ford presidency, at which time he entered corporate America.[10]

In 1988 Rumsfeld floated his name for the Republican nomination for the presidency. But the field offered several stronger candidates, Rumsfeld's stump speeches were wooden (in the words of one reporter, "His campaign style is about as colorful as a CEO's wardrobe"), and he couldn't raise anywhere near enough money to match Bush. Rumsfeld withdrew in April 1987, long before the first primary. In 1996 he worked as the national campaign chairman for Bob Dole, where Paul Wolfowitz served as his deputy for foreign policy issues.[11]

Rumsfeld barely knew the president-elect. But for Bush, Rumsfeld brought to the table a deep set of experiences that would be useful as he strategized major changes in the military. Rumsfeld's memory was that Cheney, Rice, and Powell all agreed that he should be considered for the position. Rove, however, counseled caution, arguing that the choice of Rumsfeld would feed the media narrative that Cheney was in charge.[12]

On 22 December 2000, responding to an invitation from Cheney, Rumsfeld flew to Austin, met with Bush, and discussed several issues, from his thoughts on restructuring the military to his views on the new role of the CIA. No job was offered on the spot, but both Card and Cheney later remembered that Rumsfeld's interview outshone those of all his competitors. On 26 December, Cheney phoned Rumsfeld with the offer for Defense; Rumsfeld accepted that same day. Rumsfeld chose two neo-conservatives as his closest aides: Paul Wolfowitz as deputy secretary of defense, and Douglas Feith, a former Middle East specialist on the Reagan NSC, as his undersecretary of defense for policy.[13]

The appointment of the director of the CIA had a personal angle. Bush remembered how his father had been treated by Jimmy Carter in 1977— the elder Bush had been head of the CIA and was fired by Carter to make room for a political appointment. Bush spoke to his father about the appointment, then decided to retain George Tenet, a Clinton appointee, as his CIA director in order to "send a signal of continuity and nonpartisanship in an important national security post." Tenet was a force of nature. A hands-on administrator if ever there was one, the burly, gregarious he was prone to wandering the halls and dropping in on unsuspecting analysts, just to have a chat. A believer in personal diplomacy, Tenet had forged relationships with most of the major players in the Middle East and would often be sent by the administration to have one-on-ones with, say, the crown prince of Saudi Arabia.[14]

Paul O'Neill, Bush's choice for secretary of the Treasury, had served in the Office of Management and Budget during the Nixon and Ford administrations. From 1977 to 1987, he worked at International Paper in New York City, the last two years as that company's president. From 1987 to 1999, O'Neill was the chairman and CEO of the Pittsburgh-based ALCOA Company. O'Neill was recommended both by Cheney, who had served with O'Neill in the Nixon and Ford administrations, and by Clay Johnson. But from the start, the independent O'Neill proved difficult to work with. In a harbinger of things to come, he grew testy when Rove asked him to keep his January calendar clear for a meeting in Austin with the president-elect and business leaders. O'Neill snapped that he, as Treasury secretary, not the president, should be holding such a meeting. Pronouncing the meeting a giant photo op, O'Neill threatened a boycott. He eventually attended the meeting, but he was conspicuously absent from the morning meeting with Bush and the business leaders. Lawrence Lindsay, who had been an economic adviser during the campaign, was named head of the National Economic Council.[15]

Names that were floated for attorney general included FBI director Louis Freeh, New York City mayor Rudolph W. Giuliani, former Missouri senator John Danforth, former Oklahoma governor Frank Keating, and Governor Mark Racicot of Montana. From that list, Racicot—a former state attorney general and two-term governor—was Bush's first choice. However, the Christian Right circled the wagons in opposition to a possible Racicot appointment, arguing that he had not done enough to oppose abortion in Montana.[16] Racicot removed himself from contention. Bush asked Rove for another choice; Rove recommended John Ashcroft.[17]

Born in Chicago, Ashcroft took his bachelor's degree from Yale University in 1964 and his law degree from the University of Chicago School of Law in 1967. He taught business law at Southwest Missouri State University and in 1972 ran an unsuccessful campaign for the House of Representatives. From 1973 to 1973, he served as Missouri state auditor, and from 1976 to 1985, he served as that state's attorney general. In 1984, Ashcroft won the first of what would be two terms as governor of Missouri, where he gained a national reputation for his strong law-and-order agenda. In 1994, Ashcroft was elected to the US Senate from Missouri; in that campaign, Karl Rove worked for him as a campaign adviser. Ashcroft was a consistent opponent of all things Clinton, and in the Senate he cemented his reputation as a darling of the evangelical Right. In 2000, he ran for reelection against Missouri governor Mel Carnahan, but Carnahan's sudden death, discussed in chapter 3, threw the race into chaos. Missouri state law precluded the removal of Carnahan's name from the ballot, and the state's new governor, Roger Wilson, promised that if Carnahan won, he would appoint his widow to the senate. Despite being deceased, Carnahan narrowly defeated Ashcroft, and Jean Carnahan was appointed the new senator from Missouri. Covering all the bases, the newly unemployed Ashcroft sent a congratulatory note to President-Elect Bush, letting it be known that he was ready to serve the new administration in any capacity. Ashcroft offered a link to the evangelical and far-right Republicans whose support Bush needed to increase before the next election. Card called Ashcroft and asked him to come to Austin to meet with Bush; Bush offered him the job at Justice, and Ashcroft accepted on the spot.[18]

The vast majority of Bush's appointments were quickly and easily confirmed in the Senate. Not so Ashcroft. Even though he had standing as a US senator himself, which usually meant an expedited approval by his colleagues, Ashcroft's confirmation was a nasty affair. As Ashcroft saw it, his opponents came after him because of his "deeply held personal beliefs that influenced my conservative record on matters regarding desegregation, abortion, and capital punishment, and they feared what I might do as a public official with such broad responsibilities" (the chapter in his memoir dealing with his confirmation was titled "A Marked Man"). But what particularly incensed Ashcroft's opponents was his refusal to support Ronnie White, the first African American judge on the Missouri Supreme Court and a Carnahan appointee, to a federal judgeship. Ashcroft, then in the Senate, led the opposition to White, claiming that he was "pro-criminal" as a result of his decisions on death penalty cases, citing support from all-white police organizations. White's nomination was rejected on a straight party vote, and Carnahan made the case a cornerstone of his campaign for the Senate, effectively labeling Ashcroft as a racist. Aside from his ultraconservative beliefs, critics brought into play Ashcroft's fundraising techniques, which they claimed would make it impossible for him to fully enforce campaign finance laws.[19]

Ashcroft was not without his supporters. Tevi Troy, then a policy director in Ashcroft's Senate office, wrote an influential endorsement of his boss for the *New Republic*. In it, Troy specifically defended Ashcroft from charges of intolerance: "Critics imply that Ashcroft, because of his strong Christian beliefs, is intolerant of Jews. Actually, he's more than tolerant; he's downright philo-Semitic." He also contended that Ashcroft "sees himself as a part of a small, sometimes scorned religious minority"—the Assemblies of God (Pentecostals). While Troy later maintained that the article changed few Senate minds, it was nevertheless widely cited and discussed.[20] Ashcroft was finally confirmed on 1 February 2001, by a vote of 58–42.

Bush wanted his cabinet to be bipartisan, but he was not as successful in that goal as he wished to be. He offered Interior to former Democratic governor Mike Sullivan of Wyoming; Sullivan declined. Bush then offered the slot to Gale Norton, a Republican who was Colorado's first female attorney general. She accepted and became the first female to head the Interior Department. Norman Mineta, a California Democrat who had served as Clinton's secretary of commerce, brought a small amount of bipartisanship to the cabinet. A Japanese American who had spent time with his family in the Heart Mountain internment camp, during World War II Mineta served as Bush's first secretary of transportation.[21]

For his secretary of education, Bush chose Rod Paige, a former trustee, officer, and superintendent of the Houston Independent School District. For Agriculture, he chose former deputy secretary of agriculture Ann Veneman as the first woman to head that department. Donald Evans, Bush's campaign director, became secretary of commerce. Former Wisconsin governor Tommy Thompson got Health and Human Services. Mel Martinez, the former mayor of Orange County, Florida, became secretary of the Department of Housing and Urban Development. Spencer Abraham, who had been defeated for reelection in 2000 as a US senator from Michigan, was chosen to head the Department of Energy. Anthony

Principi, a Vietnam veteran and deputy secretary of the Department of Veterans Affairs under the elder Bush, was chosen to head that department. Rounding out the cabinet were former New Jersey governor Christine Todd Whitman as head of the Environmental Protection Agency, former Vulcan Robert Zoellick as US trade representative, and Mitchell Daniels, former director of political and intergovernmental affairs under Reagan, as director of the Office of Management and Budget.

On one appointment, the Bush team stumbled badly. Linda Chavez had worked for the American Federation of Teachers, had held a number of appointive positions under Reagan and George H. W. Bush, and had served as the head of a task force on immigration issues for the Bush campaign in 2000. First Clay Johnson and then Bush interviewed her for the position of secretary of labor; Bush announced her nomination on 1 January 2001. However, Chavez did not disclose that she kept an illegal immigrant from Guatemala in her home and paid her money to do household chores and childcare. The *Wall Street Journal* discovered her secret, and in light of previous related events in the 1992–1993 Clinton transition, Chavez's nomination was doomed. When she met with the press to announce her withdrawal from consideration, Chavez waxed defiant: "I've not led a perfect life. I don't think anybody has. I'm not Mother Theresa [*sic*]." Bush then turned to Elaine Chao, who had previously served as secretary of transportation under the first Bush; Chao served the entirety of the Bush's two terms as his secretary of labor.[22]

The diversity of the cabinet was well noted. There were two African Americans (Powell and Paige), one Hispanic (Martinez), two Asian Americans (Chao and Mineta), and one Arab American (Abraham). One of the things that is often missed about the Bush White House is the level of gender diversity that was present. Three women—Norton, Veneman, and Whitman—ultimately joined the first cabinet. Had Chavez survived her vetting, there would have been four. This was the largest concentration of women with cabinet-level rank in any administration to that point in American history. One academic study found that the early Bush White House was made up of 28 percent women and 11 percent minorities (as compared with 29 percent women and 8 percent minorities under Clinton).[23]

The role of Dick Cheney in the Bush White House is the most examined, and most misunderstood, facet of the administration of George W. Bush. A close working relationship between president and vice president was nothing new. It was Walter Mondale in 1976 who had fundamentally altered that relationship, as he documented in "The Role of the Vice President in the Carter Administration." Carter's acceptance of all recommendations made in that memo led to an unprecedented amount of access being granted to Mondale, access that has been retained to the present day.[24]

Where Cheney broke new ground was with his expectation that his staff would be, in his own words, "aggressive." More so than any previous (or subsequent) vice president, Cheney integrated his staff with that of the president. Card took part of the credit for this—"I wanted to have complementary staffs . . . the vice president's staff was considered to be a part of the president's staff." So did Cheney: "What I wanted to do was . . . have some dual-hatting of certain people." Mary Matalin, Cheney's communications director, also served as an assistant to the president. John McConnell, Cheney's key speechwriter, also served on the speechwriting staff of the president. I. Lewis "Scooter" Libby, a former student of Wolfowitz, served as Cheney's chief of staff and assistant to the vice president for national security affairs, as well as an assistant to the president. In addition, Cheney found jobs for the neocons—Wolfowitz, Feith, Bolton, and others. In this, he was aided and abetted by the often-bullying, equally assured David Addington. A graduate of Duke University School of Law and former general counsel to the Defense Department, Addington had served as Cheney's chief of staff and general counsel; his outsize personality sucked the air out the room whenever he entered. For all intents and purposes, this put a Cheney staffer in the room for virtually every meeting of substance. Hughes remembered that the arrangement was "seamless"; time would quickly tell if this unique arrangement would bear fruit.[25]

The extension of the reach of the vice president under Cheney went beyond meeting attendance. Two days after the inauguration, Hadley told the senior staff that copies of every email sent to Bush, Rice, or himself would automatically be rerouted to Cheney. Breaking with precedent, Cheney took an office in both the House (his prerogative as a former House member) and Senate (his prerogative as president of that body) wings of the Capitol. He also structured his schedule so that the President's Daily Brief (PDB) from the CIA arrived on his desk at the vice president's residence early, usually by 6:30 a.m. There, Cheney, often with Libby, would read the PDB in order to be prepared to discuss it by the time the president got his morning briefing at the White House—a meeting that Cheney also attended. But there was more to it than this. Cheney would routinely move briefs "in front of the tab" so that that president might more readily see them (although Cheney later emphasized to an interviewer, "I don't recall I ever recommended taking something *out*").[26]

None of this, however, bespeaks of either a "co-presidency" between Bush and Cheney or, more nefarious, a situation in which Cheney actually controlled Bush. It cannot be ignored that every memoir and every interview with administration alumni—whether or not they are positive to the administration—completely dismisses such characterizations, often with a laugh. But many academics and journalists, with the flimsiest of evidence, have chosen to advance this characterization of the Bush-Cheney relationship. On the surface, Cheney looked like he *should* be in control. With the exception of Rumsfeld, he had worked the levers of power in Washington longer than anyone in the Bush administration. His use of the intelligence briefings, the structure of his staff, and his unwillingness to accept a second-tier position as vice president made his voice immensely influential. During the first term at least, Bush often—but not always—followed that advice. But acceptance of advice does not translate to control. As noted earlier, Cheney had long believed that the prerogatives of the presidency had eroded since Vietnam, and he hoped to help Bush regain those proper prerogatives in the due course of his presidency. But this did not mean that Cheney believed the prerogatives of the *vice* president should be increased. This was something Cheney never claimed, and never acted upon. Cheney privately gave the president his advice, and the president either took it or didn't take it.

Indeed, Cheney lost one of the first turf battles he fought. He wanted to break with tradition and chair the meetings of the Principals Committee of the NSC (made up of the vice president, the secretaries of state and defense, the head of the CIA, and other department heads) himself. Were he to win this fight, Cheney's prerogatives would have been significantly increased. But Rice argued that this role had long been established as belonging to the head of the NSC. Bush agreed with Rice, and his national security adviser continued to chair the Principals Committee instead of his vice president. As Cheney himself remarked in a 2014 interview, "I mean, he never guaranteed me that he was always going to do what I wanted him to do."[27]

The Bush-Cheney relationship was much more like the president–vice president relationship that Carter and Mondale had created, and the one Ronald Reagan had had with Bush's father, than it was some nefarious, conspiratorial abrogation of power. On this subject, let Gen. Richard

Myers, chairman of the Joint Chiefs of Staff from 2001 to 2005, have the last word: "The alpha male in the White House was the president."[28]

Saturday, 20 January 2001, dawned cold and wet in the nation's capital. The weather had been cold and miserable—it had been raining on and off for almost forty-eight hours, and that evening there would be a light snow. Nevertheless, some 300,000 people stood on the Mall in thick mud to catch a glimpse of the inaugural action. For the past several days, the Bush family had been staying at the Blair House. They started their day at 9:15 a.m. with a prayer service at St. John's Church, just across Lafayette Square and adjacent to the White House. At 10:30 the Bushes arrived at the White House; the Clintons were standing outside to greet them. They had coffee, then left for the Capitol. Cheney rode with Gore. Cheney remembered Gore as being "relaxed and in good humor," but he also remembered him commenting on why they had been late—because Clinton had been signing last-minute pardons (Gore mused, to no one in particular, "How many more do you think he can get signed before noon?").[29]

On the dais, the drizzle and the cold made for widespread discomfort among the platform party. Several of the participants had to don plastic raincoats over their semiformal apparel, and space heaters were at the feet of Bush, Cheney, Clinton, and Gore. Chief Justice William H. Rehnquist administered the oath of office to the fifty-four-year-old president-elect. Bush's hand rested on a small family Bible (he was to have used the same 1767 King James Version of the Bible that his father had used at his 1989 inauguration, but the wet weather made that impossible). As soon as the oath was administered, Bush's father was observed shedding a tear.[30]

Bush's inaugural address was, by comparative standards, very brief— it lasted only fourteen minutes. Delivered in the classic Bush monotone, it channeled the spirit of John F. Kennedy, both in its call to service, and in its warning to any world leader who might oppose the interests of the United States. The new president began by thanking Clinton for his service and praising Gore for "a contest conducted with spirit and ended with grace." Pivoting into the body of his speech, Bush invoked his view of the "American story—a story of flawed and fallible people, united across the generations by grand and enduring ideals." Bush then spoke about the need for civility ("the determined choice of trust over cynicism"); courage ("The enemies of liberty should make no mistake. . . . We will meet aggression and bad faith with resolve and strength"); compassion ("In the quiet of the American conscience, we know that deep, persistent poverty is unworthy of our nation's promise"); and character ("Our public interest depends on private character . . . on uncounted, unhonored acts of decency which give new direction to our freedom"). He asked Americans to join in a "commitment to principle with a concern for civility. . . . Civility is not a tactic or a sentiment. It is the determined choice of trust over cynicism, of community over chaos." Bush closed by asking his countrymen to be "citizens: citizens, not spectators; citizens, not subjects; responsible citizens, building communities of service and a nation of character."[31]

It had only happened this way once before in American history. On 14 February 1824, John Adams gathered with family and friends to celebrate the victory of his son, John Quincy Adams, over Andrew Jackson in that fall's presidential election. The election had been bruising and had gone to the House of Representatives. The issue was decided only when Jackson's enemy, Henry Clay, allegedly tossed his support to Adams in exchange for being named secretary of state. Wounds were still raw on both sides. But this was not a day for political postmortems, but for celebrations. Josiah Quincy, Abigail's cousin, surveyed the scene. The senior Adams, he later observed, was "considerably affected by the fulfillment of his highest wishes." Quincy's mother spoke to the family and compared the former president to "that old man who was pronounced by Solon to be the highest of mortals when he expired on hearing of his son's success at the Olympic games." Upon hearing of the comparison between his situation and that of the ancient Athenian, Adams was, according to Quincy, "visibly moved . . . and tears of joy rolled down his cheek."[32]

On 20 January 2001, George H. W. Bush attended the presidential inauguration of his son, and despite the dismal weather, the seventy-seven-year-old former president sat through the entire inaugural parade in the outdoor reviewing stand, getting chilled to the bone. Following the parade, he returned to the White House as an overnight guest. It was his first visit to the Executive Mansion since he left in defeat eight years earlier. But now he was a cold and damp private citizen; for the moment, all he wanted was a hot shower.

While Bush was drying off, a valet knocked on the door of his room. With some urgency, Bush was told that the president wanted to see him at once in the Oval Office. Bush quickly changed into a suit and tie and hurried to his old workplace. There waiting for him was the newly inaugurated forty-third president of the United States. A photographer captured the moment, almost unique in American history. The moment was so personally poignant and rich in history that neither man needed to say much to the other. All that was said was a repeated greeting, as each man looked at each other and, with an air of formality and finality, addressed the other as "Mr. President."[33]

# 6

★ ★ ★ ★ ★

# "FULL SPEED AHEAD"

Patience had never been a part of George W. Bush's makeup. On 12 December 2000, the Supreme Court came down with its decision in *Bush v. Gore*. The very next day, Cheney met with five moderate Republicans on the Hill (Arlen Specter of Pennsylvania, Susan Collins and Olympia Snowe of Maine, James Jeffords of Vermont, and Lincoln Chafee of Rhode Island). The vice president–elect surprised them when he stated that the incoming administration didn't want to wait for things to settle down before sending its agenda to Capitol Hill. Moreover, even though his numbers on the Hill were tenuous at best, Bush was not going to trim his sails or reach out to the political center to govern. His agenda was coming to the Hill exactly as it had been pitched in the campaign—the decision, as Cheney would later tell a reporter, was to move "full speed ahead."[1]

In 2016, Josh Bolten waxed philosophical for an interviewer: "All the other stuff, peace and prosperity and so on—those were all things that every president aspires to." But, as Bolten remembered, Bush's "passion" was tax cuts and education reform. Quite the opposite of his father, Bush wanted to be, and expected to be, a president who concentrated on domestic policies.[2]

As we have seen, Bush had advocated tax cuts since the beginning of his political career; indeed, they had been a key focus of his presidential campaign. Clinton left Bush with a projected ten-year budget surplus of $4.2 trillion—an amount that journalists dubbed the "peace dividend." The surplus made Bush's move for a tax cut a bit easier—Bush could now argue that tax cuts would not necessarily lead to budget deficits, and his advisers pitched the tax cuts both as a pump primer for an economy that was starting to drift into inflationary territory and as an opportunity to share the surplus with taxpayers.[3]

Treasury secretary Paul O'Neill recommended that Bush create a tax cut package that included triggers that would reduce the cuts if the economic situation got worse. But Bush wouldn't hear of it—he was all in. The question was who was going to get their taxes cut, and how much. Telling his advisers, "I will not negotiate with myself," Bush settled on a package that would include $1.6 trillion in total tax cuts. On 3 April, Cheney cast his first tie-breaking vote in the Senate to preserve those cuts. Now efforts turned to writing the actual legislation, and Bush had to defend his $1.6 trillion from Democrats who were trying to cut its size. To do so, Bush shifted his concentration from tax cuts for businesses to tax cuts for individuals. He also backed off from the desired amount of the cuts. At one early meeting in the office of Senate minority leader Trent Lott (R-MS), Cheney did some math on a napkin. He wrote down what the Republicans wanted ($1.6 trillion), what the Democrats wanted ($1.25 trillion), and the middle point between the two ($1.425 trillion), which he circled. But it was going to be close, and Bush would once again need every Republican vote.[4]

One vote in particular had become problematic. Vermont's Jim Jeffords, who held the longest continually held Republican Senate seat in US history, believed that the Bush White House had slighted him. Long interested in education reform, Jeffords was unhappy that he had been left off the guest list of the announcement of the Teacher of the Year at the White House. Rove believed that Jeffords was also displeased because of the close relationship that had developed between Bush and Judd Gregg, a New Hampshire senator who was working closely with Bush on education reforms. Most egregious to Jeffords was his belief that the impending tax cut would hurt an issue dear to his heart—funding for special education. While he promised that he would vote in favor of the tax cut, he nevertheless wanted the size of the cut to be pared back, and that $200 billion be earmarked for special education. Jeffords was rebuffed by the Bush team; Jeffords would later write that "privately, the White House made clear that any Republican who thought otherwise [about the cuts] was morally or mentally deficient."[5]

Jeffords began to consider changing his party affiliation. If he did so, the Democrats would have a one-vote majority in the Senate and would thus get majority control of that body. Naturally, the Democratic leadership dangled some incentives. On 14 May, Jeffords spoke with both minority leader Tom Daschle (D-SD) and Senate minority whip Harry Reid (D-NV). Reid promised Jeffords that if he made the switch, he would chair the Environment and Public Works Committee (if the Democrats took control of the Senate, Reid would be up for that chair), and Jeffords could bring over his entire staff. Daschle would later write that "with that we shook hands, and the deal was done."[6]

But that was not the case. Olympia Snowe got wind of Jeffords's impending switch. She informed Card, and a meeting was set up between Bush and Jeffords. During a 22 May meeting in the Oval Office, Jeffords made the president aware that he was thinking of switching parties, and he asked that Bush reconsider his tax bill to make available close to $200 billion in special education funds, funds that would become automatic in future budgets. Bush balked, saying that he would be deluged with new requests for special deals if he reopened the bill.[7]

On 24 May, in an emotional speech on the floor of the Senate. Jeffords announced that he was switching parties. As he had been promised, he was immediately made chairman of the Environment and Public Works Committee (Hughes would later write: "Listening to him frame his decision as a matter of principle made several of us . . . sick. We felt he had sold out his party in exchange for a committee chairmanship").[8] On that same day, Daschle assumed control of the Senate as the new majority leader. As important for the long-range plans of the administration, Jeffords's move made Patrick Leahy (D-VT) the chairman of the Judiciary Committee; Bush's choices for the federal bench were now in peril.

Bush lost the Senate, but he won his tax cut. Jeffords honored his commitment to support the tax cut, which on 19 May passed the House 240 to 154, as 29 Democrats defected to support the package. Later that day, it passed the Senate 58 to 33; while Republicans John McCain and Lincoln Chafee defected, twelve Democratic votes changed sides and supported the bill, which was signed into law on 7 June. The largest tax cut since those of Ronald Reagan, it lowered the top rate from 39.6 percent to 35 percent, and the next three highest rates by 3 percentage points apiece. Critics noticed that the bulk of the cut would go to the wealthiest Americans, but the Bush team countered with the fact that the bill created a new tax bracket for the working poor, an increase in the child tax credits, and a plan to phase out the estate tax.[9]

In the very first sentence of the position paper put together by the White House on the legislation that would become known as No Child Left Behind (NCLB), Bush expressed his hope that "bipartisan education reform will be the cornerstone of my administration." Any such reform would require a significant overhaul of the Elementary and Secondary Education Act of 1965, which was coming up for reauthorization in 2001. But like the tax cut, NCLB needed significant bipartisan support—indeed, in the introduction to his position paper on the subject, Bush mentioned bipartisanship six times.[10]

The road to any reform of the American education system went directly through Ted Kennedy's office. Bush's courtship of the Massachusetts icon began with a one-on-one meeting during Bush's second day as president. Two weeks later, he hosted Kennedy at the White House (together, they watched a movie—*Thirteen Days*, no doubt strategically chosen—about the 1962 Cuban Missile Crisis). The attention seemed to work; in a handwritten note sent to Bush the next day, Kennedy thanked his hosts for their graciousness. He also told Bush exactly what he wanted to hear: "Like you, I have every intention of getting things done, particularly in education and health care. We will have differences along the way, but I look forward to some important Rose Garden signings." But this was just the beginning of the wooing, as Bush endorsed a bill to name the Department of Justice building after Kennedy's brother and former attorney general, Robert F. Kennedy.[11]

Margaret LaMontagne Spellings, the head of Bush's Domestic Policy Council, oversaw bringing the disparate congressional players together on education reform. But the true "father" of what would become NCLB was B. Alexander ("Sandy") Kress. In 1994, Texas lieutenant governor Bob Bullock appointed him to serve on the interim committee to study the Texas Education Agency. It was that committee that produced the Public-School Accountability System in Texas, which was at the heart of the "Texas Miracle" discussed in chapter 2. Prior to the start of the Bush administration, Kress had written out in longhand what would become the outline for NCLB. The legislation was based on one of Bush's fundamental beliefs: that neither the liberal solutions of creating more programs nor the conservative solutions of cutting federal involvement in education had served to solve the problem of underperforming schools. To deal with this, NCLB would focus on accountability. In its original form, the legislation required the states to test students in reading and math each year between the third and the eighth grade, and once in high school. Moreover, in any school that for three years had underperformed on those examinations, a student could use Title I funds from the Elementary and Secondary Education Act to transfer to another school or to get tutorial help—this became known as the Voucher Program. Underperforming schools could, at the discretion of the secretary of education, receive financial aid as an incentive toward improvement, or be financially penalized. Similarly, high-performing states could receive No Child Left Behind bonuses in the form of financial incentives. The plan also included a new reading program for grades K-2—Reading First—that would be "anchored in scientific research."[12]

Several groups, including the National Education Association, argued that as written NCLB gave too much power and authority to the federal government at the expense of the states, which should, in their view, have had the final say over any education policy. Many conservative observers found themselves in the difficult position of disagreeing with a Republican-proposed bill that would both increase federal spending and increase federal involvement in what many felt was a state prerogative. And leaders in the African American and Latino American communities charged that any tests would be biased in favor of white students.[13]

In February 2001, NCLB went to the Senate Health, Education, Labor, and Pensions Committee, then chaired by Jim Jeffords. Kress remembered that Jeffords was dragging his feet on the progress of the bill; thus, Kress and others in the White House were privately pleased when Jeffords switched parties—his defection gave the committee chair to Ted Kennedy, a Democrat but a leader who was much more favorably inclined toward the bill. With the significant support of Kennedy in the Senate and George Miller (D-CA) in the House, the two houses passed their respective bills with comfortable margins. But the process of reconciliation was slow—the bill was actually in reconciliation on 11 September 2001, when the president was peddling NCLB in Florida and Mrs. Bush was scheduled to testify in favor of the bill on Capitol Hill. Despite the fallout from the terrorist attacks that occurred that day, NCLB maintained a place of pride for Bush, who continued to push for its passage. Helped by the support of Kennedy, NCLB passed both houses of Congress in December 2001 by overwhelming margins. Bush signed the bill into law on 8 January 2002.[14]

The final iteration of NCLB kept the concept of accountability by test but smoothed over the promise of repercussions if a school did not achieve the accepted standards of excellence. It kept annual testing for grades three through eight in reading and math and added a plan to add a science test by 2007–2008. The threat of denying Title I money to schools that did not administer those tests was, however, removed. The revamped bill allowed states to design and select their own assessments and added a test—the National Assessment of Educational Progress—that would be administered every other year in order to assess the state's tests. The time-line for academic improvement was also loosened: states had to reach aca-demic proficiency—as each state chose to define the term—within twelve years. Corrective action was less punitive, with a series of incentives given to schools that underperformed. Added to the bill was a requirement for the states to submit an annual "report card" of their progress toward state-wide and a requirement that all teachers hired under Title I, beginning in 2002–2003, be "highly qualified" (meaning, in most cases, certified by the state). The Reading First Program was retained and was budgeted for $900 million in 2002. And in a point of contention for doubting conservatives, vouchers were missing from the final bill.[15]

On 12 December 2001, Bush sent a photo of himself and Kennedy to the senator. In it, Bush was seen coming up behind a beaming Kennedy and clasping him on the shoulders. The photo was inscribed: "No Ted, Money Doesn't Solve Everything. George."[16]

Like NCLB, Bush's faith-based programs had roots in his Texas experience. As with NCLB, he moved fast to implement them on the federal level. Nine days after his inauguration, Bush issued an executive order creating the Office of Faith-Based and Community Initiatives in the White House and in five executive departments. The opening statement of the guidance document to the departments held the key to the program: "The guiding principle behind President Bush's Faith-Based and Community Initiative is that Faith-Based charities should be able to compete on an equal footing for public dollars to provide public services." That same day, Bush wel-comed thirty leaders of community, faith-based, and philanthropic groups to the White House, where they were briefed on his initiative—a program that would free up close to $20 billion a year in federal funding to grant-based competition from faith-based groups.[17]

Bush clearly saw his faith-based programs as a form of welfare reform, as he expected that the competitive grant money would be used to fight poverty. But rather than revel in the possibility of newfound funds and influence, many evangelicals believed that by not simply *giving* federal funds to religious-based organizations, the government was, in essence, discriminating against them. Richard Cizik of the National Association of Evangelicals articulated this view when he told an interviewer, "We believe there has to be equality of treatment towards religious social service providers in America. That is what America ought to be all about—equality of treatment." Evangelicals were not comforted by the words of John Dilulio Jr., a professor of political science at the University of Pennsylvania and the faith-based program's first director. A Democrat and a Catholic who had advised Bush on faith-based issues during the campaign, Dilulio rattled evangelicals with pronouncements such as his belief that ministries could never replace public assistance programs, and that federal money should not be used to help church organizations evangelize. One observer quoted Dilulio: "Bible-thumping doesn't cut it."[18]

But evangelicals weren't the only group that was wary of Bush's faith-based initiatives. Others argued that such initiatives violated the traditional line of demarcation between church and state. They, in the words of Amy Black of Wheaton College, believed that "there's a prophetic role for religion, and [they] don't want to be corrupted by government." Along those same lines, other critics charged that any earmarking of taxpayer money for *any* private organization violated the constitutional separation between church and state.[19]

Bush took to the road to defend one of his pet projects. On 20 May 2001, he delivered the commencement address at the University of Notre Dame. Bush billed the speech as being about welfare reform, and he began by giving credit to both Lyndon Johnson's War on Poverty and Bill Clinton's 1996 welfare reforms.[20] Then he looked forward:

> For the task ahead, we must move to the third stage of combating poverty in America. Our society must enlist, equip, and empower idealistic Americans in the works of compassion that only they can provide. Government has an important role. It will never be replaced by charities. My administration increases funding for major social welfare and poverty programs by eight percent. Yet, government must also do more to take the side of charities and community healers, and support their work. We've had enough of the stale debate between big government and indifferent government. Government must be active enough to fund services for the poor and humble enough to let good people in local communities provide those services. So, I've created a White House Office of Faith-Based and Community Initiatives.

The speech generated little excitement. Bush now needed a promi-nent ally, so he reached out to the nation's largest charity. On 10 July 2001, the *Washington Post* reported the existence of an internal Salvation Army memo claiming that the Bush administration had made a "firm commit-ment" to the organization to issue a regulation protecting it from state and city efforts to prevent discrimination against gays and lesbians in hiring and domestic partner benefits; in return, the Salvation Army agreed to support Bush's faith-based initiative. Dilulio swore that there had never been a deal. But the Salvation Army admitted that it had discussed the deal with Rove. Exposed, on 16 August, Bush issued a statement condemning bias against religious organizations in the awarding of federal grant mon-ies. The next day, Dilulio resigned from the faith-based office—it was an-nounced that he would depart on 11 September of that year. Bush replaced Dilulio with James Towey, another Democrat who had led Florida's social services department. In the summer of 2001, the faith-based initiative was modified under proposed legislation called the Community Services Act. On 19 July the bill was approved by the House; it was then sent to the Senate, where it stalled in committee. The bill never passed.[21]

But Bush was not to be denied. He issued executive orders allowing federal funds to flow directly to churches and limiting the capability of the government to interfere with the religious substance of the programs that received the funding. Bush was criticized for diverting federal fund-ing without congressional oversight and for using it to essentially buy the black vote by diverting much of those monies to black churches. A bitter Dilulio could only watch from a distance, telling a reporter in December 2002, "What you've got is everything—and I mean everything—being run by the political arm. It's the reign of the Mayberry Machiavellis."[22]

During the presidential campaign, Bush had laid out his general princi-ples for Social Security reform. Those principles, discussed in chapter 3, called for more choice in how citizens invested their Social Security ben-efits and a promise to form a commission on Social Security reform. On 2 May 2001, by executive order, Bush formed the President's Commission to Strengthen Social Security. Cochaired by former Democratic senator Daniel Patrick Moynihan and Republican businessman Richard Parsons, president of AOL/Time Warner, the commission had little independence of movement. In his executive order, Bush charged the commission to "submit to the President bipartisan recommendations to modernize and restore fiscal soundness to the Social Security system according to the following principles"—worded almost exactly as Bush had worded them in his Rancho Cucamonga speech in May 2000:

> that modernization must not change existing benefits for retirees or near retirees; that the Social Security surplus must be locked away only for Social Security; that Social Security payroll taxes must not be increased; that the government must not invest Social Security funds in the stock market; that modernization must preserve the disability and survivor's components; [and that] modernization must include individually controlled, voluntary personal retirement accounts, which will augment the Social Security net.

In effect, the conclusions of the committee were forced upon it in its charge.[23]

As a result, the commission came under immediate attack, both from those who opposed any kind of voluntary personal accounts (largely, but not exclusively, Democrats) and from those who opposed any kind of reform of Social Security (led by the American Association of Retired Persons [AARP]). The interim report, released in August 2001, contained three options for the creation of the private accounts and argued that it would take $2 trillion in start-up funds over the next seventy-five years to set up those accounts. It also claimed—without offering any specifics—that any reform would need a combination of benefit reductions and tax increases to work. At best, the report was a halting first step.[24]

In 2001, the western United States was in the grip of a mature and growing energy crisis. The causes were many: market deregulation, the lack of an adequate number of energy plants, and the financial collapse of major energy companies all contributed to a situation, particularly in California, where energy was now in extremely short supply (over the previous ten years, not one new power plant had been built in the state). As a result, the state was suffering through a series of rolling brownouts and blackouts that limited consumer use of energy. Chairman of the Federal Reserve Alan Greenspan predicted that the energy shortages in California could plunge the entire nation into recession.[25]

On 29 January 2001, Bush named Cheney—the former head of Halliburton, a major energy company—as the head of a task force to explore the nation's energy problem. The report of the National Energy Development Task Force (NEDTF), released in May 2001, recommended a "wiser" use of energy, the expansion of energy infrastructure, and an increase in the nation's energy supplies. Nevertheless, the crisis in California rolled largely unabated into 2003, when it was a significant contributing factor in that state's vote to recall its governor, Gray Davis.[26]

The release of the NEDTF report also had an unanticipated side effect. It showed the extent to which Cheney would go to protect what he saw as the prerogatives of the presidency. Two watchdog groups—Judicial Watch and the Sierra Club—demanded the release of the names of all individuals and companies that the NEDTF had consulted. After filing several unsuccessful Freedom of Information Act requests, they filed suit in federal court. Despite pressure in the press, Cheney refused to release the names. As he explained in his memoir: "I believed, and the president backed me up, that we had the right to consult with whomever we chose—and no obligation to tell the press or Congress or anybody else who we were taking to." The fight lasted for much of Bush's first term and occasionally made news, but Bush and Cheney eventually won this particular battle. In June 2004 the Supreme Court remanded the lawsuit to the district court. In defeat, the head of Judicial Watch could only wax optimistic: "Ultimately, we can't believe courts will endorse the Bush administration's assertion of unchecked executive secrecy and power."[27]

Unlike his father, Bush had no experience in diplomatic or foreign affairs. Like his father, however, Bush preferred direct, face-to-face personal diplomacy rather than farming out negotiations to either his staff or his cabinet. The first opportunity for Bush to practice his brand of personal diplomacy was with the nation that shared a border with Texas. In July 2000, Vincente Fox, then the governor of the northern Mexican state of Guanajuato, won election as president of Mexico. He and Bush had known each other while they were both governors. While Fox initially felt that Bush was "quite simply the cockiest man I have ever met in my life," the bond between the two men soon grew close.[28] Bush was anxious to strengthen that relationship. He was also eager to woo Mexican American voters and advance his support of free trade in the Americas. Thus, Bush made a powerful statement by making Mexico his first state visit on 16 February 2001.

After Bush had been meeting with Fox for about an hour, the phones of his aides started buzzing. One by one, the aides hurriedly left the room. Incensed, but in the dark, Bush demanded to know what was going on. He soon learned that in response to the latest instance of Saddam Hussein's targeting of UN planes patrolling the "no-fly zone," twenty-four American and British aircraft launched an attack on five Iraqi defense sites. But that was not the end of the story. What Bush later called "a relatively routine mission" was decidedly not that. Saddam counterattacked with a vengeance, his antiaircraft guns illuminating the sky over Baghdad. The scene recalled the early images of the American air strikes on Baghdad during the first Persian Gulf War in January 1991. Indeed, the parallel was so great that a Mexican reporter asked Bush, "Is this the beginning of a new war?" The trip was now a bust, instantaneously becoming more about Iraq than about free trade.[29]

The press was generally favorable—the young Bush administration was seen as being strong enough to stand up to Saddam (in the *New York Times*: the response "sent a timely signal to Saddam Hussein that the Bush administration . . . will not shy away from using force to contain any new Iraqi military threat"). But Bush was furious. He had not been told about the attack in advance and was caught completely off guard when he learned about it in Mexico City. The incident shone a light on just how much the Bush national security team had yet to learn.[30]

Indeed, before the administration was two months old, the secretary of state had made a significant blunder. In 1994, the Clinton administration had negotiated what became known as the Agreed Framework with North Korea. In exchange for agreeing to freeze and dismantle his nation's nuclear program, North Korean president Kim Jong-il received energy substitutes—heavy fuel oil, and two light water reactors—from the United States that could not be used to build fuel for a nuclear weapon. The agreement, however, did not stop North Korea from flexing its muscles. In 1998 North Korea fired a missile over Japan; the following year, its ships fired on South Korean ships patrolling in the Yellow Sea.[31]

Bush believed the Agreed Framework to be flawed, giving advantages to North Korea that were not counterweighed by appropriate precautions, and he was not planning to return to it. However, on 7 March 2001, the *Washington Post* ran a story, quoting an interview with Powell, that claimed the administration was "picking up Clinton talks on North Korea." Bush was furious, and he ordered Rice to speak to Powell. Powell retracted his statement, sheepishly admitting that he "had gotten out a little forward on his skis."[32]

On 1 April 2001, an American EP-3 surveillance plane—propeller-driven, weighted down with technology, and without much maneuverability—left Kadena Air Base in Okinawa on a routine reconnaissance mission. While over Hainan Island, a province of the People's Republic of China

(PRC), the plane was intercepted by two PRC fighter jets, both of which buzzed too close to the EP-3. One of the Chinese pilots flew into one of the EP-3's propellers and was killed. The American plane made an emergency landing on Hainan Island, and the twenty-four-man crew was captured. The Chinese demanded a public apology from the United States before they would even consider releasing the crew.[33]

The next day, Bush discussed the Chinese demands with Rumsfeld, Powell, and Rice. Rice and Powell supported some kind of statement of contrition; Rumsfeld was adamantly against either a sign of apology or a promise to suspend the reconnaissance flights. Three days later, Bush publicly declared that he "regret[ed] that a Chinese pilot is missing," but he would go no further. On 8 April, Powell proclaimed that "we're sorry" about the death of the Chinese pilot, but that his statement "can't be seen as an apology accepting responsibility." Rumsfeld reportedly mocked Powell's performance, remarking that Powell should instead say "pretty please" to the Chinese. On 11 April, a letter was delivered to the Chinese that said the United States expressed "sincere regret" that the Chinese pilot had died. The Chinese chose to call the letter a "letter of apology" for the entire incident, and the crisis was allowed to fade away. Bush later made light of the affair ("The Chinese sent us a $1 million bill for the American crew's food and lodging. We offered them $34,000"). But many neoconservatives were upset that yet another Bush had allowed the Chinese to save face after an international incident.[34]

In 1997, Clinton signed the Kyoto Protocol, which committed signatory nations to reduce their greenhouse gas emissions so as to reduce global warming. Supporters of the treaty positioned it as a major step forward in the battle against climate change. Critics noted that the treaty left out nations such as China, India, and Brazil, all of which were major emitters of greenhouse gases. They also argued that the treaty as written was virtually unenforceable. Both Congress and the president had their doubts—while Clinton signed the protocol, Congress voted 95–0 in a nonbinding resolution to reject the accord, and Clinton never formally submitted it to the Senate for ratification.

Bush had made it clear throughout the 2000 campaign that he was not in favor of the treaty. He believed it contained too many exemptions, which would ultimately hurt the American economy. Nevertheless, once in office he formed a cabinet-level working group, charged with giving the president its recommendation. Once those recommendations were in, on

11 June Bush met the press in the Rose Garden. With Cheney by his side, he pronounced that the Kyoto Protocol was "fatally flawed" and that, like Clinton before him, he would not submit it to the Senate for ratification.[35]

However, Bush chose not to formally consult America's allies about his decision to withdraw from Kyoto. This was the first hint of a charge that would follow Bush for the rest of his presidency—that he was a unilateralist, less concerned with being a member of the brotherhood of nations than he was with developing a policy that took the United States in its own autonomous direction. Certainly, this was how French president Jacques Chirac saw the situation, and he told Bush so. Rice would simply write that "we handled it badly."[36]

On 16 June 2001, Bush traveled to Ljubljana, Slovenia, to meet with the newly elected Russian president, Vladimir Putin. Bush had gotten some inside information on Putin from John Danforth, who had just returned from Russia, where he had candid conversations with an official who knew Putin well. The official described Putin as "absolutely a man of his word" and said that he liked jokes. Danforth also wrote that while he had heard that Putin wore a cross around his neck, the official would not confirm this. Danforth recommended that Bush make it clear from the start that he believed Putin was a leader who the other nations should treat with respect. He also suggested "exploring Putin's personal side to see whether he is someone you might have more in common with than pundits might suggest . . . and not to be prejudiced against him by his KGB background."[37]

At the heart of Bush's agenda with Putin was the issue of missile reductions. Bush had come to believe that such cutbacks were not only necessary but also very possible to achieve in a post–Cold War environment if the United States withdrew from the 1972 Anti-Ballistic Missile (ABM) Treaty. At Ljubljana, Bush told Putin that he would indeed withdraw from the ABM Treaty, and that following that withdrawal, Bush would cut the American nuclear arsenal by two-thirds. Putin agreed to match those cuts.[38]

This was the most significant foreign policy decision of the first eight months of the Bush administration. And yet it was not what most people remembered about the first Bush-Putin summit. Bush later remembered that at the beginning of their meeting, Putin seemed tense, rarely deviating from his notecards. In an attempt to break that ice, Bush used the information provided him by Danforth and asked Putin: "Is it true your mother gave you a cross that you had blessed in Jerusalem?" Taken aback, Putin stumbled through a story: that his home had caught fire, but the cross had been spared from destruction—as if, according to Putin, "it was meant to be." Bush was later asked by a reporter if he trusted Putin; he replied, "I looked the man in the eye. I found him to be very straightforward and trustworthy. We had a very good dialogue. I was able to get a sense of his soul."[39]

Perhaps. Cheney certainly didn't think much of Bush's ability to read into Putin's soul: "When I looked into his eyes, I saw an old KGB hand. I didn't trust him and still don't." Setting aside Bush's dime-store psychoanalysis, Ljubljana had brought about real change in missile reductions; perhaps even more important from the long range, Bush walked away from the meeting believing that Putin was a man he could deal with. Immediately following their meeting, Bush sent Putin a handwritten note: "Dear Vladimir: Our meeting was excellent today. Thank you for your willingness to lead and thank you for your friendship. I look forward to hearing reports of the discussion in Moscow. With respect, George Bush." This perception would play an important part in the days following the terrorist attacks of 11 September.[40]

On 29 January, Margaret LaMontagne Spellings, the head of Bush's Domestic Policy Council, met with the president. One of the items on her agenda was the issuance by the Clinton administration of new rules that might allow embryonic stem cell research to move forward with federal funding. Bush quickly interrupted her: "First of all, what exactly is a stem cell?"[41]

What Bush soon learned was that stem cells have the potential to develop ("differentiate") into many different kinds of cells in the human body. Scientists believe that this quality of differentiation might lead to a stem cell playing a role in replacing any defective part of the body. As that cell divides, it creates more and more stem cells, known as lines. These lines can then be used in research. Scientists believed that stem cell research could unlock previously closed doors and offer ways to treat diseases such as Parkinson's and Alzheimer's. Such research was already underway when Bush took office. Indeed, developments in stem cell science were moving at a rapid pace—in 1998, a University of Wisconsin researcher was the first to isolate an individual stem cell.[42]

There was, however, a serious roadblock in the way of stem cell research—the only way to get an embryonic stem cell was to destroy the embryo. As such, the issue of stem cell research melded closely with the white-hot debate over abortion. While no federal law prohibited the use of private funds to support stem cell research, Congress had passed a law—the Dickey-Wicker Amendment (named after its champions, Republicans Jay Dickey of Arkansas and Roger Wicker of Mississippi)—banning the use of federal funds for research that involved the use of human embryos that had somehow been destroyed. The Clinton administration had dealt with the issue through a rather permissive interpretation of the amendment—that it might permit some public funding for research if the embryos had been previously destroyed through the use of private funds.[43]

Three events in the spring of 2001 shone a public spotlight on the issue and placed it squarely on the president's desk. On 21 February, eighty Nobel laureates signed a letter to Bush, urging him to expand federal funding for stem cell research. Then, on 6 March, Tommy Thompson, secretary of the Department of Health and Human Services, told a Senate panel that if such a law were passed, he would be troubled by it. The next day, 7 March, Nightlight Christian Adoptions, a group dedicated to protecting frozen embryos and helping possible parents to adopt, filed suit in federal court to prevent the government from implementing the Clinton administration rules for research. Rove remembered that "we were in danger of having this issue decided for us."[44]

Bush could have simply taken a pass on the issue and let Clinton's policy take its course. But for Bush, nothing in his first eight months as president—not tax cuts, not Chinese aircraft, not the terror warnings that we will encounter in the next chapter—engaged him as did the stem cell debate. Indeed, he was involved to the point of obsession. He simply could not get enough information on the subject. Josh Bolten charged Jay Lefkowitz, the general counsel of the Office of Management and Budget (which would supervise any funding project), with running point on the issue. Bush and Lefkowitz hit it off, and the president kept Lefkowitz busy with requests and questions on the issue. As Lefkowitz later remembered, "Once I began turning in my memos, a day rarely passed when he did not call with a follow-up request or a question about something he had read." Lefkowitz organized private sessions in the Oval Office, where many proponents and opponents of stem cell research got the president's ear. The president was energized—not unlike a graduate student preparing a thesis. "The more I learned," he recalled, "the more questions I had."[45]

The president also consulted his wife on the issue. The First Lady responded as one might expect of a woman whose father had died of

Alzheimer's disease and whose mother was a breast cancer survivor—she counseled the president to be cautious with the promises of groups that saw stem cell research as the panacea for all of life's problems, only to leave those suffering with the diseases to bear great disappointment when the science did not immediately provide solutions. Bush was also moved by his July 2001 audience with Pope John Paul II in which, among other things, the two men discussed stem cell research—the pontiff made clear his view that human life, in all its forms, must be protected.[46]

In his memoirs, Bush presents the debate as a classic moral conundrum. On the one hand, Bush empathized with those who argued for using all available knowledge in the search for medical advancement. The death of Bush's sister, Robin, to leukemia (an event that he would reference in his speech to the nation announcing his decision), as well as his long-standing support for various medical foundations, helped support this side of the argument. The other side, however, was Bush's admitted fear of that increase in knowledge: "I felt that technology should respect moral boundaries. . . . I envisioned researchers cloning fetuses to grow spare body parts in a laboratory. I could foresee the temptation of designer babies." This side of the issue was fed by Bush's long-standing opposition to abortion. Indeed, early on in his administration, Bush had reinstated the Mexico City Policy, which prevented the granting of federal funds to any organization or group that promoted abortions overseas (known by its detractors as the "Global Gag Rule," the policy had been announced by Reagan in 1984 and rescinded by Clinton as one of his first acts in office on January 22, 1993).[47]

Perhaps the moment that best demonstrates Bush's agony over the issue was when Lefkowitz brought in his copy of Aldous Huxley's dystopian novel *Brave New World* (1932) and began to read the opening chapter, which describes humans one day being artificially bred in the Hatchery and Conditioning Center. As Lefkowitz remembered it, "a chill came over the room." Bush responded: "We are on the edge of a cliff. And if we take a step off the cliff, there's no going back. Perhaps we should only take one step at a time."[48]

Bush was also under great political pressure. The conservatives in his party wanted a flat rejection of any stem cell research. Republican moderates, however, wanted something more flexible. Amo Houghton of New York, one such House moderate, penned his concerns to Andy Card: "Please, please don't let us pro-choice northeast Republicans hang out to dry on this one. Ours will be the House battleground in 2002. We need some positive signals from the president. Medically the difference between 'cloning' and 'research' is not difficult to explain. . . . if the DeLay, Armey, Watts[49] position prevails—it's going to be well-nigh impossible to explain next fall to *our base* here in the Northeast."[50]

On 10 July, Bush met with Daniel Callahan of the Hastings Center for Bioethics and Leon Kass, a person whose position at the University of Chicago—as both a physician and a philosophy professor—bridged the two sides of Bush's conundrum. Kass suggested that Bush authorize federal funding for stem cell research, but only on already existing stem cell lines—those lines taken from previously destroyed embryos. Bush was intrigued, but he worried that Kass's solution would encourage researchers to simply destroy more embryos. Kass had a ready response: Bush must reaffirm his support for human life and make it clear that federal funding could not be used in the destruction of future embryos. As Kass put it, "If you find research on lines that have already been developed, you are not complicit in their destruction." Bush then met with officials from the National Institutes of Health and asked them how many embryonic stem cell lines already existed; they told him there were sixty such lines ready for research. Bush had found a solution to his dilemma.[51]

Kass's suggestion was the basis for what Bush announced as his policy on 9 August in his first prime-time address to the nation. Bush announced that federal funds could be used for research on sixty existing stem cell lines, "where the life and death decision has already been made," but no human embryos "that have at least the potential for life" would be destroyed and used for federally funded research." For Bush, the decision "allows us to explore the promise and potential of stem cell research without crossing a fundamental moral line."

The reaction to Bush's decision was immediate and fierce. Dr. Lee Witters, a professor of medicine and biochemistry at Dartmouth College, lamented: "The scientists are operating with at least one hand tied behind their backs by this. . . . When I walk into my lab to do an experiment, I like to be able to try all the angles, and it's very tough to proceed if you know you can do only a certain kind of experiment." Other scientists, however, sided with Dr. Elaine Fuchs of the University of Chicago, who stated: "The president's decision gives renewed hope to nearly 100 million Americans who suffer from some of the most debilitating illnesses." Several celebrities—most notably Nancy Reagan, Mary Tyler Moore, and Christopher Reeve (whose support for the decision would turn into opposition just

before his 2004 death)—announced their support of the president's decision.[52]

But the conservative Right was apoplectic. Lefkowitz recalled being
"battered" at conservative activist Grover Norquist's weekly meeting of
various conservative organizations.[53] Ken Connor of the conservative
Family Research Council compared some kinds of stem cell research to
experiments done by Nazi doctor Josef Mengele. Bay Buchanan, sister of
and political adviser to presidential candidate and conservative commentator Pat Buchanan, observed, "If it is wrong to kill, why did he not say
he will ban all federal funds?" Bush was proud of his Solon-like decision,
remembering that it was the first decision by a president that allowed stem
cell research to move forward.[54]

Yet the debate showed no signs of abating. One month after Bush's
announcement, a panel of scientists announced that for any research to
approach validity, new lines of stem cells would be necessary. That announcement was carried on the front page of the *New York Times*—on 11
September 2001.[55]

Bush later claimed that it was Rice who put the AIDS pandemic in Africa
onto the president's priority list, but the mind-numbing statistics spoke for
themselves. As compared with North America, which had 900,000 people
infected with HIV/AIDS, Africa had 24.5 million. The continent had sixteen nations in which more than one-tenth of the adult population aged
fifteen to forty-nine was infected; in seven of those countries, one in every
five people had HIV/AIDS. In Botswana, 35.8 percent of the population
was infected; South Africa, with a total of 4.2 million people infected, had
the largest number of people living with HIV/AIDS in the world.[56]

As we will see, there was never any love lost between George W. Bush
and the United Nations. But Bush shared Secretary-General Kofi Annan's
concern about AIDS in Africa. Annan had spearheaded the creation of the
UN Global Fund to combat HIV/AIDS, tuberculosis, and malaria throughout the world. Bush stepped gingerly into the fray. At the G8 summit in
Genoa, held on 20–22 July 2001 (where Bush and Jacques Chirac disagreed
over Kyoto), the United States pledged $200 million to the Global Fund.
By 2002, the US commitment to the now-renamed World Health Fund had
risen to $500 million. However, despite Bush's public and private cajoling
(and a pledge to the fund of $100 million from the Bill and Melinda Gates
Foundation), Congress had yet to pony up the money for any of Bush's

pledges. But the pandemic showed no real signs of abatement—more than sixty-eight million people were projected to die of AIDS by 2020—and Bush was becoming increasingly impatient.[57]

The trauma of 11 September 2001 did nothing to abate Bush's interest in the issue. Sometime early in 2002, Bush asked Bolten to form a group that would recommend an initiative to confront the pandemic. The group was initially composed of Jay Lefkowitz, now a deputy domestic policy adviser, Dr. Anthony Fauci, who since 1984 had been the head of the National Institute of Allergy and Infectious Diseases, deputy national security adviser Gary Edson, and deputy assistant to the president for domestic policy Kristen Silverberg. According to Lefkowitz, it was Fauci who steered the group away from putting its money toward vaccine research and instead putting it toward the issue of transmission of the disease from mother to child, in utero (each year, some 700,000 African babies were being born with HIV). Fauci's plan centered on making nevirapine, a new drug that could halve the rate of transmission of AIDS from mother to child, more readily available. The group proposed an initial start-up budget of $500 million over five years. Bush bought in. On 19 June 2002, he announced the creation of the International Mother and Child HIV Prevention Initiative, directing funds to select African and Caribbean nations. Bush had been in office eighteen months and was now prosecuting a foreign war in Afghanistan, but he had also doubled the amount that the United States was spending on the AIDS crisis.[58]

However, Bush still was not satisfied. He ordered Bolten to take his team back to the drawing board and "come up with something bigger." He was clear what "bigger" meant: "Assume that money is no object." The result of this second round of deliberations, championed at first by Fauci, was a massive expansion of the Mother and Child Initiative that was budgeted at $15 billion over five years. A new director of the AIDS office, Joseph O'Neill, who had managed the Clinton administration's AIDS initiative, was chosen. O'Neill began to sketch out the details of the new program. Based on a model already in place in Uganda, Edson mapped out a "network" plan for getting the new drugs that could dramatically increase the life expectancy of a person infected with HIV to an exponentially increased amount of people. As Bush swatted away congressional requests for him to increase American contributions to the World Global Fund, the meetings of the expanded group were kept secret. By November 2002, the group had a plan ready for the president. It proposed funding three programs: a prevention campaign that emphasized both abstinence and condom usage; a treatment program that would get medicines to the afflicted using Edson's network; and a program for caring for the victims of AIDS, particularly orphans.[59]

Bush scheduled one final December meeting with the group to iron out details of the plan. That meeting was scheduled on the day of the second annual White House Hanukkah party. Before the group's meeting, Bush met with about twenty Jewish leaders who were guests at the gathering. One, Dr. George Klein, told the president that his father had been a member of a delegation that asked to meet with Franklin Roosevelt to discuss the plight of Jews in Adolf Hitler's Reich, only to be told by White House counsel Sam Rosenman that the president did not want to see them. Now, Klein said to Bush, "If you had been president at the time, with the moral clarity you have displayed in the war against terrorism, there would be millions more Jews alive today." Lefkowitz remembered that Bush was "visibly moved" by this statement. Bush then went into the meeting on AIDS and, after some discussion, asked speechwriter Mike Gerson, who had been on the President's Emergency Plan for AIDS Relief (PEPFAR) planning team, for his thoughts. Gerson responded: "If we can do this and we don't, it will be a source of shame." Bush then told the assembled group, "We are too wealthy a nation, and too compassionate a nation, not to take this step. It's a chance to save millions of lives. We have to do this."[60]

Bush announced the PEPFAR initiative in the January 2003 State of the Union address. When it was formally proposed, the bill called for a five-year, $15 billion (including almost $10 billion in new funds) initiative that was focused on prevention, treatment, and care in fourteen African nations. The program was immediately assailed from both sides of the political spectrum. The Right attacked the prevention program for its use of condoms, with many arguing that the program violated the Mexico City Policy; the Left criticized the abstinence program as a "war on condoms." Both sides were concerned with the cost—the plan would quadruple American foreign aid to African countries. As a result, the bill was modified to guarantee that federal monies would not be turned over to the UN Global Fund but would remain under the control of a director appointed by the president (the first director was former Eli Lilly CEO Randall Tobias, and that 3 percent of the monies earmarked for the prevention program would be used for an abstinence-until-marriage program. In the House, the bill was sponsored by Republican Henry Hyde of Illinois and Democrat Tom Lantos of California; it passed, 375 to 41. In the Senate, the bill was shepherded by majority leader Bill Frist of Tennessee—himself a surgeon—and Richard Lugar of Indiana. It passed by an overwhelming voice vote. On 27 May 2003, PEPFAR became law.[61]

PEPFAR was one of the biggest successes of the Bush administration. Lefkowitz concluded his article on the decision-making surrounding the issue with a summary of PEPFAR's impact. By the end of 2008, PEPFAR

> had provided antiretroviral treatment for two million individuals, a dramatic increase from the 50,000 who were receiving treatment in 2002. As of March 2008, the program had provided transmission-prevention services for women during approximately 13 million pregnancies and given antiretroviral prophylaxis in more than one million pregnancies, Health officials estimate that this has resulted in the prevention of approximately 200,000 infant infections. Finally, PEPFAR supported care for approximately 6.6 million individuals, including 2.7 million orphans and vulnerable children, and offered more than 33 million counseling-and-testing sessions for men, women, and children. Prevention outreach programs have helped 60 million people. Over 20 million have received condoms.[62]

Moreover, the success of PEPFAR transcended political boundaries— President Barack Obama included consistent increases in expenditures for PEPFAR in his budgetary requests, and a 2019 attempt by President Donald Trump to cut funding for PEPFAR met with bipartisan opposition.[63]

# 7

★ ★ ★ ★ ★

# "AMERICA IS UNDER ATTACK"

Afghanistan has more than earned its nickname as the "graveyard of empires." Landlocked, but strategically placed at the intersection of South Asia and East Asia (its largest borders are to the west with Iran and to the south and east with Pakistan), its unforgiving mountain terrain and tribal balkanization had for centuries protected it from invasion or swallowed up its invaders. The Soviet Union ignored these lessons of history when, on 25 December 1979, it invaded Afghanistan, ostensibly to protect that nation's communist government from a growing insurgency. The Soviets quickly found themselves mired in a guerrilla war fought on treacherous ground for which its army was both ill-suited and ill-prepared. Moreover, they found themselves fighting not just the Afghan rebels but also their followers. In the early 1980s, young Muslims from all around the world flocked to Afghanistan to join the "holy war"—jihad—against the Soviet attacker. One such fighter was Usama bin Laden.[1]

Born in 1957 in Riyadh, Saudi Arabia, Usama bin Laden[2] was the seventeenth of fifty-six children of a prominent Saudi construction tycoon who died in a plane crash when Usama was eleven years old. A shy child who had a religious conversion experience while in high school, as his father's sole male heir Usama received the bulk of his father's wealth. He attended King Abdul-Aziz University, where he may have earned a degree in civil

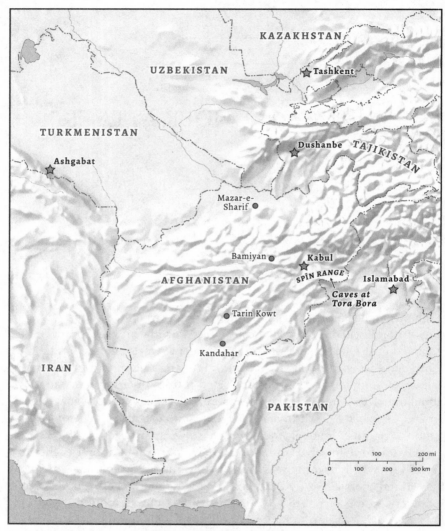

Afghanistan, ca. 2001. (Credit: Erin Greb Cartography)

engineering in 1979. At college, bin Laden was strongly affected by the sermons of Abdullah Azzam, a Palestinian who preached that all Muslims must take up arms in the struggle between God and Satan. In 1984 Azzam issued a formal ruling on Islamic law—a fatwa—that called for every Muslim to join the fight against the Soviet invader in Afghanistan. Bin

Laden raced to be a part of the crusade; over the next decade his contribution was to tap into his family's fortune to help fund the resistance. He did, however, fight at the battle of Jaji, with a zeal that led one admirer to comment that he was "really brave. . . . [He] fought in this battle like a private."[3]

On 10 September 1988, with the Soviets all but expelled from Afghanistan, bin Laden and Azzam founded Al-Qaida (The Base) as a center of operations from which to plan the next jihad.[4] The nature of that jihad was a subject of deep discord within the group. Bin Laden had met Ayman al-Zawahiri, an Egyptian doctor who had been arrested and tortured for his role in the 1981 assassination of Anwar Sadat. Now a hardened assassin who was the leader of the Egyptian Islamic terrorist organization al-Jihad, Zawahiri argued for mounting a jihad not just against invaders of Muslim territory but throughout the Middle East. Azzam, however, saw this as violence between Muslims, and did not approve. Bin Laden came to accept Zawahiri's view of jihad, and the November 1989 assassination of Azzam—a murder that was never solved—left bin Laden and Zawahiri in complete control of Al-Qaida.[5]

The 1991 Persian Gulf War, in which the United States drove an invading Saddam Hussein out of Kuwait and back within the borders of Iraq, radicalized bin Laden with a hatred of the United States, which he believed had defiled the holy land of Saudi Arabia by its military presence there. He returned to Saudi Arabia, only to be expelled from that country in 1992 both for his open criticism of the Saudi government and for smuggling. In that year, bin Laden moved first to Pakistan and then to Sudan. There, his desire to attack American targets grew and matured. Journalist Steve Coll, one of the most prescient observers of the rise of bin Laden, describes him during this period as "soft, scholarly, and more of a tycoon and a lecturer than a hardened terrorist tactician." Regardless, bin Laden and Al-Qaida were linked to several terrorist attacks during the period, most notably the December 1992 bombing of a hotel in Yemen (the bombing killed a tourist but no Americans).[6]

On 25 January 1993—116 hours after President Clinton had taken office—Mir Aimal Kansi ambushed five CIA employees as they drove to work at Langley; two were killed, and three were wounded, only one hundred feet from a security station. A Pakistani national, Kansi was able to escape and fly to Pakistan the next day, where he remained at large until 1997. Almost one month to the day later, on 26 February 1993, a 1,336-pound bomb hidden in a Ryder truck exploded in the parking garage of the World Trade Center in New York City, killing six people and injuring more than a thousand. The plot was carried out by six Islamic terrorists and financed by Kuwaiti-born Khalid Sheikh Mohammed (soon to be known by his sobriquet, KSM), the uncle of one of the plotters.[7]

Neither the CIA ambush nor the World Trade Center bombing was an Al-Qaida operation. There is also some doubt regarding the role played by Al-Qaida in the October 1993 attacks on US servicemen in Somalia, where in the capital city of Mogadishu two American helicopters were destroyed and eighteen American soldiers were killed, along with close to five hundred Somalis. The bloody battle led to the American withdrawal from Somalia and became the flash point for five years of Al-Qaida planning for strikes at US targets in Africa.

In 1996, American pressure led Sudan to expel bin Laden, and he moved Al-Qaida back to Afghanistan. On 23 August 1996, Al-Qaida publicly declared war on both the United States and Israel. The thirty-page fatwa, entitled "Declaration of War against the Americans Occupying the Land of the Two Holy Places," appeared in a London newspaper. After listing the Americans' transgressions—the greatest of which, in his mind, was their occupation of Saudi Arabia—bin Laden called for recruits to fight a holy war:

> Our youths believe in paradise after death. They believe that taking part in the fighting will not bring their day nearer; and staying behind will not postpone their day either. . . . Those youths know that their rewards in fighting you, the USA, is [sic] double than their rewards in fighting someone else not from the people of the book [the Koran]. They have no intention except to enter paradise by killing you.[8]

Bin Laden prepared for this war by striking up a wary partnership with another fundamentalist Muslim group in Afghanistan. Headed by Mullah Muhammad Omar, the Taliban filled the political vacuum created after the Soviet Union withdrew its forces in 1989, seizing Kabul in September 1996. Largely made up of Pashtuns, the principal ethnic group in Afghanistan, the Taliban quickly became known for its sadistic brutality, particularly toward women and girls. Donald Rumsfeld later observed that, thanks to the Taliban,

> women could not attend school, could not leave their homes without a male family member, and could not see male doctors, which made medical treatment for them next to impossible. Citizens could be jailed for owning a television. A man could be imprisoned in Afghanistan if

his beard were not long enough. It was illegal for youngsters to fly kites. Afghan soccer stadiums were used for stonings and beheadings.[9]

The Taliban carried out its brand of justice in public. Executions, floggings, amputations, and stonings were routine. The Taliban was also known for its participation in terrorist activities. In 2001 it blew up two huge sixth-century Buddhas at Bamiyan in Afghanistan, arguing that the figures represented immoral idols. A pariah in most world quarters, in 2001 the Taliban had diplomatic relations with only Pakistan, Saudi Arabia, and the United Arab Emirates. For his part, bin Laden grew close to Mullah Omar, who supported him even when other Taliban leaders would not. Bin Laden exploited this relationship to build training camps in Afghanistan for Al-Qaida recruits. Between 1996 and 11 September 2001, US intelligence placed the number of fighters who were trained in bin Laden's camps at between ten and twenty thousand. From there, he orchestrated several more terrorist attacks, most notably the June 1996 bombing of the Khobar Towers residential complex in Dhahran, Saudi Arabia, where 19 Americans were killed and 372 were wounded.[10]

On 23 February 1998, bin Laden issued a second fatwa. Entitled "Declaration of the World Islamic Front for Jihad against the Jews and the Crusaders," it was again published in an Arabic newspaper in London. After listing three perceived transgressions of the United States—that since 1991 its troops had taken residence in the Arabian Peninsula, that the Americans were attempting to repeat the massacre of the Palestinians that had been perpetrated by Israel, and that the overall aim of the United States in the region was to occupy the entirety of the Arabian Peninsula—bin Laden declared that "all these crimes and sins committed by the Americans are a clear declaration of war on Allah, his messenger, and Muslims," and that Muslim clerics, in the past, have "unanimously agreed that the jihad is an individual duty if the enemy destroys Muslim countries." Therefore, bin Laden called for all Muslims "to kill the Americans and their Allies—civilians and military" and made it clear that it was "an individual duty for every Muslim who can do it in any country in which it is possible to do it."[11]

Both the Reagan administration and the first Bush administration viewed terrorism through two lenses. First, when dealing with foreign terrorism, they believed that a military response should be the last resort. On 23 October 1983, a Hezbollah suicide bomber drove a truck with two thousand pounds of explosives into the marine barracks at Beirut International Airport; 220 marines, 18 sailors, and 3 soldiers, all part of a multinational peacekeeping mission, were killed. Reagan's response was to completely withdraw the marines from Lebanon, an action that Dick Cheney would later claim to be one of the events that allowed terrorism to expand and develop in the Middle East. On 21 December 1988, a Boeing 747, bound for New York City from London's Heathrow Airport, was blown out of the sky over Lockerbie, Scotland. All 259 passengers aboard Pan American Flight 103, as well as eleven residents of Lockerbie, were killed. A terrorist bomb, hidden inside checked luggage, was responsible for the slaughter. In response, the senior Bush created the President's Commission on Aviation Security and Terrorism. He also promised a victims' group that once he had evidence to support the identity of the terrorists, the United States would retaliate. But even when it was learned that the Libyans had orchestrated the bombing, the Bush administration did not strike back.[12]

Second, and related to the first, both administrations viewed terrorism—both domestic and foreign—as a law enforcement issue. In this view, terrorists should be caught and prosecuted, not hunted down and killed. Codifying this stance, the Reagan administration issued National Security Decision Directive (NSDD) 30, which assigned the international terrorism portfolio to the State Department and the FBI, a policy initially continued by the first Bush.[13] Moreover, the Reagan administration set up formal procedures that were followed by both the first Bush administration and the Clinton administration that regulated the sharing of information between the intelligence and criminal divisions. These regulations became known colloquially as "The Wall"—a concept described in 2004 by FBI director Robert Mueller:

> Before 9-11-01, Special Agent Smith, assigned to the intelligence side of a terrorism case (designed to detect and prevent future acts), was forbidden to discuss the case with Special Agent Jones, right across the hall, who was working the criminal side of the same case (focused on violations of the criminal code). For example, if SA Jones discovered crucial intelligence through her court-ordered criminal wiretap, she was not allowed to share it with SA Smith—she could not even suggest that SA Smith might want to seek a wiretap to collect the information for himself. For example, if SA Jones served a grand jury subpoena to a suspect's bank, she could not tell SA Smith what she found in the bank records. Instead, SA Smith would have to issue a National Security Letter to get that same information.[14]

Although the Clinton administration did not rescind NSDD 30, both the CIA ambush and the World Trade Center bombing of 1993 spurred it into an action that the previous two administrations had avoided. Clinton decided to keep Richard Clarke, a Bush administration staffer, as national coordinator for security, infrastructure protection and counterterrorism. Clarke sat on the cabinet-level Principals Committee when it met to discuss an issue dealing with terrorism. Under his guidance, several plans were made to strike back at international terrorism. For but one example, in spring 1998 a scheme was developed to capture bin Laden and bring him to justice (formally known in the intelligence community as a "rendition," better known as a "snatch"). The plan went through several dress rehearsals, but on 29 May, citing the considerable risk of civilian casualties, CIA director George Tenet turned off the plan.[15]

Such was the American attitude toward terrorism when Usama bin Laden finally made good on his fatwa. On 7 August 1998, Al-Qaida suicide squads using truck bombs attacked two US embassies—one in Nairobi (Kenya) and the other in Dar es Salaam (Tanzania). The Nairobi attack killed 12 Americans and 201 others; the Dar es Salaam attack killed 11 people, none of the Americans. When asked if Al-Qaida was behind the attacks, bin Laden replied that he had issued a "crystal clear" fatwa, and that if a jihad against the Jews and Americans to liberate the holy places was a crime, "let history be a witness that I am a criminal." In a portent of the future, Khalid Sheikh Mohammed, who had joined the anti-Soviet jihad in Afghanistan in 1986, saw the embassy bombings as a sign that bin Laden's organization was strong enough to get things done. He now approached bin Laden with a plan for attacking American landmarks with hijacked passenger planes. Sometime in late 1998 or early 1999, bin Laden approved the plan.[16]

Following the bombing of the US embassies, an intense debate within the administration culminated in Clinton's changing of US policy toward terrorism. For the moment, at least, the strategy of capture and adjudicate was replaced by that of search and destroy. On 20 August 1998, navy vessels in the Arabian Sea fired seventy-nine cruise missiles into terrorist training camps in both Afghanistan and Sudan. The intent of Operation Infinite Reach was to destroy Al-Qaida's leadership, but in this, as historian James D. Boys pointed out, "the operation must be considered a failure."[17]

Clarke hoped that this strike would be just the beginning of a concerted, long-term effort to eradicate Al-Qaida. In this, however, he would be disappointed. Both Clinton and Sandy Berger, his national security adviser, worried that air attacks that did not kill bin Laden only served to enhance his stature and to win him converts to his cause. In December 1998, despite a report that placed bin Laden on the road to Kandahar, well within the reach of cruise missiles, the administration decided not to launch an attack on his entourage. Two other opportunities to strike at bin Laden with cruise missiles—one in February 1999 and one in May 1999—were not executed.[18]

In fall 1999 Tenet revealed a new CIA strategy to deal with bin Laden. In-house, it was known simply as "The Plan." It proposed the continuation of disruption and rendition attempts; requested the hiring of more agents with counterterrorism skills; and argued for the penetration of Al-Qaida with human intelligence agents, as well as for pursuing a closer relationship with the Northern Alliance—a loosely knit group of opposition militias under the command of the "Lion of Panjshir," Ahmad Shah Massoud, so as to put more pressure on the Taliban, which was acting as Al-Qaida's protector.[19]

None of the plans or steps taken by the administration stopped bin Laden's next move. On 12 October 2000, using a small boat filled with explosives, Al-Qaida operatives rammed the USS *Cole*, then docked off the shore of Yemen. The blast tore open a hole in the side of the vessel; seventeen sailors died, and about forty more were wounded. Bin Laden personally planned the attack—from target choice to the choice of operatives to personally financing the mission. But this information was not readily available in real time. Indeed, initially there was a debate within the administration as to whether the attack was conducted by Al-Qaida or another terrorist group. Clinton would later tell the 9/11 Commission that it was this uncertainty that kept him from ordering a retaliatory strike in the wake of the bombing of the *Cole*.[20]

The Clinton administration, then, did not unilaterally adopt passive resistance as a strategy to terrorism. However, neither did it completely adopt a policy of military retaliation. It had, as indicated in one of its final statements on national security policy, emphasized the need to incorporate both "preventative and responsive measures" to augment the efforts of "enhanced law enforcement and intelligence gathering, vigorous diplomacy and, where needed, military action."[21]

Regardless, bin Laden now believed he could see a pattern of hesitancy. The withdrawal of American forces from Vietnam in the 1970s, the

1983 withdrawal of American forces from Lebanon after the bombing of the marine barracks, the withdrawal of US forces from Somalia, and the refusal of the Clinton administration to retaliate for the bombing of the *Cole* all left bin Laden to conclude that the United States was, in his words, a "paper tiger" that was as weak as the Soviets had been when they were expelled from Afghanistan. By June 2001, Al-Qaida was ready to strike at the mainland United States; it had fully developed a plan that would become known within the organization as the "Planes Plot."[22]

The place to begin an understanding of the Bush administration's reaction to terrorism in the eight months before the attacks of 11 September is with a study of Bush's National Security Council. There is no question but that Condoleezza Rice was the closest to Bush of all his advisers, and that she spent more time with him than any other White House staffer or cabi-net member (indeed, a case can be made that Rice was the closest to the president of any national security adviser). Perhaps because of her ease of access, Rice butted heads with her colleagues. Both Cheney and Rumsfeld were critics of Rice's organization and style. They believed that she spent too much time trying to broker consensus among the often-feuding ele-ments in the NSC, as opposed to presenting Bush with all those differ-ing points of view so that he could make an informed decision. Rumsfeld also pointed to how disorganized NSC meetings were and to the fact that they were often called at the last minute, forcing attendees to rework their schedules. For his part, Cheney told an interviewer it was his belief that as a result of Rice's style, "I did think that there were occasions when Condi told the president there was a consensus where there was none."[23]

Along with a predilection for presenting consensus rather than op-tions, Rice's NSC simply moved slowly. She once described her NSC as "low-key, very much more of a coordinating function, much less opera-tional, smaller." An academic at heart, Rice ran a deliberate process that seemed to convey no sense of urgency. She did not seem to believe that corralling a contentious interagency bureaucracy and bringing home a quick decision was her job. Rather, her NSC took a great deal of time to hold lengthy meetings, to write position papers, and to discuss. In this, she had Bush's full support (at the first NSC meeting, held on 30 January 2001, the president was clear: "Condi will run these meetings. . . . She's my national security adviser"). Yet a case can be made that this methodical, scholarly policy process contributed to an inability to see a crisis coming that was staring the NSC in its face.[24]

Some in the administration wanted the NSC to move faster. On 25 January 2001—only five days after Bush took office, Richard Clarke submitted a thirteen-page proposal to Rice. In it, Clarke pleaded for a "Principals level review on the al Qida [sic] network." Clarke offered a plan, based on "massive support" to anti-Taliban groups, such as the Northern Alliance. He also called for "special teams ready for covert entry into destroyed camps to acquire intelligence for locating terrorist cells outside Afghanistan," forces that would be supported by Predator drones. However, Rice nixed the idea for a meeting on Clarke's proposal. She remembered that she called Clarke to her office and "essentially told him that he had a green light to develop a strategy. There was no need for a Principals Committee meeting because Don, Colin, and the Vice President had all been briefed on al Qaida."[25]

By the summer, intelligence reports were spiking. They all pointed to what one CIA briefer called a "spectacular" attack—but on foreign soil (possible targets included Saudi Arabia, Israel, Kuwait, Rome, and the G8 summit in Genoa). On 10 July 2001, Tenet met with Rice, deputy national security adviser Steve Hadley, and Clarke. He told them that the system was "blinking red" and that they needed to go on an immediate war footing. In her memoir, Rice recalls this meeting much more vaguely ("My recollection of the meeting is not very crisp because we were discussing the threat every day"). Rice remembered that Bush was getting impatient: "I'm tired of swatting at flies. I'm tired of playing defense. I want to play offense. I want to take the fight to the terrorists." But the result of the 10 July meeting was Bush asking the CIA to "reexamine Al-Qaida's capabilities to attack inside the United States." To Clarke, this was passing the buck to one more study group. In May or June, he asked for a transfer to a position that dealt with cybersecurity (Rice told the 9/11 Commission that if, indeed, Clarke was frustrated, he never conveyed that to her).[26]

Bush did indeed press his CIA briefers on whether any of the threats could possibly be aimed at targets inside the United States. In direct response to these questions, the CIA wrote a memo that was included in the President's Daily Brief (PDB) for 6 August. Its headline—"Bin Laden Determined to Strike in U.S."—shifted the ground. When the PDB was made public in May 2002, many used it to buttress their argument that on 6 August, Bush was warned for the first time about an impending attack (the 16 May 2002 headline of the *New York Post* screamed, "9/11 Bombshell: Bush Knew"). But the memo contained no information that Bush did not already know. It said that bin Laden "has wanted to conduct terrorist attacks in the United States," but there were no specifics about an attack coming in New York or anywhere else. The memo also referred to ongoing FBI field operations that were following leads that were "bin Laden related," operations of which Bush was most certainly aware. Press reports would quote the memo as saying that bin Laden was planning "to hijack a U.S. aircraft," but most did not give the full quote—that bin Laden was planning "to hijack a U.S. aircraft to gain the release of the 'Blind Shaykh,' 'Umar' Abd al-Raham and other U.S. held extremists." In short, this was an informational memo without much new information in it. It was not a call to action, and it was not a warning of a specific impending attack. Despite the memo's jarring headline, it generated little buzz in the White House, and, in retrospect, there is no reason it should have.[27]

There is also no evidence that the memo led to the convening of the first cabinet-level Principals meeting of the Bush presidency on the subject of terrorism, held on 4 September 2001. At the meeting, the group approved a plan to go after Al-Qaida. One week later, on 10 September 2001, Rice forwarded the Al-Qaida strategy to Bush. Such sluggishness, particularly on the part of Rice and the NSC, infuriated Clarke, who sent Rice a terse note: "Are we serious about dealing with the al Qida [sic] threat? . . . Is al Qida a big deal? Decision makers should imagine themselves on a future day when the CSG [Coordinating Sub-Group of the Deputies Committee] has not succeeded in stopping Al-Qaida attacks and hundreds of Americans lay dead in several countries, including the U.S." And then for good measure: "The fact that the U.S.S. Cole was attacked during the last Administration does not absolve us of responding for the attack. . . . One might have thought that with a $250m hole in a destroyer and 17 dead sailors, the Pentagon might have wanted to respond." There is no record of any response from Rice.[28]

The conclusion of the bipartisan commission that investigated the events leading up to the events of 11 September (discussed in chapter 11) was that on 10 September 2001 "the pieces were coming together for an integrated policy dealing with al-Qaida, the Taliban, and Pakistan." But an equally valid conclusion was that the president was receiving generalities rather than specific warnings that might have spurred action. Also, it seems clear that the president, the CIA, and the NSC all dragged their feet through bureaucratic quicksand. Thus, the 9/11 Commission was correct in another conclusion: that while "numerous actions were taken overseas to disrupt possible attacks. . . . Far less was done domestically . . . the domestic agencies never mobilized in response to the threat. They did not have direction, and did not have a plan to institute." Ultimately, in the words of the commission report, "time ran out."[29]

The plot was code-named Holy Tuesday. Between 6:45 and 7:40 on the morning of Tuesday, 11 September 2001, at Boston's Logan Airport, five members of Al-Qaida boarded American Airlines Flight 11. In another terminal at Logan, between 7:31 and 7:40, five more Al-Qaida operatives boarded United Flight 175. All had passed through security checkpoints; each had walked through a metal detector; none of the checkpoint supervisors remembered noticing anything suspicious about their actions. At Dulles International Airport, just outside Washington, DC, at about 7:50 a.m., five more Al-Qaida operatives boarded American Airlines Flight 77. This time, however, two of the men set off an alarm at the security post. Both were escorted through the metal detector a second time. One was wanded, and both were eventually allowed to pass through, even though video footage would later show that one of the men was carrying an unidentified item in his back pocket. To the north at Newark International Airport, between 7:03 and 7:39, four members of Al-Qaida boarded United Airlines Flight 93. Between 7:59 and 8:42, all four flights were in the air. All four flights were headed to Los Angeles; all four carried up to 11,400 gallons of jet fuel.[30]

As soon as the airplanes reached their assigned cruising altitude, all four were seized by the terrorists (American 11 at 8:14, United 175 at 8:42, American 77 at 8:51, and United 93 at 9:28). The clashes were bloody and brief; the terrorists now piloted the planes.

At 8:44 a.m., Madeline "Amy" Sweeney, an attendant on American 11 who was in contact with the American Flights Service Office in Boston, coolly reported: "We are in a rapid descent. . . . We are all over the place. . . . We are flying low. We are flying way too low. Oh my God we are way too low." At 8:46:40, American 11 crashed into the North Tower of the World Trade Center in New York City.[31]

At 9:00 a.m., Peter Hanson, a passenger on United 175, spoke to his father on the ground in Easton, Connecticut: "It's getting bad, Dad—a stewardess was stabbed. . . . The plane is making jerky movements. . . . I think we are going down—I think they intend to go to Chicago or someplace and fly into a building—Don't worry, Dad—If it happens, it'll be very fast—My God, my God." At 9:03:11, United 175 crashed into the South Tower of the World Trade Center.[32]

Sometime between 9:16 and 9:26 a.m., Barbara Olson, a conservative commentator, and wife of Theodore Olson, the solicitor general of the United States who had argued Bush's case in *Bush v. Gore*, made two calls to her husband from American 77. She told him that the plane had been hijacked, and the hijackers had knives and box cutters. According to the report of the 9/11 Commission, Olson "did not display signs of panic and did not indicate any awareness of an impending crash." Her second call was cut off. At 9:37:46, American 77 crashed into the Pentagon's western wall, flying at 530 miles per hour.[33]

At 9:57 a.m., one of the passengers on board United 93 abruptly ended her phone call with a loved one on the ground: "Everyone's running up to First Class. I've got to go. Bye." In an attempt to regain control of the aircraft, the passengers had begun an assault on the plane's cockpit. The Al-Qaida pilot began to roll the airplane in an attempt to throw the passengers away from the door; he then pitched the nose of the aircraft sharply up and down; then he stabilized the aircraft. One terrorist shouted to his partner, "Is that it? Shall we finish it off?" His partner responded, "No. Not yet. When they all come, we finish it off." As the passengers broke through to the cockpit, the pilots, shouting, "Allah is the greatest," rolled the plane on its back. At 10:03, United 93, which had been headed for either the White House or the US Capitol, plowed into an empty field in Shanksville, Pennsylvania.[34]

At 9:59 a.m., the South Tower of the World Trade Center collapsed. At 10:28 a.m., the North Tower came down.

Altogether, 2,606 were killed on the ground in New York. Also killed were 125 on the ground at the Pentagon, 246 passengers on board the four doomed aircraft, and 19 Al-Qaida terrorists.

It was the early morning of 11 September 2001. Tucker Eskew, director of the White House Office of Media Affairs, sent out a hasty email to several of his colleagues. The only message was what was written in the subject heading: "Turn on CNN. FEMA [Federal Emergency Management Agency] to NYC?"[35]

Charles Gibson, the host of *Good Morning America* (ABC News): "We're joined by the entire network just to show you some pictures at the foot of New York City. This is at the World Trade Center. Obviously a major fire there. And there has been some sort of explosion. We don't fully know the details. There is one report, as of yet unconfirmed, that a plane has hit the World Trade Center. And you can see that there is smoke coming out of at least two sides of the building."[36]

It was to be a quick trip for the president. On 10 September he had flown to Longboat Key, Florida. The next day he would travel by motorcade to nearby Sarasota to visit Emma E. Booker Elementary School. The president was going to read to the students and make remarks that would highlight his developing education reform (from the Presidential Action Paper sent to all staff at 7:32 a.m. on 11 September 2001: "Message: There is a reading crisis among America's children. . . . *More funding without real reforms will not solve our nation's education challenges*"). He planned to be back in Washington by 12:30 p.m., where he would stop at the Pentagon and return to the White House by 1:05. After several meetings—including one with Catholic Hispanic leaders, one with leaders of the Muslim community, and a drop-by with the president of Lithuania, Bush would finally be able to relax a bit at the congressional barbeque, to be held on the South Lawn of the White House.[37]

When the presidential party arrived at Emma Booker, Karl Rove was the first to inform the president that an airplane had crashed into the World Trade Center. Bush nodded and said, "Get more details." Bush's first thought: "I envisioned a little propeller plane horribly lost." He was ushered into a classroom that served as a communications center, where Rice informed him by phone that the airplane that had struck the Trade Center was a commercial airliner. Still convinced that it was an accident, Bush told Rice to keep him apprised and ordered Dan Bartlett to start work on a speech that promised federal aid to the accident area. The purpose of the trip was instantly discarded. Sandy Kress, who had accompanied the president on this showcase for his education program, was ordered to get a chart that was going to be used to explain "No Child Left Behind" out of the classroom and out of the eye of the press.[38] Bush made his way into the classroom, took a seat at the front of the class, and watched as the students went through a reading exercise. At 9:05 a.m., Andy Card approached the president. Bending over, he whispered in Bush's ear: "A second plane hit the second tower. America is under attack." Card later recalled, "I knew what I was delivering was a very rare message . . . in a very unusual environment. . . . I knew that no matter what I did or no matter what the president did it was going to be somehow recorded, so I didn't want to do anything that would startle him."[39]

The moment is frozen in time. A photo taken just as Card whispered the horrific news to Bush shows a president who looks bewildered. This, however, is not how Bush remembered it for his memoir: "My first reaction was outrage. Someone had dared attack America. They were going to pay." Of course, it could have been both. Either way, Bush sat perfectly still. He had decided that if he left too quickly, he would scare the children and perhaps start a national panic. In this decision, he was abetted by his press secretary Ari Fleischer, who was in the back of the room holding up a handwritten sign that read "Don't Say Anything Yet." About seven minutes went by before Bush excused himself and went back to the communications center. It was there that he watched for the first time the video that was already defining the moment, as the networks were already beginning to replay video of American 11 crashing into the North Tower. To his staff, he quietly said, "We're at war. Get me the director of the FBI and the Vice President."[40]

Bush addressed the nation from Emma Booker. Speaking for less than one minute, he said, "This is a difficult moment for America. . . . Two airplanes have crashed into the World Trade Center in an apparent terrorist attack on our country." He ended his message by echoing his father's promise—virtually word for word—made after Iraq's invasion of Kuwait in August 1990: "Terrorism against our nation will not stand."[41] Bush left Emma Booker at 9:35 a.m. As the presidential limo raced to its rendezvous with Air Force One, Rice called Bush to tell him that American 77 had slammed into the Pentagon. At 9:54, Air Force One was wheels up. To get to its cruising altitude in as short an amount of time as possible, it shot straight up into the air like a rocket. It had, as yet, no destination.

Within moments of takeoff, Bush faced what he characterized as his "first decision as wartime commander in chief." It was also a decision that years later would come to define for many just how well the White House managed the crisis on that fateful day.[42]

Just before 10:00 a.m. the vice president was literally lifted from his chair at a meeting by Secret Service agents and whisked to the Presidential Emergency Operations Center (PEOC), a bunker underneath the East Wing of the White House that provided secure communications and protection in case of an emergency. With the president in transit, Cheney faced the very real possibility that there were other hijacked commercial airliners in the air, speeding at that very moment toward another fiery attack. The Combat Air Patrol (CAP), trained to intercept and shoot down any incoming attack planes, had scrambled from Otis Air National Guard Base on Cape Cod and Langley Air Force Base in Virginia and were in the air. All they needed was an order to attack.

In the days following 11 September, critics of the president charged that it was Cheney, not the president, who unilaterally gave the order for the CAP to attack if necessary. This is at best a half-truth. The record is clear that before he acted, Cheney sought Bush's authorization to issue an order to the CAP. *The 9/11 Commission Report* recorded Cheney's statement on the issue: "The Vice President stated that he called the President to discuss the rules of engagement for the CAP. He recalled feeling that it did no good to establish the CAP unless the pilots had instructions on whether they were authorized to shoot if the plane would not divert. He said the president signed off on that concept." In his memoir, Bush agreed with that assessment: "I told Dick that our pilots should contact suspicious planes and try to get them to land peacefully. It that failed, they had my authority to shoot them down." Rove, who was with the president at the time, remembered the call and Bush's "forceful" reply to Cheney: "Yes. You have my authorization."[43]

Having secured that authorization, the vice president was now empowered to act. At 10:02 a.m., only minutes after Bush authorized the CAP intercept, communicators in the bunker received reports from the Secret Service that an inbound aircraft was headed for Washington—it was United 93. Sometime between 10:10 and 10:15, a military aide told Cheney that the plane was eighty miles out. *The 9/11 Commission Report* recounted that "Vice President Cheney was asked for authority to engage the aircraft. . . . The Vice President authorized fighter aircraft to engage the inbound plane." Bush's memory is slightly different. In his memoir, Bush remembered that before giving the order, Cheney had once again called him: "Dick asked me to confirm the shootdown order I had given. I did." Either way, Cheney had been authorized by Bush to give the order to engage, and he did so. Once the order was given, it took an agonizing few moments to find out if it had indeed been carried out. Again, the commission report: "Minutes went by and word arrived of an aircraft down in Pennsylvania. Those in the shelter wondered if the aircraft had been shot down pursuant to this authorization." Those in the bunker thought that the CAP had, indeed, intercepted the passenger flight; Rumsfeld remembered in his memoir that Cheney told him over the phone, "It's my understanding they've already taken a couple of aircraft out." Indeed, Bush himself had to call Cheney to find out if the plane had been shot down.[44]

While all this was happening, the commander in chief was still in the air. Bush wanted to return to Washington at once, but no one, either on board Air Force One or at the PEOC, supported bringing the president back to a capital city that was under attack. An angry Bush pushed back (growling at Card, "I am the president!") but eventually he backed down. Instead, Air Force One headed to Barksdale Air Force Base in northwestern Louisiana—a location chosen not only because it was located far away from Washington but also because it was already on a high state of alert, as it was participating in a nuclear training exercise. As the plane sped west, the president, like every other American, was watching with horror the televised images from New York City and the Pentagon.[45]

According to one account, while still headed for Louisiana, Bush spoke to Cheney: "We're going to find out who did this and we're going to kick their asses." This was certainly the president's mindset when Air Force One landed at Barksdale. There, he spoke to Rumsfeld for the first time. Rumsfeld remembered that the president's first words were: "Make no mistake, the United States will hunt down and punish those responsible for these cowardly acts." Bush told his secretary of defense that he considered the attacks an act of war and ordered the nation's command readiness to be raised to DEFCON 3. He also told Rumsfeld to be ready: "The ball will be in your court and Dick Myers's [chairman of the Joint Chiefs of Staff] court to respond" to the attacks.[46]

Bush continued to urge his team to take him back to Washington, but they maintained their objections. Once again, Bush gave in. After culling the flight of nonessential personnel and a large number of reporters (only five members of the press, now acting as pool reporters, were allowed to stay on board), at 1:37 p.m., the president flew to US Strategic Command at Offutt Air Force Base at Bellevue, Nebraska. Upon his arrival at Offutt, Bush was taken to the command center there, where he was immediately greeted by a voice over the sound system: "Mr. President, a non-responsive plane is coming in from Madrid. Do we have authority to shoot it down?" Although the plane was not hijacked and eventually landed in Lisbon, it was, as Bush remembered, "another example of the fog of war." Bush then met with his national security team via teleconference and, in a word, declared that his first term of office had effectively come to an end: "We are at war against terror. From this day forward, this is the new priority of our administration." He then asked Tenet who was responsible for the morning's attack. Tenet responded, "Al-Qaida."[47]

When he finally arrived in Washington at 6:30 that evening, Bush took a rather harrowing ride on Marine One from Andrews Air Force Base to the White House—to maximize security, the speeding helicopter zigged and zagged the entire route, keeping perilously close to the ground. From the air, Bush saw smoke billowing from the Pentagon. He turned to Andy Card and said, "You're looking at the first war of the twenty-first century."[48]

At 8:30 p.m., Bush addressed the nation from the Oval Office. Karen Hughes remembered in her memoir that Bush's speech that evening "steadied a shaken nation." Many others saw it differently. While the words were bold—"Our way of life, our very freedom came under attack in a series of deliberate and deadly terrorist acts . . . [the terrorists] intended to frighten our nation into chaos and retreat. But they have failed. . . . Terrorist attacks can shake the foundations of our biggest buildings, but they cannot touch the foundation of America"—Bush spoke hesitatingly, and his eyes seemed to drift beyond the camera to an unseen place in the room. He also looked disheveled, wearing a crooked tie and an ill-fitting shirt. All told, Bush was unable to convey a feeling of either reassurance or control. But one line would stand out as a statement not just of defiance but of a future strategy: "We will make no distinction between the terrorists who committed these acts and those who harbor them."[49]

Following the speech, at 8:37 Bush walked with Hughes to the PEOC to meet face-to-face with his national security team for the first time that day. At this meeting, Bush made it clear that the line in his speech was not just rhetoric; he would demand not merely that the attackers be punished, but also those who sheltered them. He then met with the heads of FEMA, the FBI, the Department of Transportation, and others and held a two-minute meeting with the Joint Chiefs and his senior advisers. Bush was then informed by his Secret Service detail that he and Laura would be spending the night in a small room adjacent to the conference room in the PEOC. An exhausted Bush angrily refused. At 9:50 p.m., Bush returned to the residence.[50]

Bush would have been excused for thinking that this was the end to the most harrowing day of his presidency—perhaps of his life. But if he thought that, it was not to be. Just as he was about to fall asleep, his Secret Service detail burst into his bedroom, shouting, "Mr. President, the White House is under attack. Let's go!" Bush, Laura, and the family dog, Spot—along with Rice, who was spending the night at the residence—were whisked back to the PEOC, where they learned that it was a false alarm; an F-16 fighter flying down the Potomac had sent out the wrong transponder signal.[51]

The world responded as one to the events of 11 September. The North Atlantic Treaty Organization (NATO) unanimously and for the first time invoked Article V of the North Atlantic Treaty, which stated that "an armed attack against one . . . shall be considered an armed attack against them all." The United Nations Security Council passed a resolution sponsored by the French that equated acts of terrorism to acts of war and recognized that states that were victims had a right of legitimate defense. But there was a notable outlier to this feeling of unanimity—one whose words were not missed by anyone in the White House. Iraq's Saddam Hussein rejoiced: "The United States reaps the thorns its rulers have planted in the world."[52]

The next day, 12 September, Bush's first order of business was returning phone calls. The first was to Tony Blair, then one to Jean Chretien, prime minister of Canada. He then had an intelligence briefing in which Tenet confirmed what had been suspected since the early moments of the attacks—that it had been an Al-Qaida operation. Following an NSC meeting, Bush spoke briefly with the press and defiantly laid down the gauntlet: "They were acts of war." Then Bush met with the congressional leadership, at which time Tom Daschle expressed concern about Bush's overuse of the term "war" ("War is a very powerful word"). Bush was indignant, later remembering, "I listened to his concerns, but I disagreed. If four coordinated attacks by a terrorist network that had pledged to kill as many Americans as possible was not an act of war, then what was it? A breach of diplomatic protocol?" At the end of the meeting, Robert Byrd, Democrat from Virginia and scion of the Senate (who would later write a scathing indictment of the Bush presidency entitled *Losing America: Confronting a Reckless and Arrogant Presidency*) addressed the president: "I congratulate you on your leadership in this very difficult, unique situation. . . . There is still an army who believe in this country, believe in the divine guidance that has always led our nation . . . mighty forces will come to your aid."[53]

That afternoon, Bush visited the still smoldering Pentagon, where the work of recovering bodies was still underway. He surveyed the damage and, with Rumsfeld, walked through the recovery area. He also addressed the military leadership: "We want to make sure when we do something, we are not pounding sand. . . . We want it to have consequences. . . . We're not trying to remove a mole; we're after a cancer . . . and we will win."[54]

It was while viewing the devastation at the Pentagon that Bush decided he had to visit New York. The next day, 13 September, shortly after his intelligence briefing, Bush placed a phone call to New York governor George Pataki and New York City mayor Rudolph Giuliani. Bush told them how proud the nation was of their efforts (in his talking points for the conversation, Bush penciled in "and angry" next to the word "proud"); he thanked the first responders; and he told them he had directed Attorney General John Ashcroft to expedite the payment of any legal benefits to family members of the public safety officers who had fallen. Bush then told the two exhausted leaders that he was planning to visit the World Trade Center site the next day.[55]

That same day, Rice chaired a Principals meeting to begin the conversation on how the counterattack against Al-Qaida would be conducted. The role of Pakistan, which shared much of its western border with Afghanistan, was a key agenda point. All agreed that if Pakistan, well known to be sympathetic to the Taliban, dragged its feet, it too would be in jeopardy of becoming a target. To underscore that message, later that day, Deputy Secretary of State Richard Armitage met with the Pakistani ambassador to the United States, Maleeha Lodhi. Later that afternoon, Powell announced at a meeting of the full NSC that Pakistan's president, Gen. Pervez Musharraf, had agreed to every US demand. The meeting also produced some amount of melodrama. Cofer Black, the head of the CIA's counterterrorist center (whom Al-Qaida had tried to assassinate while he was the chief of the CIA station in the Sudan), told the assembled group that it would take only a matter of weeks to extinguish both Al-Qaida and the Taliban, and that they all would soon have "flies dancing across their eyeballs."[56]

Later that morning, Bush visited the Washington Hospital Center to visit those who had been wounded in the attack on the Pentagon. When he returned to the White House, Card met the limousine and then made what he would later characterize as a "big mistake"—he jumped into the limo, thereby calling press attention to his actions, and told Bush that there was another credible threat on the White House. An irritated Bush told Card he wasn't going anywhere. A few moments later, a still angry Bush informed his staff, "I'm not leaving. If a plane hits us, I'll just die." Then Bush asked his mess steward for a hamburger. Remembering Bush's desire to lose weight, which in view of the recent events now held little importance to the president, Karen Hughes quipped: "You might as well add cheese."[57]

The morning of 14 September began with a national security meeting. Bush learned that the CIA believed there were operatives still at work in the United States, planning a second strike with biological, chemical, or even nuclear weapons. After getting an update from director Robert Mueller on the progress of the FBI's investigation into the background of the hijackers, a visibly agitated Bush demanded of the group what would become a mantra for the rest of his administration: "What are you doing to stop the next attack?"[58]

That day was also proclaimed a National Day of Prayer and Remembrance. Rove remembered that there was a discussion regarding whether the president should participate in a religious service, but the consensus came down in favor of his attendance. At 12:00 noon, the National Cathedral was packed. Present in the front row were all living former presidents and their wives, save for the Reagans (Ronald Reagan was battling Alzheimer's). Before the president arrived, the elder Bush asked a favor of Bill Clinton—would he be willing to break protocol (moving from the president's left down the pew, the presidents sat in order of their time in office) and allow him to sit next to his son? Clinton readily agreed. After several welcomes, an invocation, prayers, and a sermon from Billy Graham, the president was the last to deliver remarks. He began with a certain amount of introspection: "We are here in the middle hour of our grief. . . . We have seen the images of fire and ashes and bent steel. Now come the names. . . . We will linger over them, and learn their stories, and many Americans will weep." But then Bush became openly aggressive, to the point where some critics would later charge that his remarks were out of place in a house of prayer: "Our responsibility to history is already clear: to answer these attacks and rid the world of evil." He then closed with either a promise or a threat, depending on where you stood, when he said that the coming war would "end in a way and at an hour of our choosing." When Bush sat down, his father, visibly moved, reached over Laura's lap and grasped his son's hand.[59]

The rest of the day centered around Bush's trip to New York City. Cheering rescue workers, police, and other responders lined the motorcade route between McGuire Air Force Base near Trenton, New Jersey, and Manhattan. Mayor Giuliani, who was riding in the car with the president, remembered turning to Bush and saying, "If you catch this guy, Bin Laden, I would like to be the one to execute him" (a statement that Giuliani remembered was not rhetorical: "I was serious"). When the motorcade reached lower Manhattan and approached the smoldering pile that was once the World Trade Center complex, Bush was aghast: "They hit us even harder than I had comprehended."[60]

But what affected Bush even more than the sight of the physical carnage before him at Ground Zero was the attitude of the workers and first responders, many of whom had been on the scene digging for possible survivors for three days straight. They were not prone to niceties, and they were anything but reflective. One looked straight at Bush and growled, "George, find the bastards who did this and kill them." Another yelled, "Do not let me down!" Another, with what Bush remembered as a "bloodlust," shouted, "Whatever it takes!"[61]

Nina Bishop, a member of the White House advance team, shouted to Rove, "They want to hear from their president. He needs to speak." Card asked Bush if he wanted to address the crowd. When Bush said that he did, Card pointed him to the best available spot—a smashed-up fire truck from Engine Company 76. Bishop found a bullhorn, then being used by a utility worker, and gave it to Bush. Atop the truck was Bob Beckwith, a retired firefighter and rescue worker; he reached down and pulled Bush up with him. When Beckwith tried to jump off the truck, Bush stopped him: "Where are you going? No, no, you stay right here."

Thus began the most iconic moment of the Bush presidency. The president began slowly, echoing his words from the National Cathedral—"I want you all to know that America today is on bended knee in prayer for the people whose lives were lost here." But the crowd was in no mood for prayerful contemplation. The clamor of the recovery machinery made it difficult to hear, and that only ratcheted up the crowd's already fighting spirit. Somebody screamed, "Go get 'em, George!" Others shouted, "We can't hear you!" Bush shot back: "I can hear you. The rest of the world hears you. And the people who knocked these buildings down will hear all of us soon!" The crowd exploded into applause and chants of "USA! USA!"

Bush then rode to the Javits Center, now a holding area for people waiting for news about their loved ones. The presidential party was now woefully behind schedule, but Bush refused to be hurried. He spoke with every person inside the building who wanted to speak with him. One, Arlene Howard, the mother of a Port Authority police officer who had run into the second tower and perished in its collapse, gave Bush her son's badge. Bush kept George Howard's badge with him every single day for the remainder of his presidency.[62]

That same day, by votes of 98–0 in the Senate and 420–1 in the House, Congress passed a joint resolution: "That the President is authorized to use all necessary and appropriate force against those nations, organizations, or persons he determines planned, authorized, committed, or aided the terrorist attacks that occurred on September 11, 2001, or harbored such organizations or persons, in order to prevent any future acts of international terrorism against the United States by such nations, organizations or persons." The formal title of this resolution was the Authorization for Use of Military Force.[63] Tellingly, Bush referred to it in his memoirs as the "congressional war resolution."[64]

Many Americans immediately looked for someone to blame. Some accusations, like those of Revs. Jerry Falwell and Pat Robertson, who blamed the attacks on supporters of the American Civil Liberties Union, abortion, and homosexuals, were simply ludicrous. Other commentators blamed the Clinton administration. For example, conservative radio commentator Rush Limbaugh demanded that Clinton "be held culpable for not doing enough when he was commander in chief," and television commentator Sean Hannity charged that "had Clinton and Gore understood the importance of national security, it's quite possible that 9/11 could have been avoided."[65]

Bush knew exactly who to blame. On 17 September, after visiting the Islamic Center of Washington (a visit that was reportedly Laura Bush's idea), Bush was asked by a reporter what result he was looking for in developing his response to the attacks. The response was Bush at his cockiest: "There's an old poster out west as I recall, that says 'Wanted Dead or Alive.'"[66]

On Saturday, 15 September, at Camp David, Bush met with sixteen members of his national security team, as well as chief of staff Andy Card, in what can arguably be called the most important meeting of his administration.[67] Present were Cheney, Libby, Powell, Rumsfeld, Wolfowitz, Ashcroft, O'Neill, Rice, Hadley, Tenet, Gonzales, Card, Cofer Black, FBI director Robert Mueller, assistant CIA director John McLaughlin, chairman of the Joint Chiefs of Staff Hugh Shelton, and vice chairman of the Joint Chiefs of Staff Richard Myers. Tenet went first and proposed that the CIA be given more latitude in both the capturing and the killing of Al-Qaida operatives. Bush granted the CIA this authority at once. Tenet then made the first concrete proposal for an American retaliatory strike: that CIA teams be deployed to join forces in Afghanistan with the Northern Alliance (even though the leader of that group, Ahmad Shah Massoud, had been assassinated by Al-Qaida on 9 September) as the first wave of the attack. Bush liked the idea: "By mating up our forces with the local opposition, we would avoid looking like a conqueror or occupier. America would help the Afghan people liberate themselves." So did Rumsfeld, who stated, "I concluded it would be far better to position ourselves as the allies of indigenous Afghan forces."[68]

The military went next. Hugh Shelton was a short-timer—he had only one more month as chairman of the Joint Chiefs. Vice Chairman Richard Myers, also present at Camp David, had been nominated by Bush to succeed Shelton. The two chiefs offered Bush three options for what could be done after the CIA joined forces with the Northern Alliance. The first was a cruise missile strike with no boots on the ground. This was a no-go from the start, as it smacked of Clinton-era responses like the 1999 Kosovo campaign of bombing and Operation Infinite Reach. The second alternative was a combination of missile strikes with manned bomber attacks. The third possibility was to use cruise missiles, bombers, and troops; this option was the most aggressive, but as Bush remembered it, the military did not yet have a specific plan in place for it. Rumsfeld was more caustic in his later assessment of all three options: "The shock of 9/11 had not provoked much originality or imagination from the Chairman or his staff."[69]

A wide-ranging discussion followed. Tenet warned of a second wave of terrorist attacks against the United States. Cheney opined that any American retaliatory strike could eventually involve Pakistan, possibly causing the Musharraf government to lose control of its nuclear capabilities to the terrorists. Then, as Gonzales remembered, "of course we considered Iraq." Not surprisingly, it was Paul Wolfowitz who turned the conversation in that direction, arguing that the time was ripe to confront Iraq at the same time that the United States punished the Taliban. But the balance of the room was against involving Iraq so soon. Powell, McLaughlin, Tenet, Rumsfeld, and Cheney all spoke out against the idea. Some sources have Bush snapping at Wolfowitz ("How many times do I have to tell you we are not going after Iraq this minute? We're going to wait to go after the people we know did this to us. Do you understand me?"). Rice disputes this observation, remembering that with all presenters, Bush "listened but did not comment." In a later interview, Andy Card maintained that Bush did not show his anger with Wolfowitz in front of the group but instead turned to Card and told him to privately tell Wolfowitz that if he brought up Iraq one more time, he was not going to be invited to any future meetings.[70]

Bush ended the lengthy morning meeting without articulating a decision. But during the break, he spoke privately to a state department official who, within earshot of two CIA officials—deputy director Michael Morell and Cofer Black—reminded the president that it was important for the first reaction of the United States to be diplomatic in nature. As the official left the conversation, Bush looked at Morell and Black and growled, "Fuck diplomacy. We are going to war."[71]

The team met again from 4:33 to 6:15 p.m. Bush asked each person in attendance for a specific recommendation as to a course of action; all were in favor of a military strike against the Taliban. Two days later, Bush announced his decision to his war cabinet: he had decided to go with Shelton's third option and specified that the plan as developed include the seizure of Iraqi oil fields.[72]

On 20 September, Bush spoke to a joint session of Congress. The moment was laced with drama. In the gallery with Laura Bush were Tony Blair, Tom Ridge, Rudy Giuliani, George Pataki, representatives from the New York City fire and police departments, and Lisa Beamer—the pregnant widow of Todd Beamer, who had led the passenger counterattack on the cabin of American Flight 93. Bush spoke with a forcefulness of delivery and with a conviction that few Americans had heretofore heard from him. His opening words—"In the normal course of events, presidents come to this chamber to report on the state of the Union. Tonight, no such report is needed. It has already been delivered by the American people. . . . My fellow citizens, we have seen the state of our Union—and it is strong"—were met with thunderous applause. Bush made it clear that the upcoming conflict would be a "lengthy campaign," and he reiterated the threat made in his speech from the Oval Office on 11 September: "Every nation, in every region, now has a decision to make. Either you are with us, or you are with the terrorists." Of the Taliban, Bush demanded: "They will hand over the terrorists, or they will share in their fate" (the response of Mullah Omar, the leader of the Taliban, was dismissive: "We cannot do that. If we did, it means we are not Muslims; that Islam is finished").[73] The speech ended with both a tribute and a promise:

I will carry this: It is the police shield of a man named George Howard, who died at the World Trade Center trying to save others. It was given to me by his mom, Arlene, as a proud memorial to her son. This is my reminder of lives that ended, and a task that does not end. I will not forget this wound to our country or those who inflicted it. I will not yield; I will not rest; I will not relent in waging this struggle for freedom and security for the American people.[74]

The next day, 21 September, Bush met with Cheney, Rumsfeld, and his military leadership—to discuss the American counterattack. There, Bush was introduced to General Tommy Franks, the head of Central Command (a theater that included Afghanistan) for the first time. Franks, like Bush, had grown up in Midland, Texas. Indeed, Franks and Bush had something else in common—Franks had gone to high school with Laura Welch Bush. (When the president noted that fact, Franks quipped, "Yes sir, graduated one year before her. But don't worry, Mr. President. I never dated her." That cut through a bit of the tension in the room, as Bush exploded in laughter.) Franks then laid out a three-step plan for Afghanistan. Phase one: join Special Forces with the CIA teams. Phase two: air bombardment, joined with humanitarian airdrops. Phase three: the insertion of ground troops. Bush bought into Franks's plan, as long as the military footprint was light. The initial step happened five days later, on 26 September, when the first CIA paramilitary operators—a seven-man team code-named JAWBREAKER—entered Afghanistan and positioned themselves to connect with the Northern Alliance.[75]

Bush put together an impressive coalition to support his counterattack. Led by the cooperation of Blair and Great Britain, fifty-nine nations contributed either troops or financial support to the operation. Next to Great Britain, the most important of these was Russia. Here, the Slovenia summit meeting of only three months earlier between Bush and Putin paid dividends. Putin was the first foreign leader to call Bush after the terrorist attacks; Bush later remembered that Putin assured him that "good will triumph over evil," and that Russia would not respond in kind to Bush's decision to take American defense readiness to DEFCON 3. Putin was then instrumental in gaining the support of the former Soviet republics of Uzbekistan and Tajikistan—both of which bordered Afghanistan, and both of which could be helpful as the United States prepared to deploy its forces from the north.[76]

On 5 October, Myers told Bush that the military was ready to go. The next day, by secure video from Camp David, Bush gave the order:

"Go. This is the right thing to do." That same day, Bush used his radio address to speak directly to the Taliban, demanding that they turn over the terrorists: "Full warning has been given, and time is running out." The following day, 7 October, Bush announced that Operation Enduring Freedom had begun—coalition forces led by the United States had begun their counterattack against Al-Qaida in Afghanistan.[77]

The first part of the war in Afghanistan favored the coalition. After only two hours of aerial bombardment, the coalition had destroyed what little there was of the Taliban's air defense, as well as several Al-Qaida training camps. Bush also remembered that the coalition "dropped thirty-seven thousand rations of food and relief for the Afghan people."[78]

But soon, Afghanistan itself struck back. Snowstorms, dust storms, freezing temperatures, and the logistics of flying over the forbidding Afghan mountain ranges delayed the insertion of Special Forces troops. Impatient, Bush demanded action. But his national security staff was feuding. On 16 October, at a meeting of the NSC, Rumsfeld clashed with Tenet over the question of command—each man claimed that the other was in charge of what was, for the moment at least, a strategy that wasn't working. Bush asked Richard Armitage, the deputy secretary of state who was attending the meeting for Powell, what he thought. Armitage retorted, "Well sir, I think it's all FUBAR" (a military abbreviation for "fucked up beyond all recognition"). An angry Bush turned to Rice and said, "Condi, fix it." It was not until 19 October that the first Special Forces troops were able to land in Afghanistan—a twelve-man unit landed near Mazar-e-Sharif, close to Afghanistan's northern border, and a two-hundred-man unit of Army Rangers took an airstrip code-named Objective RHINO near Kandahar in the south. But the intramural sniping continued, and it got to the point where Bush got all his advisers together and polled them: "I just want to make sure that all of us did agree on this plan, right?" Everyone agreed that they had.[79]

But the lack of a quick victory led many to parallel the situation in Afghanistan to an old American wound. On 31 October, R. W. "Johnny" Apple used the word "quagmire" in a front-page story in the *New York Times* entitled "Could Afghanistan Become Another Vietnam?" The White House also thought that it might be a quagmire, but it wasn't likening the situation to Vietnam. Rather, many advisers thought the United States would be stuck in Afghanistan like the Soviets had been stuck in the 1980s. But both observations were born of the same frustration—in Afghanistan, nothing seemed to be happening. On 2 November, during an NSC meeting, an exasperated Cheney asked Franks: "What do you need to speed it up?"[80]

By early November, things started to change. The weather improved, and coalition troops, Special Forces, and Northern Alliance fighters began to race toward Taliban-held cities. The first to fall was Mazar-e-Sharif on 9 November. Then, on 13 November, Kabul fell. Northern Afghanistan was soon under coalition control, and the remaining Taliban forces retreated southward. The mood in the White House changed as well. Bush crowed to Putin, who was visiting Washington on the day that Kabul fell, that "this thing might just unravel like a cheap suit."[81]

As coalition attention turned to southern Afghanistan, its hopes lay partly on the shoulders of Hamad Karzai, whose father had been killed by the Taliban and who had long led the anti-Taliban resistance in the south, particularly around the city of Kandahar. A Pashtun tribal leader and academic who had been living in Pakistan, Karzai had been plotting against the Taliban for years and was confident that other Pashtun tribal leaders would join his cause, if only he could get to them. On 8 October, in melodramatic fashion, Karzai and three of his lieutenants roared on their motorcycles across the Pakistan-Afghanistan border and headed for Kandahar. The "army" he met was small, and the Taliban was strong; rather than face annihilation, Karzai asked the CIA to get him back to Pakistan, which it did on 5 November. However, Karzai regrouped and returned to Afghanistan on 16 November, reinforced by American Special Forces and CIA operatives. With Karzai as their champion, the people of the city of Tarin Kowt rose up and defeated their Taliban occupiers. Karzai personally led the defense of Tarin Kowt when the Taliban mounted a last-ditch effort to retake the city. Karzai was treated as an instant hero, both in Afghanistan and in some quarters of Washington. On Sunday, 25 November, US Marines landed near Kandahar. It did not take long for the Taliban to evacuate the city, which was declared under coalition control on 7 December. The remnants of the Taliban now sped east toward the Tora Bora (translation: "Black Dust") mountains that formed part of the border between Afghanistan and Pakistan. Operation Anaconda pushed them into a labyrinth of caves that pierced the mountainous terrain. Bush was ecstatic, later claiming that the coalition put "a serious dent into Al Qaida's army."[82]

But being dented did not translate to being defeated. On 16 December bin Laden and his fighters escaped Tora Bora and fled into Pakistan. The explanations for their escape are varied. Bush blamed faulty information: "Several times we thought we might have nailed him. But the intelligence never panned out." Rumsfeld blamed the commanders in the field: "I was prepared to authorize the deployment of more American troops into the region if the commanders requested them." Journalists Barton Gellman and Thomas Ricks reported in 2002 that bin Laden had indeed been in Tora Bora in December 2001, but the Bush administration decided not to commit the troops to hunt him down. Journalist Peter Bergen claims that the coalition did not move fast enough to seal off the obvious escape routes and instead relied on a small contingent of Special Forces (about seventy total) who were quickly overwhelmed by the distance and the terrain. Moreover, Bergen speculated that the Pentagon may have been distracted from the matter at hand in Tora Bora by planning for war in Iraq. One thing was certain—the first stage of Operation Enduring Freedom had pushed the Taliban out of Afghanistan. But, as time would show, the Taliban had lived to fight another day.[83]

At the end of December 2001, twenty-seven Americans had been killed in Afghanistan since the start of action in Operation Enduring Freedom. The first of those American fatalities was killed some 560 miles to the north of Kandahar. On Sunday, 25 November, two CIA agents were interrogating several of the prisoners at the Qala-i-Jangi prison, a fortress-turned-jail under the command of the Northern Alliance and located near Mazar-e-Sharif. Suddenly the inmates erupted into what became a bloody three-day battle. One of the CIA agents, Johnny Micheal Spann, was killed (according to Rumsfeld, his body was booby-trapped with a hidden grenade, so that when the body was moved it would kill or maim those who were attempting to retrieve it), making him the first American killed in action in Afghanistan. The agents eventually subdued the inmates with high-pressure hoses. Of the three hundred Al-Qaida and Taliban prisoners at Mazar-e-Sharif, eighty-six survived the uprising. One of the survivors, John Walker Lindh—an American citizen who had joined the Taliban—was taken into custody.[84]

Yet another American fatality served to demonstrate that the routing of the Taliban did not equate to the defeat of Al-Qaida. On 23 January 2002, Daniel Pearl, the Southeast Asia bureau chief for the *Wall Street Journal*, was abducted in Karachi, Pakistan's largest city. A Jew, Pearl had begun reporting on Pakistani militant groups; his capture was the first act of anti-American terrorism perpetrated by Al-Qaida since 9/11. The abductors demanded the release of all Pakistani prisoners who were then imprisoned by the United States. One week later, on 1 February, Pearl was beheaded by three of his abductors; a videotape of his execution would be released on 22 February. On 16 May 2002, Pearl's mutilated body was found in a shallow grave near Gadap, about thirty miles north of Karachi. Khalid Sheikh Mohammed, the architect of the "Planes Plot" of 11 September, would later claim that it was he who killed Pearl.[85]

41 and 43 (New Haven, Connecticut, 10 April 1947). (George H. W. Bush Presidential Library and Museum)

41 and 43 (Oval Office, 20 January 2001). (George W. Bush Presidential Library and Museum)

George and Laura Bush campaigning for Congress, 1978. (George H. W. Bush Presidential Library and Museum)

Bush in the Texas Air National Guard (ca. 1968–1973). (George H. W. Bush Presidential Library and Museum)

First Bush Cabinet (9 April 2001). *Front row, left to right*: Donald L. Evans, Commerce; Gale A. Norton, Interior; Donald H. Rumsfeld, Defense; Colin Powell, State; President George W. Bush; Vice President Richard B. (Dick) Cheney; Paul H. O'Neill, Treasury; Attorney General John Ashcroft, Justice; Ann M. Veneman, Agriculture; Elaine Chao, Labor. *Back row, left to right*: Robert B. Zoellick, US trade representative; Christine Todd Whitman, Environmental Protection Agency; Roderick R. Paige, Education; Norman Mineta, Transportation; Tommy G. Thompson, Health and Human Services; Mel Martinez, Housing and Urban Development; Spencer Abraham, Energy; Anthony Principi, Veterans Affairs; Mitchell E. (Mitch) Daniels Jr., Office of Management and Budget; and Andy Card, chief of staff. (George W. Bush Presidential Library and Museum)

Bush and Sen. Edward M. Kennedy (Oval Office, 23 January 2001). (George W. Bush Presidential Library and Museum)

Bush and Vice President Richard B. Cheney (Oval Office, 26 January 2001). (George W. Bush Presidential Library and Museum)

Bush and national security adviser Condoleezza Rice (Oval Office, 11 April 2001). (George W. Bush Presidential Library and Museum)

9:05 a.m., 11 September 2001, Emma Booker Elementary School, Sarasota, Florida (Andy Card and Bush). (Reuters Pictures, Photographer: Win McNamee)

National Day of Prayer and Remembrance (Washington Cathedral, 14 September 2001). (George W. Bush Presidential Library and Museum)

Ground Zero, New York City (14 September 2001, Bush with Bob Beckwith). (George W. Bush Presidential Library and Museum)

Game 1, World Series (Yankee Stadium, New York City, 30 October 2001). (George W. Bush Presidential Library and Museum)

Watching Colin Powell speak to the United Nations on Iraq (5 February 2003). (George W. Bush Presidential Library and Museum)

Aboard the USS *Abraham Lincoln* (1 May 2003). (George W. Bush Presidential Library and Museum)

Laura Bush roasting the president (White House Correspondents' Dinner, Washington, DC, 30 April 2005). (George W. Bush Presidential Library and Museum)

Surveying the damage from Hurricane Katrina (Air Force One, 31 August 2005). (George W. Bush Presidential Library and Museum)

John G. Roberts Jr. sworn in as seventeenth chief justice of the Supreme Court (East Room, 29 September 2005. *Left to right*: Bush, Roberts, Jane Sullivan Roberts, Senior Associate Justice John Paul Stevens). (George W. Bush Presidential Library and Museum)

The Club (Oval Office, 7 January 2009). (George W. Bush Presidential Library and Museum)

# 8

★ ★ ★ ★ ★

# "DON'T EVER LET THIS HAPPEN AGAIN"

The events of 11 September 2001 changed the trajectory of the presidency of George W. Bush. Indeed, one could argue that it became a brand-new presidency, with one overriding purpose. That purpose was first articulated on 12 September during a meeting of the Principals Committee, when Bush turned to John Ashcroft and ordered, "Don't ever let this happen again." Bush expressed it again during a 14 September meeting with his national security team, when he angrily demanded, "What are you doing to stop the next attack?"[1]

To a person, each alumnus of the Bush administration who was interviewed for this book agreed with the proposition that following the attacks, the overriding purpose of the Bush administration—one that took precedence over every action, every policy, every decision of the administration until its end—was to prevent another attack. To Bush, this took the form of a compact with the American people—*he*, personally, would not let this happen again. As he later wrote: "After 9/11, I felt my responsibility was clear. For as long as I held office, I could never forget what happened to America that day. I would pour my heart and soul into protecting the country, whatever it took."[2]

Hands would get dirty in the process, a fact that, at least early on, the administration did little to hide. On Sunday, 16 September, Dick Cheney appeared on NBC's *Meet the Press*. After echoing the president's oft-articulated threat ("If you provide sanctuary to terrorists, you face the full wrath of the United States"), Cheney then warned Americans what to expect in the coming months: that their public officials would "have to work on the Dark Side. . . . We've got to spend time in the shadows in the intelligence world. A lot of what needs to be done here will have to be done quietly, without any discussion, using sources and methods that are available to our intelligence agencies."[3]

The actions taken by the Bush administration to keep this promise have been attacked from all sides. Many have argued that the administration's actions were a clear violation of civil liberties. Many have argued that inhumane treatment of imprisoned detainees was not justified under any circumstances. Many have argued that Bush appropriated executive powers far beyond what was constitutionally allowed. Many have argued that the administration lied to the world to justify its invasion of Iraq.

Each of these charges rolls off the backs of most alumni of the Bush administration. With rare exceptions, those who addressed Bush's compact do not evade their role in its implementation; rather, they speak of their actions with pride. They waste no time in pointing out the ultimate outcome—that there was, indeed, only one successful terrorist attack on the United States during the rest of the Bush administration, and its effects were largely contained. Since Al-Qaida did not take responsibility for that attack, the alumni argue that their actions effectively neutered the terrorist threat that had levelled the spirit of the United States on 11 September. To them, they kept the compact. They protected America—thus, they believe that their service to the country should be respected and honored.

This is, of course, a classic "ends versus means" argument. For many, the story of the Bush administration is whether it is the keeping of the compact, or *how* the administration kept that compact, that is the foundation of the legacy of the second Bush presidency. It is this argument that informs the rest of this book, as it was the argument that enveloped the American people for the rest of the Bush presidency.

Every member of the Bush administration believed, along with Ashcroft, that "our firm expectation was not *if* terrorists would strike again, but when, where, and how." The expected second wave of attacks started in the mail. On 18 September 2001, five letters laced with a white powder containing spore-forming bacterium *Bacillus anthracis*—anthrax—were mailed from Princeton, New Jersey. Four were addressed to media companies in New York City, including the office of NBC News anchorman Tom Brokaw. A fifth was delivered to American Media International, a company located in Boca Raton that published the tabloid newspaper the *Florida Sun*. The contents of that letter were inhaled by photo editor Bob Stevens; he died on 5 October. On 12 October anthrax was found in the offices of all three major news networks. On 15 October the attack hit Washington, as letters containing anthrax had been sent to the Senate offices of Tom Daschle and Patrick Leahy. Offices on Capitol Hill were closed, but two postal workers who had handled the mail would die from inhaled anthrax. Panic grabbed hold of the nation. The Postal Service began to test a wide selection of mail, and packages delivered to local, state, and federal buildings were all subject to search. The majority of general correspondence to the White House was delayed for weeks before reaching its addressee: inevitably, the mail was stamped "Received Late Due to Anthrax Screenings." The perpetrators of the attack were never found.[4]

This did not, however, end the threat of germ warfare. On 18 October, both Cheney and Powell learned that they, the president, Rice, and many other White House staffers might have been exposed to botulinum toxin—Botox—the most poisonous substance known to man, and for which there was no known antidote. The only way to determine if the substance found in the White House was, indeed, Botox was to test it on laboratory mice. It would take twenty-four hours to learn the results. If the mice died, the lives of all those exposed were in jeopardy. At the time, both Bush and Rice were in Shanghai for an economic summit. Cheney called Bush to relay the concern, and for twenty-four hours, American leaders in Washington and in China sweated it out, doing their jobs and wondering if they had ingested a lethal dose of poison. Steve Hadley finally called the travelers with good news; the mice were alive—"feet down, not up"—as the White House sensors had registered a false alarm.[5]

Yet the anthrax and Botox scares only scratched the surface. On 19 October, while Bush was in China, Laura was in Crawford, and news came of an impending attack on the ranch. The attack did not materialize. On 23 October, Pakistan arrested two nuclear scientists who had been in contact with bin Laden; an investigation offered evidence that they might have been helping Al-Qaida build a nuclear weapon. In late October George Tenet informed Bush that the CIA had reliable intelligence that there would be an attack on either 30 or 31 October that would eclipse that of 11 September. Upon hearing that news, Bush nonetheless refused to leave the White House and refused to cancel his plans to travel to New York City to throw out the first pitch of game three of the World Series. Bush donned a

New York Fire Department jacket with a bulletproof vest underneath and threw a perfect strike—but there was no attack.[6]

The year almost ended on another tragic note. On 22 December 2001, Richard Reid boarded an American Airlines flight from Paris to Miami loaded with 197 other passengers and crew. Some three hours into the flight, passengers smelled smoke. Reid was trying to light a fuse that would detonate explosives, which were hidden in his hiking shoes and had evaded detection at the security checkpoint. Only the quick intervention of two flight attendants saved the travelers from almost certain death over the Atlantic.[7]

George Tenet remembered that "you simply could not sit where I did and read what passed across my desk on a daily basis and be anything other than scared to death about what it portended." No threat was dismissed as insignificant. The Bush administration took every threat seriously and acted on each one with a full measure of gravity. As Cheney put it, if there was so much as a 1 percent chance of an attack occurring, the threat must be dealt with as a certainty and snuffed out before it occurred.[8]

There was never any doubt, and in retrospect virtually no internal debate, about whether or not Bush had either the power or the authority to both create and unilaterally approve measures to prevent another attack. Bush innately believed that he had the authority to conduct what had become known as the "War on Terror" not only by virtue of his constitutional powers as commander in chief but also by virtue of the overwhelming approval given by Congress to the congressional war resolution passed on 14 September.[9]

But this would not be enough, as there was a wide body of constitutional law that had come into existence since the end of the Vietnam War precisely for the purpose of limiting the president's power to make war. These acts included the War Powers Act of 1973, the Foreign Intelligence Surveillance Act of 1978, and the Torture Statute of 1994, to name just a few. Thus, the White House turned to the lawyers of the Office of Legal Counsel (OLC), which was located in Ashcroft's Justice Department and was responsible for giving legal advice to the president and to the other executive branch agencies. The opinions of the OLC had long been treated with reverence—CIA legal counsel John Rizzo later told an audience that those opinions were "gold . . . [they] were like Supreme Court opinions." The White House expected the OLC not only to defend Bush's inherent and implied powers under Article II but to explain away what one of those lawyers, Jack Goldsmith, called the "criminalization of war"—those legal restraints that limited in any way the president's power to make war. Despite the fact that several members of the OLC later admitted that they were privately worried about being exposed to either prosecution or congressional investigation for their actions, the OLC became Bush's legal spin team—explaining away, in lengthy, heavily footnoted memorandums and legal briefs, anything that would slow the president down. Again Goldsmith: "The president had to do what he had to do to protect the country, and the lawyers had to find some way to make it legal."[10]

One of the brightest lawyers at the OLC was John C. Yoo. A South Korean immigrant, Yoo had studied at both Harvard and Yale. He had clerked on the DC Federal Appeals Court and at the Supreme Court for Clarence Thomas, had served as general counsel for the Senate Judiciary Committee, and came to the OLC in 2001. On 24 September 2001, Yoo responded to the request of Timothy Flanagan, deputy counsel to the president, who had asked the OLC for its opinion on the scope of the president's authority to take military action in the wake of the 9/11 attacks. Yoo responded to Flanagan in a memorandum the next day. He was also uncompromising in his assessment: the president had "broad constitutional power to use military force." Yoo cited both the War Powers Act of 1973 and the joint resolution of 14 September 2001, but he did not stop there. His memorandum argued that the president had the constitutional power to retaliate not only against nations, persons, or groups that were suspected of involvement in those attacks but "also against foreign states suspected of harboring or supporting such organizations." Yoo also argued that the president could "deploy military force preemptively against terrorist organizations or the States that harbor or support them, whether or not they can be linked to the specific terrorist incidents of September 11."[11]

Tied closely to Yoo's opinions was the administration's unqualified acceptance of the unitary executive theory, which argued that the power of the president was the final authority in the executive branch, and that his powers were not subject to review by either the legislative or the judicial branch. To support their view, those who subscribe to this theory point to the powers granted the president in the Constitution's Executive Vesting Clause ("The executive power shall be vested in a President of the United States of America"); the Executive Oath Clause ("Before he enters on the Execution of his Office, he shall take the following Oath or Affirmation:—'I do solemnly swear [or affirm] that I will faithfully execute the Office of

President of the United States, and will to the best of my Ability, preserve, protect and defend the Constitution of the United States'"); and the Take Care Clause ("[The president] shall take Care that the Laws be faithfully executed"). Other scholars, however, have pointed out that such a belief in unfettered presidential power completely ignores Supreme Court precedents that upheld the power of regulatory agencies located in the executive branch, as well as the promise of checks and balances.[12]

But such arguments were unconvincing to Cheney. After serving in two administrations—Nixon's and Ford's—that had been, in his mind, dangerously hamstrung by congressional oversight as a result of the events surrounding Vietnam and Watergate, he had come to believe that powers that had been constitutionally granted to the president had been swallowed up wholesale by Congress, and it was time to take them back. The minority report of the congressional committee investigating the Iran-Contra Affair clearly articulated this theory. Written by David Addington and released under Cheney's signature, the report defended Ronald Reagan's actions in Iran-Contra through a spirited defense of the unitary power of the executive:

> This history speaks volumes about the Constitution's allocation of powers between the branches. It leaves little, if any, doubt that the President was expected to have the primary role of conducting the foreign policy of the United States. Congressional actions to limit the President in this area therefore should be reviewed with a considerable degree of skepticism. If they interfere with core presidential foreign policy functions, they should be struck down. Moreover, the lesson of our constitutional history is that doubtful cases should be decided in favor of the President.[13]

In a 2014 interview, when asked about the unitary theory, Cheney began his answer by claiming that the president's powers should be expanded only in wartime. When asked how far that enlargement should go, Cheney responded: "Well, Congress still retains the control over the purse. That's about the limit." Then, when pressed, Cheney doubled down: "So even the power of the purse, in that particular set of circumstances can be limited."[14]

Like Cheney, George W. Bush was a firm believer in the unitary theory of the presidency. The best example of this is his widespread use of signing statements. Following a bill receiving a presidential signature, a president often appends a declaration. The practice dates back to the mid-nineteenth century, and such statements were, until the mid-twentieth century, largely limited to pro forma, nonconstitutional observations, often extolling the particular virtues of the bill or giving directions for how the bill should be executed. But following World War II, presidents began to use signing statements to point out those portions of the bill which they had just signed with which they disagreed on constitutional grounds. In some cases, the president wrote that those provisions would be treated as recommended, rather than required. Clearly, the growing use of signing statements was a direct challenge by the executive to congressional authority, but several attempts on the part of Congress in the postwar years to harness the practice came to naught.[15]

Bush appended more constitutional signing statements to signed legislation than any other president in history. In his first six years in office, Bush challenged more than eleven hundred provisions of legislation that he signed on constitutional grounds, often writing, as he did with a statement appended to the 2007 Defense Appropriations Act, that "the executive branch shall construe sections 8095 and 8101 of the act, which purport to prohibit the President from altering command and control relationships within the Armed Forces, as advisory, as any other construction would be inconsistent with the constitutional grant to the President of the authority of Commander in Chief."[16]

As it faced a daily dose of threats, the administration, convinced not just of the righteousness of its cause but of the constitutionality of its actions, moved quickly to prevent those threats from becoming a reality. The first step, initiated in the days following the attacks, was a Justice Department dragnet that detained close to 762 people. Ashcroft borrowed a term that Robert F. Kennedy had used for his campaign to round up mobsters when he boasted that he would arrest suspected terrorists even for "spitting on sidewalks." In a speech to the US Conference of Mayors, the attorney general intoned:

> Let the terrorists among us be warned. If you overstay your visa—even by one day—we will arrest you. If you violate a local law, you will be put in jail and kept in custody as long as possible. We will use every available statute. We will seek every prosecutorial advantage. We will use all our weapons within the law and under the constitution to protect life and enhance security for America.

This they did (as Ashcroft later remembered: "Having a couple of FBI agents show up at your door has a sobering effect if you are an aspiring terrorist"). Although the detainees were primarily Muslims from Arab and South Asian nations, in his memoir, Ashcroft vigorously denied any "profiling." None of these detainees were found to have had any kind of a link with either a terrorist organization in general or the attacks of 11 September in particular.[17]

Also proposed were structural changes that would allow for more direct executive action. It took only three days after the attacks for Cheney to recommend a new White House agency that would coordinate all relevant security agencies. Bush announced the creation of the new department in his address to the Congress on 20 September, and on 8 October he established the Office of Homeland Security and the Homeland Security Council by executive order. Former Pennsylvania governor Tom Ridge became the office's first director (the office would become a cabinet-level department in January 2003, with Ridge serving as its first secretary).[18]

Yet far greater than Ashcroft's manhunt or any bureaucratic change in terms of preventing another attack was a significant piece of legislation, one that granted the federal government unprecedented power to combat both domestic and foreign terrorism. On 24 October 2001, the House passed H. Res. 3162, the Uniting and Strengthening America by Providing Appropriate Tools Required to Intercept and Obstruct Terrorism Act (USA PATRIOT Act) of 2001 by a vote of 357 to 66; the Senate followed by passing the bill with only one dissenting vote—that of Democrat Russ Feingold of Wisconsin. Of its many provisions, the act authorized the president, "when the United States is engaged in armed hostilities or has been attacked by a foreign country or foreign nationals," to confiscate any property of anyone who was suspected of aiding or abetting those attacks; loosened federal law as it applied to the steps that the secretary of the treasury could take if he suspected a foreign national to be laundering money to assist in terrorist acts; tightened security on the nation's northern border by tripling the number of Border Patrol, Customs Service, and Immigration and Naturalization Service personnel; and broadened the definition of aliens who were ineligible for admission to the United States, or subject to deportation, to include those who were "a representative of a political, social, or similar group whose political endorsement of terrorist acts undermines U.S. antiterrorist efforts . . . has used a position of prominence to endorse terrorist activity . . . or . . . has been associated with a terrorist organization and intends to engage in threatening activities while in the United States." The act also preserved benefits for the victims of the terrorist attacks of 11 September and authorized the attorney general and secretary of state to pay rewards to those who assisted in fighting terrorism. It also attacked "The Wall" by expressing the sense of Congress "that officers of the intelligence community should establish and maintain intelligence relationships to acquire information on terrorists and terrorist organizations."[19]

The most immediately controversial provision of the PATRIOT ACT was that which allowed the FBI to "make an application for an order requiring the production of any tangible things (including books, records, papers, documents, and other items) for an investigation to protect against international terrorism or clandestine intelligence activities, provided that such investigation of a United States person is not conducted solely upon the basis of activities protected by the first amendment to the Constitution." Many critics believed this meant that all their transactions at a public library, as well as their computer usage, were now subject to warrantless search. Although library usage was not specified in the act, the American Library Association thought it smelled a rat and vehemently protested the act as permitting violations of library patrons' First Amendment rights. Ashcroft's later defense of this section was notably weak: "The U.S. Justice Department has rarely used this portion of the Patriot Act to garner information—although it could."[20]

Bush remembered that when he learned that two of the 11 September hijackers who were stationed in the United States had communicated several times with their brethren overseas before the attacks, his immediate question was, "Why hadn't we intercepted the calls?" An answer came from Alberto Gonzales: "At that time in our history, not only could we not *connect* the dots, we were not even able to *collect* the dots. Worse yet, we didn't know what dots existed to collect." To the administration, the true villain in all this was the Foreign Intelligence Surveillance (FISA) Act of 1978, which required that any implementation of wiretaps or collection of communications evidence be done with a warrant issued by a FISA court. At a meeting only days after the attacks, Cheney asked Tenet if there was anything *more* he could do. Tenet called Gen. Michael Hayden, the director of the National Security Agency (NSA), the branch of the national intelligence that was charged with both producing and protecting the nation from electronic surveillance, and asked him the same question. Hayden said no, given the constraints placed on him under FISA. Cheney reported his discussion with Hayden and Tenet to the president. Bush asked the White House Counsel's Office and the Justice Department to investigate whether he could authorize the NSA to monitor Al-Qaida communications without FISA warrants. He remembered that "both told me I could." On 4 October 2001 (the same day that he learned of the Florida anthrax attack), Bush signed an order authorizing the NSA to collect calls and emails when there was probable cause that one of the callers was in Afghanistan.[21]

In his memoirs, Bush contended that the reason he didn't go to Congress to seek legislation for the program was that he already had the support of key congressional leaders who had been read into the program, and that all parties agreed that a public congressional debate would only serve to "expose our methods to the enemy." As for a legal justification, Bush once again turned to the OLC. Yoo drafted a legal opinion supporting the new NSA spying program that was dated 2 November, a full month after Bush had authorized the program's start-up.[22]

The top-secret plan, one of the most closely guarded secrets of the Bush administration, was known in the White House as the Terrorist Surveillance Program and was code-named Operation Stellar Wind at the NSA. When its existence was made known in the press in December 2005, it was referred to as the warrantless wiretap program. Bush required that Stellar Wind be reauthorized every thirty to forty-five days—David Addington drafted the reauthorization orders and personally delivered them to the NSA. At one point, Bush was out of town when the reauthorization deadline came up; Addington and Gonzales flew to California to get his signature.[23]

As was the case in all wars, the War on Terror produced prisoners. Indeed, combatant prisoners were taken in Afghanistan before the Bush administration had adequately vetted a plan for their trial and eventual detainment. It wasn't until 10 November 2001 that Cheney presented an order to Bush for the creation of military commissions—wartime courts where members of the military served as conveners, judges, and juries. A linchpin of their argument in favor of the use of commissions was that they had been used before and had been found to be constitutional by the Supreme Court. In 1942, eight Nazi saboteurs had landed in Florida and New York. The United States captured the saboteurs, who stood trial before military commissions. They were all found guilty, six of the eight were executed, and the Supreme Court unanimously upheld the constitutionality of the commissions.[24]

On 13 November, Bush signed the order creating the military commissions, and it was left to Rumsfeld to decide how they would work. On

21 March 2002, flanked by the members of a nine-person advisory group, Rumsfeld announced Military Commission Order Number One. It stipulated the following: defendants were presumed innocent; defendants had the right to counsel and the right to a public trial; guilt had to be proved "beyond a reasonable doubt"; a two-thirds vote of the commissioners was required for a guilty verdict; and a death sentence required a unanimous vote of the commissioners. It also barred the filing of habeas corpus actions to the federal district courts as a result of the actions of the commissions. Thanks to some wrangling over the types of crimes that would be granted standing, the commissions were not operational until April 2003. Nevertheless, Bush was optimistic: "I was confident the military tribunals would provide a fair trial."[25]

Related to the creation of the military commissions was a debate over whether the detainees would be granted habeas corpus rights. On first glance, this would seem to be a nonissue. The US Supreme Court had already ruled in *Johnson v. Eisentrager* (1950)[26] that nonresident enemy aliens did not have the legal right to petition US courts for writs of habeas corpus. However, there was pushback from watchdog groups in the United States which demanded that the detainees receive habeas protection. To deal with the protests, Bush once again turned to the OLC. On 28 December 2001, Patrick Philbin and John Yoo sent a legal opinion to William J. Haynes III, the general counsel for the Department of Defense. This time, however, their recommendation was less than clear: "While we believe that the correct answer is that the federal courts lack jurisdiction over habeas petitions filed by alien detainees held outside the sovereign territory of the United States, there remains some litigation risk that a district court might reach the opposite result."[27]

It would take almost three years, but the Supreme Court eventually came to that "opposite result." On 28 June 2004, two cases came down from the Supreme Court that negated the Bush administration's arguments on habeas corpus. The first was *Hamdi v. Rumsfeld*.[28] Yasir Esam Hamdi was an American citizen (born in Louisiana) raised in Saudi Arabia, who had been captured in 2001 in Afghanistan, declared an enemy combatant, and transferred to the navy brig at Norfolk, Virginia. Hamdi petitioned for a writ of habeas corpus, but a lower court dismissed his case. His lawyers challenged the government's authority to hold Hamdi without granting him due process and demanded the right to challenge his enemy combatant designation before an impartial authority. The administration argued that as an enemy combatant Hamdi was not entitled to the protection provided by habeas corpus. In a plurality opinion that gave the Bush administration half a loaf, the court ruled that the government had the right to detain enemy combatants, including US citizens, but that all detainees must be afforded due process rights. In response, the following month the Defense Department created Combatant Status Review Tribunals, which offered detainees a setting to challenge their standing as enemy combatants.[29]

The same day, the court ruled in *Rasul v. Bush*.[30] Three members of the Taliban, including Shafiq Rasul, a British citizen, had been captured in Afghanistan and transferred to Guantanamo Bay. All three argued that they had habeas corpus rights; here, the administration argued that foreign nationals should not have access to American courts. In a 5–4 decision, the Court ruled that, by statute, the detainees being held in a US internment camp at Guantanamo Bay were entitled access to American courts, thus handing the administration a clear defeat.

At the start of the war, captured enemy combatants were detained at several prisons located throughout Afghanistan. But the Qala-i-Jangi prison riot that resulted in the death of CIA agent Johnny Micheal Spann (discussed in the previous chapter) convinced many that a new system of detention was needed. But this presented a conundrum: while the administration was not about to keep its high-value prisoner assets in porous Afghan prisons, neither was it willing to transfer them to American penitentiaries, where the prisoners might be able to claim American constitutional protections.[31]

Thus was constructed a two-tiered system of detention. The first tier was operated by the Department of Defense. On 13 November 2001, Bush issued a military order appointing the secretary of defense as the "detention authority" for prisoners, as well as the point person for establishing a judicial system in which to try them. Several sites were considered for a new detention center: the Aleutian Islands; Fort Leavenworth, Kansas; the prison on Alcatraz Island; a ship permanently stationed in the Arabian Sea; and several island bases in the Pacific and Indian Oceans.[32]

The Pentagon ultimately chose Camp X-Ray, which had been built at a modified naval station at Guantanamo Bay on the southern end of Cuba. Guantanamo was on Cuban soil, but thanks to an agreement signed in 1903 after the Spanish-American War (the Platt Amendment), it was held by the United States in a long-term lease. The original purpose of X-Ray was to house Cuban refugees who were deemed ineligible to enter the United States under Fidel Castro's limited immigration policy of the mid-1990s. Rumsfeld spoke for many in the administration when he described X-Ray to reporters as "the least worst place." On 11 January 2002, the first twenty prisoners from Afghanistan arrived at Camp X-Ray, and plans were put into motion to construct a permanent facility. X-Ray soon became known by its sobriquet—Gitmo.[33]

The second tier of detention centers was controlled by the CIA and was kept top secret. Bush always knew that he had the legal authority to detain and, in some cases, try legal combatants in wartime. But, believing as he did that he had virtually unchecked executive authority to prevent another terrorist attack on the United States, Bush believed he also had the authority to capture and detain individuals before they actually committed a terrorist act, if it could be shown that they were planning such an act. On 17 September 2001, in a secret memorandum of notification, Bush authorized the CIA to "undertake operations designed to capture and detain persons who pose a continuing, serious threat of violence or death to U.S. persons and interests or who are planning terrorist activities." Throughout the following month, the CIA looked to at least four countries as possible hosts. When set up, the locations of the camps, known as "Black Sites," were not shared with any members of Congress; for the sake of deniability, they were not even shared with Bush.[34]

The fact that there were Black Sites is not in dispute—after stories broke in the press in October 2005, Bush admitted to their existence. However, while dozens of reports claim to know how many camps there were and in what countries they were located, such information is fragmented and often contradictory. Moreover, and not surprisingly, to this point the government has not fully cooperated with any effort to identify the location of the camps. Even the 2014 *Report of the Senate Select Committee on Intelligence* (*SSCI*), while naming names of several of the camps (see later discussion), was deliberately opaque regarding the specific number of camps and their locations.

In his memoirs, Bush remembered that the aborted December 2001 attack of the "shoe bomber" "had a big impact on me"—not just because it was a reminder that there were still very real threats to American security but because of how the unsuccessful terrorist was treated after his arrest. Bush was indignant:

> When Richard Reid was arrested, he was swiftly placed into the U.S. Criminal Justice system, which entitled him to the same constitutional protections as a common criminal. But the shoe bomber was not a bur-

glar or bank robber; he was a foot soldier in al Qaida's war against America . . . by giving this terrorist the right to remain silent, we deprived ourselves of the opportunity to collect vital intelligence on his plan and his handlers. Reid's case made clear we needed a new policy for dealing with captured terrorists.[35]

The debate that would set the parameters for everything that was to come was whether or not the detainees were entitled to protection under the Third Geneva Convention Relative to the Treatment of Prisoners of War (hereafter Geneva Convention). Passed in 1929 and revised in 1949, the Geneva Convention was ratified by 196 nations, including the United States. In it, there is a specific definition of prisoners of war (POW), as well as the protections that a POW would receive. Thus, if the detainees from the War on Terror were defined as POWs under the Geneva Convention, then the level, scope, and technique of their questioning would be tightly controlled and tightly circumscribed.[36]

Rumsfeld remembered that he was in favor of denying Geneva POW rights to the new detainees. Of several reasons listed, he noted that if they were treated as POWs under the Geneva Convention, they would not be legally obligated to give up any information—only their name, rank, serial number, and date of birth. For Rumsfeld, "because neither Taliban forces nor Al Qaida terrorists met the unambiguous requirements for POW status, they were not entitled to its special protections. This determination was not 'abandoning' or 'bypassing' the Geneva Conventions as many have erroneously alleged. It was, in fact, adhering to the letter and spirit of the Conventions." Tenet believed likewise. On 29 January 2002, a letter was drafted for him to send to the president, urging that any application of the Geneva Convention to detainees in the War on Terror would "significantly hamper the ability of CIA to obtain critical threat information necessary to save American lives."[37]

But once again, more support was needed than just the opinion of two cabinet members; and once again, the administration turned to the OLC. On 30 November 2001, John Yoo and fellow OLC attorney Robert J. Delahunty wrote White House counsel Alberto Gonzales, who had asked them to address "several questions concerning the application of certain treaties, domestic federal law, and customary international law to the armed conflict in Afghanistan." They concluded, first, that these treaties and laws did not protect Al-Qaida, "which as a non-State actor cannot be a party to the international agreements governing war. . . . Al Qaida is not a state." Second, they concluded that "the President has reasonable grounds to find that these treaties do not apply to the Taliban militia" because Afghanistan, in their view, was a "failed state"; thus, the Geneva Conventions did not apply. But consistent with Yoo's earlier statement of expansive presidential war-making powers, the memo also concluded that "customary international law has no binding legal effect on either the President or the military because it is not federal law, as recognized by the Constitution." On 22 January 2002, in a memo to Gonzales and William J. Haynes III, the general counsel for the Department of Defense, Jay Bybee, then the head of the OLC, mirrored the conclusions of Yoo and Delahunty. Thus, the opinion of the OLC was that the application of the Third Geneva Convention with regard to high-value detainees in the War on Terror was whatever the president wanted it to be.[38]

On 18 January, Gonzales informed the president of the OLC's opinions. Initially, Bush sided with his lawyers and decided that neither Al-Qaida nor the Taliban would receive the protection of the Geneva Convention. On 19 January, Rumsfeld conveyed Bush's decision to his commanders but made it clear that they should "treat [detainees] humanely and . . . in a manner consistent with the principles of the Geneva Conventions of 1949."[39]

Then Powell weighed in. He asked Bush to reconsider his decision and give the detainees POW status. Powell's position was supported by William H. Taft IV, the legal adviser to the Department of State, who wrote: "The President should know that a decision that the Conventions do apply is consistent with the plain language of the Conventions and the unvaried practice of the United States in introducing its forces into conflict over fifty years." On 25 January, Gonzales wrote the president, dutifully outlining Powell's objections, but making it clear that he believed "that the arguments for reconsideration and reversal are unpersuasive." Now it was Ashcroft's turn to push back. On 1 February, Ashcroft argued in a memo to Bush that denying both the Taliban and Al-Qaida fighters protection under the Geneva Convention "could well expose our personnel to a greater risk of being treated improperly in the event of detention by a foreign power."[40]

Faced with a chasm of opinion within the legal ranks of his administration, in an executive order issued on 7 February 2002, Bush split the difference. After making it clear that he could "suspend Geneva as between the United States and Afghanistan," he "decline[d] to exercise that authority at this time." Instead, Bush ordered that "none of the provisions of Geneva apply to our conflict with al Qaida," but "the provisions of Geneva will apply to our present conflict with the Taliban." Having said this, Bush then made it clear that "as a matter of policy, the United States Armed Forces shall continue to treat detainees humanely and, to the extent appropriate and consistent with military necessity, in a manner consistent with the principles of Geneva." Thus, as they faced questioning designed to extract information about future attacks, Al-Qaida detainees had little to protect them from whatever kind of interrogation came their way.[41]

On 4 February 1984, the United States had signed the United Nations Convention against Torture and Other Cruel, Inhumane, or Degrading Treatment or Punishment (UNCAT). This put the United States on record, under international law, as opposing torture. UNCAT defined torture as

> any act by which severe pain or suffering, whether physical or mental, is intentionally inflicted on a person for such purposes as obtaining from him or a third person information or a confession, punishing him for an act he or a third person has committed or is suspected of having committed, or intimidating or coercing him or a third person, or for any reason based on discrimination of any kind, when such pain or suffering is inflicted by or at the instigation of or with the consent or acquiescence of a public official or other person acting in an official capacity. It does not include pain or suffering arising only from, inherent in or incidental to lawful sanctions.[42]

In a like mind, US law made it a criminal offense for any person "outside the United States [to] commit or attempt to commit torture," defining the act of torture as an "act committed by a person acting under the color of law specifically intended to inflict severe physical or mental pain or suffering (other than pain or suffering incidental to lawful sanctions) upon another person within his custody or physical control."[43]

Then came the 28 March 2002 capture of Zein al-Abideen Mohammed Hussein, who went by the name of Abu Zubaydah. Although not a member of Al-Qaida, Zubaydah was a close associate of Usama bin Laden and had run the camps where the 11 September hijackers were trained. Without going into specifics, Bush later recounted that "the CIA believed [Zubaydah] was planning to attack America again." Zubaydah was captured in a firefight by Pakistani and American agents in the Pakistani city of Faisalabad, at a safe house operated by a Pakistani terrorist group. In the gunfight, Zubaydah was wounded—he was shot three times and lost a testicle. Because he was the highest-ranking Al-Qaida soldier captured after 11 September, the administration wanted him alive. Thus, the CIA flew an American surgeon from Johns Hopkins University Medical Center in Baltimore to operate on Zubaydah so that he might be interrogated by American officials.[44]

Zubaydah was the first detainee in the War on Terror who was sent to a CIA-run Black Site. He was taken from Pakistan to a site in Thailand, later identified in the *SSCI* as Detention Site Green and code-named Cat's Eye. Zubaydah was initially questioned by Ali Soufan, an Arabic-speaking FBI agent, who utilized what might be called "soft" techniques. He addressed Zubaydah as "Hani"—a nickname given him by his mother—and worked slowly and cautiously to build Zubaydah's trust. But Zubaydah's medical condition worsened, and he was taken from the site to a nearby hospital. While there, on 10 April 2002, Zubaydah gave up an important revelation: he identified Khalid Sheikh Mohammed, who had been known to investigators since 1993 as KSM, as one of the masterminds of the 11 September attacks and as the trainer of the hijackers—something that neither the FBI nor the CIA had previously known.[45]

Despite this important revelation, CIA personnel advocated a different approach to the interrogation of Zubaydah. It was proposed that while at the hospital, Zubaydah "be kept in an all-white room that was lit 24 hours a day, that [he] not be provided any amenities, that his sleep be disrupted, that loud noise be constantly fed into his cell, and that only a small number of people interact with him." This meant that the FBI agents who had been originally interrogating Zubaydah would be pulled off the case—a point to which they strenuously objected. Nevertheless, the new methods were implemented on 13 April 1002, while Zubaydah was still in the hospital. During the initial session, Zubaydah told one of his CIA interrogators that he "had a most important secret that [the interrogator] needed to know"—a "secret" that the interrogators later wrote was about "impending future terrorist plans against the United States"—but gave them no further information.[46]

It was this admission on Zubaydah's part—that he held a secret about a future attack—and his refusal to elaborate on its specifics that seem to have led to a further ratcheting up of interrogative methods. On 15 April, an interrogator told Zubaydah that he was disappointed in him. He was then sedated and taken back to Detention Site Green. The next day, a whole new set of methods began. Zubaydah awoke to find himself in an all-white cell with no windows, lit by four halogen lamps and with an air conditioner. Next to his cell was an interrogation room, locked with three padlocks. His guards wore black uniforms and goggles, so that they could not be identified. Zubaydah was handcuffed and shackled. Loud rock music was played in his cell to deprive him of sleep. Zubaydah was now on a twenty-four-hour interrogation schedule, and as a result the FBI agents were allowed to once again join the questioning. To them, Zubaydah protested that he knew nothing about an upcoming attack. On 20 April 2002, Zubaydah told his FBI interrogators about two men who had told him about a plan to detonate a uranium-based explosive in the United States. Zubaydah did not know the men's names, and he had judged them incapable of pulling off such an attack, but he did offer physical descriptions.[47]

Still unsatisfied with the information obtained, his captors kept Zubaydah in isolation from 18 June through 4 August. During that forty-seven-day period, his interrogators sought permission from their superiors to utilize what they called a "novel" set of interrogation techniques that had been a part of the US military's Survival, Evasion, Resistance and Escape (SERE) training. Twelve highly intrusive methods of interrogation were proposed for use on Zubaydah—the attention grasp, wailing, facial hold, facial slap, cramped confinement, wall standing, stress positions, sleep deprivation, waterboarding, use of diapers, use of insects, and mock burial.[48]

While the CIA was inclined to grant its approval for these enhanced interrogation techniques (EITs), such a change required presidential approval. Thus, the agency sought legal cover. First, the CIA's legal team drafted a letter of declination of prosecution, to be signed off by the attorney general, which protected the interrogators from any prosecution for their actions.[49] Then, on 13 July, John Rizzo, acting general counsel for the CIA, met with attorneys for the NSC and the OLC, along with Michael Chertoff, the head of the Justice Department's Criminal Division, and Daniel Levin, the chief of staff to the FBI director. Rizzo gave them an overview of the proposed EITs, and the attorneys present advised Rizzo that the CIA was on solid legal ground because, for acts to qualify as torture there had to be a "specific intent" to cause severe physical or mental suffering. Not satisfied with a verbal opinion, Rizzo asked for a written statement from Justice.[50] Later that day, John Yoo, who was at the meeting, wrote to Rizzo and in so doing gave a fuller definition of "specific intent":

> To establish that an individual has acted with the specific intent to inflict severe mental pain or suffering, an individual must act with specific intent, i.e., with the express purpose of causing prolonged mental harm in order for the use of any of the predicate acts to constitute torture. Specific intent can be negated by a showing of good faith. Thus, if an individual

undertook any of the predicate acts for severe mental pain or suffering, but did so in the good faith belief that those acts would not cause the prisoner prolonged mental harm, he would not have acted with the specific intent necessary to establish torture.[51]

At this point, Rice stepped in to try to slow things down. On 17 July she requested a delay in the approval of the interrogation techniques until Ashcroft had issued his opinion; the next day she requested that Justice delay its decision until the CIA could provide more information. More information was soon forthcoming. On 23 July, Gonzales met with Bush to "update him on the legal analysis." Gonzales told him that Justice would soon complete its evaluation; Gonzales later recalled that Bush "responded that he was comfortable with the administration going forward with the enhanced techniques."[52]

On 24 July, Ashcroft approved ten of the twelve proposed methods—he did not approve waterboarding and mock burial. But the CIA interrogation team indicated that they were willing to wait for the approval of waterboarding to restart their interrogation of Zubaydah. On 26 July, Ashcroft verbally approved the use of the waterboard. On 31 July, Rice informed deputy director of central intelligence John McLaughlin that she would not object to the new techniques if the attorney general found them to be legal.[53]

On 1 August, the OLC finished its analysis. In a series of three memorandums—two to Gonzales and one to Rizzo—the OLC justified its opinions of 13 July. First, in a memo addressed to Gonzales, Jay Bybee argued that the EITs were not acts of torture as defined by UNCAT because the pain inflicted by those EITs was not "severe." The conclusions of his opinion deserve to be quoted at length:

> We conclude that torture as defined in and proscribed by Sections 2340–2340A, covers only extreme acts. Severe pain is generally of the kind difficult for the victim to endure. Where the pain is physical, it must be of an intensity akin to that which accompanies serious physical injury such as death or organ failure. Severe mental pain requires suffering not just at the moment of infliction but it also requires lasting psychological harm, such as seen in mental disorders like post-traumatic stress disorder. Additionally, such severe mental pain can arise only from the predicate acts listed in Section 2340. Because the acts inflicting torture are extreme, there is significant range of acts that though they might constitute cruel, inhuman, or degrading treatment or punishment fail to rise to the level of torture. . . . Finally, even if an interrogation method might violate Section 2340A, necessity or self-defense could provide justifications that would eliminate any criminal liability.[54]

Next, in a much shorter memo to Gonzales, John Yoo signed on to Bybee's interpretation of the word "torture" and argued that even if the world did not agree, there was no basis for a prosecution by the International Criminal Court.[55]

Finally, in the most illuminating of the three memos, Bybee wrote to John Rizzo to indemnify the CIA. It is this memo that, with some justification, has become known as the "torture memo." In it, Bybee summarizes the facts as he knew them at that moment, about Zubaydah's capture and incarceration, and then notes that "you would like to employ ten techniques that you believe will dislocate his expectations regarding the treatment he believes he will receive and encourage him to disclose the crucial information mentioned above." Bybee then not only lists those ten techniques—from the original twelve, mock burial and diapers had been removed, but, notably, waterboarding was now included—but also makes it clear that the CIA had promised it would start with the least intrusive technique (attention grasp) and move toward waterboarding as the most extreme technique. He then goes into graphic detail as to what those techniques entailed; witness Bybee's description of waterboarding:

> Finally, you would like to use a technique called the "waterboard." In this procedure, the individual is bound securely to an inclined bench, which is approximately four feet by seven feet. The individual's feet are generally elevated. A cloth is placed over the forehead and eyes. Water is then applied to the cloth in a controlled manner. As this is done, the cloth is lowered until it covers both the nose and the mouth. Once the cloth is saturated and completely covers the mouth and nose, air flow is slightly restricted for 20 to 40 seconds due to the presence of the cloth. This causes an increase in carbon dioxide level in the individual's blood. This increase in carbon dioxide level stimulates increased effort to breathe. This effort plus the cloth produces the perception of "suffocation and incipient panic," i.e., the perception of drowning. The individual does not breathe any water into his lungs. During those 20 to 40 seconds, water is continuously applied from a height of twelve to twenty-four inches. After this period, the cloth is lifted, and the individual is allowed to breathe unimpeded for three or four full breaths. The sensation of drowning is immediately relieved by the removal of the cloth. The procedure may then be repeated.

Bybee concluded that none of the proposed EITs, including waterboarding, constituted "torture" because there was no "prolonged mental harm, no severe pain or suffering would have been inflicted." Since, in Bybee's view, there was no specific intent, "the absence of specific intent negates the charge of torture."[56]

The ball was now squarely in Bush's court. Bush remembered that he told Justice and CIA lawyers to look over the list of techniques that had been drawn up by CIA experts. Bush saw two techniques that he felt, in his words, "went too far, even if they were legal." He ordered that they be struck from the list. Of waterboarding, a practice that dated back to the Philippine-American War of 1899–1902, Bush remembered: "No doubt the procedure was tough, but medical experts assured the CIA that it did no lasting harm." From the perspective of his compact with the American people, Bush had no qualms: "My most solemn responsibility as president was to protect the country. I approved the use of the interrogation techniques."[57]

From 4 August until 23 August 2002, CIA agents interrogated Zubaydah using the EITs. Despite the team's reporting to the NSC that their methods were "producing meaningful results," Zubaydah never divulged further information about any imminent attacks.[58] It took another four years for him to be transferred to Gitmo on 5 September 2006.

According to the *SSCI*, this period was the most active for the CIA Black Sites: "Of the 199 detainees identified by the Committee as held by the CIA, fifty-three were brought into custody in 2003, and of the thirty-nine detainees the Committee has found to have been subjected to the CIA's enhanced interrogation techniques, 17 were subjected to such techniques between January 2003 and August 2003." The presence of the sites caused tension with the host countries, but the sites stayed open. Indeed, they expanded, as four more sites opened up. The EITs continued to be used—one detainee at Detention Site Blue was threatened with a gun and a cordless power drill.[59]

On 1 March 2003, Khalid Sheikh Mohammed (KSM), the architect of the 11 September attacks, was captured in Rawalpindi, near Islamabad. He was hiding within the line of sight of the headquarters of the Pakistani army (a diplomat quipped: "What the fuck was this guy going just down the road from GHQ [army headquarters]?"). He was held by Pakistani authorities for several weeks. While under Pakistani control, KSM was interrogated without use of the most extreme forms of EITs—he was, according to the *SSCI*, only subjected to sleep deprivation—and he gave up "limited information."[60]

But as soon as KSM was transferred to Detention Site Cobalt, he was subjected to the full gamut of EITs, exclusive of waterboarding. This treatment led to KSM giving his captors information that directly led to the arrest of two individuals; however, it was later shown that KSM had given his interrogators false information and the individuals arrested by the CIA were innocent. Subsequently, KSM was transferred to Detention Site Blue, where he was once again subjected to EITs—this time including water-boarding. Overall, KSM was waterboarded at least 183 times, and the information he gave to his interrogators was largely fabricated.[61]

Kept top secret, the CIA's interrogation program went on for seven more years. In 2005, Jose Rodriguez, who had replaced Cofer Black as the head of the CIA's Counterterrorist Center in May 2002, ordered the destruction of dozens of videotapes of the EIT sessions. The order was conveyed by Gina Haspel, his chief of staff, who in her 2018 confirmation hearings to become director of the CIA claimed that the tapes were destroyed because of the "security risk" they posed.[62]

As always, for Bush, one thing mattered and one thing only: "The CIA interrogation program saved lives. Had we captured more al Qaida operatives with significant intelligence value, I would have used the program for them as well."[63]

# 9

★ ★ ★ ★ ★

# PREVENTATIVE WAR

Saddam Hussein Abd al-Majid al Tikriti was born in 1937 near Tikrit, Iraq. He never knew his father, his brother died of cancer before Saddam was born, and his grieving mother tried to commit suicide. Then, after Saddam's birth, she abandoned him to abusive relatives, one of whom radicalized him with a hatred of British imperialism. In 1956, Saddam, now a member of the radical Ba'ath Party, participated in a coup attempt against Iraq's King Faisal II as well as a plot against the Iraqi prime minister in 1959. Both plots failed, and Saddam fled first to Syria and then to Egypt, where he finished high school and began a course of study at the University of Cairo Law School. Upon his return to Iraq, Saddam rose quickly through the ranks of the Ba'ath Party; in 1968, when the party seized control of the Iraqi government, he held the second-highest position in government. On 16 July 1979, the leader of the party either resigned or was murdered, and Saddam became president of Iraq. The following year, in an attempt to consolidate his power, Saddam invaded neighboring Iran. The bloody war that followed lasted eight years and decimated both the Iranian and the Iraqi economy.[1]

On 1 August 1990, Saddam invaded neighboring Kuwait. Within twelve hours that nation's capital fell to the Iraqi army. It took George H. W. Bush less than twenty-four hours to proclaim that the invasion "will

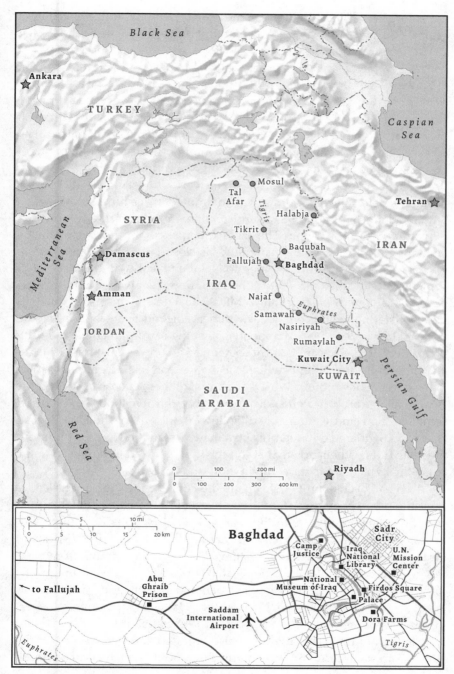

Iraq, ca. 2003. (Credit: Erin Greb Cartography)

not stand," and to begin to assemble an international military coalition against Saddam. After a near constant air bombardment of Baghdad that lasted for five and a half weeks, on 24 February 1991, coalition troops left their basing points in Saudi Arabia and began to force the Iraqi army out of Kuwait. The Iraqis were quickly routed, and a cease-fire was declared exactly one hundred hours after the fighting began. However, in a decision that would be immediately second-guessed, Bush decided not to drive all the way to Baghdad and chase Saddam out of power. As national security adviser Brent Scowcroft put it in a later interview, getting Saddam out of power was "never a goal—only a hopeful by-product."[2]

That Saddam Hussein was one of the world's most vicious dictators is beyond debate. His first murder was committed at age nineteen. He was a Sunni Muslim, his regime was a Sunni regime, and it had brutally repressed his country's Shi'a Muslims. The list of atrocities committed personally by Saddam, or in his name by his family, his closest aides, and members of his Ba'ath Party, is simply too long to include here. But in the wake of 11 September 2001, the ones that hit home hardest revolved around his use of weapons of mass destruction (WMDs), most notably his use of mustard gas, a blistering agent, combined with nerve agents such as sarin, tabun, and VX. In his 1987–1988 campaign against the Kurds, an ethnic minority in northern Iraq, Saddam launched chemical attacks against forty villages and thousands of innocent civilians, using them as testing grounds for his lethal cocktail of vaporous WMD. The worst of these attacks destroyed the city of Halabja on 16 March 1988, where in one day five thousand died and some ten thousand were maimed. Following the end of the First Persian Gulf War, Saddam continued his brutal attacks on the Kurds with impunity—he utilized helicopters that the coalition allowed him to keep in the cease-fire agreement to mow down thousands of Kurds.[3]

Iraq had been handily defeated in the Persian Gulf War, but its leader was still in power and was taunting the rest of the world. In an attempt to check Saddam's influence in the region, United Nations Resolution 687, passed on 3 April 1991, demanded that he destroy both his WMDs and his long-range missile delivery systems. It also prohibited Iraq from making or processing biological, chemical, or nuclear weapons or the means to produce them. The resolution also demanded that Saddam submit his arsenal to the verification of UN inspectors. However, demands to inspect the sites were met with intransigence; in 1998 Saddam kicked all UN inspectors out of Iraq. The resolution also imposed "no-fly zones" over the Kurdish areas of northern Iraq and the Shi'a-populated areas of southern

Iraq. These did little to help either minority, both of which were continually harassed by Saddam's forces.[4]

On 14 August 1998, Congress passed a resolution urging the president
to take "appropriate action in accordance with the Constitution and relevant laws of the United States, to bring Iraq into compliance with its international obligations." Three months later, Congress was more specific,
passing the Iraq Liberation Act of 1998. The policy of the United States was
now "to support efforts to remove the regime headed by Saddam Hussein
from power in Iraq and to promote the resurgence of a democratic government." On 29 October 1999, President Clinton acted under his new authority, directing up to $5 million in defense items to be made available to the
Iraqi National Congress, a political party headed by wealthy Shi'a Ahmed
Chalabi and whose goal was to overthrow Saddam's government. Clinton
further responded with Operation Desert Fox, a four-day bombathon
starting on 16 December and ending on 19 December 1998 that involved
650 air sorties and four hundred cruise missile launches and was designed
to neutralize Saddam's WMD capacities. On 17 December, Clinton spoke
to the American people and defended his actions: "If Saddam defies the
world and we fail to respond, we will face a far greater threat in the future.
Saddam will strike again at his neighbors. He will make war on his own
people. And mark my words, he will develop weapons of mass destruction. He will deploy them, and he will use them."[5]

But Saddam Hussein had no WMDs. Indeed, Iraq had once had such
weapons and had used them against both the Iranians and the Kurds. But
after his December 2003 capture by coalition troops, Saddam admitted to
his interrogators that all his WMDs had been destroyed in the 1990s by
either UN inspectors or his own government. In the words of two close
students of these events, by 2002 the Iraqi "cupboard was bare." However,
Saddam kept this fact a closely guarded secret, so as to allow him to per-
petuate the belief that Iraq was a nuclear power—if the Americans and
others interested in the region saw him as having, and being willing to
use, WMDs, they might leave him alone. In an attempt to preserve the illusion of having WMDs, Saddam had leaked false information and allowed
UN weapons inspectors only part of the access and material to which
they were entitled. The reason for his doing so was self-preservation—it
was, in the words of one of Saddam's corps commanders, a strategy of
"deterrence by doubt." But there was no ambiguity with his generals. In
December 2002, Hussein informed his top aides that Iraq did not possess
WMDs.[6]

In 1993 Saddam had conspired to assassinate George H. W. Bush and his family while they were visiting Kuwait. The assassination attempt left a foul taste in the mouth of Bush's eldest son, who for years afterward would puncture any conversation on Saddam by remarking, "He tried to kill my Dad." But Saddam was able to attempt that assassination because the elder Bush had decided not to try to topple his regime. In his memoir, Bush gave a pointedly backhanded compliment to his father on his conduct of the war: "I was proud of Dad's decisiveness. I wondered if he would send troops all the way to Baghdad. He had a chance to rid the world of Saddam once and for all. But he stopped at the liberation of Kuwait. That was how he had defined the mission. That was what Congress had voted for and the coalition had signed up to do. I fully understood his rationale." This statement says many things; what it does not say is that Bush agreed with his father's decision—by all accounts he did not.[7]

In this, Bush agreed with the neoconservatives, who had long pilloried his father for his refusal to enter Baghdad. The most vocal in this regard had been Paul Wolfowitz, who argued in a 1994 review, for example, that "Saddam Hussein's continuation in power is a problem. . . . [He] will remain a threat to all the governments that supported us and particularly to the Arab Gulf states." Saddam was on Bush's plate from the first days of the administration—Iraq was discussed at the very first meeting of his National Security Council, held on 30 January 2001. The following month brought the clash in the sky over Saddam's violation of the no-fly zone. And then came 11 September. As Bush remembered, following the attacks, "we had to take a fresh look at every threat in the world."[8]

Many scholars have concluded, along with military historians Michael R. Gordon and Gen. Bernard E. Trainor, that the Iraq War was "a war of choice, not necessity."[9] The Bush administration believed the exact opposite. As had his father and Clinton before him, the second Bush needed no convincing that Saddam Hussein posed a certain threat to international security. He believed that he could not keep his promise to the American people—"never again"—unless the threat of Saddam Hussein was eliminated. There is no better statement of this than the one given by Cheney in his memoirs:

> When we looked around the world in those first months after 9/11, there was no place more likely to be a nexus between terrorism and WMD capability than Saddam Hussein's Iraq. With the benefit of hindsight—even considering that some of the intelligence we received was

wrong—that assessment still holds true. We could not ignore it or wish it away, hoping naively that the crumbling sanctions regime would contain Saddam. The security of our nation and of our friends and allies required that we act. And so we did.[10]

Bush was convinced that Saddam's brutality was enough of a reason to finish the job that his father had left undone. But Bush also knew that in the court of public opinion, simply the fact that Saddam was a bad guy would not be enough to justify war—the world was full of bad guys who the United States had allowed to remain standing. What was required was a casus belli, and the events of 11 September presented Bush with an opening. If it could be proved that Saddam was connected in any way to the 11 September attacks, the administration would have immediate justification for invading Iraq. The day after the attacks, Bush told Richard Clarke and a few other members of his staff, "See if Saddam did this. See if he's linked in any way."[11]

But until there was proof of the linkage, Bush was not willing to discuss a strike against Iraq. At the 15 September meeting at Camp David, discussed in chapter 7, Bush muzzled Wolfowitz when he attempted to argue in favor of an immediate attack on Iraq. The next day on NBC's *Meet the Press*, Cheney told his interviewers that the administration would act against Saddam Hussein if there was any evidence—but as of yet there was none. Bush reiterated this point at a 17 September meeting of the war cabinet where he admitted that while he believed that Saddam was involved with 11 September, he could not immediately strike Iraq because he didn't have the evidence.[12]

Such evidence was hard to come by. On 18 September, responding to Bush's request, Clarke's office sent a memo to Rice. Entitled "Survey of Intelligence Information on Any Iraq Involvement in the September 11 Attacks," the memo found no "compelling case" that Iraq had either planned or committed the attacks. Then, on 21 September, Bush's daily intelligence briefing informed him that there was no evidence of Iraqi complicity in the 11 September attacks, and little evidence of any link between Iraq and Al-Qaida. Nevertheless, Bush's team pressed the case. Between October and December 2001, two analysts who reported to Douglas Feith at Defense (calling themselves "Team B") dug through CIA and Defense Intelligence Agency (DIA) files and concluded that there was "consultation, training, financing and collaboration" between Iraq and Al-Qaida. However, Michael Scheuer, the head of the bin Laden team at the CIA, conducted his own investigation and found no evidence of collusion.[13]

Then, on 26 October 2001, it looked like the smoking gun had been found. The Czech interior minister confirmed that Ahmed Khalil Ibrahim Samir al-Ani, an Iraqi intelligence officer, met in Prague prior to 11 September with Mohamed Atta, one of the planners of the "Planes Plot" and one of the hijackers of American Flight 11, which had smashed into the North Tower of the World Trade Center. On *Meet the Press* on 9 December, Cheney publicly acknowledged the Prague meeting for the first time. (Host Tim Russert: "What we do know is they—Iraq is harboring terrorists." Cheney: "Correct.") But that information soon rang hollow. In early 2002, Czechoslovakian president Václav Havel called the White House and told administration officials that there was no credible evidence that Atta had met with Samir al-Ani.[14]

Frustrated, the administration turned away from trying to link Saddam to 11 September and concentrated instead on gathering evidence showing that he possessed WMDs and would soon use them again. The pivot began on 15 October 2001, when American intelligence learned of a possible agreement between Niger and Iraq for the sale of yellowcake uranium. If true, the evidence was damning—once fully processed, yellowcake can be used to produce weapons-grade uranium, appropriate for nuclear weapons. However, there were holes in the intel from the start. On 20 November the US embassy in Niger released a cable dealing with a recent meeting between the American ambassador and the director general of Niger's French-led consortium. In that cable, the director general was quoted as saying there was "no possibility" that the government of Niger had diverted any of the yellowcake produced in its uranium mines.[15]

Bush was undeterred. Saddam was seen as too much of a threat to American security to be left in power, and he would be taken out, with or without a casus belli. On 21 November 2001, Bush ordered Rumsfeld to direct Gen. Tommy Franks to begin exploring what it would take to remove Saddam. To be specific, Bush told journalist Bob Woodward that he told Rumsfeld, "I want to know what the options are." Soon after the Christmas holidays, Franks presented his plan to the national security team: using a light footprint as had been done in Afghanistan, Franks argued that Iraq could be taken with a limited number of troops by a swift invasion from Kuwait in the south, Saudi Arabia and Jordan in the west, and Turkey in the north. Bush told them to keep working on it.[16]

Now fully immersed in planning an invasion of Iraq, Bush started the new year with an attempt to soften the ground of public opinion. He did so by directly addressing the question that was on the mind of many of his critics: How could the United States invade a nation that had not attacked it and, moreover, had shown no outward sign of preparing for such an attack? Bush's answer was clear: if Iraq *might* attack us, we must neutralize them *before* they attack.

On 29 January 2002, in his State of the Union address, Bush uttered one of the more enduring lines of his presidency. But included in that speech was the beginning of a rationale for attacking a nation that threatened the United States:

> Our ... goal is to prevent regimes that sponsor terror from threatening America or our friends and allies with weapons of mass destruction. Some of these regimes have been pretty quiet since September 11, but we know their true nature. North Korea is a regime arming with missiles and weapons of mass destruction, while starving its citizens. Iran aggressively pursues these weapons and exports terror, while an unelected few repress the Iranian people's hope for freedom. Iraq continues to flaunt its hostility toward America and to support terror. The Iraqi regime has plotted to develop anthrax and nerve gas and nuclear weapons for over a decade. This is a regime that has already used poison gas to murder thousands of its own citizens, leaving the bodies of mothers huddled over their dead children. This is a regime that agreed to international inspections then kicked out the inspectors. This is a regime that has something to hide from the civilized world. States like these, and their terrorist allies, constitute an axis of evil, arming to threaten the peace of the world. By seeking weapons of mass destruction, these regimes pose a grave and growing danger. They could provide these arms to terrorists, giving them the means to match their hatred. They could attack our allies or attempt to blackmail the United States. In any of these cases, the price of indifference would be catastrophic.

Bush fleshed out this theme in a graduation address given at the US Military Academy at West Point on 1 June 2002. In that speech, which went through twenty drafts,[17] Bush made even clearer his belief that any nation that threatened the United States should be neutralized before it can act:

> For much of the last century, America's defense relied on the Cold War doctrines of deterrence and containment. In some cases, those strategies still apply. But new threats also require new thinking. Deterrence— the promise of massive retaliation against nations—means nothing against shadowy terrorist networks with no nation or citizens to defend. Containment is not possible when unbalanced dictators with weapons of mass destruction can deliver those weapons on missiles or secretly provide them to terrorist allies.

We cannot defend America and our friends by hoping for the best. We cannot put our faith in the word of tyrants, who solemnly sign non-proliferation treaties, and then systemically break them. If we wait for threats to fully materialize, we will have waited too long. . . . Our security will require transforming the military you will lead—a military that must be ready to strike at a moment's notice in any dark corner of the world. And our security will require all Americans to be forward-looking and resolute, to be ready for preemptive action when necessary to defend our liberty and defend our lives.

This viewpoint, now dubbed the "Bush Doctrine," would be codified in September 2002 in the National Security Strategy (NSS) that the administration was required to present each year. Rice would later remember that for this iteration, she took NSC-68—the Truman administration's bellicose statement of the need for an arms race with the Soviet Union—as her model. The NSS was crystal clear: the United States "will not hesitate to act alone, if necessary, to exercise our right of self-defense preemptively."[18]

Despite Bush's word choice, the step he was considering was not "preemptive"—an attack that was, in the words of one of the leading scholars on the subject, made "in the face of an imminent threat of armed attack." Rather, this was an act of "prevention," which was "undertaken in order to forestall . . . the acquisition of threatening capabilities."[19] Moreover, preventative war was hardly a new idea. The concept may have its origins in John Locke's seminal 1690 work on the liberal mind, *Treatise of Civil Government*:

> Being reasonable and just, I should have the right to destroy that which threatens me with destruction. . . . This makes it lawful for a man to kill a thief who has not in the least hurt him, nor declared any design on his life. . . . I have no reason to suppose that he who would take away my liberty would not, when he had me in his power, take away everything else. And, therefore, it is lawful for me to treat him as one who has put himself into a state of war with me—i.e., kill him if I can.[20]

There were also American precedents. Ironically, sixty years to the day before the attacks of 11 September, Franklin D. Roosevelt preached preparedness against the Nazi menace. In a Fireside Chat to the nation, Roosevelt warned that were Hitler not stopped, America might well strike first: "When you see a rattlesnake poised to strike, you do not wait until he has struck to crush him." Roosevelt was followed some twenty years later by John F. Kennedy. In his speech to the nation on the Cuban Missile Crisis on 22 October 1962, Kennedy made it clear that the United States would fire the first shot, if that is what it took to eliminate the missiles: "Neither the United States of America nor the world community of nations can tolerate deliberate deception and offensive threats on the part of any nation, large or small. We no longer live in a world where only the actual firing of weapons represents a sufficient challenge to a nation's security to constitute maximum peril."

For Bush, this was the lesson of 11 September. In order to protect the American people from a second attack, Bush was ready to invade a nation that had not yet struck at the United States but *might* do so in the near future. And by spring 2002, that die had been cast—plans to invade Iraq were in development. In March 2002 Bush interrupted a meeting between Rice and three senators, barking, "Fuck Saddam. We're taking him out."[21]

But affairs in the Middle East could intrude on the progress of any policy. On 28 September 2000, Ariel Sharon, the leader of Israel's conservative Likud Party, visited the Temple Mount complex—both Judaism's holiest place and the third holiest site in Islam—with more than a thousand police in tow. Sharon avowed that the complex would forever remain under Israeli control. Not surprisingly, the Palestinians responded to Sharon's claim with violence. In September 2000, what became known as the bloodshed of the "second intifada" began. Palestinian suicide bombings led to retaliations by Sharon, who had been elected prime minister in February 2001. Israeli helicopters attacked Arafat's headquarters in Ramallah, and on 3 January 2002 the Israeli navy stopped the *Karine A.*, a Palestinian freighter headed for Gaza with some fifty tons of munitions. Yasir Arafat, the chairman of the Palestine Liberation Organization, denied any involvement, but Bush had evidence to the contrary. He would later write, "Arafat had lied to me. I never trusted him again. I never spoke to him again. By the spring of 2002 I had concluded that peace would not be possible with Arafat in power."[22] However, Powell favored a more malleable approach, hoping to jump-start talks between the Israelis and the Palestinians. But such talks were not in the immediate future, and the violence of the intifada showed no signs of abatement.

On 27 March 2002, Abdel-Basset Odeh, a Palestinian affiliated with the militant organization Hamas, bypassed security at the Park Hotel in Netanya, Israel, walked into a dining room filled with some 250 people celebrating the Passover seder, and detonated an explosive device. The suicide bombing killed 28 and injured about 140 more. On 31 March, in response to what had been dubbed the "Passover Massacre," Israeli troops entered the city of Bethlehem, which was in Palestinian territory. Palestinian militants retreated into Bethlehem's Church of the Nativity, demanding sanctuary. As important from a diplomatic point of view, the Israelis surrounded Arafat's compound in Ramallah, leading to a standoff.

Despite his disgust with Arafat, Bush tried to resolve the situation. In a Rose Garden statement given on 4 April, Bush looked at the camera and pleaded, "Enough is enough." But it wasn't enough for Sharon, who refused to withdraw his troops from either Ramallah or Bethlehem. Bush sent Powell to the Middle East to defuse the crisis. Powell spent ten days there, and at the end of his trip Israeli troops had not retreated. To break the logjam, and without consulting the White House, Powell announced that there would be a peace conference on the Middle East. Cheney, who believed that the United States should stand firm with Israel over the matter, was furious. He told Rice to contact Powell, who was flying back from Israel, and inform him that his idea for a conference was "dead on arrival." Bush also felt that Powell had gone too far with his announcement. The president invited Sharon to visit the White House on 18 April, where he publicly referred to the prime minister as a "man of peace." This angered Powell, who felt that Sharon, who had ignored American requests to pull back forces, was simply playing the Americans.[23] But Powell was forced to stand down.

Besides, Bush had another plan to end the crisis—he would prevail upon the Saudis to act as brokers in the matter. On 25 April, Crown Prince Abdullah visited Bush at the Crawford ranch. The atmosphere was tense: Abdullah demanded, "When will the pig leave Ramallah?" After more discussion, the prince asked to be excused to talk to his advisers. Powell came back in the room and told an incredulous Bush that the Saudis were getting ready to leave. The situation was grave—not only did Bush need Abdullah's help in ending the standoff in Bethlehem and Ramallah, but he would need him as at least a silent partner when he invaded Iraq. Bush needed to buy himself some time, so he literally put himself between the prince and the door and, before the prince could take his leave, offered to give him a tour of the ranch. Abdullah agreed, and the two men got into a pickup truck with their interpreter and took off. As Bush remembered it, somewhere along the dirt road a large game bird blocked the path of the truck. Abdullah asked what it was, and Bush told him that it was a hen turkey. Abdullah grabbed Bush's arm: "My brother, it is a sign from Allah. This is a good omen." When they returned to the ranch, Abdullah agreed to stay for lunch. Abdullah returned to his country and was instrumental in negotiating an end to the crisis that involved a few of the Hamas extremists being sent into exile.[24]

On 9 July 2002, British prime minister Tony Blair met with his chief advisers. Blair could not have been pleased with the report from his chief of intelligence, who informed the room that in Washington, "intelligence and facts were being fixed around the policy" of invading Iraq and that "military action was now seen as inevitable." But by the summer of 2002, this was hardly a secret. The drift to war was barely concealed from the American people, as the rhetoric from the administration became more accusatory and bellicose toward Iraq. Indeed, by August, Quonset huts had arrived at Camp Doha in the Kuwaiti desert—preparations for an invasion had already, quietly, begun.[25]

That summer, however, Bush had to contend with several substantial denunciations of his policy. On this, Brent Scowcroft, the senior Bush's national security adviser, ran the point. On 4 August Scowcroft appeared on CBS's *Face the Nation*, where he projected that attacking Iraq "could turn the whole region into a cauldron and, thus, destroy the war on terrorism." A little over a week later, on 15 August, the *Wall Street Journal* carried an opinion piece written by Scowcroft, entitled "Don't Attack Saddam." Here, Scowcroft argued that "Saddam's strategic objective appears to be to dominate the Persian Gulf, to control oil from the region, or both. That clearly poses a real threat to key U.S. interests. But there is scant evidence to tie Saddam to terrorist organizations, and even less to the Sept[ember] 11 attacks. Indeed, Saddam's goals have little in common with the terrorists who threaten us, and there is little incentive for him to make common cause with them." He concluded that "our pre-eminent security priority—underscored repeatedly by the president—is the war on terrorism. An attack on Iraq at this time would seriously jeopardize, if not destroy, the global counterterrorist campaign we have undertaken."[26]

The younger Bush was furious, expressing incredulity that instead of going public, Scowcroft didn't pick up the phone and vent his concerns to one of his many contacts on the White House staff. Bush also called his father, who tried to calm his son as well as protect Scowcroft: "Son, Brent is a friend." But the link that many pundits saw was in the reverse, as many opined that Scowcroft was acting as a stalking horse for the antiwar opinions of Bush the elder (in the *New York Times*, columnist Maureen

Dowd sniffed, "Junior Gets a Spanking"). Bush the younger, who saw this as "ridiculous," commented, "Of all people, Dad understood the stakes. If he thought I was handling Iraq wrong, he damn sure would have told me himself." Scowcroft's most thorough biographer agrees: "Scowcroft wasn't writing on behalf of his friend or for anyone else. In fact, it would have been out of character for the former president to ask Scowcroft to write a dissenting op-ed."[27]

Regardless, the younger Bush delegated to Rice the task of personally admonishing Scowcroft. She did so, and according to Rice he expressed his regret, protesting that he never meant to criticize the president. However, the meeting did not completely calm the waters. In her memoir, Rice makes an oblique reference to repeat performances of Scowcroft's criticisms ("several more times the same thing happened"), but she offered no elaboration. Rice did note, however, that the "level of trust between the President and Brent plummeted until there was nothing left."[28]

But Scowcroft was not the only alumnus of the first Bush administration to publicly vent his displeasure at the escalating rhetoric of war. On 25 August, in a *New York Times* op-ed, James Baker argued that Bush should seek a UN resolution requiring Iraq to submit to elections. He advised the president not only to not "go it alone" in Iraq but to "reject the advice of those who counsel doing so."[29]

The second bit of pushback came from within the administration itself. While he had made it clear that he would support a decision to invade Iraq, Tony Blair had long been pressing Bush to seek a United Nations resolution that directly outlined the world's concerns about his intent and required a timeline for turning over any WMDs. Rumsfeld and Cheney did not consider it necessary to seek a UN resolution. But Colin Powell was just as steadfast in its favor. On 5 August, Powell and Bush had a private meeting in the White House residence. Powell argued that most of the briefings that Bush had received had focused on how to invade Iraq and depose Saddam. Powell felt that, in his words, "not enough attention had been given either to non-military options or the aftermath of a military conquest." Powell remembered warning Bush, "If you break it, you own it," and he strongly recommended that Bush take the issue to the United Nations. However, at no point in any of these discussions did Powell say that he did not, or would not, support an invasion if that was the president's decision, and at no point in the meeting did Bush make a decision one way or the other on a UN resolution.[30]

Nothing that he heard in the summer of 2002 changed Bush's mind about the need to use the American military to depose Saddam. On 4 September he met with congressional leaders and asked for a resolution of force against Iraq. But Bush had come to believe that there was something to be gained by going to the United Nations. On 6 September, over dinner with Bush and Cheney, Tony Blair made his final push for the president to seek a UN resolution in opposition to Saddam. Cheney repeated his opposition, arguing that any new set of inspections "could too easily be a source of false comfort" for Saddam. Nevertheless, Bush promised Blair that he would seek a UN resolution. After dinner, Bush quipped to Blair's communications director: "I'll say this, and I don't want it on the record, and with apology to the mixed audience but your guy's got balls." The next day at Camp David, Bush told the NSC of his decision. But he made it clear that this would be the final break given to Saddam: "Either he will come clean about his weapons, or there will be war."[31]

Bush decided to travel to New York and personally ask the United Nations to pass a resolution that condemned Saddam for being in material breach of past resolutions and give him a specific timetable to identify and destroy his WMDs. However, Bush was not in a diplomatic mood. Instead, in a 12 September speech to the General Assembly, he berated and threatened that body. The audience applauded only one time—when Bush pledged to renew American membership in the United Nations Educational, Scientific and Cultural Organization (UNESCO). Other than that, those in attendance sat stone-faced and listened to a speech that Jacques Chirac called "both an ultimatum to Iraq and a formal notice addressed to the Security Council."[32] The speech was an indictment of Iraq ("Our greatest fear is that terrorists will find a shortcut to their mad ambitions when an outlaw regime supplies them with the technologies to kill on a massive scale. In one place—in one regime—we find all these dangers, in their most lethal and aggressive forms, exactly the kind of aggressive threat the United Nations was born to confront"); an explanation of preventative war ("The history, the logic, and the facts lead to one conclusion: Saddam Hussein's regime is a grave and gathering danger. To suggest otherwise is to hope against the evidence. To assume this regime's good faith is to bet the lives of millions and the peace of the world in a reckless gamble. And this is a risk we must not take"); a declaration of war ("The purposes of the United States should not be doubted. The Security Council resolutions will be enforced—the just demands of peace and security will be met—or action will be unavoidable. And a regime that has lost its legitimacy will also lose its power"); and a resounding critique of the United Nations itself ("All the world now faces a test. . . . Will the United Nations serve the purpose of its founding, or will it be irrelevant?").

However, bullying would not work with the US Congress. There, as he began to lobby for a resolution approving American use of force in Iraq, Bush faced a political conundrum. The nation was skidding into its first post-9/11 national election, and putting pressure on members to give their support to an invasion of Iraq was a delicate gambit. If the White House managed things correctly, it could paint all who opposed war—particularly Democrats—as either naive or unpatriotic. However, the same strategy could boomerang, tarring Bush with a warmonger image that the Democrats could exploit.

A strategic lapse by the Democrats gave Bush an opening. Looking to gain some cover for those in his party who were inclined to vote in favor of the force resolution or who felt they had to in order to preserve their chances at reelection, Sen. Bob Graham (D-FLA), the vice chairman of the Senate Intelligence Committee, pressed the intelligence communities to prepare a new National Intelligence Estimate (NIE), presenting the available evidence on Saddam Hussein and WMDs. Graham requested the report by 1 October. That gave the analysts little over a month to complete the task—nowhere near enough time by Washington bureaucratic standards. The ninety-page report, entitled "Iraq's Continuing Programs for Weapons of Mass Destruction," stated that the Bureau of Intelligence and Research and the Department of Energy believed that Iraq did, indeed, have an active chemical and biological weapons program, and that it was "reconstituting its nuclear weapons program . . . [and ] could make a nuclear weapon within several months to a year." The NIE was written in an incredibly short time frame; on 1 October it was delivered to Congress, and the CIA delivered a one-page summary to Bush on the same day.[33]

Tenet would later blame the short time frame for errors in the report, but this was far from the biggest problem. The conclusions of the NIE were largely based on information given by an Iraqi defector codenamed Curveball, who was being held by the German intelligence agency and had not let the CIA interrogate him. A decidedly unreliable source, Curveball was, according to future director of national intelligence Michael McConnell, "saying what that group [the Germans] wanted to hear," and his intel was later found to be largely false. Moreover, there is evidence that everyone in the chain of command knew that Curveball was a dubious source. One CIA official, Tyler Drumheller, later claimed that he told his superiors, specifically deputy director John McLaughlin, that Curveball was mentally unstable (Drumheller: "Everyone in the chain of command knew exactly what was happening"); in his memoir, Tenet disputes Drumheller's account.[34]

Whether or not they knew about the weakness in the sourcing of the report, everyone jumped to pronounce the NIE as authoritative. Indeed, it was in their best interest to do so—both the administration, which had sponsored the force resolution, and the members who had to vote on it could now point to an official document that read as if Saddam had the wherewithal to either prosecute or support an attack against the United States. Moreover, thanks to the NIE, it had now become harder for a member not to support the force resolution, and it was in Bush's best interest to push for an immediate vote. On 2 October, the day after the release of the NIE, Bush came to an agreement with House Democratic leader Richard Gephardt (D-MO) on bringing the resolution to the floor for a vote. Bush appeared in the Rose Garden with Gephardt and Connecticut Democratic senator Joe Lieberman, who supported the resolution. Senate majority leader Tom Daschle refused to attend the ceremony.[35]

In order to push the deal through, as well as lay down a marker with voters, Bush decided to give a speech to present his case. On 7 October Bush spoke to the nation from the Cincinnati Museum Center in Cincinnati, Ohio. Throughout the speech, Bush presented the strained intelligence that had been the foundation of the NIE. But it was the image that Bush evoked of the necessity for a preventative war with Iraq that was the most haunting: "We cannot wait for the final proof, the smoking gun that would come in the form of a mushroom cloud."

Three days later, the House voted in favor of the force resolution, 296–133. Ten hours later, the Senate approved it, 77–23. In their memoirs, Bush, Cheney, and Rove took pains—using virtually the same language— to note that these margins were greater than those of the votes for the Gulf War in 1990.[36] For Bush the level of Democratic support for the resolution—including Gephardt and Daschle from the House, and Senators Hillary Clinton (NY), Joe Biden (DE), John Kerry (MA), John Edwards (NC), and Harry Reid (NV)—must have been particularly satisfying. Only one Republican, Lincoln Chafee of Rhode Island, opposed the resolution (in 2007, Chafee would switch to the Democratic Party). For many of these Democrats, themselves hoping to run for the presidency, this vote would soon come back to haunt their ambitions. On 16 October, Bush signed the resolution, reminding his audience, "I have not ordered the use of force," and protesting, "I hope the use of force will not become necessary."

The image of the "mushroom cloud"—eerily reminiscent of Lyndon Johnson's "Daisy Girl" television ad of 1964[37]—was the high point of a political campaign that had skated away from Daschle's hope for a referendum on the economy and instead became a referendum on the War on Terror. Bush and his surrogates contended that the Republicans were better equipped than the Democrats to prosecute the war on terror. Bush campaigned vigorously, traveling 10,000 miles to 15 states, making 108 campaign visits supporting 26 House candidates and 20 Senate candidates. He was also fundraising manna—the Republican National Committee held a $30 million to $5 million advantage over its Democratic counterpart. The Republicans also outorganized the Democrats on the ground. The "72 Hour Task Force" (so named because GOP research had shown that GOP voters were underperforming, giving the Democrats an advantage in the final seventy-two hours of a race) pushed GOP turnout, particularly with evangelical voters—a key constituency that Rove had been concentrating on since 2000.[38]

Bush was also able to use opposition to his proposed Department of Homeland Security against the Democrats. The proposal called for the Office of Homeland Security, then headed by Tom Ridge, to be expanded into a new cabinet-level department, one that incorporated twenty-two government agencies under its bureaucratic umbrella. The bill was held up in committee debate, as Democrats charged that every agency in the new department had to be subject to collective bargaining, and Republicans charged the Democrats with playing politics with a department that was needed to improve national security.[39]

The turnout in 2002 was higher than it had been in the 1998 midterms—39 percent of the voting age population went to the polls. The result was a stunning victory for the Republicans—it was only the third time since the Civil War that the president's party had picked up seats in an off-year election (the other three being those held in 1902, 1934, and 1998). The Republicans had a net gain of two seats in the Senate; that gave them a majority of 51–49; they also picked up eight seats in the House, thus expanding their control of that body, 229–204. Democratic analyst James Carville was so mortified that he covered his head with a trash can while scrutinizing election night returns on CNN. *Time* magazine gushed, "It was nothing short of astonishing. George W. Bush's relentless campaigning had paid off big time for his party."[40]

Two of those campaigns stand out. Only eleven days before the election, liberal Democrat Paul Wellstone, campaigning for reelection, was killed in a plane crash in Eveleth, Minnesota, along with his wife and daughter. Former vice president and presidential candidate Walter Mondale agreed to replace Wellstone on the ticket. Mondale ran a spirited campaign, showing a surprising willingness to attack his opponent, former mayor of St. Paul Norm Coleman, in the final senatorial debate. Nevertheless, Coleman won the election, receiving 49.5 percent to Mondale's 47.3 percent of the vote.

The most infamous chapter in the 2002 campaigns was the campaign for reelection to the Senate by Max Cleland, Democrat of Georgia. Cleland had lost both his legs and his right forearm in Vietnam. He had been in the Senate since 1996 and had been one of the twenty-nine Democrats who had voted in favor of the force resolution. In 2002, Cleland faced a reelection challenge from four-term congressman Saxby Chambliss. An ad paid for by the Chambliss campaign opened with clearly identifiable images of Saddam Hussein and Usama bin Laden, followed by a voice-over: "As America faces terrorists, and extremist dictators, Max Cleland runs television ads claiming he has the courage to lead." Thus, the Chambliss campaign had called Cleland's patriotism into question by linking him with America's enemies. To hammer the point home, the ad went on to observe that Cleland had voted against the Homeland Security measure eleven times. The ad closed by branding Cleland as a liar: "Max Cleland says he has the courage to lead. But the record proves Max Cleland is just misleading." Vietnam veterans of both parties, including John McCain, loudly protested the ad, and it was soon pulled from the airwaves. However, the damage had been done. Cleland lost to Chambliss, 55–46 percent. Cleland later blamed Karl Rove for the ad; Rove maintained his innocence.[41]

Bush used his moment of triumph to dispense with what had become a problem within his cabinet. Bush planned to propose a second round of tax cuts in advance of the 2004 presidential campaign. Treasury secretary Paul O'Neill had not been in favor of the first round of cuts, nor was he in favor of the second. A frustrated Bush later remembered with some bitterness that "by late 2002, nearly two million Americans had lost jobs in the past year, and Paul wasn't conveying our determination to get them back to work." Instead, O'Neill used his time in the Oval Office with Bush to talk about tangential topics, like his plan to improve workplace safety at the US Mint. Bush decided that a change was necessary. On 5 December Cheney called O'Neill to tell him that his services were no longer needed. The next day, O'Neill had a subordinate drop off his resignation letter. O'Neill was succeeded at Treasury by John W. Snow, the former CEO of CFX Corporation. Snow would join another new member of the cabinet. On 25 November, the Congress broke its logjam and approved the creation of the Department of Homeland Security. Tom Ridge, who had served since September 2001 as Bush's homeland security adviser, became its first secretary.[42]

On 8 November 2002—three days after the upset win in the off year, the UN Security Council voted 15 to 0 in favor of Bush's resolution. UN Resolution 1441 held Iraq in "material breach" of previous UN resolutions and gave Saddam a "final opportunity to comply." He was given until 7 December to disclose his weapons and disarm them—if he did not, he would face "serious consequences."[43] In response to the resolution, on 7 December, Saddam submitted a twelve-thousand-page statement, the gist of which was his claim that he had no banned weapons. The leader of the inspection team, Swedish diplomat Hans Blix, chairman of the United Nations Monitoring, Verification, and Inspections Commission, called Saddam's response "rich in volume but poor in information." British foreign secretary Jack Straw called it "an obvious falsehood." On 19 December, the administration announced that it found Saddam's explanation to be "inadequate."[44]

Nevertheless, Bush was worried that nations which were on the fence about whether to support an invasion of Iraq would be convinced by Saddam's explanations. He decided it was time to release some of the closely held intelligence that had concluded Saddam had WMDs. Bush asked the CIA to take the first cut at developing a presentation that could be made public. On 21 December, George Tenet and John McLaughlin attended a White House meeting on Iraq. McLaughlin gave the presentation as requested by the president. However, his presentation was academic and somewhat dense (Cheney called it "fuzzy"), and Bush brushed it aside with a dismissive "Nice try." Bush told the group that in his mind, the facts were clear, and that if packaged better they would ultimately convince the American people. Bush remembered telling the group, "Surely we can do a better job of explaining the evidence against Saddam." Tenet replied: "It's a slam dunk." Following the meeting, Bush ordered Scooter Libby and Steve Hadley to create a better draft of the indictment against Saddam.[45]

Tenet's basketball metaphor, which has achieved the status of folklore among students of the ramp-up to war in Iraq, has been used by many of those observers as evidence to support an argument that the administration believed it had an airtight case that would justify its removing Saddam from power. Bush himself seems to believe this—he remembered that his reaction to the "slam dunk" comment was that "I believed him [Tenet]. I had been receiving intelligence briefings on Iraq for nearly two years. The conclusion that Saddam had WMDs was nearly a universal consensus." But that is not how Tenet remembers the moment. He argued in his memoirs that the comment was meant to refer specifically to Bush's disappointment with the CIA's presentation, and that it was a "slam dunk" that it could be improved.[46]

Regardless, the "slam dunk" flap served to highlight the fact that the administration had yet to articulate a coherent, defensible case for war against Saddam's Iraq. Wavering nations and shaky American public opinion both needed bolstering. In his second State of the Union address, delivered on 28 January 2003, Bush laid out a bill of particulars against Saddam. But when he maintained that "from three Iraqi defectors we know that Iraq, in the late 1990s, had several mobile biological weapons labs. These are designed to produce germ warfare agents, and can be moved from place to a place to evade inspectors. Saddam Hussein has not disclosed these facilities. He's given no evidence that he has destroyed them," he was using information from the NIE, which based its conclusions on the testimony of Curveball—an unstable source who no one in American intelligence had yet met, and who only two weeks later would be completely discredited. When he used what would be dubbed the "sixteen words" to link Saddam to a search for uranium—"The British government has learned that Saddam Hussein recently sought significant quantities of uranium from Africa"—he was making a claim based on evidence that, as we have seen, had also been brought into question. The administration followed the speech by raising the terrorism threat level from yellow (elevated risk) to orange (high risk), and newly minted secretary of homeland security Tom Ridge urged people to plan for an emergency. Families raced out to buy canned food and bottled water, as well as plastic sheeting and duct tape to cover windows in case of a chemical attack.[47]

Bush next turned to Colin Powell to make the American case. Two days after the State of the Union address, in an act that bypassed his representative to the United Nations, John Negroponte, Bush told Powell that he would be addressing that body.[48] After Powell's meeting with the president, his staff received the WMD case that the Hadley and Libby staff had been preparing since 21 December. Powell would later characterize that case as being primarily authored by Libby, and as a "disaster," stating, "It was incoherent." Libby's draft had tied Iraq to international terrorism, but it also tied Saddam to the 11 September attacks. It did so on the flimsiest of evidence—the Prague meetings that Václav Havel had already reported to the White House as being highly questionable. Powell decided to scrap Libby's draft and begin anew. Powell now had four days before he had to deliver his speech, so he brought his staff to the CIA. There, they worked with Tenet, McLaughlin, and their analysts in the daytime; in the evenings, Powell and Rice joined the group. Powell would later write that Cheney "urged us to tilt our presentation back towards Scooter Libby's by adding assertions that had been rejected months earlier to links between Iraq and 9/11 and other terrorist acts." The working group removed the reference to the Prague meetings. On 5 February, Libby called Col. Lawrence Wilkerson, Powell's chief of staff, to try one last time to get the Prague story into Powell's speech; Wilkerson didn't take the call.[49]

On 5 February, Powell addressed the General Assembly of the United Nations. Although he had excised the references to the Prague meeting from the speech, references to the existence of WMDs remained. Powell was anything but obtuse: "My colleagues, every statement I make today is backed up by sources, solid sources. These are not assertions. What we are giving you are facts and conclusions based on solid intelligence." To support his assertion that Saddam did, indeed, possess WMDs, Powell cited the "eyewitness account" of an Iraqi defector that "has been corroborated by other sources"—the notorious Curveball—as well as three other Iraqi sources. Powell assessed the situation as being ripe for preventative war:

> We know that Saddam Hussein is determined to keep his weapons of mass destruction. He's determined to make more. . . . [S]hould we take the risk that he will not someday use these weapons at a time and place and in a manner of his choosing, at a time when the world is in a much weaker position to respond? The United States will not and cannot run that risk to the American people.[50]

Tenet would later admit in his memoirs that "despite our efforts, a lot of flawed information still made its way into the speech." This was an understatement, and for Powell, this most likely offered little consolation. Powell would later claim to the *Los Angeles Times* that he had never been warned during those three days of briefing at the CIA that he was using material that both the Defense Intelligence Agency and the CIA knew to be false: "I was not pleased. What really made me not pleased was they [the CIA and DIA] had put out a burn notice on this guy [Curveball], and people who were even present at my briefings knew it." In his memoir, Bush largely dismisses the fallout from Powell's speech: "Later, many of the assertions in Colin's speech would prove inaccurate. But at the time, his words reflected the considered judgement of intelligence agencies at home and around the world." In his own memoir, Rumsfeld was less sanguine: "Powell was not duped or misled by anybody, nor did he lie about Saddam's suspected WMD stockpiles. The President did not lie. The Vice President did not lie. Tenet did not lie. Rice did not lie. I did not lie. The Congress did not lie. The far less dramatic truth is that we were wrong."[51]

Amid this high diplomatic drama came a split second of almost unbearable tragedy. On Saturday, 1 February, the space shuttle *Columbia* exploded in descent from its orbit. Seven astronauts were killed, including the first Israeli to fly in space.[52] In his remarks from the Oval Office, Bush reflected, "The same Creator who names the stars also knows the names of the seven souls we mourn today. The crew of the shuttle Columbia did not return safely to Earth; yet we can pray that all are safely home."

It was soon clear that the administration's attempts to convince wavering nations that Saddam possessed WMDs, and that a preventative war against Iraq was necessary, had fallen on many deaf ears. On 8 February, Germany, France, and Russia—all three permanent members of the UN Security Council, any of which could veto a possible resolution—announced their opposition to an American attack on Iraq. Powell professed in his memoir to being "blindsided" by the French announcement. On 1 March, the Turkish government refused to allow American troops to use its territory to mount a northern front. On 7 March, Blix reported to the Security Council that was "no evidence" of mobile biological production facilities in Iraq, and he asked for more time for Saddam to comply with the resolution.[53]

The events of early 2003 put a great strain on Tony Blair's support for Bush's planned invasion. Blair had long been on Bush's side, and he had made it clear to Bush that if the United States invaded Iraq, Great Britain would be a coalition partner for the long run. But now it seemed that Blair would not be able to keep that promise, as his own Labour Party was showing signs of breaking with the prime minister over the issue. With his government in crisis, Blair pleaded with Bush to support a second UN resolution, one that gave Saddam more time to comply with the first resolution, but one that Blair felt would give him the cover necessary to both support the United States and keep his government in power. Virtually no one in Bush's administration supported Blair's request. Nevertheless, on 31 January, Bush met with Blair in the White House and told him that even though war was "penciled in for March 10," Bush would nevertheless try to get a second resolution to protect Blair. On 7 March, the United States, Britain, Spain, and Bulgaria put forth a resolution, giving Saddam until 17 March to completely disarm. It soon became clear that Bush did not have the votes on the Security Council to pass this second resolution. In the face of certain defeat, on 17 March Bush withdrew his resolution. Nevertheless, the same day Blair won a parliamentary vote of support for the US position, and his government remained intact.[54]

On the evening of 17 March, Bush addressed the American people: "The United Nations Security Council has not lived up to its responsibilities, so we will rise to ours. . . . Saddam Hussein and his sons must leave Iraq within forty-eight hours. Their refusal to do so will result in military conflict, commenced at a time of our choosing."[55]

Two days later, on 19 March, Bush met with his NSC and all his field commanders via teleconference. Bush asked each of them if they had what they needed. They all replied in the affirmative. Tommy Franks went last: "Mr. President: This force is ready." Bush turned to Rumsfeld: "Mr. Secretary, for the peace of the world and the benefit and freedom of the Iraqi people, I hereby give the order to execute Operation Iraqi Freedom. May God bless the troops." Franks saluted—"Mr. President, may God bless the troops." Bush returned his salute.[56]

Bush then went to his desk in the Treaty Room and composed a handwritten letter to his father: "In spite of the fact that I had decided a few months ago to use force, if need be, to liberate Iraq and rid the country of WMD, the decision was an emotional one. I know I have taken the right action and do pray few will lose life. Iraq will be free, the world will be safer. . . . I know what you went through. Love, George." Several hours later, the elder Bush faxed a handwritten reply: "Dear George: Your handwritten note, just received, touched my heart. You are doing the right thing. . . . It is right to worry about the loss of innocent life be it Iraqi or American. But you have done that which you had to do. . . . Remember Robin's words 'I love you more than tongue can tell.' Well, I do. Devotedly, Dad."[57]

# 10

★ ★ ★ ★ ★

# "CATASTROPHIC SUCCESS"

Then the well-oiled American war machine came to a screeching halt.

On the afternoon of 19 March 2003, at a hastily called meeting of the president's national security team, Rumsfeld and Tenet told Bush that intelligence showed Saddam Hussein and his sons Uday and Qusay—both psychopaths in their own right—were at that moment on their way to a family compound outside Baghdad called Dora Farms. The opportunity to kill Saddam even before the war even began was tempting but also particularly risky. Since the military believed there was an underground bunker at Dora Farms, a missile attack would not do the trick. Instead, the military would have to use two F-117 bombers, both of which would have to fly over Iraqi air defenses in order to drop a series of bunker-busting bombs. The reliability of the intelligence was also a question. Bush quizzed Tenet about his level of confidence; Tenet replied that it was high. Bush went around the room; everyone agreed that bombing Dora Farms was a chance worth taking. Bush decided to take the chance, and he approved the raid. At 9:30 p.m., two 2,000-pound bombs were dropped on Dora Farms; thirty-nine Tomahawk missiles followed. One hour later, Bush addressed the nation. In a solemn voice, he announced, "On my orders, coalition forces have begun striking selected targets of military importance to undermine Saddam Hussein's ability to wage war. These are the opening stages of what will be a broad and concerted campaign."[1]

The next morning, Bush learned that although the bunker at Dora Farms had been obliterated, along with every nearby structure, Saddam Hussein had been spared—he had left the bunker before the missiles struck. Within hours, Saddam had retaliated, launching a surface-to-air missile at the place of deployment for the 101st Airborne Division in northern Kuwait. While there were no coalition casualties, the missile had flown so low to the ground that it had been completely undetected by coalition radar.[2]

The ground war against Iraq began on 21 March. The First Marine Division, under the command of Gen. James Mattis, crossed the border between Kuwait and Iraq, captured the oil fields at Rumaylah, and then pushed north toward Baghdad along the eastern banks of the Euphrates. Mattis was to protect the right flank of the army's V Corps, which was heading in the same direction on the other side of the Euphrates. As the Americans got closer to Baghdad, they literally outran their supply lines—Mattis's marines were told to eat every ounce of their field rations because the rations might soon be limited.[3]

Just outside of Nasiriyah, some 215 miles southeast of Baghdad, troops either wearing partial uniforms or completely dressed in black fired on coalition forces. These were the Fedayeen, armed guerrillas who for years had stored weapons in every city and town in order to put down any uprising against Saddam. Now, strengthened by foreign jihadists who flocked to the cause, the Fedayeen turned their rage on the invader. The strength and tenacity of the Fedayeen caught the coalition forces by surprise. They had expected mass surrenders of Iraqi troops on the road to Baghdad; instead, they would be peppered by paramilitary forces the entire way. At Nasiriyah, eleven American soldiers were killed, and army PFC Jessica Lynch was captured (imprisoned in a hospital in Nasiriyah, she would be freed one week after her capture by a Special Operations Task Force, which retrieved both Lynch and the bodies of eight dead American soldiers; it was the first successful rescue of a POW since World War II). The battle for Samawah was just as fierce, as the 101st Airborne Division, under the command of Gen. David Petraeus, engaged the Fedayeen for control of that city.[4]

As had happened in Afghanistan, weather played a crucial role in the advance to Baghdad, as a massive sandstorm slowed down the advance. One week after the start of the invasion, the order was given for a seventy-two-hour pause to resupply. When the attack resumed, troops from the 101st Airborne Division were airlifted to Najaf, where they conducted street-by-street warfare to secure that city. They then moved north to Hillah, where they demolished the vaunted Hammurabi Division of the Iraqi Republican Guard. The road to Baghdad was now clear.[5]

When the 101st arrived in the capital city, it met not the organized Republican Guard forces that it had expected but heavily armed Fedayeen jihadists. Fierce fighting took place around Saddam International Airport, and it was a slugfest to break into the city. When, on 9 April, the Americans reached Firdos Square in the center of Baghdad, they effected one of the most iconic moments of the War on Terror. In the heart of the square was a thirty-nine-foot-tall statue of Saddam Hussein. After several attempts to destroy the statue and having one Marine momentarily drape an American flag over Saddam's bronze head, they tied a rope around the statue's neck and pulled it down. But the real Saddam Hussein had escaped, leaving memories of Usama bin Laden's escape from Tora Bora some two years earlier.

Bush's response to the initial success of the coalition mirrored that of his father in November 1989, when he refused to gloat over the fall of the Berlin Wall. As the younger Bush told Spain's prime minister José Maria Aznar: "You won't see us doing any victory dances or anything." But the administration was taken in by a false sense of finality in Iraq. On 1 May 2003, forty-three days after the war had begun, Bush proclaimed victory. He did so in dramatic fashion aboard the USS *Abraham Lincoln*, then docked off the coast of San Diego. Bush flew to the ship in a US Navy S-3B Viking fighter jet that, while over the Pacific, he had piloted for a few moments. Once on deck, he exuded optimism: "My fellow Americans, major combat operations in Iraq have ended. . . . The transition from dictatorship to democracy will take time, but it is worth every effort. Our coalition will stay until our work is done. Then we will leave, and we will leave behind a free Iraq." Later, Bush claimed that he had not seen a large banner behind him, hanging from the ship's bridge, proclaiming "Mission Accomplished." It had been hung out there, according to Bush, by his staff: "Our stagecraft had gone awry. It was a big mistake."[6]

The bigger mistake was in not recognizing that the war in Iraq was far from over. Despite Bush's confidence, the second phase of the Iraq War had already begun.

Rumsfeld would later label it a "catastrophic success."[7] That was putting lipstick on a pig. It was quickly clear that while Iraq had been liberated from Saddam, no one was in control of the new Iraq.

The first indication of a post–"mission accomplished" chaos in Baghdad was a wave of widespread looting. Along with supermarkets and other stores, the looters stripped the National Museum of Iraq of some 170,000 of its irreplaceable artifacts, many of which were either stolen or destroyed. Looters burned both the Iraq National Library and the National Archives to the ground; countless manuscripts dating back thousands of years were destroyed. Officials put the cost of the looting at close to $12 billion. At an NSC meeting, an irritated president growled: "Why isn't anybody stopping these looters?" The main reason was that, as Rumsfeld later observed, the Iraqi army and police force had for all intents and purposes disappeared, and the overwhelmed American troops were now, de facto, expected to act as local police—a job they did not expect to do and one for which were not adequately trained. As a result, the looters were left to their revelry largely unchecked. As frustrated as was the president, at an 11 April press conference Rumsfeld barked: "Think what's happened in our cities when we've had riots, and problems, and looting. Stuff happens!" The ill-advised comment was immediately spun as a lack of empathy on the part of the secretary of defense.[8]

But things would soon go from bad to worse. The undisciplined looting soon morphed into an organized insurgency against the coalition forces. When the United States invaded Iraq and overthrew Saddam's Sunni regime, the resulting power vacuum created an opportunity for two radical leaders. Shi'a cleric Muqtada al-Sadr's fiery anti-Sunni sermons appealed to the more destitute of Iraqis, allowing him to form a Shi'a militia to oppose the Americans. And Abu Musab al-Zarqawi, a veteran of the insurgency against the Soviets in Afghanistan, had developed a terrorist network that, while separate from Al-Qaida, nonetheless received funding and support from Usama bin Laden. However, the American invasion of Iraq effectively drove bin Laden and Zarqawi together into a more formal alliance. By May 2003, a Zarqawi-led group called the Organization of Monotheism and Jihad had begun organized resistance against the coalition forces in Iraq. The insurgency had begun.[9]

Before the invasion, the assumption in Washington was that it would be a quick war, and that the Iraqi people would accept the Americans not as foreign conquerors but as liberators. Therefore, the prevailing logic was that the troops would be home quickly (Rumsfeld's spokesman, Larry Di Rita: "All but twenty-five thousand soldiers will be out by the beginning of September").[10] This would leave postwar reconstruction of Iraq largely to the Iraqi people. As a result, an inadequate amount of time and planning was given to postwar Iraq. The result was a government for postwar Iraq that was wholly inadequate for the task and contributed to the violence that was to follow.

On 20 January 2003, three months before the launch of Operation Iraqi Freedom, Bush issued National Security Presidential Directive (NSPD) 24 on the subject "Iraq Post War Planning Office." Labeled secret, the directive declared:

> If it should become necessary for a U.S.-led military coalition to liberate Iraq, the United States will want to be in a position to help meet the humanitarian, reconstruction, and administration challenges facing the country in the immediate aftermath of the combat operations. The immediate responsibility will fall on U.S. Central Command; overall success, however, will require a national effort. . . . To support this effort, the Department of Defense shall establish a Post-War Planning Office."

That office was the Office of Reconstruction and Humanitarian Assistance (OHRA), which was charged by the NSPD with deploying to Iraq "to form the nucleus of the administrative apparatus that will assist in administering Iraq for a limited period of time. This administrative apparatus will seek to involve the Iraqis themselves, initially in an advisory role."[11] To run OHRA, Rumsfeld chose Jay Garner, a retired general and a veteran of the Vietnam War. Garner commanded the humanitarian efforts in northern Iraq (Operation Provide Comfort) that followed the Persian Gulf War in 1991. After his retirement, he had settled in as president of SYColeman, Inc., a defense contractor that made Patriot and Arrow missiles.

The clock was working against OHRA's success—Garner was given only seven weeks to prepare to deploy. As one wag at the Pentagon was quoted as saying, "That's what it takes to get a computer connection at the Pentagon."[12] Once in Iraq, Garner established OHRA in the opulent Republican Palace in Baghdad. But looks were deceiving. The OHRA never got hold of the situation, insurgent attacks and looting continued virtually unchecked, and as a result Garner never had the full confidence of the administration.

Several of Bush's advisers recommended that he replace Garner with former ambassador Paul Bremer III. Bremer had joined the State Department in 1966, serving at postings in Afghanistan and Malawi until 1971. Upon his return to the States, he served as an assistant to two secretaries of state, Henry Kissinger and Alexander Haig, and in 1986 he served as ambassador to the Netherlands. From 1989 to 2000, Bremer served as the managing director for Kissinger Associates, and from 2000 to 2003 he served as the chairman and CEO of Marsh Crisis Consulting Company, a business whose offices had been located in the South Tower of the World Trade Center.[13] Bush met Bremer for the first time at the White House on 6 May 2003, where the two men had a private lunch—somewhat of an anomaly for what was essentially a job interview. Bush's first words to Bremer: "Why would you take this terrible job?" Bremer liked Bush's candor; Bush was impressed and offered Bremer the job, which was immediately accepted.[14]

On 12 May, Bremer arrived in Baghdad, and OHRA was folded into the new Coalition Provisional Authority (CPA), an organization that had been created a month before Bremer's arrival and was funded by the Department of Defense. As the chief executive of the CPA, Bremer interpreted his luncheon conversation with Bush as indicating that he was Bush's personal representative in Iraq, and that he reported directly to the president alone. This rankled many in the administration; Rumsfeld, for one, remembered that Bremer was given a great deal of latitude in his decision-making, but he dryly observed that Bremer "had a robust definition of the term 'latitude.'"[15]

Bremer came into Iraq with guns blazing. On 16 May he issued Order 1, which banned the Ba'ath Party from service in the postwar Iraqi government. This was instantly problematic, since all bureaucrats who served under Saddam were required to belong to the Ba'ath Party; thus, thousands of Iraqi officeholders were instantly unemployed. One week later, on 23 May 2003, Bremer issued Order 2, which disbanded the Iraqi army. As did the first order, this command put thousands of angry, unemployed, armed men onto the streets. While subsequent histories of the period would hold Bremer personally responsible for these decisions, both programs had been goals of the neoconservatives and several Iraqi exile groups, and the evidence suggests that they had been discussed and approved by Bush even before the invasion. Regardless, Orders 1 and 2 served primarily to add thousands of furious soldiers to the ranks of the insurgents.[16]

Bush's original reaction to the increasing violence in Iraq was initially one of defiance. On 2 July he met with reporters in the Roosevelt Room. Referring to the insurgents, he sniffed, "There are some who feel like the conditions are such that they can attack us there. My answer is, 'Bring 'em on.'" They came. In August, Zarqawi spearheaded a truck bombing on the UN Mission Center, killing the UN envoy to Iraq, Sergio Vieira de

Mello, and twenty-one other UN officials and prompting to UN to close its mission in Iraq. Zarqawi's forces also attacked the Jordanian embassy in Baghdad, and at the end of the month a Zarqawi-sponsored suicide bomber detonated his weapons on a Shi'a mosque, leaving ninety-five dead. In addition, foreign fighters flocked to Iraq to join Zarqawi's forces. In the first twelve months after the US invasion, there were 78 terrorist attacks. In the second twelve months, there were 302.[17]

As the insurgency picked up steam, so did the search for evidence to justify the American invasion. This quest centered on the elusive WMDs. On 28 May 2003, the intelligence community published a white paper arguing that two trucks loaded with lab equipment found after the invasion were part of Hussein's biological warfare program. But laboratories were not, in and of themselves, weapons. In an attempt to find actual WMDs, on 11 June 2003 Bush formed the Iraq Survey Group. David Kay, a former evaluator for the International Atomic Energy Agency who, as UN chief weapons inspector, had led the search for WMDs in Iraq after the Persian Gulf War, was placed in charge of the group, which reported directly to Tenet. In July, Kay briefed the White House on the group's progress, leaving his audience with the impression that the group would eventually find chemical weapons hidden in Iraq, but that there was doubt as to the existence of biological weapons. However, the search for both weapons systems ultimately proved fruitless, and word soon leaked that Kay was going to inform the president that there were no WMDs in Iraq.[18]

As noted in the previous chapter, Saddam had no WMDs, at least not in 2003. On 2 October, Kay confirmed this for the world, as he issued his report to Congress, which stated:

> We have found substantial evidence of an intent of senior-level Iraqi officials, including Saddam, to continue production at some future point in time of weapons of mass destruction. We have not found at this point actual weapons. It does not mean we've concluded there are no actual weapons. It means at this point in time, and it's a huge country with a lot to do, that we have not yet found weapons.[19]

Kay returned to Washington from Iraq on 3 December and reported to the CIA; he remembered his new office was windowless and without a telephone. Ostracized, on 23 January Kay resigned. Five days later he appeared before the Senate Armed Services Committee and provided testimony that confirmed what many had come to believe about the administration's arguments proclaiming the existence of WMDs in Iraq: "We were almost all wrong."[20]

Ironically, Bush later found himself agreeing with Kay—in his memoir, he admitted, "Nobody was lying. We were all wrong." But ultimately this did not matter to Bush. What mattered was his promise to protect the United States from a second attack—"The absence of WMD stockpiles did not change the fact that Saddam was a threat."[21]

Short of finding actual WMDs, the administration held on to what it knew to be a fiction—that Niger had supplied uranium to Iraq for the manufacture of nuclear weaponry. But the truth on that story was beginning to get out.

On 6 May 2003, Nicholas Kristof wrote in the *New York Times* that he had been told by a person involved in the Niger caper that more than a year ago the vice president's office asked for an investigation of the uranium deal, so a former US ambassador to Africa was dispatched to Niger. In February 2002, according to someone present at the meetings, that envoy reported to the CIA and the State Department that the information was unequivocally wrong and the documents that pointed to Niger's complicity had been forged. If Kristof's story was correct, it directly contradicted the "sixteen words" in Bush's 2003 State of the Union address.[22]

In his memoir, Cheney protested that he was "surprised" by the stories about the unnamed ambassador: "In all my years working with the intelligence community . . . I had never seen anything like this." He called Tenet, who claimed that neither he nor McLaughlin had been aware of any envoy being sent to Niger. Regardless, the agency moved quickly, starting an internal "fact gathering." But Kristof was just getting warmed up. On 13 June 2003, he asserted that documents that seemed to support the Niger uranium deal had been forged. He wrote, "Moreover, I hear from another source that the CIA's operations side and its counterterrorism center undertook their own investigations of the documents, poking around in Italy and Africa, and also concluded that they were false—a judgement that filtered to the top of the CIA."[23]

The White House soon learned that the "former U.S. ambassador to Africa" was Joseph C. Wilson IV. Wilson had joined the US Foreign Service in 1976 and from 1976 to 1998 had served in five African nations; from 1992 to 1995 he had served as US ambassador to Gabon and São Tomé and Príncipe. The administration now had a target: it sought to discredit Wilson by outing his wife, Valerie Plane Wilson, who was working as a covert agent for the CIA. The information worked its way from the top. On 12 June 2003, Cheney told Scooter Libby that Plame Wilson worked for the CIA. Then the administration started talking to reporters. That same day, Richard Armitage, described by one reporter as "an inveterate gossip," gave that tidbit to journalists Bob Woodward and Robert Novak, while talking about other subjects. On 23 June, Libby met with *New York Times* reporter Judith Miller; while Libby claimed that Cheney did not know about Wilson or the subject of his trip to Niger, Libby nevertheless told Miller that Plame Wilson worked for the CIA. One week later, on 27 June, Woodward met with Libby in his office. Woodward testified that "Joe Wilson's wife" was in his notes, but it didn't come up in the interview. Each of the leakers may well have broken the law: the Intelligence Identities Protection Act (1982) made it a crime to deliberately reveal the identity of a covert agent.[24]

As the administration systematically leaked the identity of Wilson's wife to selected reporters, all Washington was abuzz, trying to figure out the name of Kristof's "retired ambassador." Recognizing that reporters were hot on his trail, but not yet aware that the administration was leaking his wife's true identity to the press, Joe Wilson decided to out himself. On 6 July 2003, in an op-ed in the *New York Times* entitled "What I Didn't Find in Africa," Wilson revealed that it was he who had gone to Niger, and he who had found no evidence of Iraqi attempts to get uranium. According to Wilson, the office of the vice president had sent him to Niger, in order to find the answer to "a serious question. . . . I did so, and I have every confidence that the answer I provided was circulated to the appropriate officials within our government." Wilson concluded that "some of the intelligence related to Iraq's nuclear weapons program was twisted to exaggerate the Iraqi threat."[25]

The White House now had to explain why it had not acted on Wilson's supposed advice. If Wilson was telling the truth, then the White House knew that the Niger sale was bogus, while at the same time using that supposed sale to buttress its various justifications for invading Iraq. The administration tried to dismiss Wilson as a publicity hound: at his 7 July briefing, press secretary Ari Fleischer stated that "there is zero, nada, nothing new here. Ambassador Wilson, other than the fact that people now know his name, has said all this before."[26]

As the White House equivocated, it stepped up its campaign to discredit Wilson by leaking claims that it was his wife who recommended him for the trip to Niger. The day after Wilson's op-ed appeared, Novak spoke to Armitage. In the course of that phone call, Armitage observed:

"Well, you know his wife works at the CIA, and she suggested that he be sent to Niger." The next day, Novak spoke to Karl Rove. They began their conversation talking about Frances Townsend, the new homeland security adviser, and how, as a Democrat and an adviser to former attorney general Janet Reno she might be seen as an inappropriate pick for the job. But then, according to Rove, "Novak brought up Wilson's wife and told me she worked at the CIA in counterproliferation and that she—not Vice President Cheney—had suggested Wilson be sent to Niger. Novak recalled I then said, 'Oh, you know that, too.' I remember saying, 'I've heard that, too.'" In his memoir, Rove indicates he does not recall how he heard of Wilson's identity: "Novak hadn't asked me to confirm anything; it sounded to me like he had his story and was running with it, and had even talked with the CIA." But that was not the end of Rove's connection with the story. *Time* magazine reporter Matthew Cooper would later tell a grand jury that on 11 July Rove told him not to "get too far out" on the uranium story; without naming her, Rove told Cooper about Plame Wilson's job at the CIA (ending the interview with "I've already said too much"). The next day, Walter Pincus of the *Washington Post* was told by an "administration official" that the Wilson trip was "set up as a boondoggle by his wife, an analyst with the agency working on weapons of mass destruction."[27]

Of all the reporters to whom the White House had leaked Plame Wilson's identity, it was Novak who would be first to publicly reveal the administration's message. On 14 July, in his nationally syndicated column, Novak reported that "[Joe] Wilson never worked for the CIA, but his wife, Valerie Plame, is an agency operative on weapons of mass destruction. Two senior administration officials told me his wife suggested sending Wilson to Niger." Three days later, Cooper posted his version of the story on *Time*'s website.

But rather than instantly destroying Wilson's credibility, the White House plot only succeeded in leaving the White House itself open to charges of breaking the law—if it could be proved that Novak's two sources were, indeed, White House employees. A mad scramble ensued to try to find the leakers. On 28 September, the *Washington Post* reported that two unnamed White House officials had called at least six reporters to out Wilson before Novak's column ran. The source for that story was also quoted as saying, "Clearly it was meant purely and simply for revenge."[28]

In the end, the White House leaking of Plame Wilson's identity did infinitely more damage to the White House than it did to Joe Wilson. As the administration headed toward an election year, it was now faced with a Justice Department investigation of the affair, headed by a special prosecutor. For the first five months of 2004, Patrick Fitzgerald, who had tried terrorism and organized crime cases as a deputy US attorney in Manhattan, brought Rove, Novak, and Libby before his grand jury. In May he met with Cheney, and in June he met with Bush. The melodrama extended into 2005. In July of that year, Judith Miller spent seventy-five days in jail before she revealed to the grand jury that Scooter Libby had been the source for her story.[29]

On 28 October 2005, the grand jury indicted Scooter Libby for lying to federal investigators and obstructing justice. On 6 March 2007, Libby was found guilty of all charges; he was sentenced to two and a half years in prison and a $250,000 fine. On 7 July 2007, the appeals court ruled that Libby had to begin serving his sentence immediately. On the way home from Kennebunkport that day, Bush commuted the sentence but did not pardon Libby. Fitzgerald ultimately indicted Libby, decided not to bring charges against Rove, and both Armitage and Novak avoided the special prosecutor's net altogether.[30]

As the Plame Wilson scandal dogged the White House in the second half of 2003, the insurgency in Iraq only worsened. In October, during the Muslim holy month of Ramadan, four synchronous suicide attacks, including one on the International Red Cross, presaged a new phase of the carnage. Dubbed the "Ramadan Offensive," attacks increased to nearly fifty per day, at a cost of eighty-two American dead for the month of November. The administration's response was twofold. The first element was an increase in airstrikes against suspected insurgent enclaves—Operation Iron Hammer. The second was a plan to return the government of Iraq to the Iraqi people as quickly as possible. Rumsfeld presented a proposal to Bush, calling for the selection of an interim prime minister, the drafting of a constitution, and plans for parliamentary elections. The proposal also set a 30 June 2004 deadline for transferring sovereignty to the Iraqis. Rumsfeld offered Bush an analogy: "We have to take our hand off the bicycle seat."[31] For the moment, Bush agreed with Rumsfeld, and Bremer announced the timetable for the transfer of sovereignty in Iraq on 15 November.

Three weeks later, Bush decided to make a surprise visit to see the troops in Iraq. The trip, which was Card's idea, was carried out in complete secrecy. Indeed, as they went to the car that would take them from Crawford to the airport in nearby Waco—without benefit of lights or sirens—both Bush and Rice wore baseball caps to disguise their identities (prompting Bush to quip that they looked like a couple on their way to shop at Wal-Mart). They flew Air Force One from Waco to Andrews Air Force Base in Washington, where they joined Card, Joe Hagin, and Dan Bartlett and boarded a second plane designated as Air Force One, which had been made ready and shielded from the press. After evasive nighttime maneuvers that gave all aboard a queasy stomach, the presidential party landed at the newly renamed Baghdad International Airport at 5:52 p.m. on Thursday, 27 November—Thanksgiving Day. Bremer greeted the president with a jaunty "Welcome to a free Iraq." At the Bob Hope Dining Facility, where six hundred troops had gathered for a Thanksgiving dinner, Bremer and coalition commander Gen. Rick Sanchez soft-shoed their way through an intricate ruse. Both went out to the front of the hall, pretending to be the main speaker; Bremer protested, saying that he thought that the most "senior person present' was supposed to read a message from the president. Sanchez deadpanned that, since they could not agree, they might want to get someone from backstage to read the message. In response, Bremer dramatically asked, "Is there anybody back there who's more senior than us?" With that, Bush appeared from offstage, and the mess hall exploded in cheers. Bush responded by tearing up. He stayed for two hours, ate with the soldiers, and posed for every request for a photo. Then Bush got back in the air before the Secret Service in Texas was even aware that he had left.[32]

On 13 December 2003, Rumsfeld informed Bush that the military might have captured Saddam Hussein. After a twelve-hour wait to be sure they had not apprehended a double (his DNA was tested against that of one of his late sons), Rice called Bush at about 3:00 a.m. to tell him they indeed had Saddam in custody. Delta Team had found him on a farm near his hometown of Tikrit, hiding in a spider hole. After he was pulled out, the filthy but defiant prisoner announced: "My name is Saddam Hussein. I am the president of Iraq and I want to negotiate." His captor shot back, "Regards from President Bush." Within hours, Bremer announced the capture to the press—"Ladies and gentlemen, We got him." Rumsfeld was angry that Bremer made the announcement, rather than the generals who led the search or an Iraqi official. In his defense, Bremer remembered that the story "wasn't going to hold," that "we had an obligation to show the Iraqi people we actually had him," and that he informed Bush of his intentions in advance of the announcement.[33]

Regardless, the takedown of Saddam had region-wide implications. Cheney would later remark that once Saddam fell, Libya's Muammar Gaddafi "got religion"—indeed, six days after the capture of Saddam, on 19 December, Bush announced that Gaddafi had agreed to international inspections of his supposed nuclear stockpile.[34]

In his 20 January 2004 State of the Union address, Bush used the capture of Saddam Hussein to justify his invasion of Iraq:

> Had we failed to act, the dictator's weapons of mass destruction programs would continue to this day. Had we failed to act, Security Council resolutions on Iraq would have been revealed as empty threats . . . Iraq's torture chambers would still be filled with victims, terrified and innocent. The killing fields of Iraq, where hundreds of thousands of men and women and children vanished into the sands, would still be known only to the killers. For all those who love freedom and peace, the world without Saddam Hussein's regime is a better and safer place.

Yet while Bush took a brief bow, a moment of bureaucratic ineptitude that was kept from the American people showed not only that the war was far from over but also the lengths to which the Bush administration would go to keep parts of the prosecution of that war a secret.

In October 2003, Jack Goldsmith, who had clerked for Supreme Court justice Anthony Kennedy and had taught law at both the University of Virginia and the University of Chicago, replaced Jay Bybee as head of the Office of Legal Counsel (OLC). One of Goldsmith's first tasks would be to oversee the scheduled reauthorization of Operation Stellar Wind—the NSA's warrantless wiretap program (see chapter 8). The surveillance program had been reauthorized twenty-two times since its inception, and very few changes had been made in its operation. Indeed, reauthorization had been, to that point, rather pro forma. As the program had been written and approved, the OLC gave its recommendation to the attorney general, who gave his recommendation to the president, who then reauthorized the program. The deadline for the next scheduled reauthorization was 11 March 2004.[35]

On 4 March, John Ashcroft was admitted to the hospital with a particularly painful case of gallstone pancreatitis. In his absence, Ashcroft had placed James Comey, his deputy, in charge of the Justice Department. On 5 March, with Ashcroft in the hospital, Goldsmith went to the White House and informed both Alberto Gonzales and David Addington that the OLC could not reauthorize the surveillance program unless a basic change was made. Goldsmith believed that the president did not have the authority to order the collection of some of the metadata collected by the program; while he was not immediately recommending the cancellation of Stellar Wind, he made it clear that unless the scope of the program was restricted, neither could he recommend reauthorization. Addington exploded: "If you rule that way, the blood of the hundred thousand people who die in the next attack will be on your hands." Goldsmith calmly responded: "The president is free to overrule me if he wants."[36]

Three days later, on 9 March, a meeting was held in Card's office to discuss the matter. Cheney was firm: "The president may have to reauthorize without blessing of [the Department of Justice]." Robert Mueller, the director of the FBI, responded grimly: "I could have a problem with that." Later that afternoon, Cheney met with Comey, Goldsmith, and several other lawyers, demanding to know why they could not recommend reauthorization. Comey, who shared Goldsmith's concerns about the metadata, argued that despite the importance of the program, its legal basis was, "in fact, facially flawed. No lawyer reading that could reasonably rely on it." Addington stopped him: "Well, I'm a lawyer and I did." Comey shot back: "No good lawyer."[37]

The next day, 10 March—the day before Stellar Wind was set to expire—Bush was delivering a speech in Cleveland. In Washington, Cheney met with the congressional leadership to discuss the situation with the OLC. Pat Roberts of Kansas, the chairman of the Senate Intelligence Committee, retorted: "You ought to get yourself some new lawyers." Cheney then asked those in attendance if the president needed to seek additional legislative authority to keep Stellar Wind alive—the unanimous view of those in the room was that he did not. But the fact remained that nothing could be done one way or the other without Ashcroft's recommendation. Suddenly, a lot of people wanted to pay John Ashcroft a hospital visit.[38]

What followed closely resembled a Keystone Cops short film. At least half a dozen people—Card, Comey, Gonzales, Addington, possibly Patrick Philbin of the OLC, and possibly Goldsmith—all raced to the hospital, vying to be the first to make their case to the seriously ill Ashcroft. No wonder that several of the sources remember that Janet Ashcroft stuck her tongue out at them as they left. Although the memories of the principals do not agree in terms of who was in the room at what time, all sources agree that Ashcroft (who does not help the historical record here by completely ignoring the episode in his memoir) refused to sign a reauthorization of Stellar Wind.[39]

The next day, Bush overrode his attorney general and signed the re-authorization order.[40] To a president and an inner circle who believed that Operation Stellar Wind had been crucial in preventing another attack on American shores, it must have been particularly telling that that reauthorization came on the day of the most recent act of terrorism. On the morning of 11 March, four trains in Madrid's commuter system were hit by terrorist bombs—193 people were killed and about 2,000 were wounded in a pointed reminder that the War on Terror had not yet eradicated terror.

Nevertheless, when Bush reauthorized Stellar Wind over the objections of his attorney general, Comey, Goldsmith, and Mueller all drafted letters of resignation. Card made Bush aware of their plans on 12 March. After that morning's FBI briefing, Bush requested to see Comey, who had been at the meeting representing Ashcroft. Furious, Bush demanded to know why he was raising this issue "at the last minute." Comey protested: "Mr. President, your staff has known about this for weeks." Comey then told Bush that Mueller, too, was planning to resign. Moments later, Mueller confirmed that assessment in a private meeting with the president.[41]

In a scenario eerily reminiscent of the "Saturday Night Massacre," a pivotal moment in Richard Nixon's embattled presidency, Bush was now facing a major defection of troops. Should Comey, Goldsmith, and Mueller all resign, not only would it be a major embarrassment to an administration that was gearing up to run for reelection, but it was likely that another casualty of the storm that was sure to explode in the press would be the secret of Stellar Wind. In the face of what could be a serious blow to his presidency, Bush backed down. He later remembered gamely, "I was willing to defend the powers of the presidency under Article II. But not at any cost." Over the strong objections of Cheney, Bush agreed to modify those parts of the program that Justice had found problematic; the program, however, remained in place. There were no resignations over the matter, but Bush still seethed: "I made it clear to my advisers that I never wanted to be blindsided like that again."[42]

Two weeks after the imbroglio over the reauthorization of Operation Stellar Wind, the Iraqi insurgency reignited with a vengeance. The explosion came in Fallujah, a city in Anbar Province about forty miles west of Baghdad, which was well known as the hub of the insurgent resistance. On 31 March 2004, four private security agents employed in Fallujah by Blackwater USA were ambushed and killed. Their charred bodies were dragged through the streets; two of their corpses were hung from a bridge over the Euphrates. American retribution was swift. On 6 April the First Marine Expeditionary Force struck back; the new assault on the insurgents was code-named Operation Vigilant Resolve.[43]

While the Coalition hammered the insurgents, the Iraqi civilian leadership fumed. Furious that the United States had reacted to the Blackwater killings in what it believed to be a disproportionate response, the Iraqi Governing Council demanded a cease-fire—then, once one was in place, it threatened to resign if hostilities were resumed. The reaction of the Governing Council led to a debate in the White House over whether or not to halt Vigilant Resolve. Cheney wanted to continue the offensive, but Bush eventually fell on the side of diplomacy, not wanting the fragile Iraqi government to fall. On 8 April, the order came down to halt the attack; the marines who had spearheaded Vigilant Resolve were furious.[44]

Seeing an opening after Fallujah, Muqtada al-Sadr's Mahdi army attacked in southern Iraq. Another debate ensued in the White House—this time over whether to execute an arrest order on al-Sadr (an Iraqi judge had issued a warrant). The administration weighed the need to remove al-Sadr from the insurgency against the very real possibility that arresting him would make him a martyr. Rumsfeld recommended an arrest; al-Sadr was not arrested. Bremer offered his own version of why the arrest did not happen—the Iraqis wanted him arrested, but the marines did not want to provide perimeter security. As Bremer recalled: "I just think people got cold feet."[45]

Meanwhile, losses piled up. According to Bush's numbers, the United States lost 135 lives in April, and 80 more in May. Zarqawi ratcheted up the bloodshed with a series of brutal beheadings. The most notorious of these was the death of Nicholas Berg, an American radio tower technician who had been captured by Zarqawi's forces. On 7 May Zarqawi personally decapitated Berg, and on 11 May he posted the grisly execution to social media.[46]

As it was intended to do, Zarqawi's gruesome violence fanned the fires of insurgency and played a role in the decision to withdraw US forces from Fallujah on 21 May. It also played a role in speeding up the transfer of sovereignty, which had been scheduled for 30 June, to two days earlier. As the transfer was effected, Bush was attending a NATO summit in Istanbul. Rice passed him a note that read, "Mr. President Iraq is sovereign. Letter was passed from Bremer at 10:26 a.m., Iraqi time." Bush took his ever-present Sharpie pen and scribbled, "Let Freedom Reign!" on the bottom of the note. Bush then turned to his right and shook hands with his closest ally—domestic or foreign—in the war on terror: Tony Blair.[47]

The CPA was now dissolved, and the United States had divested itself of any formal role in the governance of Iraq. To paraphrase Powell, Iraq was broken, but the United States had decided not to own it. However, it soon became clear that Ayad Allawi, the new Iraqi prime minister, was no more capable of controlling the insurgency than had been the CPA. The uprising in Fallujah had left that city, as well as several others, under the control of the Sunni insurgents, and Zarqawi was now working cautiously with other rebel groups. In early August, fighting broke out between American forces and al-Sadr's Mahdi army in the city of Najaf, one of the most sacred cities of Shi'a Islam. That battle, which stretched into September, led to a truce that allowed the Mahdi to withdraw to the north, to Sadr City. That fall saw heavy fighting in Sadr City and more American losses. On 4 September the Pentagon announced that the number of American casualties in Iraq had hit one thousand. And yet, the United States still had 150,000 soldiers on the ground in Iraq, fighting an insurgency that was only growing.[48]

And it was now the middle of Bush's campaign for reelection.

# 11

★ ★ ★ ★ ★

# REELECTING A PRESIDENT

Prior to 1945, Americans had been decidedly unwilling to jettison their president in the middle of a war. Five wartime presidents had run for reelection; all five of them not only were reelected but also won more votes than they had won four years earlier (1804, Thomas Jefferson and the Barbary War; 1816, James Madison and the War of 1812; 1864, Abraham Lincoln and the Civil War; and 1945, Franklin D. Roosevelt and World War II). However, since 1945, being a wartime president did not guarantee either reelection or renomination. While two wartime presidents had been resoundingly reelected (1964, Lyndon Johnson and Vietnam War; 1972, Richard Nixon and Vietnam War), both Harry Truman (1952, Korean War) and ultimately Lyndon Johnson (1968, Vietnam War) ran for the nomination of their party and failed.

Guaranteed of his party's nomination in 2004, Bush would not meet the immediate fate of either Truman or Johnson. But Bush's reelection was far from a sure thing. Bush was now in the opposite position that he had been in in 2000, when so many Americans had been tired of Bill Clinton; thanks largely to the escalating Iraqi insurgency, they were now growing tired of Bush. Bush began his presidency with a 57 percent approval rating. That rating stayed fairly steady until the events of September 11, at which time Bush's approval rating skyrocketed to 90 percent. But from that point, it had been a gradual but steady downhill slide. By January 2004, Bush's approval rating was at 60 percent. It would continue to drop through the first half of the year, until, at the time of his renomination in August, he was at 49 percent and dropping. In the pages of the *New Republic*, pollster Geoff Garin observed that the growing antipathy toward Bush was "as strong as anything I've experienced in 25 years now of polling." Columnist Robert Novak, who had contributed to the situation by becoming a pawn in the White House skewering of Valerie Plame Wilson, described it as a "hatred . . . that I have never seen in forty-four years of campaign watching."[1]

To make matters worse, two events, both occurring in the spring of 2004 as the Bush campaign was just getting rolling, threatened to plunge his ratings even lower. The first, and by far the most damaging, were the revelations about Abu Ghraib. Located some twenty miles to the west of Baghdad, Abu Ghraib had long held a reputation as being one of Saddam's most brutal prisons, one where his enemies went to be raped or tortured, or from where they simply vanished. The US Army inherited Abu Ghraib in 2003 and renamed it the Baghdad Central Correctional Facility. Its new commander, Brig. Gen. Janis Karpinski, assured an interviewer that those prisoners still incarcerated there were receiving "the best care available."[2]

In early 2004, CBS News picked up on a story of acts of abuse perpetrated by the American military guards at Abu Ghraib. One of its sources was an army reservist and former Abu Ghraib guard, Staff Sergeant Ivan "Chip" Frederick, who was awaiting court-martial for several counts of abuse. Frederick revealed the existence of photographs that, although they were not in his possession, would document the cruelty. CBS obtained the photos, which left no doubt as to the extent of the depravity at Abu Ghraib. They showed inmates wearing hoods and connected to what seemed to be electrical wires; an inmate cowering in front of a snarling German shepherd guard dog; guards punching inmates; a hooded inmate being forced to keep his balance while standing on a box; naked inmates piled on top of each other in a human pyramid; and naked inmates being forced to masturbate in front of female guards—a deliberate breach of Muslim religious principles. Several of the photos showed guards giving the thumbs-up and laughing at the humiliated inmates.[3]

CBS kept its story under wraps for three weeks, ostensibly to get a reaction from the Pentagon. Rather than give a reaction for the record, Gen. Richard Myers, head of the Joint Chiefs of Staff, attempted to delay the publication of the story, arguing that its release would be detrimental to the morale of the troops, then fighting in the Battle of Fallujah. But soon CBS found itself in a race with the competition—investigative reporter Seymour Hersh, who also had possession of the photographs, was preparing a story on Abu Ghraib for the *New Yorker*. Despite Myers's pleas, CBS ran its Abu Ghraib story on *60 Minutes II* on 28 April 2004. The photographs caused an explosion of indignation, as did Hersh's story on the abuses, which was published two days later.[4]

In his memoir, CBS anchor Dan Rather claimed that the real story was a cover-up that kept the public from finding out that the Abu Ghraib guards had simply been following orders: "Then as now, one must conclude that shielding the higher-ups was deliberate." An alternative story is that the military kept the extent of the abuse from the administration. Bush had been told by Rumsfeld about the existence of the photos in January 2004 and was assured that the military was conducting an investigation. But he did not see the photographs until some of them were aired on *60 Minutes II*, and he did not see the complete set of photographs until the next day, when he and Cheney viewed them at the Pentagon. In his memoir, Bush claimed that he "felt sick, really sick," at the photographs; he also "felt blindsided" by the fact that he was exposed to the photographs at the same time as the viewing public. He stated, "I was not happy with the way the situation had been handled. Neither was the team at the White House." In his memoir, Powell agreed with Bush and was unsparing with his criticism of the chiefs: "The Abu Ghraib photos were available to senior Pentagon leaders, but it does not appear that Secretary Rumsfeld saw them, nor were they shown at the White House. A fuse was burning, but no one made the senior leadership aware that a bomb was about to go off. . . . The President was not told early."[5]

In the wake of the Abu Ghraib revelations, Rumsfeld found himself in the crosshairs. Matthew Dowd, one of Bush's chief reelection strategists, called for Rumsfeld's immediate dismissal, and he was but one of many.[6] Rumsfeld obliged. On 5 May he gave Bush a letter in which he wrote, "I want you to know you have my resignation as Secretary of Defense anytime you feel it would be helpful to you." Bush did not accept it. Two days later, after testifying on Abu Ghraib on Capitol Hill, Rumsfeld attempted once more to resign, handing Bush a note that read in part: "I have concluded that the damage from the acts of abuse that happened on my watch, by individuals for whose conduct I am ultimately responsible, can best be responded to by my resignation." Again, Bush refused to accept the letter, but this time he paused to seriously consider Rumsfeld's offer. After reflection, Bush concluded that "there was no obvious replacement for Don, and I couldn't afford to create a vacuum at the top of Defense." On 11 May, at the request of the president, Cheney went to the Pentagon and convinced Rumsfeld to stay on. Rumsfeld withdrew his resignation. In an awkward coda to the crisis, on 24 May, Rumsfeld banned the personal use of cameras by the US military in Iraq.[7]

The second set of revelations were nowhere near as dramatic as those surrounding Abu Ghraib, but they were damaging to Bush nonetheless in that they fed a narrative that the Democrats were sure to exploit—that the intelligence community had missed the importance of several warning signs about the 11 September attacks. There had been much wrangling over both the need for, and the structure of, an independent investigation into the events surrounding the attacks of 11 September 2001. Believing that the Democrats were planning to use such an investigation to lay the lion's share of the blame for the attacks at the White House door, the administration was adamantly opposed to such an investigation. Publicly, it argued that since the House and Senate had already established a joint inquiry into the attacks (an inquiry that concluded that the intelligence community had pertinent information that was relevant to the 9/11 attacks, and it had not "paid sufficient attention to potential for domestic attack"), another investigation would simply lead to a duplication of effort. But such arguments were in vain. Pressure from the surviving families of the 11 September victims, and the lobbying of Congressman Tim Roemer (D-IN) and Senators John McCain and Joe Lieberman led to the creation of the National Commission on Terrorist Attacks upon the United States—known to most as the 9/11 Commission.[8]

Former secretary of state Henry Kissinger was chosen as the commission's chair, but his nomination ran up against the powerful lobby of the families of victims of the attacks. They demanded that Kissinger disclose the names of any clients of his firm, Kissinger Associates, that might be either Arabs or commercial airlines. As a result of the attendant publicity, Kissinger stepped down and was replaced by Thomas Kean, the former Republican governor of New Jersey then serving as president of Drew University. Kean, described by one observer as the "humblest rich aristocrat you'd ever meet,"[9] had no foreign policy or national security experience. That was provided by his cochair, Lee Hamilton, formerly a seventeen-term Democratic House member from Indiana who had served as chair of the House Foreign Affairs and Committee and the Intelligence

Committee and was then serving as the head of the Woodrow Wilson International Center for Scholars.[10]

The commission spent its first year investigating the tragedy, as well as enduring constant struggles with the White House over the release of sensitive documents that the commission believed to be necessary for its investigation. Of particular importance to the commission were the President's Daily Briefs (PDBs); these documents took on a heightened significance after CBS News reported the existence of the 6 August 2001 PDB entitled "Bin Laden Determined to Strike in U.S." (see chapter 7). Indeed, the first interim report of the commission directly fingered the Defense Department for not being timely with answering commission requests for information, a problem the report claimed was "becoming potentially serious."[11] Kean threatened to use his subpoena power (Kean: "Any document that has to do with this investigation cannot be beyond our reach. I will not stand for it"), and the White House finally backed down, giving the commission controlled access to all PDBs. Bush and Cheney together spoke to the commission, but neither man's testimony was given under oath, and neither session was transcribed.[12]

It was the spectacle of the commission's public hearings that most directly threatened the upcoming Bush campaign. In late March and early April 2004, many of the big names of the Clinton and Bush administrations testified. The most potentially damaging to Bush was the testimony of Richard Clarke. To a cynic, Clarke's testimony might have appeared to be part of a public relations campaign. On 21 March, he appeared on *60 Minutes*; the next day, his book *Against All Enemies* was released with attendant publicity; three days later Clarke began what would be two days of testimony before the 9/11 Commission. In his opening statement, Clarke shocked everyone present and viewing the hearing by offering an apology: "It is finally a forum where I can apologize to the loved ones of the victims of 9/11. . . . Your government failed you . . . and I failed you. . . . And for that failure, I would ask—once all the facts are out—for your understanding and for your forgiveness." Clarke testified that the Bush administration "considered terrorism an important issue but not an urgent issue," and that it had been a mistake to extend the War on Terror into Iraq ("In the fifteen hours of testimony, no one asked me what I thought about the President's invasion of Iraq. And the reason I am strident in my criticism of the President of the United States is because by invading Iraq—something I was not asked about by the Commission, but something I chose to write about a lot in the book—by invading Iraq, the President of the United States has greatly undermined the war on terrorism"). The White House response to Clarke's testimony was weak. After months of wrangling between the White House and the commission, Condoleezza Rice testified on 8 April; during that tense testimony, she admitted to the existence of the 6 August 2001 PDB and agreed to declassify and release it.[13]

On 22 July 2004—one week before the start of the Democratic National Convention—the 9/11 Commission released its report, which was a scathing indictment of official ineptitude prior to 11 September 2001. From the second paragraph of the report: "The nation was unprepared." Since its inception, it had been assumed that the commission would recommend some amount of additional centralization of the nation's intelligence community, and following the public testimony it was generally assumed that the CIA would take a hit. Both things happened. Among the commission's recommendations was the creation of a National Counterterrorism Center and the strengthening of congressional oversight "to improve quantity and accountability." Most important, and ultimately most controversial, was the creation of a new director of national intelligence (DNI). If this recommendation were to be adopted, the CIA director would no longer coordinate the nation's intelligence efforts. As Kean had hoped, the recommendations were made unanimously—there was no minority report.[14]

But the war was not the only issue that was hurting Bush in the spring of 2004. Bush had also drawn the ire of many conservatives within his own party with his advocacy of a policy goal that had long been dear to his heart. As Bush saw it, Medicare was not only careening toward insolvency (in his memoir, he derisively labeled the system a "$13 trillion unfunded liability"). It was also outdated, particularly in that the program did not cover prescription drugs. Therefore, Bush recommended changes to Medicare on two fronts. First, he proposed adding a prescription drug benefit. Second, he proposed delivering that benefit through private insurance plans, thus bringing market forces to bear on the aging system. Bush proposed that any senior who wanted to use the new prescription drug benefit would have to choose a private plan instead of Medicare. This would entail changing the funding formula, so that those insurance companies and Medicare were competing fairly.[15]

The bill initially met opposition from both sides of the aisle. Republicans balked at the cost of the drug benefit—Bush's estimation in his memoirs was $634 billion over ten years.[16] Democrats were also concerned about the cost of the plan, as they cringed at the thought of seniors seeing their overall Medicare benefits decrease to help offset the cost of the drug prescription benefit. The bill was also opposed by several powerful interest groups, most notably the American Association of Retired Persons (AARP). Nevertheless, a strong White House lobbying effort led to both the Senate and the House passing separate versions of the bill in June 2003. In reconciliation, a trigger proposal was inserted—if costs rose faster than expected, Congress would be required to amend the program. The reconciled bill also emphasized health savings accounts (HSAs), which had been a part of the House bill. These HSAs combined low-premium, high-deductible insurance with a tax-advantaged savings account to pay medical expenses. Both employers and individuals could contribute to that account, which could be transferred from job to job. Largely thanks to the insertion of HSAs, the AARP withdrew its opposition and supported the conference version of the reform bill.

Yet the massive cost of the program still unnerved many Republican legislators. On 21 November 2003, the day of the final vote in Congress, Bush was flying back from London (following a state visit that included a meeting with Queen Elizabeth II); he made phone calls from Air Force One to wavering members. The first House vote, taken at 3:00 a.m., came up short of victory for Bush. However, Speaker of the House Dennis Hastert (R-IL) proved himself to be a cagy parliamentarian—instead of closing the vote, he kept it open, which allowed the president to continue his lobbying. One deal that he cut would become important two years later: in return for his support, Bush promised Congressman Trent Franks (R-AZ) that the next list of candidates to fill a Supreme Court vacancy would not include the name of Alberto Gonzales.[17] On 22 November, the House passed the measure, 220–215; three days later, the Senate passed the bill, 54–44.

On 8 December 2003, Bush signed the Medicare Prescription Drug Modernization Act into law. While the bill included much of what Bush wanted, it came with a hefty price tag, and it imposed that price tag on a budget already encumbered by the War on Terror. It also created a new level of federal bureaucracy. Many Republicans, even those who voted for the bill, began to grumble that Bush's spendthrift proclivities and seeming willingness to expand the reach of the federal government undercut his claim to being a true conservative.

In early 2004 Bush was clearly a wounded candidate, and the blood on the water brought more than the usual number of Democratic challengers.

The list of hopefuls included Ret. Gen. Wesley Clark, Ohio representative Dennis Kucinich, Rev. Al Sharpton of New York, Missouri representative Richard Gephardt, former Illinois senator Carol Mosely Brown, Florida senator Bob Graham, and Connecticut senator and recent vice presidential candidate Joe Lieberman. But each of these candidates would fade away, as the primary season quickly developed into a three-man race.

Karl Rove professed to be the most worried about the telegenic senator from North Carolina, John R. Edwards, who had made a name for himself as a successful trial lawyer with high-profile victories against the insurance industry. However, Edwards had left himself vulnerable with his vote in favor of the Iraq War Resolution, a vote that became a greater liability with every passing day of the insurgency. So too did Massachusetts senator John F. Kerry, who hoped that his service in Vietnam (two tours of duty as the officer in charge of a Patrol Fast Craft—a "Swift Boat"— and the recipient of a Silver Star, a Bronze Star with Combat V, and three qualifying wounds that earned him three Purple Hearts) would mitigate his vote on Iraq. Yet Kerry has also been a member of Vietnam Veterans against the War, and on 22 April 1971 he had testified before a Senate Committee investigating possible ways to end the war ("How do you ask a man to be the last man to die in Vietnam? How do ask a man to be the last man to die for a mistake?"). None of this concerned the loquacious former governor of Vermont Howard B. Dean III, who went all in on an antiwar candidacy. In the early going, Dean held the front-runner position. His message seemed to resonate with college students and the far-left wing of his party. Dean also proved himself to be a master of the nascent art of online fundraising—he raised $40 million on the internet alone, the vast majority of it from individual small donors.[18]

It looked as if Kerry's candidacy would be an early casualty to the Dean juggernaut. The assumption of a Kerry implosion was so widespread that when Kerry called Al Gore to question him about his endorsement of Dean, Gore hung up on him.[19] However, Kerry refused to lie down. First, he fired his campaign manager and replaced him with an aide to Teddy Kennedy. Then he mortgaged his home, which gave much needed capital to his campaign. This infusion of cash propelled Kerry to a first-place finish in the Iowa caucuses on 19 January 2004, with Edwards placing second and Dean third. A surprised and exhausted Dean faced his supporters that evening and began to gesticulate and scream at them—ostensibly to gear them up for the next contest, but in a manner that made him seem completely out of control. "Dean's Scream" was lampooned everywhere on the media, and it helped Kerry, now billing himself as "Comeback Kerry," to victory in New Hampshire on 27 February 2004, winning 38 percent to Dean's 26 percent. Edwards won South Carolina as expected, and Dean withdrew from the race. But on 2 March Kerry won nine of the ten states in play, thus becoming his party's presumptive nominee.

The Bush campaign had been privately hoping to run against Dean. Bush saw Dean as "loud, shrill, and undisciplined. I was pulling hard for him to get the nomination." According to media adviser Mark McKinnon, the Bush message against Dean would be "sort of 'steady' versus 'crazy.'" Rove earthily remembered that "we knew we could beat him like a drum." But John Kerry was now the presumptive nominee of the Democratic Party—and running against a decorated Vietnam War hero worried the Bush campaign.[20]

To combat all this, Rove set out to make Bush a hero in another war—the American culture war. One of the most influential books written on American politics in the first decade of the twenty-first century was Thomas Frank's *What's the Matter with Kansas? How Conservatives Won the Heart of America*. Released in June 2004, and written with a biting tone, the book described how Kansans had convinced themselves to vote against their own best economic interests so that they could instead defend their cultural values against what they believed was an assault by liberal elites. Frank argued that this rekindling of the "culture wars" featured a reversal of politics as usual, where the Democrats had been the "party of workers, of the poor, of the weak and the victimized," but now, in what he called the "Great Backlash," the Republicans had become the party of those who felt oppressed. To Franks, the basic focus of the new Republican Party was that "culture outweighs economics as a matter of public concern." Thus, by promising that it would protect their cultural values, the Republican Party captured the heart of working-class people and rode their votes to victory.[21]

To those who believed they had been victimized by the values of the liberal elites, two issues seemed to validate their fears. In July 2003, in *Lawrence v. Texas*,[22] the Supreme Court overturned a Texas law that criminalized sodomy. In so doing, the Court not only overturned its own precedent of only seventeen years earlier (*Bowers v. Hardwick*,[23] which had found a Georgia sodomy law to be constitutional), but it invalidated similar sodomy laws in thirteen states. In an angry dissent, Justice Antonin Scalia predicted that the Court was now going to have to consider same-sex marriage. It soon looked like Scalia was right. On 18 November 2003, in *Goodridge v. Department of Public Health*,[24] the Massachusetts Supreme Court ruled that same-sex marriage was a right under the state constitution. Conservatives now feared that the same US Supreme Court majority that had found sodomy unconstitutional in *Lawrence* would uphold *Goodridge* and find same-sex marriage to be a federally protected right.

The fight over same-sex marriage coincided with the debate over partial-birth abortion. The term refers to any abortion in which the life of the fetus is terminated after its removal from the mother's body. Getting a ban on this procedure had been a mantra for evangelicals. Republican Congresses had twice passed an act prohibiting the practice during the Clinton era; twice Clinton vetoed the bill. On 21 October 2003 the House passed a bill banning partial-birth abortion under penalty of a fine or two years' imprisonment; the Senate passed the bill on 21 October. After an unsuccessful attempt to amend the bill in conference to include a statement of support for *Roe v. Wade*, the bill went to Bush's desk.[25]

Since 2000, one of Bush and Rove's main goals had been to increase their support among conservative evangelicals. The issues of gay marriage and partial-birth abortions were made to order for this strategy. On 5 November 2003, Bush signed the Partial Birth Abortion Act into law.[26] Two months later, in his 20 January 2004 State of the Union address, he defended the "sanctity of marriage," arguing—with the justices of the Supreme Court sitting immediately in front of him in the front row of the House chamber—that "activist judges . . . have begun redefining marriage by court order, without regard for the will of the people." Lines had been drawn. On 12 February, San Francisco mayor Gavin Newsom proclaimed that the California Constitution gave him the right to allow same-sex marriages. In direct response to Newsom's announcement, on 24 February Bush announced his support for a proposal that had been introduced in Congress in May 2002, and one that Rove had been urging the president to support—an amendment to the US Constitution which would define marriage as between a man and a woman.[27]

Bush's stand on gay marriage was relatively safe politics—64 percent of Americans already opposed same-sex marriage. Moreover, that fall thirteen states would have constitutional amendments banning gay marriage on their ballots, and support for those amendments was polling strong. But Bush's stance on the marriage amendment put him at odds with his vice president. Cheney's daughter was gay, and he was on record as saying that "freedom means freedom for everyone" to enter "into any kind of relationship they want." Perhaps as a result of this, Bush didn't push hard for the marriage amendment, which never gained the required two-thirds vote to move out of the House. But Bush did endorse civil unions for same-sex couples—a stance that put him at odd with his party's platform—thus leaving the matter up to the states.[28]

Bush also profited from a Kerry misstep. On 16 March in a speech at Marshall University, Kerry tried to explain his vote for an $87 billion supplemental appropriations for the war in Iraq and Afghanistan. But what came out of his mouth was a classic political malapropism: "I actually did vote for the $87 billion before I voted against it."[29] While the Bush campaign immediately used the Marshall speech as evidence for Kerry's proclivity to flip-flop on issues, the fact of the matter was that neither Bush nor Kerry had had a particularly good spring. In an attempt to jump-start his campaign, Bush found himself considering doing something that his father had considered doing in 1992—dumping his vice president.

In mid-2003 Cheney met with Bush three times; each time the vice president offered to withdraw from the ticket. According to Cheney, the first two times Bush effectively ignored the suggestion, but the third time was the charm. Bush seriously considered this offer, later recalling in his memoirs that "accepting Dick's offer would be one way to demonstrate that I was in charge." Bush mulled over the offer with Card, Rove, and other advisers (Rove later remembered that he did not support dumping Cheney). According to Bush, Senate majority leader Bill Frist was his top choice to replace Cheney. Nevertheless, after reflection, Bush decided to keep Cheney on the ticket. He expounded on his reasons for doing so in his memoir: "I hadn't picked him to be a political asset; I had chosen him to help me do the job. That was exactly what he had done. He accepted any assignment I asked. He gave me his unvarnished opinions. He understood that I made the final decisions. When we disagreed, he kept our differences private. Most important, I trusted Dick."[30]

On 26 July, the Democratic National Convention opened in Boston. Kerry had chosen Barack Obama, then a state senator from Illinois who was running for that fall for a US Senate seat, to deliver the keynote address. Obama made the most of his moment, as he introduced himself to the American people with a speech that, as Kerry remembered it, "[blew] the roof off the Boston Garden":[31]

John Kerry believes in America. And he knows that it's not enough for just some of us to prosper. For alongside our famous individualism, there's another ingredient in the American saga. A belief that we're all connected as one people. If there is a child on the south side of Chicago who can't read, that matters to me, even if it's not my child. If there's a senior citizen somewhere who can't pay for their prescription drugs, and has to choose between medicine and the rent, that makes my life poorer, even if it's not my grandparent. If there's an Arab American family being rounded up without benefit of an attorney or due process, that threatens my civil liberties. It is that fundamental belief, it is that fundamental belief, I am my brother's keeper, I am my sister's keeper that makes this country work. It's what allows us to pursue our individual dreams and yet still come together as one American family. E pluribus unum. Out of many, one.[32]

Kerry's original choice for his running mate had been Republican senator John McCain. The negotiations reached an elevated level of seriousness before McCain finally refused the offer. With that, Kerry settled on John Edwards, who had finished second overall in the Democratic primaries that spring. Kerry's acceptance speech centered on his service in Vietnam, opening with the line: "I'm John Kerry and I'm reporting for duty."[33]

Then came what Kerry would later call the "Guns of August"[34]—the one-month period between the end of the Democratic National Convention and the convening of the Republican National Convention on 30 August that sent the Kerry campaign reeling. It began with Kerry's decision not to accept federal matching funds during the primaries. This had left his campaign cash-poor, and he had been unable to raise substantial amounts of private donations. Thus, by the time of the convention his campaign was effectively broke. While Kerry would receive federal matching funds for the fall campaign the minute after he was named his party's nominee, he now had to decide how to spread that relatively small amount over a thirteen-week period between 30 July and 2 November. On the other side, even though he, too had refused to take federal matching funds during the primaries, Bush was nevertheless flush with private donations. As Rove expected, the Kerry campaign chose to conserve its finances in August (a decision that was second-guessed by virtually everyone in the Kerry campaign after the election), thus giving the Bush campaign and its surrogates a four-week window to bash a Kerry campaign that didn't have the money to counterpunch.

Into this window of opportunity leapt the Swift Boat Veterans for

Truth, thirteen veterans who had served with Kerry on board his Patrol Craft Fast in Vietnam. These veterans had held a press conference in May during which they disputed Kerry's portrayal of his war record. Now, in August, the group that the press had dubbed the "Swifties" had raised enough money to buy advertising. The first ad, entitled "Any Questions?," ran in early August and claimed that Kerry was "lying about his record" in Vietnam. John McCain defended his fellow Vietnam vet and angrily denounced the ad, but it had traction. A second ad ran on 20 August: this one, entitled "Sellout," included footage of Kerry's 1971 testimony to Congress for Veterans against the War, intercut with commentary from the veterans who were censuring him ("John Kerry gave the enemy for free what I and many of my comrades in North Vietnam in the prison camps took torture to avoid saying").[35]

Bush never mentioned the Swift Boaters in his memoir; Rove, however, gloated: "I had no role in any of it, though the Swifties did a damned good job." Rove was right. The Swifties spent a mere $1 million on their ads. Kerry's media adviser certainly understated the case when he later quipped that "it was probably the most cost efficient million bucks ever spent in the history of presidential politics, short of the [1964 Lyndon Johnson] 'Daisy Ad.'" While it was argued that the advertisements were in violation of the Bipartisan Campaign Reform Act of 2002 (the McCain-Feingold Act), the criticism never stuck. For one thing, the Kerry campaign spent only $406,000 to respond to the Swifties that August; during the same period, the Bush campaign spent $32 million to hammer its message home. For another, Kerry himself refused to directly address and refute the claims or create response ads—decisions he would later admit to be mistakes. The Swift Boat ads, and the doubt they sowed about Kerry as a leader, resulted in Bush closing the gap in August. On 1 August, immediately following the Democratic National Convention, Kerry led Bush 48.0 to 46.3; now, exactly one month later, on the eve of the Republican Convention, Kerry had lost considerable ground and was now trailing Bush 46.0 to 45.3.[36]

The Republican National Convention, held in New York City from 30 August to 2 September, was a completely anticlimactic affair. It was obvious that the locale was chosen to allow the party and its president to try to rekindle the nationalism—and the high presidential polling numbers—that had immediately followed the attacks of 11 September 2001. Completely devoid of any drama (to hold viewer interest, Bush and

Cheney were renominated at the end of a two-day "rolling roll call"), Bush's acceptance address began as a tepid affair, with Bush talking about his plans for an "ownership society" that would allow for an expansion of HSAs and permit workers to privately invest a portion of their Social Security payroll taxes. But Bush hit his stride when he addressed the war, declaring that "freedom is on the march" in Iraq and Afghanistan. The peroration spoke to Bush's implicit compact with the American people, a promise he believed he had kept through preventative war in Iraq. It also brought the delegates to their feet: "So I forget the lessons of September the 11th and take the word of a madman? Or do I take action to defend our country? Faced with that choice, I will defend America every time."

Five days after Bush accepted his party's nomination for a second term, the death toll for American soldiers in Iraq hit one thousand.[37]

Kerry had planned a fall campaign in which he would challenge Bush's bona fides as a wartime leader and offer himself—a veteran with extensive congressional experience in foreign policy—as a more thoughtful, better-prepared commander in chief. The Swift Boat ads and Kerry's weak response put a dent in this strategy. Then Kerry got a reprieve, as Bush was hit with a media exposé of his own.

Mary Mapes, a producer for CBS's *60 Minutes Wednesday* who with Dan Rather had helped break the story of the abuses at Abu Ghraib, came into possession of six documents that appeared to call into question Bush's service in the National Guard from 1968 to 1973. The story, which had been lying in wait for decades (see chapter 1), claimed that Bush's commanding officer (then deceased), Lt. Col. Jerry Killian, had not approved Airman Bush's leave from the Guard in 1972 to work on the Alabama Senate campaign of Winton Blount, but that Bush went anyway. If true, Bush had been absent without leave. The story also claimed that Killian had ordered Bush to take a physical examination that was never completed, and that Killian had been pressured from higher up to write better reports on Bush than his performance warranted. The story also included an interview with Ben Barnes, in 1968 the Speaker of the Texas House of Representatives, who claimed that he had been pressured to show the younger Bush preferential treatment and procure for him a place in the National Guard, thus protecting him from active duty in Vietnam. Mapes's story seemed solid enough. Killian's commander, Gen. Bobby Hodges, corroborated it; moreover, a forensic document analyst pronounced the documents to be genuine. Mapes later remembered that she "felt that I was in the clear, that I had done my job."[38] On 8 September, Rather broadcast the story.

Even before the broadcast was off the air, bloggers (such as those at Freerepublic.com) were posting messages asserting that the documents on which the story was based were fakes. One blogger, who called himself Buckhead, was particularly indignant, claiming that the font was wrong and that proportional spacing, as well as the ability to produce a superscripted "th" at the end of numbers (e.g., "20th") did not exist in 1973, even though superscripts were used in the memos. Conservative websites turned their guns on CBS with a vengeance, and competitor networks began to investigate the authenticity of the documents. To make matters worse for Mapes, Hodges changed his story and claimed that now he too believed the documents to be forgeries.[39]

On 20 September CBS News president Andrew Heyward offered a public apology: "Based on what we now know, CBS News cannot prove that the documents are authentic, which is the only acceptable journalistic standard to justify using them in the report. We should not have used them. That was a mistake, which we deeply regret."[40] The network established a review panel, headed by former attorney general Richard Thornburgh. In February 2005, at the conclusion of that panel's investigation, Mapes was terminated by CBS, and the resignation of three others was demanded and received by the network. In March 2005, Rather stepped down as the anchor of the *CBS Evening News*.

In the wake of CBS's blunder, Bush began to pull away. On 27 September, he opened his largest lead of the campaign, 50.0 to 43.6.[41]

The first debate between Bush and Kerry, held on 30 September at the University of Miami, featured a tired and clearly agitated Bush, who lost on style points to an upbeat, confident Kerry. In much the same way that Gore was tagged four years earlier, a split screen showed Bush smirking and scowling, clearly disgusted by some of Kerry's answers. There was no doubt that Kerry looked presidential—a primary goal for any debater. Bush tried to laugh off the setback. Several days later, a story surfaced that a strange wrinkle in Bush's suit was actually a radio receiver connected to a transmitter controlled by Karl Rove, who was, according to the story, providing Bush with answers. Bush dismissed the story with a joke: "It's too bad I didn't have a radio, so Karl could have told me to quit grimacing." Nevertheless, Kerry regained the ground that had been lost by the

Swift Boat and National Guard imbroglios—five days after the first debate, the race was a statistical dead heat, with Bush at 47.5, Kerry at 45.9.[42] It was a now a new election.

The Bush campaign looked to Cheney to stop the bleeding by giving a strong showing in the vice presidential debate, held on 5 October at Cleveland's Case Western Reserve University). This Cheney did, giving a blunder-free performance. Kerry would later blame Edwards for not seizing the moment ("I hadn't seen the Mr. October I'd been promised").[43] Indeed, the only truly memorable exchange—one that would have significance later in the campaign—came over the expected question dealing with Bush's call for a constitutional ban on same-sex marriages. Edwards stunned both the audience and Cheney when he responded: "Let me say first that I think the vice president and his wife love their daughter. I think they love her very much. And you can't have anything but respect for the fact that they're willing to talk about the fact that they have a gay daughter, the fact that they embrace her. It's a wonderful thing. And there are millions of parents like that who love their children." Cheney declined to respond. The polls over the next few days stayed essentially the same— the best possible outcome, short of a knockout, that the Bush campaign could hope for. The second presidential debate—held three days later on 8 October at Washington University in St. Louis—was a listless affair that saw no real movement in the polls.

Like the first debate, the third and final debate, held on 13 October at Arizona State University, was a game changer—both for what was said during the debate and for the spirited postdebate response. Moderator Bob Schieffer opened the door by asking the candidates whether they believed that homosexuality was a choice. Kerry's answer was a clear attempt to peel undecided evangelicals away from Bush: "We're all God's children, Bob, and I think if you were to talk to Dick Cheney's daughter, who is a lesbian, she would tell you that she's being who she was, she's being who she was born as." The next question was Kerry's, so Bush was not afforded an opportunity to respond to his opponent's thrust. But the postdebate response to Kerry was overwhelmingly negative, so much so that his campaign manager, Mary Beth Cahill, was forced to publicly maintain that it was the Kerry campaign's view that Mary Cheney was "fair game." That did nothing to mollify the Second Lady. A livid Lynne Cheney turned on Kerry: "The only thing I can conclude is that he [Kerry] is not a good man. I'm speaking as a mom. What a cheap and tawdry political trick."[44]

In a December 2004 postmortem panel discussion on the election,

Democratic strategist Bob Shrum tried to explain away Kerry's comment as he spoke to another panelist—the vice president's other daughter, Liz: "There was no motive. There was no plan. There was no strategy. John Kerry was actually trying to pay a compliment to your family." Liz Cheney was having none of it: "I do feel that Bob and I reside on different planets."[45] Shrum's mea culpa does not hold water. When tied to Edwards's comment in the vice presidential debate, Kerry's comment in the third presidential debate strongly whiffs of a conscious strategy—one to separate Bush from social conservatives by consistent reminders that his running mate's daughter was gay.

It is equally clear that the strategy backfired. Within three days of the debate, Bush's polling numbers took a sharp uptick, and Kerry's took an equally sharp downturn. Bush now led the race 49 to 45. What the Bush campaign had taken to calling the "Mary Cheney bounce" had provided the cushion Bush would need to survive the last major body blow of the campaign.

Had the public known that, at precisely this moment, Bush was keeping the press from exposing one of his most closely guarded secrets, it is possible the election would not have been playing out so close. Early in October, the administration learned that *New York Times* reporters James Risen and Eric Lichtblau were about to publish a story that would expose Operation Stellar Wind. In an attempt to convince the *Times* to hold its story, Bush met personally with *Times* publisher Arthur Sulzberger Jr. and editor Bill Keller. They agreed to postpone its publication, but days before the election, the *Times* let the administration know that it once again planned to run the story. This time, Gonzales met with the reporters and their editors. After hearing his pitch, one of the reporters asked Gonzales, "Do you have any problems sleeping at night?" Nevertheless, the *Times* once again promised to sit on the story. That promise would hold for another year.[46]

On 29 October, five days before Election Day, Kerry caught a last-minute break. Al Jazeera, an Arabic media conglomerate, released a tape of Usama bin Laden, addressing the world for the first time since the 11 September attacks. Despite having lived in hiding for almost three years after taking flight from the mountains of Tora Bora, bin Laden looked fit, almost regal. In his fourteen-and-a-half-minute message, bin Laden purported to discuss "the ideal way to prevent another Manhattan." He blamed the United States for the attacks, specifically because the United States had allowed Israel to invade Lebanon in 1982: "The events of September 11th came as a reply to those great wrongs—should a man be blamed for defending his sanctuary?" Looking forward, he predicted more pain unless all Americans accepted Islam: "I tell you in truth that your security is not in the hands of Kerry, nor Bush, nor al-Qaida. No. Your security is in your own hands. . . . And Allah is our Guardian and Helper, while you have no Guardian or Helper. All peace be upon he who follows the guidance."[47]

The tape served as a reminder that the Bush administration had not yet caught bin Laden, and that the War on Terror was still raging on. Kerry underscored the point: "Let me make it clear, crystal clear: as Americans, we are absolutely united in our determination to hunt down and destroy Usama bin Laden and the terrorists. They are barbarians, and I will stop at absolutely nothing to hunt down, capture or kill the terrorists wherever they are, whatever it takes. Period."[48] Thanks largely to the tape, Kerry made up the ground in the polls that he had lost after the third debate: Bush now led by 48.9 to 47.4.[49] The race was too close to call.

On 2 November, Election Day, early exit polls showed Bush lagging behind in several swing states. However, Rove believed that the polling methodology was flawed—in his recollection he was "steaming"—and he began to call the networks, telling anyone who would listen that they were getting it wrong. Rove was right; Kerry's exit-poll lead was an illusion, and the election would be another nail-biter. By evening's end, it was clear that the election would hinge not on Florida, as it had four years earlier, but on Ohio, in which Bush and Kerry were running at a dead heat. At about 4:00 a.m., Bush was informed that there were rumors that Kerry planned to file a lawsuit challenging the Ohio vote. Several advisers suggested that Bush go out and declare victory—even though no network had called the race and Kerry had not conceded. Bush took the advice of his wife, who counseled him to say nothing publicly. At about 5:00 a.m., Andy Card addressed the president's supporters: "President Bush decided to give Senator Kerry the respect of more time to reflect on the results of this election. We are convinced that President Bush has won reelection."[50]

The next day found Bush leading by 136,000 votes in Ohio and all three networks having called the election for the president. But Kerry still refused to concede. Card called Jim Baker, who, thinking the campaign was asking him to relive the 2000 Florida nightmare and travel north to spearhead an Ohio recount, momentarily panicked. But Card wanted Baker to put in a call to Democratic Party fixer Vernon Jordan and ask him to nudge Kerry toward a concession. Baker made the call, reaching Jordan at Augusta National Golf Club. Jordan didn't let on to Baker as to whether or not he would call Kerry, but at 11:00 a.m., Kerry formally conceded the election.[51]

George W. Bush won 50.7 percent of the popular vote to John Kerry's 48.3. percent. The Electoral College was also close, with Bush winning 286 electoral votes to Kerry's 251. Kerry won New England, the Mid-Atlantic states, the Upper Midwest, and the West Coast. Bush prevailed in the South and in the heartland, including Ohio—had Kerry won Ohio, he would have won the presidency by one electoral vote. Bush's coattails were also surprisingly long. Bush became the first Republican incumbent since Calvin Coolidge to win a second term and carry both houses of Congress. Republicans won the Senate by a margin of 55 to 44 and the House by a margin of 232 to 202. This was largely due to Bush's readiness to campaign for down-ticket elections, as he had done two years earlier (for his part, Kerry did not devote much time to state or local races).

While turnout was up more than 16 percent from 2000, undecided voters broke almost evenly between the two candidates. But as had been the case in 2000, Bush could thank evangelical Christians for his victory. After a drop in their participation in 2000, evangelicals returned to the fray in 2004—their turnout was 9 percent greater than four years earlier, and almost 78 percent of them voted for Bush. Moreover, congressional candidates who had been supported by evangelicals, or were evangelical Christians themselves, won in the majority of their races. For evangelicals the issue that drove them was not the war but gay marriage—the issue that Rove and Bush had early on decided to put at the forefront of the debate. It was a shrewd choice. Bush's opposition to gay marriage drove evangelicals to the polls. Constitutional amendments banning gay marriage passed in each of the thirteen states in which the issue was on the ballot. In Ohio, where evangelical Christians cast 25 percent of that state's vote, "Issue One"—a constitutional amendment barring any legal status for "relationships of unmarried individuals that intends to approximate the design, qualities, significance or effect of marriage"—passed with 62 percent of the vote and may have helped Bush win that key swing state.[52]

The day after the election, David Addington emailed several staffers: "For those interested in looking to the future, here is the list of Senators whose seats will be up for reelection on November 2006."[53]

# 12

# STORMS

It is safe to say that the man that the nation reelected to the presidency in 2004 was not well known to most Americans. For the entirety of his political career, George W. Bush had studiously avoided interviews or personal appearances that led the interviewer, in Bush's words, to place him "on the couch." Assiduously avoiding introspection of any kind, Bush derisively referred to attempts to get him to analyze himself as "navel gazing." This was less a political strategy than it was a character trait. For one well-cited example: at a 13 April 2004 press conference, Bush was asked to name his biggest mistake since 11 September; he looked genuinely confused and tongue-tied as he tried to answer—he couldn't do it. There were exceptions to this, as when he observed for journalist Bob Woodward that he did not seek his father's guidance on issues because he was "the wrong father to appeal to in terms of strength; there is a higher father I appeal to." But such exceptions were rare, and they almost always involved Bush mentioning his religious beliefs, a subject on which he often spoke. Thus, the American people knew that their president was a Republican and a Christian—and they knew little else.[1]

If they had been allowed to see their president at work in the Oval Office in any manner except for the occasional press pool photograph, Americans would have found an office manager who was the anti-Clinton. Where his predecessor had allowed open-collar casual dress, even on some weekdays, Bush required suits and ties to be worn at all times in the West Wing. Where Clinton stretched the meaning of being "on time" for a meeting to mean anything within an hour or two of the appointed start time (Clinton was so habitually late that his staff referred to the trait as "Clinton Standard Time"), Bush demanded that all meetings begin and end as scheduled—to the point of locking the door after the meeting began (no one was exempt from this rule, as a tardy Colin Powell once found out when he had to knock for admittance to a meeting with the president). Most memoirs offer testimony to Bush's impatience. To this, Bush readily agreed: "I don't wait well. I have been fairly accused of being impatient." In the Bush White House, wasted time was a mortal sin.[2]

Related to his impatience—perhaps of a piece—is the belief that Bush made important decisions in haste and then adopted a "buck stops here" mentality that precluded any change of heart if the decision went bad. Journalist Robert Draper agreed with this, entitling his 2007 book—the first detailed assessment of the Bush presidency—*Dead Certain*. Bush casually referred to himself as "The Decider" (christening himself with this sobriquet when he explained to the press why, after Abu Ghraib, he had not fired Don Rumsfeld). However, Bush bristled at any characterization of him as impulsive, believing himself to be a much more thoughtful, careful decider: "I make my decisions by understanding the background of an issue first. I will read about it and ask for additional information. The history major in me comes out when I seek to understand the background behind the issue of the day." Karl Rove agreed with Bush on this point, noting that "contrary to the myth that grew up around Bush, he wanted candid advice. He encouraged people to make their case in front of others who might disagree. . . . He wanted people around him who would not back down or wilt under cross-examination." Even Hughes admitted that "he explores, prods, then carefully watches how someone reacts to his pointed questions, or orders with which they disagree. It's the way he evaluates how secure you are, how certain of your convictions." Indeed, there is more evidence for the latter characterization than the former. Virtually every Bush administration alumnus testified to Bush's clarity of purpose and probing nature when making a decision. Indeed, Bush preferred in-person briefings more than he did reading briefing books or memos: "I read a lot of memos, but I enjoy the give-and-take that comes with a substantive discussion." Bush particularly profited from what he called "deep-dives"—lengthy conversations with a wide range of staff opinions on a specific topic.[3]

Much of this belies the lore that had dogged Bush since Yale (where, to put it charitably, he underperformed) that he was an intellectual lightweight. That myth has followed Bush beyond his presidency. In 2013, Keith Hennessey, who had served as director of the National Economic Council under Bush, set off an internet blaze with his tale of informing his Stanford University classroom that "President Bush is smarter than almost every one of you." He expanded upon the point to his students: "President Bush is extremely smart by any traditional standard. He's highly analytical and was incredibly quick to discern the core question he needed to answer. . . . He would sometimes force us to accelerate through policy presentations because he so quickly grasped what we were presenting. . . . In addition to his analytical speed, what most impressed me were his memory and his substantive breadth."[4] This was more than some could bear. For but one example, commentator Jonathan Chait responded directly to Hennessey in the pages of *New York* magazine: "All the public evidence available to us shows a man who thinks in crude, simplistic slogans. . . . His way of discussing policy bore all the hallmarks of a highly simplistic mind."[5]

Bush was hardly the first president to be saddled with the label of being slow on the uptake. In the postmodern period, perhaps the best known is Gerald Ford, who was labeled by Lyndon Johnson as a guy who had played football once too often without a helmet, and judged by a Nixon staffer as being not "excessively bright." Ford simply laughed off the label, letting his humor defuse any real political damage. However, Bush refused to address the charge, either during or after his presidency (see "navel gazing," mentioned earlier). But Bush administration alumni never tire of talking about how smart their boss was. When they do, they make several observations. The first, as pointed out by Hennessey, is that Bush had a phenomenal memory (Frances Townsend noted that in a meeting, Bush was always "extraordinarily sort of dialed in"). The second was that it was all just an act. Rove certainly believed this: "He likes to play the 'Good Ol' Boy' from Midland. But he was a Harvard MBA and a Yale history undergraduate."[6]

The third, and one that seems to have surprised many of his critics the most, is that outside the Oval Office, Bush was a voracious reader. Five days after 11 September, while at dinner with friends, Bush sighed: "I read books though nobody thinks I do." This seems to have been quite true. In a section of his study of presidential reading habits entitled "Misunderstanding Bush's Reading," former White House staffer

Tevi Troy points out that in 1986 a liberal journalist found books by John Fowles, F. Scott Fitzgerald, James Joyce, and Gore Vidal "lying about" in the Midland house; the same journalist would report that between 2006 and 2008 Bush read 186 books, 95 in 2006 alone. Both Bush and Rove love telling the story of their book-reading contest (Bush lost, 110 to 95 books read over the course of a year). Bush's reading often informed his policy choices, as we have seen with the development of the concept of "compassionate conservatism," his coming to a decision on stem cell research, and, as will become apparent, his shift in focus on Iraq. Bush's reading took him outside the box on issues that have a more recent relevance. Bush's reading of John M. Barry's *The Great Influenza* (2004) led him to form a strike force on pandemics and, with a fair amount of prescience, issue a warning in November 2005 that "to respond to a pandemic, we need medical personnel and adequate supplies of equipment. . . . In a pandemic, everything from syringes to hospital beds, respirator masks and protective equipment would be in short supply."[7]

Perhaps it is not surprising that as he morphed into his role as a wartime president, Bush developed an obsession with books on Abraham Lincoln (Troy claimed that Bush read fourteen biographies of Lincoln during the course of his presidency)[8] and came to see a kinship with the Civil War leader. Like Lincoln (the only other president to do so), Bush visited battlefields on American soil from the war he was prosecuting—the Pentagon in Washington and Ground Zero in New York City. Like Lincoln, who had no compunction about visiting an active war zone, Bush reveled in surprise visits to the troops in Iraq.

And, like Lincoln, Bush took his war personally. Two weeks after the attacks of 11 September, Bush met with families of passengers and crew of United Flight 93, which had gone down near Shanksville. Bush asked the White House staff to line the hallway between the East Wing and the Executive Mansion, through which the families would exit, to say thank you. He would carry George Howard's badge, given to him on 14 September 2001 by Howard's mother at the Javits Center in New York for the remainder of his presidency. Even more noticeable was how Bush obsessed over the fate of veterans of the War on Terror. Like Lincoln, Bush regularly visited veterans hospitals. He also personally answered the majority of the letters he received from soldiers and vets, mail that was brutal in its candor and horrifying in its recounting of the carnage they had faced, and more often than not answered them with a handwritten note (for example, in a note to a wounded veteran who had served in Fallujah he wrote: "It is an honor to serve. I tell people I'll not compromise my soul for the latest poll. I will finish strong and then head home. All is well. God bless"). As we will see, concern for, and advocacy for, the condition of the veteran would become the foundation of his postpresidency.[9]

But veterans were far from Bush's only obsession. Bush never accepted the word "alcoholic" as a term to describe himself, even though on the very first page of his 2010 memoirs he admitted that "drinking had become a habit." It is easy to understand why a man with dreams of political advancement would not want such a label—it would have effectively destroyed his career. Nevertheless, Bush showed many of the traits of a person who had battled substance abuse. He admitted to having a "habitual personality," and he could—and did—obsess when making a decision. While there were many instances of such behavior, the best example of how his obsessive personality affected the development of policy was Bush's single-mindedness when it came to researching and debating the stem cell issue, recounted in chapter 6.[10]

This type of personality would never have succeeded in politics were it not for a dedicated support system. Without question, Bush's emotional support system consisted of one person. Laura Bush has been dismissed by many observers as being irrelevant as First Lady. Part of this is because of her low-key personality. Part of it is because she has, in the main, been compared unfavorably with her two immediate predecessors in the East Wing—the gregarious Barbara Bush and the activist Hillary Rodham Clinton. Part of it is because there were no significant Bush-era policies advanced either with her participation or on her behalf. There were notable moments when Laura stepped into the spotlight: as we will see, she pushed her husband, both privately and publicly, to name a woman to the Supreme Court, and she became the first First Lady to deliver a complete presidential radio address, on the topic of the Taliban's brutality toward women.[11] But these moments were the exception to a First Ladyship spent largely in the background.

And yet, except for Eleanor Roosevelt, no First Lady changed her husband more. Bush would later tell one of his mother's biographers that had it not been for Laura, he would not have become president of the United States. This observation rings true. Laura was pivotal in changing his direction as a young man, as she was the most important person contributing to his decision to stop drinking. As an adult, it was Laura who would temper her husband's addictive personality and helped to ground him in times of crisis or when a decision was pending. As we have seen, it was

Laura who got him back on the beam after the New Hampshire primary defeat. When the president started feeling sorry for himself, the First Lady gently reminded him that *he* was the one who chose to run for president.[12]

It was also Laura Bush who would be the focal point for one of the funniest moments of the Bush presidency. On 30 April 2005, she sat with her husband on the dais at the annual White House Correspondents' Dinner. The president began his speech, but was he only a few words into it when he was melodramatically interrupted by his wife, who informed the surprised audience, "I've been attending these dinners for years and just quietly sitting here. I've got a few things I want to say for a change." What followed was a slow but steady delivery of a series of one-liners that had the audience in stitches:

- Here's our typical evening: 9:00, Mr. Excitement here is sound asleep. And I'm watching "Desperate Housewives." With Lynne Cheney. Ladies and gentlemen—I *am* a desperate housewife.
- George and I are complete opposites. I'm quiet, he's talkative. I'm introverted, he's extroverted. I can pronounce nuclear.
- People think [Barbara Bush] is the sweet, motherly, Aunt Bea type. Actually, she's more like Don Corleone.
- George's answer to any problem at the ranch is to cut it down with a chainsaw. Which I think is why he and Cheney and Rumsfeld get along so well.

Then she closed with a line that was often left out in the rebroadcasts of the speech: "I want you to know that I'm happy to be here for a reason—I love and enjoy being with the man who usually speaks to you on these occasions."[13]

According to press secretary Scott McClellan, Bush did not ask the cabinet members to tender their resignations after the election—an action that was common when a president had been reelected.[14] For the most notable change in the cabinet, Bush did not think a letter was necessary—indeed, he believed that the change had all been taken care of.

On Iraq, Colin Powell had pushed for seeking a diplomatic solution through the United Nations—too hard and too long for the tastes of Rumsfeld and Cheney. As a result, as author James Mann has pointed out, the White House had largely divided itself into two "tribes"—one faction aligning itself with Cheney, and the other with Powell. For his part, by the beginning of 2004 Powell had had enough. He wrote in his memoir that "the Bush national security team had in my mind become dysfunctional, which has been well documented. Since it was obvious that my thinking and advice were increasingly out of sync with others on the team, the best course for me was to leave." This bad blood cut both ways: Cheney would later write that despite Powell's service under the first Bush, the vice president was "disappointed" in his colleague's time at State.[15]

Powell told Bush in the spring of 2004 that he wanted to step down, but Bush asked him to stay on through the election. However, immediately following the election, Powell informed Andrew Card that he no longer wanted to leave, a decision that Bush later wrote came "out of nowhere." The reason behind this change of heart is hazy. For his part, Bush speculated in his memoir that Powell had expected Rumsfeld to leave the cabinet at the same time that he did, and when Rumsfeld did not, Powell changed his mind and decided to stay. Regardless, it was too late. Bush had told Condoleezza Rice of her promotion to secretary of state on 5 November—three days after the election—while at Camp David. It was left to Card to tell Powell that whether he wanted to or not, he had to step down. On 14 November Powell delivered his letter of resignation to Bush. Two days later Bush met with the press; by his side was his new secretary of state designate. Neither Powell nor Cheney was present.[16]

There were other cabinet-level shake-ups. Rod Paige was replaced at Education by Margaret Spellings. John Ashcroft was also replaced at Justice by Alberto Gonzales. Harriet Miers, then serving as deputy chief of staff for policy, succeeded Gonzales as White House counsel. The Senate Judiciary Committee used Gonzales's confirmation hearings to explore the abuse of prisoners in general, and Abu Ghraib in particular. Specifically, in the words of committee chair Patrick Leahy (D-VT), "We want to know what the current policy on torture is."[17]

The second transition was not without its Linda Chavez–like moment. Tom Ridge had long planned on leaving Homeland Security. New York mayor Rudy Giuliani had recommended Bernard Kerik, who had served as New York City police commissioner during the 11 September 2001 attack and as the interior minister of the Iraq Coalition Provisional Authority as his replacement. But on 10 December Kerik was forced to withdraw his nomination when news of an undocumented nanny surfaced. According to journalist Peter Baker, after Kerik's withdrawal, Bush tried to get both Richard Armitage—the leaker in the Plame Wilson affair—and Democrat

Joe Lieberman, but he finally went with Michael Chertoff, then serving as a judge on the US Court of Appeals for the Third Circuit.[18]

There was also a change in the leadership of the intelligence community. On 17 December 2004, following the recommendation of the 9/11 Commission, Bush signed legislation that placed sixteen separate intelligence agencies under a single director of national intelligence. The first person to hold this position was former UN ambassador John Negroponte; his deputy director was Michael Hayden, who left the National Security Agency—and Operation Stellar Wind—to join him.

But the biggest story of the transition to the second term was the change that most observers had expected to happen but didn't. Bush had planned on replacing Donald Rumsfeld before the start of his second term. While giving him credit for "transforming the military, the mission that initially attracted me to him," Bush was frustrated with Rumsfeld's "abruptness" toward both subordinates and peers. Bush was ready, but he could not find a replacement, He once again sounded out Fred Smith to see if he wanted the job; once again, Smith declined the offer. Bush considered moving Rice to Defense; he also considered Joe Lieberman and Jim Baker for the job. But in the end, Bush decided to keep Rumsfeld. He would later remember somewhat obliquely that "the reality is that there aren't many people capable of leading the military during a complex global war. Don Rumsfeld was one of them." Rumsfeld would stay at Defense for almost two more years.[19]

As we have seen, Bush originally saw the overthrow of Saddam Hussein as a war of necessity—necessary to prevent further terrorist attacks on the United States. Since the invasion, however, Bush's view of the purpose for the war in Iraq had changed. By 2004, Bush had come to see the conflict as one whose purpose was to replace Iraqi tyranny with a truly democratic form of government. It was, as deputy national security adviser Elliot Abrams told an interviewer, a true "transformation." Many factors had led to this shift in focus. Bush had been profoundly affected by Natan Sharansky's book *The Case for Democracy: The Power of Freedom to Overcome Tyranny and Terror*, with its metaphor of a tyrannical state as a soldier pointing his gun at the head of a prisoner until the soldier's arm finally tires. Bush read the book in galleys, met with Sharansky—then a member of the Israeli Knesset—and had many of his staffers read it. Bush had also been affected by bloodless coups in two of the former Soviet republics.

The Rose Revolution was a November 2003 uprising in Georgia that overthrew the government of Eduard Shevardnadze (Bush would write the deposed president: "Your decision to resign rather than use force on the streets of Tbilisi was a crowning moment in an outstanding career") and installed the fanatically anti-Moscow Mikheil Saakashvili as president. The "Orange Revolution," in which hundreds of thousands of Ukrainians protested the results of a fraudulent election, was underway in November and December 2004, as Bush was planning his second term (these protests would lead to the installation of another anti-Russian government in the Baltic states, led by the equally anti-Russian Viktor Yushchenko and Yulia Tymoshenko).[20]

As speechwriter Michael Gerson began work on the president's second inaugural address, Bush kept referring to it as the "Freedom Speech." Impressed by a memorandum written by Yale University historian John Lewis Gaddis (encouraging Bush "to think like Wilson, Roosevelt, and Reagan" and to set as a goal "that by the year 2030—a quarter century from now—there will be no tyrants left, anywhere in the world"), Bush invited Gaddis and other scholars to the White House to discuss the speech. Gaddis doubled down on his memo, saying to the group, "I think the president should call for ending tyranny in our time." Bush agreed.[21]

This point of view was at odds with the view held by the Republican realists. Political scientist Bartholomew Sparrow recounts a dinner between Rice and Brent Scowcroft, where Rice told her mentor that she wanted to help Bush introduce democracy into Iraq. A stunned Scowcroft protested: "Condi, it's just not going to happen. You can't build democracy that way." Rice stood her ground: "Oh yes you can. . . . The world's a mess and someone's got to clean it up."[22] Both Armitage at State and Rumsfeld at Defense tried to get the president to soften the slant toward national freedom and independence in the speech, and to be, in Rumsfeld's view, more "clear-eyed about democracy's prospects" in Iraq and elsewhere.[23] But Bush was adamant, and what would later become known as Bush's "Freedom Agenda" ended up at the heart of his second inaugural address:

> The survival of liberty in our land increasingly depends on the success of liberty in other lands. The best hope for peace in our world is the expansion of freedom in all the world. . . . So it is the policy of the United States to seek and support the growth of democratic movements and institutions in every nation and culture, with the ultimate goal of ending tyranny in our world.

It is possible that this embrace of the "Freedom Agenda" led Bush to stand fast at a particularly chancy moment in Iraq. On 8 November, Operation Phantom Fury—the second Battle of Fallujah—had begun. In the midst of the mayhem that was that battle, a national election had been scheduled for 30 January 2005 to replace Ayad Allawi's interim government. Bush refused to even consider postponing the election, and it went off without serious incident. Some eight million people voted, defiantly waving their fingers in the air, fingers that had been dipped in indelible purple ink to prevent double voting. Iraqis elected a permanent government, the centerpiece of which was a new National Assembly empowered to write a new constitution for Iraq. While the purple fingers symbolized hope in a situation gone powerfully bad, none of this changed things on the ground in Iraq, a point that Bush admitted when he spoke to the nation on 31 January. While noting that "the people of Iraq have spoken to the world, and the world is hearing the voice of freedom from the center of the Middle East," Bush warned that "terrorists and insurgents will continue to wage their war against democracy, and we will support the Iraqi people in their fight against them."[24]

While speaking with the press the day after his reelection, Bush gloated: "I earned capital in the campaign, political capital, and I intend to spend it." He presented his shopping list to Congress in his fourth State of the Union address, delivered on 22 February 2005. At the top of his list was a continuation of Social Security reform. Bush was still focused on securing at least a partial privatization of the system: "As we fix Social Security, we also have the responsibility to make the system a better deal for younger workers. And the best way to achieve that is through voluntary personal retirement accounts." Bush argued that the rate of return from personal accounts would be higher than in the present system, but "Best of all, the money in this account is yours, and the government can never take it away."

Bush proposed allowing workers who were already contributing to Social Security to invest 4 percent of their wages in personal accounts, up to an annual cap of $1,000. The criticism was immediate. Some criticized the president for leading with the personal accounts, as opposed to addressing how the entire program could stay solvent at all; others cited the high administrative cost of his plan; others pointed out that the group that would benefit from such a private investment program was not the average taxpayer but the Wall Street brokers who would be selling the personal accounts. So Bush immediately hit the road, announcing that he was taking his plan directly to the people for their consideration—Rove called it the "Sixty Cities in Sixty Days" tour. But a larger reason for the tour was that it offered an opportunity to visit those states that he had won in 2004 but were nevertheless represented by at least one Democratic senator. The political logic of this was sound—assuming that all fifty-five Republican votes held, Bush would need five Democratic votes in the Senate to secure passage of his plan.[25]

But Bush's road show was counterproductive. A Gallup poll found that public disapproval of Bush's plan rose by sixteen points—from 48 to 64 percent—between his State of the Union address and the summer. In response Bush tried to make his plan friendlier for lower-income investors. He also embraced the concept of "progressive indexing." The brainchild of Robert Pozen, a Democrat and a member of Bush's original Social Security Commission, progressive indexing set retirement benefits to grow faster for poorer Americans and slower for the upper strata, with a sliding scale of benefits for the middle class.[26]

In the end it didn't matter. Congressional Democrats made it clear that they would not vote for any reform that was based on the introduction of private accounts, and their lines held firm. On 4 March 2005, forty-one Democrats—including Joe Lieberman, who had originally been thought to be in favor of the reform—signed off against it; only three Democratic senators refused to sign. But to add insult to injury, Bush's own party broke with him over the issue. John D. Graham, who worked in the Office of Management and Budget (OMB) under Bush, concluded that Social Security reform under Bush was a "debacle." That assessment rings true.[27]

Immigration reform met the same fate. While the issue was important to Bush in his attempt to improve relations with Mexico, it was pushed aside, first by the primacy of Social Security reform, then by other considerations, including Bush's Supreme Court appointments and the federal response to Hurricane Katrina. In October 2005, Bush signed a homeland security bill that supplied an additional $75 billion for border enforcement. Seven months later, in May 2006, Bush delivered the first prime-time presidential address on immigration. In it, he proposed a plan that would provide new investment in border security; a temporary worker program that would include a tamper-proof identification card; stricter immigration enforcement at businesses; requiring immigrants to learn English; and a restructuring of criteria regarding those illegal immigrants who could apply for citizenship.[28] The Senate passed a bill that incorporated much of Bush's plan, but when the Democrats won back the Senate in the 2006 off-year elections, they left Bush's immigration reform to die in committee.

Rice's argument—that "by 2007 we were out of steam and out of ammunition. . . . Maybe the battle for immigration reform came too late"—is a convincing one. It is arguable that Bush should not have led his second term with as contentious an issue as Social Security. In his memoir, Rove contended that if the administration had led its second term with immigration reform, it would have won, because the Democrats had said they would work on that issue with the administration. Indeed, many members of Bush's staff similarly argued that he should start his second term by proposing immigration reform, but he brushed them off.[29]

Regardless of the reasons, Bush simply did not have the political capital he thought he had, and he got neither Social Security nor immigration reform. But by the end of 2005 he got the opportunity to do something that would affect American society for decades to come—fundamentally reshape the Supreme Court.

Following its decision in *Bush v. Gore*, the Supreme Court slowly but noticeably moved to the left. Sandra Day O'Connor led this shift. In 2003, in *Lawrence v. Texas*[30]—the case that reversed *Bowers v. Hardwick* (1986)[31] and ruled that any law regulating the private sexual conduct of a citizen was unconstitutional, O'Connor joined with the liberal bloc to form a 6–3 majority. In the enemy combatant cases, most notably *Hamdi* and *Rasul*, decided in 2004 and discussed in chapter 8, both O'Connor and Anthony Kennedy joined the majorities. In 2005, O'Connor once again joined with the Court's liberals in finding the McCain-Feingold campaign finance law largely constitutional.[32] Legal scholar David Cole has argued that this change was a result of a deliberate Supreme Court "campaign to rehabilitate itself . . . to repair its image [following *Bush v. Gore*] as an institution guided by law and constitutional principle rather than partisan politics." Court-watcher Jeffrey Toobin ascribed the shift to O'Connor's growing alienation from her Republican Party following 11 September. But whatever the reason, the Court had indeed moved to the left—as proclaimed in the headline to a *New York Times* article by veteran legal reporter Linda Greenhouse, 2003 was "The Year Rehnquist May Have Lost His Court."[33]

In October 2004, Chief Justice William Rehnquist announced that he was afflicted with thyroid cancer. The news did not catch the Bush administration—specifically Ashcroft, Cheney, Card, Rove, and Gonzales—unprepared. Through a White House working group called the Judicial

Selection Committee, they had been vetting and interviewing possible replacements for Rehnquist since the spring of 2001.[34] Harriet Miers joined the group after Gonzales became attorney general and she replaced him as White House counsel. The possibility that Rehnquist would step down offered Bush an opportunity that had not occurred since 1994, when Clinton nominated Stephen Breyer to succeed Harry Blackmun. In fact, Bush entered his second term as one of only two presidents who had not had the chance to appoint a justice to the Supreme Court in his first term (the other being Jimmy Carter).

But it was the memory of an appointment by his father that haunted Bush. Several on his staff had represented David Souter to the elder Bush as a worthy conservative replacement for Justice William Brennan. Souter sailed through his nomination hearings, only to frustrate the administration by proving to be more liberal in his opinions than was expected. In his memoir, the younger Bush grumbled that Souter had been a "disappointment" to his father, one that he remembered when it was his turn to nominate a justice: "The only tests in my mind were personal integrity, intellectual ability, and judicial restraint. . . . I subscribed to the strict constructionist school; I wanted judges who believed the Constitution meant what it said."[35]

In April 2005, the working group informed Bush that it had narrowed down the candidates to a short list that included Third Circuit judge Samuel Alito, Fourth Circuit judge J. Michael Luttig, DC Circuit judge John G. Roberts, and Fourth Circuit judge J. Harvie Wilkerson. Screening interviews were scheduled with each justice. The group was most impressed with Roberts, a fifty-year-old honors graduate of Harvard Law School who had clerked for Rehnquist and worked in both the Reagan and the first Bush administration. Under the elder Bush, Roberts had served as deputy solicitor general and had been nominated by him to the DC Circuit Court of Appeals in 1992, but that nomination was quashed by the incoming Clinton administration. Roberts returned to private law practice until 2001, when George W. Bush nominated him to the same court to which his father had tried to name him; this time, Roberts was confirmed.

Gonzales was the first to interview Roberts. He would later remember for one of Roberts's biographers that "the main thing I was asking about was precedent . . . I came away from that conversation knowing I would be comfortable recommending him for the Court." He also noted that "one of the major advantages [in Roberts's favor was] that he had a limited paper trail in the judiciary." Roberts's performance earned him a second interview. This time Gonzales was joined by Cheney, Card, Rove, and Miers (with gallows humor, Cheney invited Roberts to "sit in the hot-wired seat"). Assuming, as did they all, that Rehnquist would soon be retiring, Cheney initially supported promoting Associate Justice Antonin Scalia to the chief justice position, and putting forth Luttig, a darling of conservative groups (this due largely to his consistent opposition to abortion rights) for the associate position. But this did not keep the group from taking Roberts's name to the next level—on 23 May he provided the group with his financial information.[36]

A retirement was soon announced, but in a shock to both the administration and the nation, it was not Rehnquist's. On 1 July 2005, Miers called Bush and announced: "It's O'Connor." O'Connor, who initially had supported Bush's election and was likely the swing vote in his favor in *Bush v. Gore* (see chapter 4), had long since changed her mind about the president. After Bush was reelected, she reportedly told Souter that Bush was "destroying the military with adventures that we aren't prepared for. . . . We've got colossal deficit spending, and the only way he got reelected was by getting states to vote on same-sex marriage. . . . Barry Goldwater never gave a damn who you slept with. Bush repudiated all that." Thus at first glance it was surprising that O'Connor was giving Bush the chance to replace her with a jurist of his own choosing. But O'Connor's husband suffered from dementia, and she wanted to retire. She had only waited this long because Rehnquist asked her to (planning his own retirement, the chief justice argued, "I don't think we need two vacancies"). But as her husband's condition grew more serious, O'Connor grew impatient with waiting for the chief to make the first move; now it was O'Connor who stepped down before Rehnquist.[37]

Bush now had his opportunity, but he threw a curveball to the vetting group—he wanted to be sure that the short list included a woman. Cheney saw the matter simply: "Diversity in hiring, both for women and minorities, was an issue about which George Bush cared deeply." But Bush was also getting some pressure from home. When traveling in South Africa on 12 July 2005, Laura Bush told the press, "Sure, I would really like for him to name another woman." The short list to replace O'Connor eventually included Edith Brown Clement of the Fifth Circuit in New Orleans; joining her were Roberts, Luttig, Alito, and Wilkerson.[38]

One name that was not on the list—despite his being a Bush favorite—was Alberto Gonzales. In his memoir, Gonzales all but admitted that he expected to be nominated. But it was not to be. After increasing their

turnout in 2004, evangelicals felt that they were owed a reliably conservative justice, and they were certain that Bush's attorney general would not
fill that bill. Citing his vote for abortion rights when he was on the Texas
Supreme Court, conservatives had been gunning for Gonzales since early
in the administration—Kate O'Beirne of the *National Review* wrote an article questioning his conservative credentials, and Gonzales was booed
by conservative audiences. Wags quipped that "Gonzales" was Spanish
for "Souter." Added to this was the 2003 deal that Bush had cut with Rep.
Trent Franks (R-AZ) to keep Gonzales off the list in exchange for Frank's
support of Bush's Medicare proposal (see chapter 11). Bush sputtered: "I
don't like it when a friend gets criticized. . . . No, I don't like it at all." But
in the end, Bush gave in to the inevitable. Gonzales's name would not be
brought forth. Gonzales would later write, "I must admit I was still somewhat disappointed."[39]

When they considered the judges on the short list, Bush remembered
that Cheney and Gonzales liked Luttig, Miers supported Alito, and both
Card and Rove supported Roberts. Bush also solicited the advice of Brett
Kavanaugh, then a White House lawyer who Bush had nominated to the
DC Circuit Court of Appeals. Kavanaugh told Bush that Luttig, Roberts,
and Alito would all be good choices, but he suggested that Bush should be
looking to see which of the candidates could be the most effective leader
on the Court. Bush met personally with all the candidates. Of all those
interviewed, Bush found Roberts to be the most impressive—indeed, the
two men hit it off from the start. On 19 July Bush announced Roberts as
his nominee. In a rare moment of innocence in the White House, Roberts's
four-year-old son, Jack, escaped the protective hold of his mother and glee-
fully danced around onstage. Bush remained stoic, Roberts suppressed a
grin, and the nomination was dutifully announced. O'Connor offered a
classic backhanded compliment: "He's good in every way, except he's not
a woman."[40]

Having dispensed with both the formality and the childhood revelry,
the White House girded itself for a confirmation fight. Roberts spent the
summer preparing for his testimony, but the White House was distracted
by two events of mammoth proportions. First, on 29 August, Hurricane
Katrina hit. Then, on 3 September—three days before Roberts's confirmation hearings were scheduled to begin before the Senate Judiciary
Committee—Rehnquist died. Bush now had the singular opportunity to
name both a chief justice and an associate justice. Moreover, he had been

handed the opportunity to affect the ideological balance of the court for decades to come.

Bush surprised his staff by deciding to nominate Roberts, who had been thoroughly vetted and was scoring high marks with senators with whom he met, as chief justice. The White House immediately shifted gears and put together a plan to present Roberts not as an associate but as the chief. Roberts continued to shine in his one-on-one meetings on the Hill and proved to be untouchable in his public testimony. He refused to speak directly to any pending case, but he disarmed the committee with his easygoing demeanor and his gentle style. In one of the most oft-quoted statements of modern jurisprudence, Roberts used a sports metaphor to describe the role of a judge: "Judges are like umpires. Umpires don't make the rules, they apply them. The role of an umpire and a judge is critical. They make sure everybody plays by the rules, but it is a limited role. Nobody ever went to a ball game to see the umpire." Roberts cruised to confirmation on 23 September and was confirmed by the whole Senate, 78–22, six days later.[41]

Roberts's confirmation changed the dynamic for the associate seat. Initially, Bush tried to buy himself some time. Following Rehnquist's death, Bush directly asked O'Connor to stay on the Court while the White House found her replacement. She declined. The process had been opened anew, and a new short list was required. As the vetting committee prepared that list, Bush made it clear that he had every intention of nominating a woman to replace O'Connor (Card told Miers, who continued to oversee the vetting process, "No White Guys").[42]

But in the end, Bush hijacked his own vetting process. Bush would later contend in his memoirs that the idea of nominating Harriet Miers as an associate justice to the Supreme Court came from outside the White House—that "several senators had been very impressed by Harriet as she shepherded John Roberts through his interviews on Capitol Hill." Card later expanded upon this, claiming that he had a "wonderful conversation with a Democratic member of the Supreme Court" who said that what the Court needed was someone who knew commerce and corporate law; then Card quoted the justice—"someone like Harriet Miers." Bush needed no convincing: "There was no doubt in my mind that she shared my judicial philosophy and that her outlook would not change. She would make an outstanding justice." Card agreed, calling Miers a "rock star."[43] To Bush, "The decision came down to Harriet [Miers] and [associate justice of the

Texas Supreme Court] Priscilla Owen. I decided to go with Harriet." He would later give three reasons for his decision: he knew her well, she was confirmable, and she came from "outside the judicial fraternity." On 2 October, Bush offered Miers the nomination. She immediately accepted and was formally nominated the next day.[44]

It promised to be a difficult confirmation. There were so many areas of potential concern, the White House counsel's Office had no problem preparing an opposition research briefing book. The concerns ranged from "Miers lacks the experience to serve as an Associate Justice on the Supreme Court, because she has never been a judge, and did not attend an Ivy League Law School"; to her views on abortion as being "consistent with her 'fundamentalist Christian' religious beliefs"; to her endorsement of positions favoring gay rights; to her chairing an American Bar Association committee that submitted a report recommending the enactment of laws which provide that sexual orientation shall not be a bar to adoption and her being a member of a Christian group (Exodus Ministries) that ministers to homosexuals; to charges of cronyism ("She has been nominated solely because of her close connections to the Bush family"); and to the fact that she had donated to the campaigns of Democratic candidates. As if this weren't enough, her critics pointed to the fact that she had no relevant experience in constitutional law—she had never argued a case before the Supreme Court; indeed, of the three cases in which she represented clients who were petitioning for certiorari to the Supreme Court, cert was granted in none of the three.[45]

This was but a prelude to a disaster. Miers's performances when meeting with senators on the Hill were as halting and tense as Roberts's had been smooth and polished; she did nothing to make senators feel more comfortable with the fact that she was neither a constitutional scholar nor a jurist of any kind. Moreover, it was revealed that Miers had been suspended from the DC Bar because she forgot to pay her dues. The Judiciary Committee wanted further explanation of this suspension and took the opportunity to ask a series of follow-up questions in nine other areas.[46]

It took only twenty-three days for the White House to tire of the process. On 25 October, Card recommended to Bush that Miers withdraw her name from consideration for the post. Miers withdrew two days later. In her letter to Bush, she said she was withdrawing to spare the White House a protracted fight over executive privilege, as the Senate made ready to demand documents from her time as White House counsel.[47]

It was not the time for another crusade. The day after Miers dropped out, Patrick Fitzgerald's grand jury indicted Scooter Libby. Five days later, the *Washington Post* broke the story of the CIA's secret prisons—the "Black Sites."[48] At the same time, Congress was debating a bill introduced by John McCain and Lindsey Graham, which if passed would prohibit the use of torture on any individual in US custody (Bush eventually signed the bill, known as the Detainee Treatment Act, in December 2005). The need for a quick and bloodless confirmation hearing was acute. Bush turned to Samuel Alito of the Second Circuit. Bush had interviewed Alito, and although his rather grave personality did not sit well with the president, Bush knew that after Miers he had to send a dyed-in-the-wool conservative to the Hill.

But Senate Democrats were not in the mood to roll over and play dead. Although Bush nominated Alito on 31 October, hearings on his nomination were not scheduled until the new year. When they finally began on 11 January 2006, Democrats grilled Alito on his past membership in a group of Princeton alumni that supported keeping women out of that university. Lindsey Graham demanded of Alito, "Are you really a closet bigot?" Alito's wife, Martha-Ann Bomgardner, could take no more; she left the hearing room in tears.[49] On 31 January, the day of Bush's fifth State of the Union address, Alito was narrowly confirmed by the full Senate, 58 to 42, with only four Democrats in his corner. He was sworn in in time to attend Bush's address.

On 26 December 2004, an earthquake measuring 9.1 on the Richter scale detonated in the depths of the Indian Ocean some thirty miles off the coast of Sumatra, generating a tsunami that inundated the coasts of several Southeast Asian countries. More than 230,000 people were killed by waves that often exceeded one hundred feet in height. In response, Bush sent a navy aircraft carrier strike group to the Indonesian coast and a marine expeditionary strike group to the Bay of Bengal. The total military relief force numbered 20,000—the largest such effort to aid disaster victims in American history. Bush also sent the forty-first and forty-second presidents of the United States. At the behest of Andy Card, Bush asked his father and Bill Clinton to spearhead a fundraising campaign to aid the victims of the tsunami. They both agreed at once. They flew to the disaster site together, and on that trip they formed a rather unlikely "odd couple"–type bond, finding to their mutual surprise that they liked each other's company. Clinton was deferential to his older partner—even to the point of giving him the only bed available on their military transport. The Bush-Clinton Tsunami Relief Fund raised more than $1 billion.[50]

It would take only eight months for Bush to face the wrath of nature once again. This time, however, the devastation would occur on American soil.

On 23 August 2005, the National Weather Service spotted a storm forming over the Bahamas. It named the storm Tropical Depression Twelve; when it strengthened into a tropical storm, it was renamed Katrina. Two days later, now upgraded to a category 1 hurricane, Katrina hit southern Florida at 6:30 p.m. The storm moved along the Gulf of Mexico, wreaking havoc in its wake. It was also growing. On 27 August Katrina was further upgraded to a category 3 hurricane. It was headed straight for New Orleans, a city of 454,000 people, more than half of whom lived either at or below sea level, that was protected from its water borders—Lake Pontchartrain to the north and the Mississippi River to the south—by a series of federally built dams and levees.

Disaster relief was nothing new for a governor of Texas, where fires, tornadoes, and hurricanes were a regular occurrence. Bush had also responded to major hurricanes as president—four in 2004 alone, all of which hit Florida, together causing some $20 billion in damage, and all of which led to an immediate presidential visit. When Katrina hit Florida, Bush was at his ranch in Crawford, Texas, where he was kept updated by his deputy chief of staff, Joe Hagin. When he learned that the storm was headed for New Orleans, Bush put the Federal Emergency Management Agency (FEMA) on its highest level of alert. As Katrina sped west, FEMA spearheaded a massive prepositioning of services to New Orleans—drinking water, ice, ready-to-eat meals, thirty-three medical teams, disaster response teams, helicopters, and more than five thousand National Guard personnel were at the ready. Bush issued an emergency declaration covering New Orleans on Saturday evening, 27 August; he signed one covering Mississippi and Alabama the following day. That same day, 28 August, Katrina was upgraded to a category 5 hurricane; New Orleans could expect a storm with accompanying winds of 157 miles per hour and higher, with a storm surge greater than eighteen feet above normal.[51]

Yet despite the ominous nature of this rapidly intensifying storm, Bush was receiving decidedly mixed messages from the people on the ground. New Orleans mayor Ray Nagin at first issued only a voluntary evacuation order; then, later in the morning, Louisiana governor Kathleen

Blanco told Bush that Nagin had been dragging his feet with regard to making the evacuation order mandatory. Nevertheless, Blanco assured Bush, "We've got it under control." One hour later, Nagin announced a mandatory evacuation. As for possible damage, Max Mayfield, the director of the National Hurricane Center, told Bush there would be negligible flooding. But in the same videoconference, Michael Brown, the new director of FEMA, told Bush, "This is the big one, I think."[52]

At 6:10 a.m. on Monday, 29 August, packing winds of 150 miles per hour, Katrina made landfall at Buras, Louisiana, some 60 miles southeast of New Orleans. The storm moved northeast over the Gulf and hit land again near Pearlington, Mississippi, some 44 miles to the northeast of the Big Easy.

Bush and his staff believed that New Orleans might be spared the brunt of the storm. Thus, that day Bush honored a long-standing commitment and traveled to Arizona, where he presented John McCain with a birthday cake that immediately melted in the southwestern heat. Then he flew to San Diego, where he was to take part in a ceremony commemorating the end of World War II in the Pacific. From there, Bush spoke once again to Blanco, who had shed her earlier optimism and implored the president, "We're going to need everything you've got," but was not specific about her needs. Staying the night in San Diego, Bush went to bed in the mistaken belief that the locals had everything under control.[53]

He was soon disabused of that notion. Early on Tuesday morning, 30 August, Katrina slammed into New Orleans. Bush was awoken at 5:00 a.m. and told that the Seventeenth Street Canal levee had been breached, and water from Lake Pontchartrain was surging into the city.[54] Rather than immediately depart for Crawford, Washington, or Louisiana, Bush chose to go ahead with business as usual in San Diego. He made his speech as scheduled, and a photographer caught him strumming a guitar that he had been given as a gift. When juxtaposed with scenes of destruction in the French Quarter, Bush looked disengaged; it also fed the developing narrative that he simply did not care about the suffering caused by Katrina.

By the time Bush arrived that evening for an overnight in Crawford, the destruction in New Orleans was too much to calculate. Ninety percent of the population of that city had been driven from their homes; 80 percent of New Orleans would, within hours, be under six to twenty feet of water. It was, as one writer entitled her 2018 novel on New Orleans after the hurricane, "the floating world."[55]

The next day, Bush took the advice of both his staff and Blanco and decided against encumbering the recovery effort with a presidential visit. Instead, on the suggestion of Rove, Bush ordered the pilots of Air Force One that when they reached New Orleans, they were to do a low-altitude flyover. Bush remembered that as he stared out the plane's window, "what I saw took my breath away." But Rove understated the case when he later wrote that the flyover was a "mistake." While Bush surveyed the damage, photographers were brought into his cabin. A photograph of Bush wearing his cabin windbreaker, staring out the window while flying safely above the carnage, dominated the news cycle. In a 2010 interview with NBC News, Bush acknowledged that permitting the photo to be taken was a "huge mistake" because it made him look as if he was "detached and uncaring." That image of indifference was reinforced by the former First Lady. When commenting on the refugees from the storm who had taken shelter in the Houston Astrodome, Barbara Bush quipped: "What I'm hearing, which is sort of scary, is they all want to stay in Texas. Everyone is so overwhelmed by the hospitality. And so many of the people in the arena here, you know, were underprivileged anyway, so this is working very well for them."[56]

Along with the initial devastation of Katrina's impact, and the devastation of the flooding, another crisis soon presented itself: looting and lawlessness in New Orleans, with the local authorities powerless to stop it. There were already some four thousand National Guard troops at the scene, but they would be nowhere near enough. Later that Wednesday, Blanco asked Bush to mobilize forty thousand additional troops from the Eighty-Second Airborne Division and send them to New Orleans. Two things stood in the way. The first was Blanco herself, who made it clear that while she wanted the troops sent immediately, she was opposed to any plan for the federalization of those troops. Second was the Posse Comitatus Act of 1878,[57] which made it illegal for active-duty troops to conduct law enforcement duties within the United States. Thus, even if deployed, the troops could not legally assist in containing the looting. Rumsfeld spoke against sending in the Eighty-Second Airborne, arguing that Americans would recoil at seeing the military in the streets of New Orleans; Rice countered with her belief that given the situation, the military would be welcomed. There was, however, a way for Bush to get around Posse Comitatus: if he declared New Orleans to be in a state of insurrection, he did not need the permission of the governor. It had been done before—that was how Dwight Eisenhower justified sending troops to Little Rock in 1957, and how the senior Bush had sent federal troops to Watts in 1992. But, as Bush remembered it, this would put him in the unenviable political position of overruling a female governor and an African American mayor. He decided to fly to New Orleans to speak with the governor in person.[58]

On Friday, 2 September, Bush flew south. His first stop was in Mobile, Alabama, where he met with Governor Bob Riley of Alabama and Governor Haley Barbour of Mississippi. Finding the situation there under manageable local control, Bush was pleased. When he asked if they were getting what they needed, Riley responded, "That Mike Brown is doing a heck of a job." Moments later, standing with the press, Bush found himself repeating Riley's words, turning to Brown and gushing, "Brownie, you're doing a heck of a job"—a comment that was used to demonstrate that Bush did not have a proper appreciation for, or understanding of, the gravity of the situation. Next Bush flew to Biloxi, Mississippi, where he walked through what he later called a "wasteland."[59]

Finally, Bush landed in New Orleans. In the conference room aboard Air Force One, he met with Nagin, Blanco, Brown, and Louisiana senator Mary Landrieu. Rove remembered that the mayor and the governor "both seemed shell-shocked, scattered, and without a clue as to what they needed." According to Bush's recollection, the meeting degenerated into demonstrative outpourings and blame assessment—Blanco thought that Nagin was in charge; Nagin thought that Blanco was in charge. Bush then met with Blanco alone. He told her that she needed to ask the federal government to take charge of the response; she said she needed twenty-four hours to consider what to do. Bush snapped: "We don't have twenty-four hours. We've waited too long already." Then Bush met privately with Nagin, who had just finished showering and eating a hot meal for the first time in four days. Nagin was clear: "Nobody's in charge." Bush then took a helicopter tour of the city before returning to Washington. But at trip's end, no decision had yet been reached about sending in federal troops.[60]

Bush met that evening at the White House with Card and Miers, who presented him with a solution: send troops into New Orleans under the command of a three-star general. On all matters pertaining to the active-duty troops, that general would report to the president; on all matters pertaining to the National Guard, he would report to the governor. The proposal was immediately transmitted to Blanco; the next day, she contacted the White House and declined the offer. Bush had had enough. Without the approval of the governor of Louisiana, he announced the deployment of some seven thousand active-duty troops to New Orleans. Those troops, under the command of Gen. Russel L. Honoré, would not have law enforcement powers (Bush: "I decided that sending troops with diminished authority was better than not sending them at all"). As a Louisiana native and an African American, Honoré easily won the support of the local population. And Honoré's no-nonsense, take-charge attitude was a perfect match for the situation. He won the trust of elected officials, and the situation in the streets was stabilized. Nevertheless, Bush would write that "my biggest substantive mistake was waiting too long to deploy active-duty troops."[61]

He might have added that his actions had left his administration exposed to charges that it did not care about the African American population of New Orleans. As Katrina washed away the majority black Upper Ninth Ward of the city, the Bush administration was charged with looking the other way and speeding federal aid to white neighborhoods. In the year following Katrina, more than 175,000 black residents left New Orleans; 75,000 of them never returned. In 2015, four of five white citizens of New Orleans believed that the city had mostly recovered, while three out of five blacks maintained that it has not. Bush faced accusations of racism; the most damning of these came from musician Kanye West, who stated, "George Bush doesn't care about black people."[62]

The final tally was gruesome: 1,833 people were killed by Katrina along the Gulf coast, with most of them from New Orleans. The storm had also caused an estimated $151 billion in damage. Josh Bolten, then the director of the Office of Management and Budget, requested fiscal year 2005 supplemental appropriations totaling $10.5 billion to fund immediate emergency response and relief needs associated with Katrina. While most in government found their way clear to support what one group of Republican senators termed a "Marshall Plan for the Gulf Coast," not everyone supported the expenditure. Conrad Burns, Republican senator from Wyoming, wrote the president: "It is true that the people of the Gulf Coast are hurting, and there is no question that they need our help. Unfortunately in my experience, whether we are feeding cattle or moving money, it seems that when in a rush, we end up spilling more out of our buckets than we get to the trough." Other states that were sending aid to Louisiana and the Gulf after Katrina requested that Bush declare a state of emergency for *their* state as well. One senator asked for more volunteer medical personnel to be sent to areas hit by Katrina. In a letter to Bush, Illinois senator Barack Obama observed that many of the victims he had spoken to had not had their calls to FEMA returned—"bureaucratic red tape and runarounds should not prevent these people from getting the help they need."[63]

Bush's postmortem was grim: "The problem was not that I made the wrong decisions. It was that I took too long to decide. I made an additional mistake by failing to adequately communicate my concern for the victims of Katrina." In 2015, Bush revisited New Orleans to participate in ceremonies commemorating the tenth anniversary of the storm. Not surprisingly, protesters turned out. One held a sign of the famous photo of Bush looking at the devastation from Air Force One; below it was written: "You're Early. Come Back in a Week."[64]

# 13

★ ★ ★ ★ ★

# SURGES

The second Battle of Fallujah—Operation Phantom Fury—began six days after Bush's reelection on 8 November 2004. Several days of intense bombing resulted in large numbers of insurgents abandoning the city. But this did nothing to quell the violence in Iraq; in fact, it only worsened. The insurgents relocated into other cities, most notably Mosul and Baghdad, and a wave of new fighting began. Suicide bombings increased in frequency, and by March 2005 some seven hundred civilians and eighty US soldiers were dead. As a result, fifteen thousand American troops had their tour of duty extended and were required to stay in Iraq. The creation of a new government, chosen by the new National Assembly, did nothing to reduce the violence. Ibrahim Jaafari, the new prime minister, was as incapable of dealing with the insurgency as had been his predecessor, Ayad Allawi. The second half of the year saw another major offensive by the insurgents, with the bloodiest battles taking place in Anbar Province—the home of the city of Fallujah.[1]

The situation in Afghanistan was becoming as bleak. Largely forgotten by the American people after the fiasco at Tora Bora in December 2001, Operation Enduring Freedom was pushed off the front pages by the war in Iraq, and it remained an underreported conflict for several years. But by mid-2005 it was clear that the Taliban was making a resurgence in Afghanistan. On 28 June 2005, four Navy SEALs were ambushed by the

Taliban; three of the SEALs were killed, as were all sixteen Army Special Forces reinforcements who had been sent on a rescue helicopter. That one engagement resulted in the greatest number of American deaths in a single day since the Afghan War had begun.[2]

The primary cause of the revival of the Taliban was the fact that Pakistan allowed it to happen. Despite significant amounts of American aid given to Pakistan to secure its help in the original war against Al-Qaida, Pakistan had always been an unwilling partner. The main reason for this was Pakistan's fear of India, which was only worsened by a March 2006 agreement between India and the United States to begin nuclear cooperation between the two nations. Thus, Pakistani president Pervez Musharraf looked elsewhere for security. He negotiated a peace accord with northern Afghan tribal leaders that allowed for a certain amount of border stability in return for his ignoring the movement of terrorists across the Afghan border. This allowed both Al-Qaida and the Taliban to operate from Pakistan with impunity (bin Laden and his followers were encamped in Pakistan with the full knowledge of the Pakistani government). By the end of 2006, the number of Taliban attacks in the eastern provinces had risen by 300 percent and showed no signs of stopping.[3]

On 28 June 2005, Bush traveled to Fort Bragg, North Carolina, to deliver a televised address on the escalating violence in Iraq and Afghanistan. The afternoon before the speech, Bush spent three hours meeting with the relatives of slain American soldiers. The experience exhausted him, and his delivery that evening was flat and listless. His question of the American people, designed to rally support, came across more like a tired plea: "I know Americans ask the question: 'Is the sacrifice worth it?'"[4]

Bush clearly believed that it was, but many Americans disagreed. Cindy Lee Sheehan of Vacaville, California, had lost her son, Casey, in Sadr City, a suburb of Baghdad. The tragedy led Sheehan to start what was at the time a one-woman protest against Bush's policies in Iraq. On 5 August 2005, Sheehan took her protest to Crawford, setting herself up some five miles outside the entrance to the presidential ranch. She refused to leave until she received an audience with the president. With her came the national media, which soon dubbed her outpost, and the tent she slept in at night, "Camp Casey." For his part, Bush refused to meet with Sheehan, choosing instead to respond to her through the press. On 1 September Sheehan left Crawford to spearhead a national antiwar tour, but overnight she had become the face of the antiwar movement, a movement that was gaining in numbers. That fall, thousands took part in antiwar protest marches in San Francisco, Los Angeles, and Washington, DC.[5]

Some on Capitol Hill had also begun to say no—if not to the War on Terror itself, then to the methods used by the administration to prosecute that war. By mid-2005, John McCain was spearheading a push for an amendment to the defense appropriations bill that would ban torture and limit the techniques used by interrogators with detainees by restricting their options to those laid out in the Army Field Manual. In an attempt to save the enhanced interrogation techniques (EITs), Cheney and CIA director Porter Goss met with McCain to try to convince him to withdraw his legislation. As Cheney remembers it, McCain was not interested in their point of view and stormed out of the meeting.[6] Besides, McCain had the votes. The Detainee Treatment Act passed the Senate on 5 October by a vote of 90 to 9.[7] Cheney argued for a veto, but Bush endorsed the bill on 2 November and signed it on 31 December.

However, Bush's endorsement of the act meant little. He did not intend to surrender a weapon that he believed had been important in keeping his compact with the American people after 11 September. Thus, Bush added a signing statement to the bill, clearly proclaiming that his view of the unitary presidency allowed him to ignore the provisions of this act if he deemed it necessary in order to prevent another attack:

> The executive branch shall construe . . . the Act, relating to detainees, in a manner consistent with the constitutional authority of the President to supervise the unitary executive branch and as Commander in Chief and consistent with the constitutional limitations on the judicial power, which will assist in achieving the shared objective of the Congress and the President . . . of protecting the American people from further terrorist attacks.[8]

One wonders if Bush would have signed the proposed law at all had it not been for two revelations in the press about his conduct of the War on Terror published at the exact moment he was presented with the bill. Bush publicly endorsed the Detainee Treatment Act on the same day that the *Washington Post* published a story disclosing the existence of the CIA Black Sites—a story that, only the day before, Bush had personally tried to squelch by meeting with the publishers. One of the most contentious debates in the administration's history came over whether Bush should publicly acknowledge the existence of the CIA's Black Site prisons and close the sites. Rice favored closing the secret prisons and transferring the prisoners to Guantanamo. But there, they would have more rights, and Cheney was decidedly against any such transfer. Rice carried the day. On 6 September 2006, Bush publicly acknowledged the CIA prisons for the first time and announced that fourteen high-value detainees, including Khalid Sheikh Mohammed (KSM), would be sent from there to Gitmo.[9]

Also, the *New York Times* shocked the world with a story of its own. As noted in chapter 11, in the fall of 2004 *Times* reporters James Risen and Eric Lichtblau had unearthed the existence of Operation Stellar Wind. At that time, Bush had been able to convince the *Times* to sit on its story. But this had not stopped Risen from authoring a book entitled *State of War*, which was about to be published in December 2005 and which included information about the warrantless surveillance program. Not wanting to be scooped by its own reporter, the *Times* informed the administration that it was ready to run its story on Stellar Wind. Once again, Bush tried to kill the story. Once again, he called publisher Arthur Sulzberger Jr. and editor Bill Keller to the Oval Office. Bush tried to convince the journalists that the nation was still in danger and that outing the program would put American lives at risk. Sulzberger said he would consider his request, but this time, Bush lost. On 15 December 2005, the *Times* published its story.[10]

Not surprisingly, following the events of 2005, Bush's polls went into a free fall. He began the year with a postelection 52 percent approval rating; by mid-November his approval rating had plummeted to 37 percent.[11] In an attempt to reverse his slide, in November and December Bush struck out on a confidence offensive, delivering a series of speeches around the country designed to show that he was starting to think about the endgame in Iraq. This began at the US Naval Academy at Annapolis on 30 November, where for the first time Bush publicly hinted at plans for a phased withdrawal from Iraq: "We will continue to shift from providing security and conducting operations against the enemy nationwide to conducting more specialized operations targeted at the most dangerous terrorists. We will increasingly move out of Iraqi cities, reduce the number of bases from which we operate, and conduct fewer patrols and convoys." The last of these talks was a televised broadcast from the Oval Office on 18 December 2005. While making it clear that "to retreat before victory would be an act of recklessness and dishonor and I will not allow it," Bush once again signaled that he had begun to think about pulling out: "As these achievements come, it should require fewer American troops to accomplish our mission. I will make decisions on troop levels based on the progress we see on the ground and the advice of our military leaders—not based on artificial timetables set by politicians in Washington. Our forces in Iraq are on the road to victory—and that is the road that will take them home." In all these speeches, Bush pleaded for the American people to have "patience."

The new year brought the latest test of American patience. On 22 February 2006, the al-Askari mosque in Samarra, located some sixty miles from Baghdad and one of the holiest sites in the Shi'a Muslim world, was attacked. Insurgents overwhelmed the guards, planted two bombs, and set them off from outside the mosque's compound. Intelligence was quickly convinced that it was a Zarqawi-led operation. But the bombing signaled a new phase of the insurgency. Rather than inflicting casualties—no one was killed in the bombing—the attack was designed to make Zarqawi and his forces the target of the wrath of other Iraqis. He had used symbolic violence to spike Shi'a hatred of his followers, thus throwing the country into sectarian violence that could, with a great deal of accuracy, be termed a civil war. That conflict could engulf the Americans, making them targets from all sides of Muslim Iraq.[12]

In the personal papers of George Bush is found a single piece of paper, with a single sentence typed on it. That sentence shows Bush's mindset in February 2006: "U.S. Service Member Deaths (as of February 16, 2006): Operation Iraqi Freedom: 2,270; Operation Enduring Freedom: 257."[13]

It was time to make some changes.

Those changes began with a series of personnel shifts within the administration. This may well have been sparked by a conversation Bush had with his friend Clay Johnson, who had served as his director of personnel until 2003 and was presently the deputy director of the Office of Management and Budget. The subject of the meeting—a meeting that came about at Johnson's request—was the White House staff, which Johnson believed had morphed into a mess. He tried to sketch out the lines of reporting on a napkin, but he couldn't do it. Johnson then used a term to describe the chaos; as Bush recalled, "It started with 'cluster' and ended with four more letters."[14]

Bush decided that the first step was "to take Andy up on his offer to move on." On 28 March 2006, Bush announced the appointment of budget director Josh Bolten as chief of staff, replacing Andy Card, who resigned. Bolten took over on 14 April and immediately began to make changes. On 26 April, journalist and frequent Bush critic Tony Snow replaced Scott McClellan as press secretary.[15] Porter Goss was replaced at CIA by NSA director Michael Hayden. Karl Rove was eased out of his position as deputy chief of staff for policy and was left with the elections/electoral strategy portfolio.[16]

But the most important long-term decision that Bolten made on the domestic policy side was a cabinet-level move. Bolten later remembered that he "had a fairly strong conviction that we would not survive the final three years of the Bush presidency without a financial crisis, and that John Snow, being a corporate leader but not a financial markets person, was ill suited to be in the role of Treasury Secretary through a major international financial crisis." Snow was replaced by a Bolten recruit, Henry M. Paulson Jr, who had grown up on a farm near Chicago and had graduated from Dartmouth College with a degree in English literature. Hardly ostentatious, he wore a plastic running watch. An Eagle Scout and an environmentalist, in 2006 he donated 680,000 acres of land to the Wildlife Conservation Society, a group he served as its chairman. Paulson had served in the Nixon White House both as a member of the Domestic Council and as staff assistant to the assistant secretary of defense. In 1974, after being recruited by Robert Rubin, who would serve as Clinton's secretary of the Treasury, Paulson began a tenure with Goldman Sachs that would last almost three decades. Beginning as an investment banker (at a salary of $30,000 per annum), in 1999 he became the CEO. By 2005 he was the highest-paid CEO on Wall Street, and by 2006 he was a senior partner.[17]

Bolten was much warier of change when it came to Bush's national security team. It has been reported that one of his long-term goals was to effect the resignation of Rumsfeld; if that was so, Bolten began his tenure by biding his time, and Rumsfeld stayed on. But there was little need to juggle the rest of the team. Bush was clearly more comfortable with Rice at State and with Steve Hadley as her successor as national security adviser than he had been with Colin Powell at State and Rice at the NSC.[18]

In an attempt to stabilize the situation in Iraq, Bush directed Rice to push the Iraqis to select a permanent prime minister (Ibrahim al-Jaafari had been selected prime minister following the 2004 elections, but he was universally seen to be a placeholder until the Parliament could elect a permanent prime minster). On 20 May 2006, Nouri al-Maliki, a Shi'a leader who had lived in exile in Syria, became prime minister of Iraq. But Maliki, a novice in politics, was just the most recent weak Iraqi leader who was powerless to stop the insurgency. With a sigh, Cheney called him a "disappointment. Problem."[19]

Nevertheless, the summer of 2006 began with a notable victory in Iraq. On 7 June 2006, in a targeted killing, an American F-16 dropped two five-hundred-pound bombs on a safe house some five miles north of Baqubah. The house was obliterated, and all six individuals inside were killed—including Abu Musab al-Zarqawi. The reaction of the coalition to the news was positively euphoric. Maliki said, "Today we have managed to put an end to Zarqawi. They [the insurgents] should stop now. They should review their situation and resort to logic while there is still time." For his part, Bush mused: "Now Zarqawi has met his end and this violent man will never murder again."[20]

But Zarqawi's death was only a temporary triumph. Bush later contended that "the summer of 2006 was the worst period of my presidency. . . . For the first time, I worried we might not succeed. . . . We could be looking at a repeat of Vietnam." Certainly from the perspective of casualty figures, this was not hyperbole, as the numbers kept increasing with no signs of abating (June 2006: 61 US military casualties; July: 51; August: 70; September: 77). By fall, Bush was getting reports of some one thousand attacks per week in Iraq.[21]

Bush's long summer of 2006 was distinguished not just by continuing problems in Iraq. On 29 June the Supreme Court announced its decision in *Hamdan v. Rumsfeld*.[22] Salim Hamdan, a Yemini detainee at Guantanamo, had filed a habeas corpus petition after his capture. Following the decision in *Hamdi v. Rumsfeld* (discussed in chapter 8), Hamdan was granted his petition and was tried before a military commission. He then argued that the military commission itself was unconstitutional. The court agreed. Writing for a 5–3 majority (Roberts did not participate in the case), John Paul Stevens argued not only that the military tribunals violated Hamdan's rights as a prisoner of war but that their very existence violated the tenets of the Uniform Code of Military Justice. But Stevens went further, maintaining that all protections of Common Article III of the Geneva Conventions—which forbade torture and inhuman or degrading treatment of detainees—applied to Hamdan specifically and to the War on Terror between the United States and Al-Qaida in general.

Stevens's use of international law in an American case was certainly novel. It was also noted that Stevens's opinion directly challenged Bush's signing statement appended to the Detainee Treatment Act, a statement which claimed that if the president saw fit, the use of EITs could be continued. A furious Bush saw this as an example of "judicial activism." In her memoir, Rice obliquely argued that "some members of the administra-tion"—without specifically naming them—wanted Bush to push for legis-lation that would override the decision of the Court. She then remembered that in an Oval Office meeting, she implored Bush, "Mr. President, you cannot reverse the Supreme Court." Bush complied. On 7 July, in a memo-randum for the secretaries of the military departments, Rumsfeld ordered, "You will ensure that all DoD [Department of Defense] personnel adhere to these [Article III] standards." On 6 September Bush announced that he was sending legislation—the Military Commissions Act—to Congress to create new military commissions that satisfied *Hamdan*—the Military Commissions Act. The same day, the Department of the Army released "Human Intelligence Collector Operations" (Army Field Manual 2-22.3), which included revised directives on the questioning of suspects.[23]

The situation in Afghanistan was also deteriorating. Throughout 2006, the Taliban continued to reinsert itself into Afghanistan. In September, a Taliban suicide bomber assassinated the governor of Paktia Province; the next day, another suicide bomber attacked the governor's funeral, killing six mourners. Bush dealt with the escalating situation by ordering an al-most 50 percent increase in the American troop presence in Afghanistan; troop levels in the country jumped from twenty-one thousand to thirty-one thousand. Bush called this a "silent surge," and it was largely missed by the press. Not surprisingly, his coalition partners contributed little to the increased troop presence.[24] But in his decision to send more troops to Afghanistan, Bush had hit on a strategy for Iraq.

Sometime in the spring of 2006, Bush spoke to Steve Hadley, then his na-tional security adviser, about Iraq. The president finally confessed, "This is not working. We need to take another look at the whole strategy." Hadley's NSC was unlike that of Rice, in that it was more conditioned to bring in a quick decision than it was to present options for discussion. Hadley immediately began a comprehensive assessment of the Iraq policy. That study revealed that Bush's commanders held two mutually exclu-sive viewpoints on how best to win in Iraq. One view, held by coalition commander in chief Gen. George W. Casey (who had replaced Gen. Rick Sanchez in that role) argued that the heavy troop presence in Iraq, particu-larly in Baghdad, was largely responsible for the violence. Casey believed that the United States looked like an occupying force, acted like an occu-pying force, and, as a result, was being treated like an occupying force by the insurgents. Therefore, the way to win in Iraq was to continue doing what Bush had been doing—cut back on the number of American troops and slowly turn the conflict over to the Iraqis.[25]

But others argued the opposite—that to win in Iraq, Bush needed to shift to a different strategy, and for that he would need more, not fewer, troops. Of those, Bush was most impressed with Col. Herbert L. McMaster, who had commanded a regiment in the northern Iraqi city of Tal Afar. McMaster's troops had pacified that city by going door to door in search of the insurgents. They not only succeeded in weeding out the insurgents, but their very presence put a stranglehold on the territory and helped rebuild local government. Bush later described McMaster's strategy as "clear, hold, and build"; military strategists called it the strategy of counterinsurgency. McMaster was not the only commander who had succeeded by using counterinsurgency tactics. In Mosul, Gen. David Petraeus, who had rewritten the army's counterinsurgency manual, had done much the same thing. Bush was quick to observe that once the number of troops in Tal Afar and Mosul was reduced, the violence flared up again. The experience of McMaster and Petraeus argued that counterinsurgency as a tactic worked, but for counterinsurgency to be given a chance to work, more troops—a surge—would be needed.[26]

The death knell for the old strategy of gradual withdrawal of troops came in the fall of 2006. Casey launched two missions—Operation Together Forward—to secure Baghdad. Both missions were conducted with a lighter American military footprint; both missions failed. Bush decided that a shift to a strategy of counterinsurgency, joined by a significant increase in the number of troops, was necessary in Iraq. But this decision would be a closely guarded secret.

The reason for the secrecy was pure politics. The 2006 midterm elections were fast approaching. Beleaguered Republicans, tied to an unpopular president, argued that the only way to win in November was for Bush to begin to withdraw troops from Iraq. In September, Bush Senate majority whip Mitch McConnell (R-KY) said this to Bush in no uncertain terms: "Your unpopularity is going to cost us control of the Congress." McConnell asked Bush to bring some troops home from Iraq. Bush was noncommittal, and he did not tell McConnell that he had already decided on a surge.[27]

In retrospect, it seems highly unlikely that any abrupt shift in military strategy—either withdrawal or surge—would have helped the Republicans in the midterm elections of 2006. There was no chance that a strategy positioning the Republicans as holding the best hope for victory in Iraq—in essence, the core of Bush's 2002 and 2004 strategies—could ever work again. Moreover, the war had taken Bush out of the ring. With plummeting approval ratings, he had become persona non grata for Republican candidates who had welcomed a visit from the president in 2002 and 2004 and, as we have seen, profited from those visits. Bush did little campaigning in 2006, and it is clear that even if he had taken to the road, his presence would have done little to help Republican candidates.

But along with the war, Bush's domestic policies since his reelection hurt Republican chances. The clumsy rollout of social security reform alarmed older voters, traditionally a core group for Republicans. The Miers nomination had unnerved social conservatives, who were now even more convinced that Bush was a moderate like his father. Despite the fact that the administration was limited in what it could do by feuding and incompetent state officials, its response to Katrina seemed ham-handed, and it offered no shortage of opportunity for the Democrats to paint the administration as uncaring about the people of New Orleans. And ballooning budget deficits offered a convenient target for the Democrats, as well as an area of concern for social conservatives. Add to this a number of scandals that touched Republican members of Congress (Randall Cunningham of California and Bob Ney of Ohio were convicted of accepting bribes, Mark Foley of Florida was found to have sent sexually explicit emails to House pages, and Speaker of the House Dennis Hastert was accused of covering up the existence of those messages) and the choice of fundraiser extraordinaire Illinois congressman Rahm Emanuel as head of the Democratic Congressional Campaign Committee, a decision that fattened Democratic coffers and left Republicans twisting in the wind.

There was, however, one thing that Bush might have done that could have made a difference in the outcome of the elections. During the last few weeks of the campaign, speculation ran rampant on the fate of Donald Rumsfeld. Many analysts argued that the only way for the Republican Party to get any traction in the election was for the president to dump his secretary of defense and one of the chief architects of the War on Terror. Bush had, indeed, decided to replace Rumsfeld, and he had once again begun a search for Rumsfeld's replacement. Bush began by offering the position to Jim Baker, who turned down the offer. Regrouping, the president spoke with Jack Morrison, a classmate of Bush's while at both Andover and Yale and a member of the President's Foreign Intelligence Advisory Board. Morrison suggested a successor for Rumsfeld, and as Bush remembered it, "I immediately called Steve Hadley and asked him to feel out Bob."[28]

The career of Robert M. Gates had spanned the better part of three decades. In 1971 he began his service at the CIA as a support staffer on arms control issues. Brent Scowcroft brought him on to Gerald Ford's NSC as a junior staffer, and Gates continued to serve on the NSC under Jimmy Carter. Gates returned to the CIA for the entirety of the Reagan administration; in 1986 Reagan nominated him as deputy director, but persistent questions about Gates's role in the Iran-Contra affair led him to withdraw his name. In 1989, Scowcroft brought Gates back to the NSC as his deputy. During the Persian Gulf War, Gates was a member of the senior Bush's war cabinet, known as the "Gang of Eight." In May 1991 Bush nominated Gates as the director of the CIA; he was confirmed in November 1991 and served until the end of the Bush administration in 1992. In 1999 Gates began a tenure of service at Texas A&M University, first as the dean of the George Bush School of Government and Public Service and then as that institution's president. Gates was still at A&M when the younger Bush offered him the job at Defense. While Gates had turned Bush down for the new post of director of national intelligence in 2005, he was interested in Defense. Hadley asked him if he would accept if Bush offered him the position; Gates gave him an immediate yes.[29]

On 31 October Bush told Cheney that he had decided to accept Rumsfeld's resignation and that he was thinking about asking Gates to be his replacement. Cheney later remembered that Bush was "informing me of his decision, not soliciting my views. . . . He turned and was out the door fast. He knew I'd be opposed, and I suspect he didn't want to hear the arguments he knew I'd make." But the same day, Bush told the news gaggle that Rumsfeld had his full support. Bush would later justify this deception by arguing, "If I were to change Defense secretaries at that point, it would look like I was making military decisions with politics in mind. I decided to make the move after the election." Be that as it may, Bush's refusal to dismiss Rumsfeld before the election may have been a missed opportunity to pick up some votes among those who opposed Bush's prosecution of the war. On 4 November Bush told Ken Mehlman, Bush's 2004 campaign manager and now chair of the Republican National Committee, that he was ready to fire Rumsfeld. Mehlman asked Bush to do it the next day—two days before the elections.[30]

The next day, Gates met with Bush at the Crawford ranch. Among other things, Gates told Bush that he supported a surge, and he protested to the president that the war in Afghanistan had been all but ignored. At the end of the interview, Bush asked Gates if he had any questions. Gates said no, but Bush volunteered: "Cheney?" Gates smiled in reply, and Bush was blunt: "He is a voice, an important voice, but only one voice." Gates accepted the position before he left the meeting. But despite Mehlman's recommendation, Gates's nomination was not immediately announced. After speaking with Gates, Bush called Cheney that same day and gave him the opportunity to tell Rumsfeld. Cheney did so (according to Cheney, Rumsfeld's response was "Okay. I got it." Rumsfeld remembered that he said "Fair enough"). Two days later, on Election Day, Rumsfeld delivered his letter of resignation to Bush.[31]

On 7 November, the Democrats ran the table. Both houses of Congress had been under Republican control since 1994. Now, the Democrats won a net gain of six seats in the Senate and took control of that chamber by a 51–49 margin. In the House, the Democrats picked up thirty-one seats; their margin of control was now 232–203. This shift led to the election of Nancy Pelosi (D-CA) as the first female Speaker of the House in the nation's history.

The day after the elections, with both Rumsfeld and Gates by his side, Bush announced that Rumsfeld was stepping down, and he would nominate Gates as his replacement.

The unmistakable message of the 2006 elections was that the American public wanted change in Iraq. The release of the final report of the Iraq Study Group reinforced that message. In early 2006, Congressman Frank Wolff, a Virginia Republican, had proposed the creation of an independent bipartisan group charged with exploring the possibility of new strategies in Iraq. Chaired by James Baker and Lee Hamilton, the study group released its report on 6 December. Calling the situation in Iraq "grave and deteriorating," it proposed that Iraqi Army Brigades to take over much of the security in their country. It also recommended that while the United States should increase the number of advisers who were then working with the Iraqi Army—a limited surge, of sorts—"U.S. combat forces could begin to move out of Iraq" as "the primary mission of U.S. forces . . . evolve[d] to one of supporting the Iraqi army, which would take over primary responsibility for combat operations." Cheney in particular was highly critical of the report: "The only place the word *victory* appeared in the document was in connection with the chances for an Al-Qaida victory. This was not a strategy for winning the war."[32]

The report was also a preview of the criticism that would follow Bush's announcement of a policy of counterinsurgency backed by an increase in troops. Some of that criticism came from within the White House itself. Rice agreed with a counterinsurgency strategy but was not initially in favor of a troop surge. At an 8 December 2006 meeting, Bush snapped at her—"So what's your plan, Condi?" When Gen. Ray Odierno, then the commander of Multi-National Corps–Iraq, told Rice that it was his opinion that more troops were needed, she came around.[33]

On 13 December, Bush and Cheney went to the Pentagon to convince the Joint Chiefs. Gates and Rumsfeld (who had stayed on at Defense until Gates's confirmation by the Senate) were both in attendance. The Chiefs were a harder sell than Rice. They believed that the surge would, in their words, "break the military"—it would put such a strain on supplies, as well as on families through extended deployments, that the military would crack under the pressure. Gates remembered being surprised by the fact that "not one [of the members of the Joint Chiefs of Staff] uttered a single sentence on the need for us to win in Iraq."[34] In part to mollify the Chiefs and to win their approval for the surge strategy, on 19 December Bush announced that he supported an increase in the size of the military. Concurrent with that announcement was the news that Casey had been removed from command and promoted to army chief of staff; Gen. David Petraeus was now in command in Iraq, with Gen. Ray Odierno as his deputy.[35]

On 30 December 2006 Saddam Hussein was executed at the joint Iraqi-American military base, Camp Justice. A special tribunal made up of five Iraqi judges had found him guilty of crimes against humanity. Immediately before his hanging (he had requested an execution by firing squad, in line with his position as commander in chief, but that request was denied), Shi'a partisans sneered at him and bellowed their allegiance to Muqtada al-Sadr. A grainy cell phone video of the execution was immediately seen around the world. The next day, 31 December 2006, the American casualty toll in Iraq hit three thousand.[36]

On 10 January 2007, admitting that "it's clear that we need to change our strategy in Iraq," Bush announced the surge to the American people. A total of 21,500 more troops would be sent to Iraq to spearhead what would become a counterinsurgency strategy. All troops were to be embedded with Iraqi troops. Bush also called on Congress to increase the size of the army and Marine Corps by 90,000 troops.

And then, as Gates remembered, "All hell broke loose."[37]

At his confirmation hearings in late January 2007, Petraeus was asked by John McCain, who supported the surge, if the newly defined mission in Iraq could succeed without more troops. He responded, "No, sir."[38] But any call for an increase in troops to support what had, to that point, been a losing effort was bound to meet with congressional opposition. On 16 February, the House passed a nonbinding resolution opposing the surge, 246 to 182. The next day, the Senate tried to do the same, but Democratic majority leader Harry Reid could not break a filibuster.

Following the implementation of the surge, initial casualty figures were not promising. In February 2007, 81 American troops were killed; in March, 81 more; April, 104; May, 126; June, 101. Democratic presidential candidates pounced. Joe Biden pronounced the new strategy as "a tragic mistake"; Barack Obama mused: "The fundamental question that American people . . . are having to face now is, at what point do we say 'enough'?" After an angry White House meeting between Bush and congressional leaders to discuss the surge, Reid told reporters: "This war is lost. The surge is not accomplishing anything."[39]

But angry rhetoric aside, Bush had put the opposition into a box. On 5 February 2007, Bush sent a $93 billion spending request to Congress to support both the counterinsurgency and the surge.[40] Remembering how in 2004 the Republicans had beaten them up over their votes against the war resolution, few Democrats—certainly not any of those running for president in 2008—were about to vote against the spending bill. As a result, they tried to make the bill acceptable to their interests. On 25 April, the House passed Bush's $95 billion spending bill to subsidize the wars in Iraq and Afghanistan. However, a rider was attached to the bill, mandating a complete withdrawal of American troops by March 2008. The next day, the Senate concurred with that bill. On 1 May Bush vetoed it. Not having the votes necessary to override, a chastised Congress sent him back his spending bill without the troop withdrawal rider attached; Bush signed the bill on 25 May.

By the fall, there was evidence that the counterinsurgency strategy, backed by the troops of the surge, was working. This was first apparent

in Anbar Province, where thanks to the troops of the surge, which reinforced an already present tribal revolt against the insurgents, violence in
Anbar dropped by 90 percent. In Anbar alone, insurgent attacks fell from
thirteen hundred in October 2006 to about two hundred in August 2007.
Soon, much the same results as had been seen in the "Anbar Awakening"
were reported from the Diyala Province and the Sunni neighborhoods of
Baghdad. Gates remembered that civilian casualties were down 17 percent
from December 2006, total deaths were down 48 percent, and murders
were down 64 percent. Such successes gave Bush an opening to explore
timetables for withdrawing the surge troops. That September, he announced that if the circumstances were acceptable, all surge forces would
be withdrawn from Iraq by summer 2008. On 10 April 2008, Bush confirmed that he would withdraw the last surge brigades from Iraq by July.[41]

In September 2008, US forces handed over control of Anbar Province
to the Iraqi government—the first Sunni province to be returned to the
Shi'a-led government. Maliki began to pressure Bush to commit to a date
for the withdrawal of all American troops from Iraq, and Bush agreed to
begin negotiations for a timetable of a phased-in withdrawal. Both sides
hammered out a Status of Forces Agreement (SOFA) that allowed troops
to stay in Iraq past the expiration of the United Nations mandate at the
end of 2008, and a Strategic Framework Agreement (SFA) that provided
for a close relationship between the two nations even after troops had been
withdrawn. The original hope was to sign the agreement by 31 July, as the
surge forces were being withdrawn, but that deadline was soon missed. It
took until 3 November to finish the deal. The final agreement: American
troops would begin a withdrawal in June 2009—when Bush was out of the
White House—a withdrawal that would be complete by the end of 2011.
The pact was endorsed both by Petraeus, who was now head of Central
Command, and by his successor in Iraq, Ray Odierno, and signed by Bush,
now a lame-duck president, and Maliki in Iraq on 13 December 2008. Thus,
George W. Bush bequeathed to his successor an unfinished war.[42]

# 14

★ ★ ★ ★ ★

# BAILOUTS

The US district attorneys represent the United States in matters that come before the US district courts and the US courts of appeals. There are ninety-three US attorneys, each of whom was a presidential appointee who served for a four-year term. On 7 December 2006, through his attorney general, Alberto Gonzales, Bush fired seven of them—Daniel G. Bogden (Las Vegas Office); Paul K. Charlton (Phoenix); Margaret Chiara (Grand Rapids); David C. Iglesias (Albuquerque); Carol S. Lam (San Diego); John McKay (Seattle); and Kevin Ryan (San Francisco). On 20 December, H. E. "Bud" Cummins, US district attorney for Arkansas, resigned; he had been told in June that his resignation was needed.[1]

The firing of US attorneys at the beginning of a new administration was a common occurrence; theirs was a political appointment, and they served at the pleasure of the president. But their firing in the middle of Bush's second term raised eyebrows. While Gonzales remembered in his memoirs a reason for each of the firings, seven of the eight fired attorneys had received good to excellent performance reviews (Ryan's San Francisco office was said to be in "crisis"). Soon, however, reports surfaced in the press that suggested their dismissal seemed to be motivated less by their performance in office than by their disagreements with the Bush administration. Charlton had clashed with Washington over the death penalty and FBI interrogation rules, and Lam had argued with the White House over immigration and firearms cases. Most troubling was the fact that several of the attorneys seemed to have been fired for purely political reasons: Iglesias had been contacted by Sen. Pete Domenici (R-NM) and Rep. Heather Wilson (R-NM) to inquire about initiating a federal corruption probe into New Mexico Democrats, and the replacement for Cummins was J. Timothy Griffin, a former aide to Karl Rove. Moreover, a clause in the newly reauthorized (9 March 2006) USA PATRIOT Act allowed for the appointment of interim US attorneys without a specified time limit to their term in office.[2]

It was, in retrospect, foolish to fire the attorneys less than a month after the Democrats had seized back control of both houses of Congress in 2006, a point to which Gonzales would later agree. Spoiling for a fight, the Congress shifted into full investigatory mode. Before the new year was three weeks old, Gonzales had been called to testify before the Senate Judiciary Committee ("I would never, ever make a change in a United States attorney position for political reasons, or if it would in any way jeopardize an ongoing, serious investigation"). On 6 March the dismissed attorneys testified before Congress, with some of them claiming they were fired for political reasons. On 13 March Gonzales held a news conference; after admitting that "mistakes were made," he claimed that he "never saw documents. We never had a discussion about where things stood." The next day, Bush, who was in Mexico to meet with President Felipe Calderón, was forced to defend his beleaguered attorney general, insisting that he had confidence in him. On 19 April Gonzales testified on the Hill about the firing of the attorneys—sixty-four times he said he could not remember the particulars of the decision.[3]

The story descended into a typical Washington melodrama, one that lasted well into 2008: Congress demanded pertinent records from the files of both Josh Bolten and Harriet Miers . . . the White House dug in, invoking executive privilege in both cases . . . Gonzales was required to produce any emails from his files regarding Rove's role in the matter . . . Miers was subpoenaed to testify but refused to show . . . Congress charged both Miers and Bolten with contempt . . . John Conyers (D-MI) invited John Ashcroft, John Yoo, Karl Rove, and David Addington to testify . . . By mid-2008, the country's attention was on the upcoming presidential election, and the US attorneys scandal died of its own weight, but not before claiming a key administration victim—on 27 August, Alberto Gonzales announced his resignation.[4]

In the midst of the US attorneys scandal, a second scandal, one that hit close to Bush's beloved wounded veterans, hit the front page. On 18 and 19 February 2007, the *Washington Post* reported on the conditions present at the outpatient facilities at Walter Reed Army Medical Center in Washington, DC. To be sure, the facility was overburdened. Outpatients, many of whom showed severe physical and psychological ailments, outnumbered admitted patients seventeen to one; some had been outpatients for more than two years. But the part of the story that struck home dealt with the sickening conditions of the outpatient facilities. Called the "Other Walter Reed" by patients, these facilities consisted of five buildings that were near the main hospital. In one, a patient said he could "see the bathtub on the floor above through a rotted hole. The entire building, constructed between the world wars, often smells like greasy carry-out. Signs of neglect are everywhere: mouse droppings, belly-up cockroaches, stained carpets, cheap mattresses." Added to this was patient neglect. Records were routinely lost; one soldier had to produce his Purple Heart to prove his service before he would be admitted.[5]

Prior to the revelations, the army had announced that in 2011 it would be closing Walter Reed. But this did not stop the story from becoming a cause célèbre. It was also the first public test of Robert Gates as secretary of defense. Gates moved quickly, setting up an investigatory body chaired by Togo D. West Jr., who had served as secretary of the army and secretary of the Department of Veterans Affairs under Clinton, and former congressman Jack Marsh, who had served as secretary of the army under Reagan. The commandant of Walter Reed was forced to resign on 1 March; the next day, so too was Bush's secretary of the army, Francis J. Harvey. Bush and Gates were given points in the press for acting quickly and decisively, but when congressional investigations found like conditions in other VA hospitals throughout the country, the story continued into 2008.[6]

Hampered by unpopularity, war, political stalemate, and scandal, the administration also had to face several international crises of some import.

As was the case for each of his immediate predecessors, Bush was wary of North Korea's desire to produce a weapon of mass destruction—in this case, a nuclear weapon. In 1994, Clinton had negotiated the Agreed Framework—North Korea agreed to hold up on its threat to withdraw from the Nuclear Non-Proliferation Treaty and freeze its nuclear program, in exchange for energy aid from the United States. It didn't stay frozen for long—the United States was slow to deliver on its aid, and North Korea built a uranium-enrichment reactor.[7]

In the shadow of 11 September, Bush came to view North Korea as an imminent threat to American security. In January 2002, Bush included North Korea as one of the charter members of his "axis of evil." But rather than launch a preventative war against North Korea, as he was planning to do against Iraq, Bush chose diplomacy. Spinning North Korea as an out-of-control rogue nation that threatened the stability of Southeast Asia, if not the world, Bush pressured China to intervene. Undeterred, on 10 January 2003 North Korea withdrew from the Nuclear Non-Proliferation Treaty, thus turning the Agreed Framework into a dead letter by allowing North Korea to accelerate its program without fear of treaty sanctions. In April 2003, at a trilateral meeting held in Beijing between North Korea, China, and the United States, North Korea admitted for the first time that it was in possession of a nuclear weapon.[8]

Amid all this saber-rattling, and despite Cheney's adamant opposition, Bush agreed with Rice, who wanted to proceed with the Six-Party Talks (involving the United States, China, North Korea, Russia, South Korea, and Japan), which had been instituted to effectuate the end of North Korea's nuclear arms program. Those talks began in Beijing in August 2003 and went through three rounds until February 2005, when North Korea publicly announced that it possessed a nuclear weapon and that it would no longer attend the talks. However, Bush and Rice were wedded to the process. In September 2005, after extracting a statement from the United States that it had no plans to invade their nation, the North Koreans came back for a fourth round of talks, which ended with North Korea's agreement to abandon all nuclear weapons. Bush later remembered, "I was skeptical."[9]

He had a right to be. On 4 July 2006—a date no doubt chosen with irony in mind—North Korea fired seven missiles into the Sea of Japan. Three months later, it detonated its first nuclear weapon. Both actions were in direct violation of the agreement of September 2005. Bush publicly promised to hold North Korea "fully accountable" for any further nuclear proliferation, but being committed to negotiations, this was empty rhetoric. The administration pressed on with the Six-Party Talks, which led to a February 2007 deal negotiated by assistant secretary of state (and former ambassador to South Korea) Christopher Hill, one that Rice presented to Bush without informing Cheney. In it, North Korea agreed to shut down its chief nuclear reactor and also agreed to allow United Nations inspectors to reenter the country to verify that shutdown. In return, the Six-Party powers agreed to give energy assistance to North Korea and to take that country off their list of terrorist nations. Bush agreed to the deal, but with the exception of the North Koreans, it had few friends, even within the six parties: on our shores, Cheney and his allies had long been perturbed with North Korea, and they made it clear that they hated the deal.[10]

It was soon apparent that the North Koreans were in secret violation of, at the very least, the spirit of that deal. On 24 April 2007, Meir Dagan, the director of Israeli intelligence (Mossad), and two aides to Israeli prime minister Ehud Olmert flew to Washington. There, they showed Cheney and Hadley photographic evidence that Syria was building a nuclear re-actor—often referred to as the Al-Kibar reactor—in the Deir ez-Zor region of Syria. That reactor bore a striking resemblance to the North Korean reactor at Yong-byon, which had produced plutonium for use in nuclear weaponry. To hammer the point home, Mossad's photos clearly showed North Korean workers inside the Syrian facility. North Korea was helping Syria build a nuclear weapon. Olmert called Bush and asked him point-blank to bomb the reactor.[11]

It took until 17 June for Bush to meet with his national security team in the White House residence to discuss the situation. Despite Bush's prom-ise to hold North Korea "fully accountable" for any further proliferation, there were several variables to be considered. Cheney remembered that Bush's first question was "How good is the intelligence?"—a clear indi-cation of an administration that had been, in Cheney's words, "snakebit" on the intelligence over WMDs in Iraq. Director of national intelligence Michael McConnell then replied, "It's about as good as it gets," saying that the intelligence community had "high confidence" that this was, indeed, a nuclear reactor.[12]

There was never any doubt where Cheney would come down on the issue. He remembered for one interviewer that he had, indeed, "felt strongly that we should take [the reactor] out," but he also remembered that his was a "lone voice." Indeed, Cheney was the only one of Bush's ad-visers who thought that bombing the suspected reactor was a good idea. Cheney recalled that Rice opposed the strike because she was trying to get Syria to attend the upcoming peace conference on the Middle East, to be held at Annapolis. On 19 June, Olmert came personally to Washington to try to convince Bush to bomb the reactor. Bush told Olmert that he had decided against a military strike. Olmert's response: "This is something that hits at the very serious nerves of this country." On 6 September 2007, the Israelis took matters into their own hands and bombed the nuclear reactor. The code name for the Israeli mission was, appropriately enough, Operation Outside the Box. Gates wryly noted that events had turned into a victory for Cheney: "By not confronting Olmert, Bush effectively came down on Cheney's side. By not giving the Israelis a red light, he gave them a green one."[13]

After visiting Afghanistan in January 2007, Gates returned convinced that the "silent surge" was not enough. He began to advocate for more troops—both American and NATO—to be sent to Afghanistan. Facing the needs of the Iraqi surge, the best that Gates could get from Bush was an extension of the deployment of the Tenth Mountain Division for an additional 120 days, and the hastening of the deployment of units of the Eighty-Second Airborne Division. But NATO refused to commit any more than a handful of troops, and Pakistan balked at ending its dalliance with the Taliban. Afghan president Hamid Karzai was also intransigent, fearing a backlash from his people if there was a pronounced increase in the foreign military footprint. In January 2008, thirty-two hundred new marines were sent to Afghanistan on what Gates termed a "one-time deployment." But as the Bush administration ended its tenure, the War in Terror in Afghanistan was far from concluded.[14] And it was about to face its greatest domestic crisis.

The fall of the "dot.com" economy of the 1990s and the recession of 2001 had done little to shake the prevailing confidence in the American economy. Nowhere was that confidence more prevalent than in the housing market. Since the early 1980s, both the demand for and the price of American housing, particularly in the South and the Southwest, had skyrocketed. At the peak of the housing boom, 69 percent of the population owned a home, and between 1993 and 2007, the average price of a home in the United States doubled. All of this, of course, was financed on credit, and along with the housing boom came a corresponding boom in the US mortgage market. Virtually anyone could get a mortgage, regardless of their income. Subprime mortgages—mortgages that were made available to low-income borrowers and others who had trouble keeping a regular payment schedule—were plentiful, but they carried great risk. Subprimes came with higher interest rates; if the housing bubble burst, and home prices dropped, families could find that their home was now worth less than the mortgage they held on it. While there was little to stop the banks from feeding the credit boom, but there was virtually nothing to stop the noncommercial banks (investment banks such as Bear Stearns and Lehman Brothers) and the government-sponsored enterprises (GSEs)—private lending institutions with federal charters, most notably two mortgage goliaths: the Federal National Mortgage Association (Fannie Mae) and the Federal Home Loan Mortgage Corporation (Freddie Mac)—all of which operated and lent massive sums with the barest of government regulation. Quite simply put, banks found ways to loan money to just about anybody—damn the torpedoes, full speed ahead. And if the value of a home fell, then a homeowner would owe more on their mortgage than their home was worth.[15]

The Bush administration had largely surfed the crest of the housing boom, seeing it as a badly needed shot of optimism for a country fixated on the War on Terror. It was also not missed that in 2004, mortgage bankers and brokers donated close to $847,000 to Bush's reelection campaign, more than triple what they had donated in 2000. Nevertheless, in 2005 Ben Bernanke, then the chair of Bush's Council of Economic Advisers, attempted to strengthen the oversight of Freddie Mac and Fannie Mae, only to have his attempts stymied (depending on who you read, they were stymied either by a recalcitrant Congress or by the president himself, who refused to approve a compromise with Congress that had been negotiated by then Treasury secretary John Snow). Quite simply put, in the words of one of Bush's economic advisers, even with the post-9/11 warning signs, "No one wanted to stop that bubble."[16]

The first hint that the good times were over for the housing market came in the summer of 2007, when subprime lender Countrywide Financial showed signs of declining liquidity, and its closest competitor went bankrupt. In August the mortgage market continued its meltdown when BNP Paribas, France's largest bank, announced that it was freezing any withdrawals from several of its funds that were backed by US subprime mortgages. The response of American policymakers was to refuse any request for direct federal intervention (such as the request that came from Countrywide, which was ignored, leaving it to be swallowed up by Bank of America).[17] While this action led to a deceptive lull in the crisis, it was not long before other financial giants started to teeter. Merrill Lynch and Citigroup both wrote down their troubled assets, both took huge losses for 2007, and both fired their CEOs. In January 2008, the administration proposed a temporary $150 billion in tax cuts to stimulate the economy, but by that point, such an action was like the Dutch boy's finger in the dike.[18]

The housing bubble had burst. Home prices plummeted, and the number of foreclosures skyrocketed (from 71,507 in January 2005 to 261,255 in May 2008). The collapse of the US housing market destroyed some $11 trillion in household wealth. In Toledo, Ohio, one in every ten homeowners was either in arrears or in foreclosure. The markets lost 10 percent of their housing stock over a two-and-a-half-year period, leading to a nationwide loss of $4 trillion in wealth in retirement accounts.[19]

As a result, mortgage brokers tried desperately to sell out—those who could not find a buyer now faced financial ruin. Bear Stearns, one of the nation's oldest (founded in May 1923) and the nation's seventeenth-largest investment bank, was heavily leveraged; for every dollar that Bear had in capital, it had borrowed thirty-three dollars to invest, most of it in mortgaged-based securities. And as an investment bank, Bear had been allowed to operate in the market largely unfettered by any effective government regulation. When the bubble burst, Bear was overexposed, and on 10 March, investors began to pull their money—the run on Bear had begun. On 13 March its cash reserves dropped from $18 billion to $2 billion, and Bear was ready to declare bankruptcy.[20]

Bush later claimed that his and Treasury secretary Henry Paulson's first inclination was to let Bear fall of its own weight. But the fact of the matter was that the administration could not step in to save Bear. Because Bear Stearns was an investment bank, the Federal Deposit Insurance Corporation (FDIC) could not seize its assets as it could if it was a commercial bank. Nevertheless, Paulson argued that there was a very real chance that the tremor caused by the crash of Bear would cause the fall of other equally vulnerable financial firms—the result could be a serious shock to the world financial system. So Paulson went shopping for a buyer for Bear Stearns. He found one at JPMorgan Chase, which was interested in buying Bear but was wary of being saddled with Bear's mortgage-backed securities. But Chase could not do it alone. As a result, Bernanke, Paulson, and Timothy Geithner, the president of the New York Federal Reserve, agreed to lend JPMorgan Chase $30 billion from the New York Fed. On 14 March, Bear Stearns was taken over by JPMorgan Chase at a cost of $2 dollars per share.[21]

Later that same day, Bush spoke to the Economic Club of New York. He warned that things were about to get worse, and that the government's action in the purchase of Bear was only the beginning of federal involvement in the crisis: "The temptation of Washington is to say that anything short of a massive government intervention in the housing market amounts to inaction. I strongly disagree with that sentiment. I believe there ought to be action, but I'm deeply concerned about law and regulation that will make it harder for the markets to recover." Following the acquisition of Bear by JPMorgan Chase, the markets calmed down a bit, but few insiders thought it was over.

The next shoe to drop would land on the GSEs. Fannie Mae and Freddie Mac had been full-fledged participants in the mortgage boom. It was assumed by most insiders that if they ran into the same type of trouble that sank Bear Stearns, the government, which owned their charter, would have no choice but to bail them out. But this could happen only if Congress approved. It is a measure of the fear of the day that despite Bush's low approval ratings, and despite the oncoming presidential election, Congress gave Bush the power to save both Fannie and Freddie even before they ran out of capital. On 30 July Bush signed the Housing and Economic Recovery Act, which created the Federal Housing Finance Administration, which could, under certain circumstances, make up to $300 billion in mortgages available to both Freddie and Fannie. But it would not be enough. In early August, both Freddie and Fannie announced huge quarterly losses. Faced with the impending crash of the two mortgage giants, Bush made the decision to nationalize their dwindling assets. On 5 September, Paulson and Bernanke told the CEOs of Fannie Mae and Freddie Mac that their companies were being seized by the federal government, which would now back their insured mortgages. The nationalization of the two largest GSEs was as bold a move as any decision that Bush had made as president, and it effectively stopped the run on Fannie and Freddie. In his announcement of the takeover, Paulson argued that "nothing about our actions today in any way reflects a changed view of the housing correction or the strength of other U.S. financial institutions."[22] Few people believed him, and the worst was yet to come.

According to journalist Peter Baker, Bush expected Hillary Clinton to succeed him in 2008. This was hardly an appealing prospect for Bush, who reportedly remarked to aides, "Wait 'til her fat ass is sitting at this desk."[23] But the Democratic Party had other ideas. In a stunning upset, Illinois senator Barack Obama defeated Clinton for the Democratic nomination (the race was so close that after all the primaries, neither Clinton nor Obama held a majority of delegates; the matter would be decided by a large bloc of delegates not chosen in the primaries—"superdelegates"—who would go to the convention undecided, and eventually supported Obama). In his own party, old Bush rival John McCain held off a crowded field of candidates, including former governors Mitt Romney of Massachusetts and Mike Huckabee of Arkansas, to become the presumptive nominee of the Republican Party.

This left McCain with the thorny problem of what to do with an unpopular incumbent. McCain's initial strategy was to completely distance himself from Bush. He kept Bush away from the convention, held in St. Paul, and reduced the president to addressing the delegates via video. Bush was also given no advance notice of the 29 August 2008 choice of Alaska governor Sarah Palin as McCain's running mate. But within days of McCain's nomination, the financial crisis would take a particularly precipitous turn, one that would change the trajectory of his campaign, as well as affect the immediate future of the American economy.[24]

Founded in 1850, Lehman Brothers was the nation's fourth-largest investment bank. In 2007 it ranked number one on *Fortune* magazine's list of "Most Admired Securities Firms." But like Bear, Lehman had bet heavily on subprime mortgages, and when the housing bubble burst, Lehman found itself vulnerable. Despite earning for itself the sobriquet of being "Too Big to Fail," on 10 September Lehman stunned the nation and the world by announcing quarterly losses of $3.9 billion.[25]

Paulson was quoted as being "adamant" that no government money be used in any deal resolving the Lehman crisis.[26] Thus, as they had done with Bear, Bush and Paulson tried to find a buyer for Lehman. There were soon two banks in the mix: Bank of America and Barclay's. But neither firm was willing to take on Lehman's noxious assets. At 1:45 a.m. on 15 September, Lehman declared bankruptcy—it was the biggest bankruptcy in American history, and there would be no federal bailout for Lehman. The crash of Lehman sparked a market sell-off. On 15 September, the Dow dropped some 500 points. Securities were sold off at bargain prices; what profits there were from those sales bought Treasury Bills and gold as investors abandoned their investment banks.

Close on the heels of Lehman's bankruptcy, the American International Group (AIG), the nation's largest insurance company, also faced default. Fearing a complete collapse of the nation's insurance system, Bush moved quickly and decisively—as it had done with Fannie and Freddie, the federal government took over AIG. On 16 September, $85 billion was pushed into AIG through the New York Fed; in return, the federal government received a warrant for 79.9 percent of AIGs shares. The amount spent by the government on the deal was indeed astounding: $85 billion was more than the Congress spent each year on transportation, and almost three times as much as the government spent on combating AIDS.[27]

The nationalization of AIG only served to save the company. On September 17, the credit markets, now in full-fledged panic, froze, as banks refused to lend money to anyone or anything. The next day, at a meeting of his economic team, Paulson informed Bush that he had no choice but to step in to save the American economy. To Paulson, this necessitated Bush's approval of what would be the largest government bailout in American history. Paulson and Christopher Cox, a former Republican congressman from California then serving as the head of the Securities and Exchange Commission, pitched a long-term solution to the crisis: the federal government would guarantee all money market deposits, introduce a new lending organization to revive the commercial paper market, and purchase hundreds of billions of dollars in mortgage-backed securities—that program would become the Troubled Asset Relief Program (TARP). The initial price tag was set at $700 billion. Bush agreed to the plan, and work began to secure congressional approval (Cheney later remembered that "we briefly contemplated not seeking congressional authority").[28]

On 24 September, Bush addressed the nation on the financial crisis, observing that "we are in the midst of a serious financial crisis, and the federal government is responding with decisive action." Bush parsed his words—the speech draft shows that he changed the line reading "So I have proposed that the federal government *help eliminate* the risk posed by these troubled assets," to "*reduce* the risk"; he also changed his reference to "the *collapse* of the housing market set off a domino effect across our economy" to "the *decline* in the housing market." After outlining the proposal for TARP, Bush promised that "once this crisis is resolved, there will be time to update our financial regulatory structures," and that "in the long run, Americans have good reason to be confident in our economic strength."[29]

The crisis took all the air out of McCain's campaign. His party was being blamed for the financial crisis, but if McCain came out in favor of Bush's plan, the conservatives in his own party would skewer him for being a big-government spender. As a result, McCain reversed his strategy of keeping his distance from Bush and instead asked the president for a favor. On 24 September McCain called Bush and asked him to convene a meeting at the White House to discuss the crisis. Bush remembered that virtually every member of his team, including Bolten and Paulson, were against having the meeting. But Bush agreed, and he called Obama, requesting that he also attend (Bush remembered that Obama replied, "Anytime the president calls, I will take it").[30]

The next day, McCain, Obama, and congressional leaders met with Bush at the White House. The administration was represented by Cheney, Paulson, Bush, and Bolten. Prior to the meeting, Bush took the House Speaker Nancy Pelosi aside and told her that after the representatives of the administration spoke, he would call on her. Pelosi surprised Bush by informing him that "Barack Obama will be our spokesman." When it was his turn, Obama spoke in a measured, thoughtful voice, making it clear that he would cooperate with the passage of a bill. Then it was McCain's turn, but rather than address the issue, McCain—who had asked for the meeting—declined to speak. The stunned room then exploded into a cacophony of argument. After a few minutes of this, McCain finally spoke, but rather than mention specifics, he gave a sweeping statement that reminded some present of campaign talking points. Bush had had enough. He later recalled that he told the candidates not to use the White House as a backdrop for political statements, "then I stood up and left"; another participant remembered that Bush's last words to the group were, "We can't let this sucker fail."[31]

Four days later, the House defeated Bush's financial rescue bill, 228 to 205. Democrats were in favor of the legislation, 140 to 95; Republicans opposed the legislation, 133 to 65. The market sell-off began before the vote was over—the Dow lost 777 points—the largest single-day point loss to that point in American history. Immediately after the vote, Bush met with his economic team, and they quickly decided they had no other choice but to try again. Bolten devised a plan to introduce the bill in the Senate first, hoping that the market sell-off would light a fire under the senators. It did. On 1 October, a slightly modified bill was approved in the Senate, 74 to 25. On 3 October, the House approved the Emergency Economic Stabilization Act of 2008, 263 to 171. On 13 October, Paulson approved the first round of TARP purchases. Three weeks later, Barack Obama was elected the forty-fourth president of the United States.

Political scientist Gary Jacobson has made a convincing case that Obama won the presidency not because of the financial crisis but "because of conditions already in place"—namely, the war in Iraq. While that may well be, even more than the invasion of Iraq, the crash of 2008 left a bigger legacy for ordinary Americans. Consider the following statistics: total US household net worth dropped by $11.1 trillion in 2008; median household wealth plummeted from $126,000 in 2007 to $97,000 in 2016; mutual funds lost more than a third of their value—38 percent—over the same period; between 2007 and 2013, wages declined for the bottom 70 percent of all workers, the racial wealth gap widened (whites: $171,000, Hispanics: $20,700; African Americans: $17,600); and, perhaps the most impactful statistic, a 2016 survey by the Fed found that 28 percent of working-age adults now had no retirement savings at all.[32]

Several years later, Bush ruefully remembered: "This was one ugly way to end the presidency."[33]

Bush's final three months in office were overshadowed by a national period of self-congratulation at the country having elected its first African American president. Bush seemed to understand this when addressed the nation the day after the election:

> This moment is especially uplifting for a generation of Americans who witnessed the struggle for civil rights with their own eyes—and four decades later see a dream fulfilled. . . . It will be a stirring sight to watch President Obama, his wife, Michelle, and their beautiful girls step through the doors of the White House. I know millions of Americans will be overcome with pride at this inspiring moment that so many have awaited so long.

By all accounts, the transition to the Obama administration ran smoothly. Stephen Hess, a Brookings Institution scholar and expert on presidential transitions, commented at the time that he was "not sure I've ever seen an outgoing administration work as hard at saying the right things. This is really quite memorable." In a like gesture, on 7 January 2008, Bush created a new tradition—one that Obama would not follow with his successor—by inviting all the former presidents to the White House to meet with Obama and to talk a bit of shop. On the inside, however, there was some amount of tension, as Robert Gates, who on 26 November had given a speech that was critical of Bush's policies in Afghanistan and Iraq, agreed to stay on at Defense for the incoming administration.[34]

Throughout the transition, Bush continued to deal with the financial crisis, which by December had spun into a new phase. The automobile industry had been languishing for years, hit hard by foreign competition. The Big Three were hit particularly hard—since 2006, Ford had already lost $24 billion; General Motors had less cash on hand than Ford; and although Chrysler did not release its financials, it was also well known to be in trouble. When the economy hit the reef in 2008, sales of new vehicles plummeted. The auto industry began to lobby for immediate federal help. In 2007 Congress had passed a bill that offered $25 billion in loans to auto manufacturers in order that they might make their product more fuel-efficient. These loans had yet to be released. Now, Bush proposed that they be distributed at once, with very few strings attached. After clearing a roadblock in the Senate, on 19 December Congress approved a $17.4 billion loan to the auto industry. The money would come from TARP, and the auto companies that took the loans had until April 2009 to demonstrate that they were fiscally sound.[35]

There was also the issue of the endgame in Iraq. On 13 December 2008, Bush flew to Baghdad to meet with Nouri al-Maliki and sign the completed Status of Forces Agreement (SOFA) and Strategic Framework Agreement (SFA), which, as discussed in chapter 13, would give a timetable for the American military withdrawal from Iraq. The two men signed the agreements and then opened the floor for questions. Suddenly Muntadhar al-Zaidi, an Iraqi journalist, stood up, shouted "This is a gift from the Iraqis! This is the farewell kiss, you dog!" in Arabic, and threw his shoe directly at Bush. As Bush ducked, al-Zaidi cried: "This is from the widows, the orphans, and those who were killed in Iraq!" and threw a second shoe in Bush's direction, only to have it deflected by Maliki. Bush would later make light of the incident when he joked, "All I can report is that it was a size 10." He concluded his day with a visit to the troops at Camp Victory, where he pronounced the surge "one of the greatest successes in the history of the U.S. military."[36]

There was another issue that gnawed at Bush, one placed squarely in front of him by his vice president. On 28 October 2005, Patrick Fitzgerald's grand jury had indicted Scooter Libby not for leaking Valerie Plame Wilson's name to reporter Judith Miller but for lying to federal investigators and obstructing justice. On 23 January 2007, his trial opened in federal court. On 6 March he was found guilty, and in early June 2007 Libby was sentenced to two and a half years in prison and a $250,000 fine. On 7 July 2007 the appeals court ruled that Libby had to begin serving his sentence immediately. A number of conservative intellectuals and media figures, including William Bennett, Irving Kristol, Gertrude Himmelfarb, Charles Krauthammer, William Kristol, and former US senator Alan Simpson, wrote Bush to ask for a "timely and well-deserved compassion." Bush commuted Libby's sentence, but he did not issue a pardon.[37]

Cheney badly wanted that pardon. He pushed Bush harder on this than he had on any other issue during his vice presidency, but to no avail. On 15 January 2008, during Cheney and Bush's final one-on-one lunch, Bush told Cheney there would be no pardon for Libby. Uncharacteristically, Cheney lost his temper with his commander in chief and snapped, "I can't believe you are going to leave a soldier on the battlefield." Bush professed in his memoir that the reason he did not choose to pardon Libby was procedural: "At first I was frustrated. Then I was disgusted. I came to see massive injustice in the system. If you had connections to the president, you could insert your case into the last-minute frenzy. Otherwise, you had to wait for the Justice Department to conduct a review and make a recommendation. In my final weeks in office, I resolved that I would not pardon anyone who went outside the formal channels." Nevertheless, for Bush, Cheney's comment "stung."[38]

A few weeks before this clash over the pardon, Josh Bolten had convened a meeting of all the former chiefs of staff, for the purpose of giving advice to Obama's incoming chief, former Illinois representative Rahm Emanuel. When his turn came, Cheney—who had been chief of staff to Gerald Ford—deadpanned: "Whatever you do, make sure you've got the vice president under control."[39]

In an irony of sorts, as well as a grim reminder of the work left to be done in the War on Terror, Inauguration Day 2009 was punctuated by a credible terrorist threat against the city of Washington, DC.[40]

After leaving Washington, the Bushes moved to a $3 million home in Preston Hollow, a tony neighborhood in North Dallas. From there, Bush settled in to attend to the two most pressing jobs facing any former president: planning his presidential library and writing his memoirs.

The George W. Bush Presidential Center, located on the campus of Southern Methodist University in Dallas, Texas, was built for a cost of $250 million. The Bush Center houses the George Bush Library and Museum and the George Bush Institute, an independent policy institute. The center was dedicated on 25 April 2013, with President Obama and former presidents Jimmy Carter, George H. W. Bush, and Bill Clinton in attendance. The Bush Library opened to researchers on 1 May 2013. Among other artifacts and memorabilia of the Bush administration, the library holds some seventy million pages of paper records, approximately eighty terabytes of electronic records, and about two hundred million email messages.[41]

In 2016, Bush told an audience, "I've written two books, which has surprised a lot of people, particularly up east, who didn't think I could read, much less write." Bush's math was off—by 2016 he had actually completed three books. *A Charge to Keep*, released in 1999, has been discussed earlier in this book. In 2010, Bush released *Decision Points*, his second volume of memoirs and a book Bush claimed he began writing as soon as he left office. Utilizing a style unique to presidential memoirs, which to that point had been written as chronological narratives (even his father's memoir coauthored with Brent Scowcroft followed a largely chronological structure), Bush decided to utilize a topical approach, with each chapter focusing on a major decision of his presidency. Bush then wrote *41: A Portrait of My Father*. Released in 2014, *41* has elements of both biography and memoir. The book was originally set to be released on the death of the senior Bush, but the younger Bush moved up the publication date so that his father, who would pass away on 30 November 2018, would have a chance to read it.[42]

Writing was not the only art form that engaged the former president. Competing for the former president's leisure time was a newfound hobby—that of a fine artist. Bush remembered that he found a love of painting after historian John Lewis Gaddis, when visiting Bush in Dallas in 2012, suggested that he read Winston Churchill's essay "Painting as a Pastime" ("Happy are the painters, for they shall not be lonely"). Bush reminisced: "For the first time in my sixty-six years, I picked up a paintbrush that wasn't meant for drywall. I selected a tube of white paint and another labelled Burnt Umber. I liked the name, which reminded me of Mother's cooking." Bush took his new hobby seriously, taking lessons from three Dallas-based artists. He started by painting still lifes, then moved to portraits of animals, pets, landscapes, and eventually world leaders.[43]

This led to Bush's paintings of ninety-eight service veterans of the War on Terror. Published in the book *Portraits of Courage: A Commander in Chief's Tribute to America's Warriors* (2017), the paintings are (to this observer, at least), stark, rough, and emotionally charged. Each portrait is accompanied by Bush's backstory of the subject of the portrait and often Bush's personal relationship with the subject. The one that affected me the most was the story of 1st Lt. Melissa Stockwell. On 13 April 2004, in Baghdad, her vehicle struck an improvised explosive device (IED). Although a medic saved her live, Stockwell became the first female to lose a limb—her left leg—in the War on Terror. Stockwell rehabilitated with a vengeance, eventually representing Team USA in the triathlon at the Summer Paralympic Games in Brazil and earning a bronze medal. Bush sent her a note of congratulations and included her in the program of the dedication of the Bush Presidential Center in 2013.[44]

For the first eight years of his postpresidency, Bush was judicious in his refusal to criticize either his successor or his Democratic predecessors. Indeed, Bush had a proper but often playful relationship with the Obamas. In June 2012, the White House unveiled the official portrait of George W. Bush. The former president went back to the White House, and the banter between Bush and Obamas seemed to bespeak the respect born of those who had had a common trial by fire. Bush reminded Michelle Obama that in 1812, the British had burned the White House, but that Dolley Madison had refused to leave without saving a portrait of George Washington; pointing to his painting, he said, "Now, Michelle, if anything happens, there's your man."[45] When the Obamas and both Bushes were present in Washington at the ceremony to open the National Museum of African American History and Culture, a photo of Michelle Obama hugging the forty-third president went viral on the internet.

Not so Donald Trump. In 2016, Bush's brother Jeb ran a lackluster campaign from the front-runner's position for the Republican nomination. As he had done to his other adversaries in the primaries, Trump attacked. He called his opponent "Low Energy Jeb," a criticism that clearly had some impact. After coming in sixth in the Iowa caucuses and fourth in New Hampshire, Jeb Bush needed a victory in South Carolina to keep his campaign alive. On 15 February 2016, George and Laura Bush came to Charleston in support of their brother. The former president attempted to use humor to defuse Trump's attacks: "There seems to be a lot of name calling going on, but I want to remind you what our good dad told me one time: labels are for soup cans." In an obvious play to evangelicals, Bush then praised his brother's "deep and genuine faith." Trump responded to the visit by opening full fire on the former president, claiming that Bush had deliberately misled the public about WMDs: "Obviously, the war in Iraq was a big, fat mistake, all right? They lied. They said there were weapons of mass destruction. There were none, and they knew there were none." Jeb Bush placed fourth in South Carolina and withdrew from the race. The hatred felt for Trump by alumni of both Bush administrations was palpable. Many of them, including Henry Paulson, Richard Armitage,

Brent Scowcroft, and Paul Wolfowitz, announced that they were voting for Trump's opponent in the general election, New York senator Hillary Clinton.[46]

On 20 January 2017, the day of Trump's inauguration, George and Laura Bush were on the dais, along with Bill and Hillary Clinton. The cameras caught Bush in a comic wrestling match with his government-issued rain poncho. Immediately following Trump's meandering and inflammatory speech, Bush turned to the Clintons and said in a stage whisper, "That was some weird shit." With Trump in office, Bush dropped his refusal to criticize a successor. He worked publicly to keep funding for PEPFAR when the Trump administration put it on the chopping block. In August 2018, after the racial violence in Charlottesville that Trump blamed on "both sides," Bush and his father released a joint statement which included the observation that "America must always reject racial bigotry, anti-Semitism, and hatred in all forms." In May 2020, at the height of the coronavirus pandemic, Bush issued a videotaped message calling for nonpartisan cooperation ("We are not partisan combatants. . . . We're human beings, equally vulnerable and equally wonderful in the sight of God. We rise or fall together. And we're determined to rise"). Trump's immediate response was to tweet an admonishment: "Oh bye [sic] the way, I appreciate the message from former President Bush, but where was he during Impeachment calling for putting partisanship aside. . . . He was nowhere to be found in speaking up against the greatest Hoax in American history!" In June 2020, the *New York Times* reported that Bush was not going to vote for Trump when he stood for reelection that fall.[47]

# 15

★ ★ ★ ★ ★

# CONCLUSIONS

A history major himself, George W. Bush never expected much from historians. In a February 2008 interview, he grumbled, "As far as history goes and all of these quotes about people trying to guess what the history of the Bush administration is going to be, you know, I take great comfort in knowing that they don't know what they are talking about, because history takes a long time for us to reach."[1]

Regardless, historians have spoken, and their assessments of the presidency of George W. Bush, to this point at least, have come with a resounding thud. The appraisal began much too early—while Bush was president—when a nonscientific poll commissioned by the History News Network (HNN), a platform for open discussion based at George Washington University, found that 81 percent of those polled judged Bush a failure. Four years later, a poll taken by the same site found not only that 98.2 percent of respondents judged him a failure but that more than 61 percent judged his presidency as the worst in American history. And HNN was hardly alone. In 2010, a Siena Research Institute poll ranked Bush thirty-ninth out of forty-four presidents; four years later, the same poll placed him at thirty-third. In 2009, a C-SPAN poll ranked Bush thirty-sixth out of forty-four presidents; in 2017, the same poll placed him thirty-third. Political scientists were no kinder. In 2015, members of the American Political Science Association ranked Bush thirty-fifth out of forty-three presidents (Abraham Lincoln sat at number one); three years later, the organization ranked Bush at number thirty (with a new worst failure at number forty-four: Donald J. Trump).[2]

The sentiment of the polls found its way into the assessments of scholars. In the very first sentence of his 2016 biography of Bush, political scientist Jean Edward Smith excoriates his subject: "Rarely in the history of the United States has the nation been so ill-served as during the presidency of George W. Bush." For sheer bluntness, one cannot beat historian Sean Wilentz, when he dubbed Bush—who at the time of the article's publication still had two years to go in his presidency—"the worst president in history." The vast majority of historical and political science studies released to date agree with Smith and Wilentz and, treating Bush as a presidential piñata, judge his administration to be an unmitigated failure.[3]

After spending eight years measuring and evaluating the evidence now available to the historian, I cannot share in that assessment.

As noted in this book's introduction, time is the ally of the serious historian. The further removed a writer is from their subject, the more sources are available for their perusal and the more nuanced their judgments will be. Studying the presidency of George W. Bush is no exception. The overwhelming majority of the early evaluations—books, articles, press accounts, and internet postings written either during or immediately following Bush's presidency—offer judgments that, because solid sources were not yet available, were supported primarily with press accounts and often selective interviewing done with members of the administration. But recent years have given the historian new sources with which to judge the Bush presidency, including a plethora of memoirs, the release of previously classified documents and interviews on the internet, and the opening of the material at the George W. Bush Presidential Library in 2013. Regardless of what the judgments of those early works were (and those conclusions were, as already noted, uniformly negative), they need to be revisited in light of newly available, more solid sources.

This leads to a second concern that needs addressing. Along with being poorly sourced, the early Bush literature—academic and otherwise—is highly reductionist. That is, the overwhelming majority of authors based their negative judgments exclusively on their view of the administration's response to 9/11 and its management of the War on Terror, particularly the invasion of Iraq. There is no question but that the War on Terror dominated the presidency of George W. Bush in a way that no issue has dominated any other presidency, save one: that of Abraham Lincoln and the Civil War. Indeed, the nation knew only nine months of peace during the eight years of the Bush presidency. There is also no question but that the administration's handling of the War on Terror leaves a great deal open to criticism—a task I will tackle in a moment. But focusing on only one area means by default that other areas will be left underanalyzed. Such a fallacy concerned no less a writer than Thomas Jefferson, when he rebuked those who advanced an intellectual position without "command[ing] a view of the whole ground."[4] When one looks at the "whole ground" of the presidency of George W. Bush—domestic, economic, administrative, national security, and foreign policies in total—the need to revise the completely dark assessments comes into sharp relief.

Unless one has no academic moorings, one does not revise for the sake of revising. The evidence presented in this book does not absolve the Bush administration of its shortcomings. It was an administration plagued with staff infighting, particularly on the national security side of the house. It was often a vindictive administration, as demonstrated by the Plame Wilson affair and the firing of the US attorneys. It was an administration that often moved too slowly, as shown by the lethargy present in the National Security Council's pre-9/11 dealings with terrorism, the failed attempts to revise the Social Security system and advance immigration reform, and the administration's sluggish reaction to Hurricane Katrina. It was often a blusterous administration, where the overtly martial tone of its rhetoric often got in the way of communicating its point in the court of public opinion. It was an administration that wholeheartedly accepted, and acted on, the highly suspect theory of the unitary executive—a theory articulated by John Yoo, advocated by Dick Cheney, and accepted by the president. That theory was used to justify many of the decisions made on the War on Terror, most notably the decision to utilize enhanced interrogation techniques. Following the horror of 9/11, it was often an overly romantic administration in which an unchecked neoconservatism—that Wilsonian belief that the world both could and should accept democracy whether the world wanted democracy or not—ran amok and often interfered with a realistic assessment of the international situation. In that same vein, it was often an obsessive administration, with a lack of open-mindedness and a decided unwillingness to debate its own preconceptions that led to tunnel vision on more than a few policies.

The criticism of the Bush administration's handling of the War on

Terror can be seen in this light and can be summarized as follows. First, the Bush administration dallied about with warnings of impending terrorist attacks in 2001, largely a result of both staffing issues present within the NSC and Bush's expectations of that body. Second, in the conduct of the War on Terror that followed those attacks, the administration actively searched for, and often found, ways to get around the strictures placed in its way by both constitutional limitations and traditional legal guarantees. Third, in the ramp-up to the invasion of Iraq, the administration lied to the American public and used the threat of Iraqi weapons of mass destruction as a pretense for war. Fourth, the administration both sanctioned and utilized torture in an attempt to glean intelligence from captured enemy combatants. Fifth, the conduct of the war in Iraq was inept and led directly to a violent insurgency against an occupying American force, and there was no clearly articulated exit strategy until 2008. Sixth, in the administration's rush to end that conflict, and then its inability to articulate an exit strategy, the war in Afghanistan was put on the back burner and would ultimately be raging beyond the end of the Bush administration.

As we have seen, there is more than enough evidence to at least indict, if not convict, the Bush administration on each of these charges. If one was to ascribe a reason for the administration's travails in the War on Terror, it seems that it was the administration's lack of an open mind that led it down a path toward military morass, particularly in Iraq. At a 21 March 2003 cabinet meeting about Iraq, Bush claimed that he had tried "everything possible to solve this through peace."[5] The evidence presented in this book contradicts this statement. At any number of times the United States might have resolved the situation without resorting to armed conflict, but it did not. It had chosen another path, and it refused to deviate from that path. The Bush administration was predisposed at an early date to invade Iraq—WMDs or no—and there was little to no debate within the administration on the issue.

The Bush Doctrine, as articulated by Bush in his June 2002 speech at West Point, rationalized this closed-mindedness. Whether or not there were WMDs in Iraq in the days following 9/11 (there clearly were not) or whether or not Iraq posed a credible threat to the United States during that same period (all available evidence shows that it did not) is quite beside the point. The Bush administration, almost to a person, believed that Iraq posed a potentially lethal threat to the security of the United States, and the Bush Doctrine of preventative war demanded his neutralization. This led to a series of destructive conflicts in the Middle East in which the nation is still active at this writing, and for which the Bush administration must take responsibility.

That being said, the evidence also makes it eminently clear that the Bush administration was responsible for many positive achievements, successes that have been largely ignored by contemporary observers. In domestic policy, some accomplishments pointed the way toward potential future Republican reforms. For example, while tinged with partisan rhetoric and goals, No Child Left Behind set the nation on the road toward effecting serious educational reform. In the same vein, Bush's faith-based policies, while limited by the same political and rhetorical baggage, showed a way toward a conservative rethinking of the welfare system. Other policies, however, brought real, immediate, and measurable improvements. The best example of this was in health care reform, as the Bush administration both strengthened the Medicare system and extended its benefits for millions of Americans. Each of these policies ran afoul of Bush's conservative critics, primarily for their cost. But expense does not erase success—it would take too long here to list the policies of, for example, the New Deal and the Great Society that were both astronomically expensive and universally seen to be successful.

Despite the plethora of evidence that shows that the administration mishandled the War on Terror, particularly in Iraq, that, too, cannot be the end of the story. In terms of national security policy, those who claim that Bush's policies in the War on Terror were an unmitigated failure must contend with two facts. First, the invasion of Iraq erased Saddam Hussein, a ruthless, corrupt, and bloody dictator, from the world stage. Second, while the Iraqi insurgency was, indeed, largely caused by the decisions of the administration, the surge—a decision made by the president himself in the face of almost unanimous opposition—had the immediate effects of both muting the insurgency and saving American lives in Iraq.

Each of these areas of success had long-term effects on both the domestic and the international situation. But in two areas the Bush administration stared down crises that, had they not been addressed, would have had disastrous consequences. While the price tag of the administration's response to the financial crisis of 2008–2009 was, indeed, astronomically high, it nevertheless saved the nation's banking and investment infrastructure and kept the nation from falling into the abyss of a second economic depression. And through PEPFAR, Bush did more to combat the worldwide scourge of AIDS than any other president; indeed, through

PEPFAR, Bush did more for Africa than any other president in American history.

All told, this is hardly the stuff of a presidential administration that is an unmitigated failure.

Any discussion of the legacy left by the Bush administration must include the input of one key group. In their memoirs and interviews, the alumni of the Bush administration advance an important assessment of their administration—one that has largely escaped the notice of previous students of the Bush presidency, but one that nevertheless must be taken seriously.

It is not surprising that both in their memoirs and in interviews with both scholars and journalists, alumni of the Bush administration argue that their administration has not yet been looked at in its complete context.[6] Nary an interview is complete, for example, without the subject reminding the interviewer that PEPFAR was a success, or that Bush erased the threat of Saddam Hussein from the face of the earth. But it is their defense of the administration's policies toward the War on Terror that bids the reader to pause. Here, they show themselves to be a very self-assured bunch. With the exception of Richard Clarke, no mea culpas have been issued, either in memoirs or in interviews. To a person, they feel they have nothing to explain away, nothing to apologize for. When pressed by an interviewer, they simply ignore the criticisms. Instead, they unanimously have made it clear that only one thing mattered—George Bush kept his promise to the American people.

In his memoir, Bush recollected, "In a single morning [11 September 2001], the purpose of my presidency had grown clear: to protect our people and defend our freedom that had come under attack."[7] He had entered into a compact with the American people, one that he articulated both on 12 September 2001, when he turned to John Ashcroft and said, "Don't let this happen again," and to his NSC on 14 September ("What are you doing to stop the *next* attack?"). Bush wrote his preferred epitaph for his administration in his memoir: "History can debate the decisions I made, the policies I chose, and the tools I left behind. But there can be no debate about one fact: After the nightmare of September 11, America went seven and a half years without another successful terrorist attack on our soil. If I had to summarize my most meaningful accomplishment as president in one sentence, that would be it."[8] In terms of historical evidence, this claim can be proved with absolute certainty. With the exception of the anthrax scare in the fall of 2001, the effects of which were largely contained and the culprits of which were never found, the widely feared second attack never happened.

To those serious students who point out the many costs of keeping this promise, Bush alumni simply offer a shrug. Three examples will suffice, speaking to the highly controversial Stellar Wind program. Alberto Gonzales: "The program worked. A tremendous amount of data was collected, and thanks to Stellar Wind, numerous potential or attempted terrorist actions were interrupted." On the same program, Dick Cheney: "The Terrorist Surveillance Program is, in my opinion, one of the most important success stories in the history of American intelligence. . . . this program is one of the things of which I am proudest." And on the enhanced interrogation program, Mike McConnell: "We have people walking around in this country that are alive today because this process happened."[9]

In arguing that the administration was a success because Bush kept his promise, the alumni are doing the opposite of what they have publicly claimed needs to be done—they are judging the administration solely on its response to the War on Terror as opposed to looking at it as a whole. Moreover, none of their claims completely erase the costs of keeping that promise, and history keeps an accurate, if not always balanced, scorecard. But as historians assess whether not the ends justified the means employed by the administration of George W. Bush, it is important to note that for Bush and virtually the entirety of his administration, the ends were all that mattered. Following the worst foreign attack ever perpetrated on American soil, George Bush made a singular promise to the American people—never again. From that point on, keeping that promise was the only focus of his presidency that really mattered to him. When assessing the successes and failures of the Bush administration, history must note that that promise was, indeed, kept.

In a 2008 interview with the *Jerusalem Post*, Bush opined, "I'll be long gone before some smart person ever figures out what happened inside this Oval Office."[10] Regardless of Bush's observation, that assessment has indeed begun. Moreover, any such judgments are a constantly moving target; as the Bush Library releases additional documents, more will become known about this tumultuous administration, and judgments on its success or failure will be refined. But at present, one leaves a reading of the story of the administration of George W. Bush unable to accept overly simplistic judgments regarding its tenure—either the judgments of its success as voiced by those who served or those of its failure as voiced by most of the academic community. Like each of its predecessors and each of its successors, the Bush presidency was a complex administration that defies simplistic judgments and stereotypical conclusions, and any verdict on its policies, successes, and failures must be a mixed one. What cannot be debated is that the administration of George W. Bush was of consequence. The actions of this presidency—not just in the War on Terror but in the whole of its endeavors—would affect the presidencies of each of his successors, as well as the trajectory of world history to the present day. Perhaps, then, the most accurate thing that can be said about the Bush presidency is that we now live in a world of its making.

# NOTES

All public statements made by George W. Bush while president can be found in George W. Bush, *Public Papers of the Presidents: George W. Bush*, 16 vols. (Washington, DC: US Government Printing Office, 2001–2009). They are also available at http://www.presidency.ucsb.edu/ws/. Thus, speeches and proclamations by Bush as president are not cited in this book unless a videotape or script of a specific speech was consulted. Any public statement by any other president can be found at the above website and remain similarly uncited in this book.

## ACRONYMS AND SHORT TITLES

| | |
|---|---|
| BGR | Gubernatorial Records of George W. Bush, Texas State Library and Archives Commission, Austin, Texas |
| BP | James A. Baker III, Papers, Seeley G. Mudd Manuscripts Library, Princeton University |
| DPC | Domestic Policy Council |
| FOIA | Freedom of Information Act request |
| GHWB | George H. W. Bush |
| GWB | George W. Bush |
| GWBL | George W. Bush Presidential Library, Dallas, Texas |
| GWBM | Museum, GWBPR |
| GWBPOH | George W. Bush Presidential Oral History, Miller Center, University of Virginia |
| GWBPR | George W. Bush, Presidential Records, George W. Bush Presidential Library, Dallas, Texas |
| *LAT* | *Los Angeles Times* |
| LOC | Library of Congress |
| NSC | National Security Council |
| *NYT* | *New York Times* |

| | |
|---|---|
| SMOF | White House Staff Member Office Files |
| *SSCI* | *Report of the Senate Select Committee on Intelligence, Committee Study of the Central Intelligence Agency's Detention and Interrogation Program. Together with Foreword by Chairman Weinstein and Additional and Minority Views*, 113th Cong., 2d Sess., 9 December 2014 |
| *TTP* | Karen J. Greenberg and Joshua L. Dratel, *The Torture Papers: The Road to Abu Ghraib* (New York: Cambridge University Press, 2005) |
| WHORM | White House Office of Records Management |
| WHSMOF | White House Staff Member Office Files |
| *WP* | *Washington Post* |
| *WSJ* | *Wall Street Journal* |

## CHAPTER 1. GEORGIE

1. John Robert Greene, *The Presidency of George H. W. Bush*, 2nd ed., revised and expanded (Lawrence: University Press of Kansas, 2015), 3–5; Joe Hyams, *Flight of the Avenger: George Bush at War* (New York: Harcourt Brace Jovanovich, 1991), 83–84.

2. Greene, *The Presidency of George H. W. Bush*, 5–6; Tom Wicker, *George Herbert Walker Bush: A Penguin Life* (New York: Penguin, 2004), 6; Herbert S. Parmet, *George Bush: The Life of a Lone Star Yankee* (New York: Scribner, 1997), 59.

3. On the G.I. Bill, see https://www.benefits.va.gov/gibill/history.asp; Barbara Bush quoted in George W. Bush, *41: A Portrait of My Father* (New York: Crown, 2014), 35. There has been a great deal of variation among writers in terms of the names used to identify George H. W. Bush and his son George W. Bush. Using "Senior" and Junior" is not accurate, except in that at several times in his life, the people around the younger Bush took to calling him "Junior," often as a sign of thinly veiled contempt when comparing his personal and political assets with those of his father. Identifying the two men as "41" and "43," a shorthand started by the elder Bush in his retirement and picked up by members of the Bush family—to the point where hats and jackets were embroidered with the number of the Bush presidency and worn by the appropriate George Bush—seems too flippant. Along the same lines, referring to the younger Bush as "W"—a favorite of press and writers alike—places a generally accepted acronym on the forty-third president (much like "FDR," "JFK," or LBJ") but seems somewhat demeaning (as in "Bush and his son, 'W'"). Thus, when necessary for clarity in the narrative, this book chooses to distinguish between the two men as either the "elder" or the "younger" Bush, and to refer to the adolescent George W. Bush by the nickname given him by his father—"Georgie."

4. Elizabeth Mitchell, *W: The Revenge of the Bush Dynasty* (New York: Berkley Books, 1999), 23; Mark K. Updegrove, *The Last Republicans: Inside the Extraordinary Relationship between George H. W. Bush and George W. Bush* (New York: HarperCollins, 2017), 29.

5. "Midland," in *The Handbook of Texas Online*, Texas State Historical Association, https://tshaonline.org/handbook/online/articles/hdm03; George W. Bush, *Decision Points* (New York: Crown, 2010), 5; Peter Baker, *Days of Fire: Bush and Cheney in the White House* (New York: Doubleday, 2013), 19; Parmet, *George Bush*, title page.

6. See many examples of Bush referring to his son as "Georgie" in his correspondence in George H. W. Bush, *All the Best, George Bush: My Life in Letters and Other Writings*, updated edition (New York: Scribner, 2013). For Bush on Midland, see Bush, *Decision Points*, 6; George W. Bush, *A Charge to Keep* (New York: William Morrow, 1999), 16–17, 56. See also Baker, *Days of Fire*, 20; James Mann, *George W. Bush* (New York: Times Books, 2015), 5; Susan Page, *The Matriarch: Barbara Bush and the Making of an American Dynasty* (New York: Twelve, 2019), 80; Updegrove, *The Last Republicans*, 16. The Bush home, located at 1412 West Ohio Avenue, Midland, Texas, is now the George W. Bush Childhood Home.

7. Bush, *A Charge to Keep*, 15–18, 182; the quote on the Greenwich Country Day School is found in many sources—for one, see Mann, *George W. Bush*, 6; GHWB to FitzGerald Bemiss, 1 January 1951, in Bush, *All the Best*, 70; the observation on Bush's personality as an act is found in Mann, *George W. Bush*, 6 ("He became skilled, indeed shrewd, at assuming the role of the small-town Texas country boy"). See also Mitchell, *W*, 38.

8. Updegrove, *The Last Republicans*, 39. Robin was initially buried at the family plot in Greenwich, Connecticut. In 2000 she was moved to the George H. W. Bush Presidential Library in College Station, Texas, and reinterred in the plot that holds George and Barbara Bush (see GHWB to Dr. Larry Gipson, 16 May 2000, in Bush, *All the Best*, 633–634).

9. Bush, *41*, 56; Baker, *Days of Fire*, 21; Jon Meacham, *Destiny and Power: The American Odyssey of George Herbert Walker Bush* (New York: Random House, 2015), 100–101; Bush, *A Charge to Keep*, 14; Myra G. Gutin, *Barbara Bush: Presidential Matriarch* (Lawrence: University Press of Kansas, 2008), 14–15. GWB's entreaty to his parents is quoted in Mann, *George W. Bush*, 7. The fullest, and most touching, retelling of Robin's torturous last days can be found in Bush, *41*, 53–57.

10. GWB quotes in Updegrove, *The Last Republicans*, 13; Bush, *41*, 56. See also Bush, *Decision Points*, 8.

11. GHWB to Hugh Sidey, 3 November 1998, in Bush, *All the Best*, 618; Bush, *Decision Points*, 8; Updegrove, *The Last Republicans*, 45; Bush, *Decision Points*, 8; GHWB to Marvin Pierce, 7 April 1955, in Bush, *All the Best*, 79.

12. Bush, *Decision Points*, 11; Bush, *A Charge to Keep*, 22.

13. Ronald Kessler, *A Matter of Character: Inside the White House of George W. Bush* (New York: Sentinel, 2004) 21; Updegrove, *The Last Republicans*, 50, 52; Mann, *George W. Bush*, 8; Baker, *Days of Fire*, 23; Bush, *Decision Points*, 13.

14. Bush, *A Charge to Keep*, 169–170; Mitchell, *W*, 83–84; Updegrove, *The Last Republicans*, 61; Kessler, *A Matter of Character*, 18; Updegrove, *The Last Republicans*, 53; Mann, *George W. Bush*, 9.

15. Bush, *A Charge to Keep*, 47; Updegrove, *The Last Republicans*, 64; Mitchell, *W*, 85, 97–98; Bush, *Decision Points*, 13–14; Mann, *George W. Bush*, 10.

16. Updegrove, *The Last Republicans*, 62; Warren Goldstein, *William Sloane*

*Coffin, Jr.: A Holy Impatience* (New Haven, CT: Yale University Press, 2004), 316; Mann, *George W. Bush*, 11; Updegrove, *The Last Republicans*, 62–63; Bush, *Decision Points*, 14. In 1998, when the story on Coffin was first published, Coffin wrote the younger Bush, protesting, "I have a hard time imagining my saying to you . . . 'your father was beaten by a better man.' But if you say so, I believe you." Bush replied, "I believe my recollection is correct. But I also know time passes, and I bear no ill will." Coffin to Bush, 15 September 1998; Bush to Coffin, 30 September 1998 (handwritten), BGR, 2002/151-352, General Counsel Public Information Request Files, 1998, Graves, Pat, folder 3 of 11. Bush would not reach out to Yale again until 1993, when he allowed his class to spend its thirty-fifth reunion at the White House.

17. Updegrove, *The Last Republicans*, 73; Bush, *A Charge to Keep*, 47–48; Kessler, *A Matter of Character*, 25–26; Mitchell, *W*, 99–100, 128–129.

18. Bush, *A Charge to Keep*, 49–50; Updegrove, *The Last Republicans*, 75. It should be noted that as he prepared for his first campaign for the presidency, Bush tried to have Vietnam both ways; as he wrote in his 1999 memoir, "My inclination [in 1968] was to support the government and the war until proven wrong, and that only came later, as I realized we could not explain the mission, had no exit strategy, and did not seem to be fighting to win" (*A Charge to Keep*, 50). He maintained this stance in the second volume of his memoirs: "My attitude toward the war was skeptical but accepting. I was skeptical of the strategy and the people in the Johnson administration executing it. But I accepted the stated goal of the war: to stop the spread of communism" (*Decision Points*, 16).

19. Bush, *Decision Points*, 16; Bush, *A Charge to Keep*, 51; Updegrove, *The Last Republicans*, 76–77.

20. Mitchell, *W*, 108; Ben Barnes, *Barn Burning, Barn Building: Tales of a Political Life, from LBJ through George W. Bush and Beyond* (Albany, TX: Bright Sky Press, 2006) 109–110. Barnes first told this story in a deposition given in a 1999 lawsuit against GTECH, a company that ran lotteries and which Barnes had lobbied. Barnes was called as a witness to speak to the charge that GTECH was allowed to keep its state lottery contacts because the younger Bush wanted to keep Barnes quiet about the National Guard question (see Mitchell, *W*, 108–109). This story is also told in Molly Ivins and Lou Dubose, *Shrub: The Short but Happy Political Life of George W. Bush* (New York: Vintage Books, 2000), 3–12; Mann, *George W. Bush*, 12–13; Updegrove, *The Last Republicans*, 77–78.

21. Bush, *A Charge to Keep*, 52, 79; Updegrove, *The Last Republicans*, 98.

22. Bush, *Decision Points*, 18; Mann, *George W. Bush*, 14. Bush does not mention either this campaign or his transfer in the first volume of his memoirs, published in 1999 while he was running for the Republican nomination for the presidency.

23. Bush, *A Charge to Keep*, 171–172.

24. Updegrove, *The Last Republicans*, 100; Bush, *A Charge to Keep*, 58–59; Meacham, *Destiny and Power*, 167.

25. This altercation has been told in so many different fashions that is impossible to accurately judge the veracity of any of them. Bush refers obliquely to this episode in *Decision Points*—without being specific as to what was said, he admits to an incident between "a boozy kid, and . . . an understandably irritated father" (21). Then, in his biography of his father, he refers once again to the altercation, claiming

that after he faced his father, no words were shared—the elder Bush "calmly took off his reading glasses, and stared right at me. Then he put his reading glasses back on, and lifted up the book" (Bush, *W*, 82). Of the many sources that have repeated the "mano a mano" retort, see Baker, *Days of Fire*, 25; Ivins and Dubose, *Shrub*, 13; Kessler, *A Matter of Character*, 35; Mitchell, *W*, 140; Jean Edward Smith, *Bush* (New York: Simon & Schuster), 25; and Updegrove, *The Last Republicans*, 101–102.

26. Bush, *Decision Points*, 22; Bush, *A Charge to Keep*, 60; Bill Minutaglio, *First Son: George W. Bush and the Bush Family Dynasty* (New York: Times Books, 1999), 154; Baker, *Days of Fire*, 26; and Mann, *George W. Bush*, 15. The former girlfriend is quoted in Mitchell, *W*, 143–144.

27. Mann, *George W. Bush*, 16; Bush, *A Charge to Keep*, 56; Kessler, *A Matter of Character*, 40; Laura Bush, *Spoken from the Heart* (New York: Scribner, 2010), 114; Mitchell, *W*, 146.

28. Bush, *A Charge to Keep*, 57, 62.

29. Diary entry, 6 July 1975, in Bush, *All the Best*, 230; Bush, *Decision Points*, 24–25; Baker, *Days of Fire*, 30; Kessler, *A Matter of Character*, 41; Updegrove, *The Last Republicans*, 114; Mitchell, *W*, 152.

30. Bush does not tell this story in his first memoir, *A Charge to Keep*, but he includes it in his second memoir, *Decision Points*, 25. See also Mann, *George W. Bush*, 18.

31. Baker, *Days of Fire*, 30; Updegrove, *The Last Republicans*, 101; Bush, *Decision Points*, 37; Bush, *A Charge to Keep*, 172; Mann, *George W. Bush*, 17; William A. Galston, "Why the 2005 Social Security Initiative Failed, and What It Means for the Future," report, Brookings Institution, 21 September 2007; GHWB to Eddie Mahe, 25 July 1977, in Bush, *All the Best*, 273.

32. Bush, *41*, 124–125; Bush, *A Charge to Keep*, 80; Baker, *Days of Fire*, 32; Bush, *Spoken from the Heart*, 94–95.

33. Bush, *Decision Points*, 26–27; Laura Bush, *Spoken from the Heart*, 95–97.

34. Baker, *Days of Fire*, 32; Updegrove, *The Last Republicans*, 130; Bush, *Decision Points*, 39–40; Ivins and Dubose, *Shrub*, 15. GWB comment on GHWB and Reagan quoted in Doro Bush Koch, *My Father, My President: A Personal Account of the Life of George H. W. Bush* (New York: Grand Central Publishing, 2006), 146. This is corroborated by GHWB in a letter to the editor of a Lubbock newspaper, where he protested that Reagan's endorsement of Reese "obviously didn't make me happy" (GHWB to Charles A. Guy, 14 July 1978, in Bush, *All the Best*, 277). GHWB letter to GWB quoted in Meacham, *Destiny and Power*, 545.

35. Shivers quoted in Bush, *Decision Points*, 39; Bush, *A Charge to Keep*, 173; and Bush, *41*, 124. Reese quotes are from Baker, *Days of Fire*, 33; Bush, *Decision Points*, 40; Laura Bush, *Spoken from the Heart*, 101; and Mann, *George W. Bush*, 17. See also Ivins and Dubose, *Shrub*, 17; Mitchell, *W*, 181–182.

36. Todd Purdum, "43+41=84," *Vanity Fair*, September 2006; Baker, *Days of Fire*, 33; Laura Bush, *Spoken from the Heart*, 102; Bush, *A Charge to Keep*, 174–175.

37. Bush, *A Charge to Keep*, 62; Bush, *41*, 137–138; Laura Bush, *Spoken from the Heart*, 102; Updegrove, *The Last Republicans*, 138–139, 146.

38. Bush, *A Charge to Keep*, 84–85, 178; Bush, *Decision Points*, 27–29; Laura Bush, *Spoken from the Heart*, 106–107.

39. Laura Bush, *Spoken from the Heart*, 115; Mann, *George W. Bush*, 16, 19; Bush, *Decision Points*, 30; Updegrove, *The Last Republicans*, 159; Bush, *A Charge to Keep*, 63.

40. Greene, *The Presidency of George H. W. Bush*, 31–33.

41. Greene, 32–33; Bush, *A Charge to Keep*, 178–179; Bush, *Decision Points*, 42–43; Bush, *41*, 156; Baker, *Days of Fire*, 36; Mann, *George W. Bush*, 22; Mitchell, *W*, 214; Updegrove, *The Last Republicans*, 163.

42. Bush, *Decision Points*, 30; Updegrove, *The Last Republicans*, 164–165; diary entry, 12 November 1986, in Bush, *All the Best*, 353.

43. Updegrove, *The Last Republicans*, 170–171; Bush, *A Charge to Keep*, 136; Bush, *Decision Points*, 30–33.

44. Laura Bush, *Spoken from the Heart*, 118; Bush, *A Charge to Keep*, 132–133; Mann, *George W. Bush*, 20; The quote from Laura is the very first sentence of Bush, *Decision Points* (1). Several sources claim that Laura gave her husband an ultimatum: "It's either Jim Beam or me." In her memoir, she denied saying the line, but she did admit to being "disappointed. And I let him know that I thought he could be a better man" (Laura Bush, *Spoken from the Heart*, 118).

45. Bush, *A Charge to Keep*, 136; Laura Bush, *Spoken from the Heart*, 119.

46. Updegrove, *The Last Republicans*, 178. The irreverent photo of Atwater graces the cover of John Brady, *Bad Boy: The Life and Politics of Lee Atwater* (Reading, MA: Addison Wesley, 1997). See also Bush, *41*, 161; Bush Koch, *My Father, My President*, 224; Baker, *Days of Fire*, 38; Mitchell, *W*, 223–224; Updegrove, *The Last Republicans*, 178. GWB's harangue at Warner is quoted in Baker, *Days of Fire*, 38; Greene, *The Presidency of George H. W. Bush*, 34; Mitchell, *W*, 220–222. Bush recounts the encounter with vagaries in *A Charge to Keep* (181); he does not quote himself, and he does not specifically name Warner. He is a bit more specific in *Decision Points*, mentioning Warner by name but still not quoting himself (43–44). In his biography of his father, Bush identifies Warner and makes reference to her story but does not make any reference to his angry reaction to the story (*W*, 162). The elder Bush mentioned the incident in his diary, recording only that his son was "giving her grief" (diary entry, 12 October 1987, in Bush, *All the Best*, 368).

47. Updegrove, *The Last Republicans*, 194–195; Greene, *The Presidency of George H. W. Bush*, 54; Minutaglio, *First Son*, 232–233. In *The President's Club: Inside the World's Most Exclusive Fraternity* (New York: Simon & Schuster, 2012), Nancy Gibbs and Michael Duffy call this group the "Silent Committee" (478). Bush does not mention this role in either of his memoirs.

48. Laura Bush, *Spoken from the Heart*, 126; GWB friend quoted in Baker, *Days of Fire*, 40; Bush, *A Charge to Keep*, 198, 201; Bush, *Decision Points*, 44–46; Updegrove, *The Last Republicans*, 214–215.

49. Updegrove, *The Last Republicans*, 215, 257; Nicholas D. Kristof, "Breaking into Baseball: Road to Politics Ran Through a Texas Ballpark," *NYT*, 24 September 2000.

50. Quoted in Greene, *The Presidency of George H. W. Bush*, 213; for a summary of the administration's travails in 1991, see chap. 10.

51. Bush, *41*, 225–227, 243; Greene, *The Presidency of George H. W. Bush*, 200–202, 224, 305n34; Meacham, *Destiny and Power*, 492–494; Bush, *Decision Points*, 49;

Meacham, *Destiny and Power*, 508–509, 512; Mitchell, *W*, 283; Updegrove, *The Last Republicans*, 24, 244; Bush, *A Charge to Keep*, 4.

52. Quoted in Page, *The Matriarch*, 265.

## CHAPTER 2. GOVERNOR BUSH

1. Katharine Q. Seelye, "Clayton Williams, Oilman Whose Gaffes Cost Him an Election, Dies at 88," *NYT*, 18 February 2020; Dave McNeely and Jim Henderson, *Bob Bullock: God Bless Texas* (Austin: University of Texas Press, 2008), 246–347; Karl Rove, *Courage and Consequence: My Life as a Conservative in the Fight* (New York: Threshold Editions, 2010), 81; George W. Bush, *A Charge to Keep* (New York: William Morrow, 1999), 23.

2. Patricia Kilday Hart, "Little Did We Know," *Texas Monthly*, November 2004; Rove, *Courage and Consequence*, 16–17. In 1981, twelve years after she left her family, Rove's mother committed suicide.

3. Rove, *Courage and Consequence*, 39.

4. James A. Baker III, *"Work Hard, Study, and Keep Out of Politics!": Adventures and Lessons from an Unexpected Public Life* (New York: G. P. Putnam's, 2006), 357; Rove, *Courage and Consequence*, 57–58.

5. It is impossible to resist quoting Rove's description of Allbaugh: "[His] hair is cut in a flattop that is roughly the size of a World War II carrier's landing deck, and when he draws up his 265 pounds and 6'4" frame and gets that I'm-going-to-pinch-your-head-off-look on his face, he is an intimidating figure. He was exactly what we needed to shape up the campaign" (Rove, *Courage and Consequence*, 89).

6. Karen Hughes, *Ten Minutes from Normal* (New York: Viking, 2004), 80; James Mann, *George W. Bush* (New York: Times Books, 2015); Bush, *A Charge to Keep*, 67; Peter Baker, *Days of Fire: Bush and Cheney in the White House* (New York: Doubleday, 2013), 43.

7. Bush, *A Charge to Keep*, 28; Mann, *George W. Bush*, 27.

8. Bush, *A Charge to Keep*, 33; George W. Bush, *Decision Points* (New York: Crown, 2010), 54; Hughes, *Ten Minutes from Normal*, 97–98; Laura Bush, *Spoken from the Heart* (New York: Scribner, 2010) 133; Hart, "Little Did We Know"; Baker, *Days of Fire*, 43; Mann, *George W. Bush*, 27–28. Chuck McDonald, the press secretary to the Richards campaign, explained to an interviewer in 2004 that the "jerk" comment was just a big misunderstanding: "She didn't call George Bush a jerk. [At an education rally, Richards said], 'You know how it is. You are working your tail off and doing a good job and then some jerk comes along and tells you it's not good enough.' . . . She was talking about the people who say Texas education isn't good enough. It wasn't too hard to make the leap to say she called him a jerk" (Chuck McDonald, in Hart, "Little Did We Know"). The sobriquet "Shrub" was popularized in the columns of journalist Molly Ivins; see Molly Ivins and Lou Dubose, *Shrub: The Short but Happy Political Life of George W. Bush* (New York: Vintage Books, 2000).

9. Hughes, *Ten Minutes from Normal*, 93–95; Bush, *A Charge to Keep*, 34–40; Rove, *Courage and Consequence*, 93–96.

10. Bush, *A Charge to Keep*, 42; Hugh Sidey, "George H. W. Bush: The *Time* Interview," *Time*, 19 December 2004.

11. Bush, *A Charge to Keep*, 42–43; Bush, *Decision Points*, 55; Mark K. Updegrove, *The Last Republicans: Inside the Extraordinary Relationship between George H. W. Bush and George W. Bush* (New York: HarperCollins, 2017), 265; Barbara Bush diary entry, in Jon Meacham, *Destiny and Power: The American Odyssey of George Herbert Walker Bush* (New York: Random House, 2015), 551; George W. Bush, *41: A Portrait of My Father* (New York: Crown, 2014), 255; and Doro Bush Koch, *My Father, My President: A Personal Account of the Life of George H. W. Bush* (New York: Grand Central Publishing, 2006), 456.

12. Bush, *A Charge to Keep*, 97–100.

13. McNeely and Henderson, *Bob Bullock*, 261.

14. Rove, *Courage and Consequence*, 102; Alberto Gonzales, *True Faith and Allegiance: A Story of Service and Sacrifice in War and Peace* (Nashville, TN: Nelson Books, 2006), 61; Bush, *Decision Points*, 56–57; Bush, *A Charge to Keep*, 110–112, 114–115; McNeely and Henderson, *Bob Bullock*, 258, 262; Ivins and Dubose, *Shrub*, xiv; Sandy Kress, interview with author, 7 August 2018.

15. Bush, *A Charge to Keep*, 116–118.

16. GWB to Phyllis Schlafly (handwritten), 9 January 1997, BGR, 2002/151-0365, General Counsel Public Information Requests (PIR) Files, 2000, Elizabeth Cavendish, folder 2. Evangelist Pat Robertson also advocated the teaching of phonics; he also contacted Bush to voice his opinion on the subject (Margaret LaMontagne to Robertson, 29 April 1997, BGR, 2002/151-0365, General Counsel PIR Files, 2000, Elizabeth Cavendish, folder 2); Bush, *A Charge to Keep*, 74–75, 120, 211.

17. Press release, 2 May 1996, BGR, 2002/151-845, Faith Based Programs, folder 1; "Faith in Action: A New Vision for Church-State Cooperation in Texas," Governor's Advisory Task Force on Faith-Based Community Service Groups, Full Report, December 1996, viii (copy of report in BGR, 2002/151-845, Faith Based Programs, folder 2, and in Anthony Lewis Papers, LOC, Part II, box 722, folder 10); Bush, *A Charge to Keep*, 214.

18. The case was *Hopwood v. Texas*, 78 F.3d 932 (5th Cir. 1996). See also Mann, *George W. Bush*, 30–31.

19. McNeely and Henderson, *Bob Bullock*, 271–273; Bush, *A Charge to Keep*, 122–130.

20. 372 U.S. 335.

21. Official memorandum, State of Texas, Office of the Governor, 20 June 1999; Lewis Papers, LOC, Part II, box 722, folder 10. See also *Austin American-Statesman*, 22 June 1999; *Dallas Morning News*, 22 June 1999; *Houston Chronicle*, 2 June 1999; "Bush Notes," undated, Lewis Papers, LOC, Part II, box 743, folder 7.

22. "U.S. Capital Punishment—Total Executions by State, 1976–2019," Statista Research Department, 18 November 2019, http://www.statista.com; Mann, *George W. Bush*, 31.

23. Archbishop Agostino Cacciavillan to GWB, 5 January 1998, BGR, 2002/151-352, General Counsel Public Information Request Files, 1998, Graves, Pat, folder 11 of 11; Bush, *A Charge to Keep*, 140–155; Gonzales, *True Faith and Allegiance*, 63, 67–68.

24. Bush, *A Charge to Keep*, 155–163; *NYT*, 27 June 1998. On 12 March 2001, Lucas died in prison of heart failure.

25. Rove, *Courage and Consequence*, 114, 132–133.

26. Bush, *Decision Points*, 399–400; GHWB to "Kids," 12 February 1999, in George H. W. Bush, *All the Best, George Bush: My Life in Letters and Other Writings*, updated edition (New York: Scribner, 2013), 629.

27. Rove, *Courage and Consequence*, 119–120; Baker, *Days of Fire*, 49; Robert Draper, *Dead Certain: The Presidency of George W. Bush* (New York: Free Press, 2007), 53–54; James Mann, *Rise of the Vulcans: The History of Bush's War Cabinet* (New York: Viking Penguin, 2004), 248–249.

28. Bullock died of cancer in June 1999. He had asked Bush to deliver the eulogy at his funeral—a favor that Bush granted. Bullock also had his widow attend the Republican National Convention in 2000 and announce her late husband's support for Bush (Bush, *A Charge to Keep*, 131; Bush, *Decision Points*, 63–64; Rove, *Courage and Consequence*, 114, 116–117).

29. Helen Thorpe, "Less Is Mauro," *Texas Monthly*, August 1998; Bush, *A Charge to Keep*, 217–223; Jean Edward Smith, *Bush* (New York: Simon & Schuster, 2016), 94n; Ivins and Dubose, *Shrub*, 55; Joyce Saenz Harris, "Harriet Miers: Reflections of a Lawyer-Politician," *Dallas Morning News*, 28 July 1991; Draper, *Dead Certain*, 55.

30. Bush, *A Charge to Keep*, 224; Rove, *Courage and Consequence*, 122; Hughes, *Ten Minutes from Normal*, 110–111.

31. Bush, *A Charge to Keep*, 1–2, 8–9, 13; Bush, *Decision Points*, 60–62; Rove, *Courage and Consequence*, 124. See also Draper, *Dead Certain*, 57; Frances Fitzgerald, *The Evangelicals: The Struggle to Shape America* (New York: Simon & Schuster, 2017), 457; Peter Schweizer and Rochelle Schweizer, *The Bushes: Portrait of a Dynasty* (New York: Doubleday, 2004), 458.

## CHAPTER 3. ELECTING A PRESIDENT

1. Karen Hughes, *Ten Minutes from Normal* (New York: Viking, 2004), 123. Allbaugh was replaced on the gubernatorial staff by Clay Johnson; Hughes by Linda Edwards (see press release, 28 June 1999, BGR, 2002/151-1846, Appointments News Releases: Governor's Office Staff, Miers, McClellan, McMahon folder).

2. John Robert Greene, ed., *Presidential Profiles: The George W. Bush Years* (New York: Facts on File, 2011), 16–17.

3. Peter Baker, *Days of Fire: Bush and Cheney in the White House* (New York: Doubleday, 2013), 51; Frances Fitzgerald, *The Evangelicals: The Struggle to Shape America* (New York: Simon & Schuster, 2017), 460.

4. Terry M. Neal, "Bush Says GOP Must Turn from Negativity," *WP*, 6 October 1999.

5. Quoted in Charles Blahous, *Social Security: The Unfinished Work* (Stanford, CA: Hoover Institution Press, 2010), 203–204.

6. Quoted in Michael J. Gerson, *Heroic Conservatism: Why Republicans Need to*

*Embrace America's Ideals (And Why They Deserve to Fail If They Don't)* (New York: Harper One, 2007), 44–45.

7. Michael Novak, ed., *Democracy and Mediating Structures: A Theological Inquiry* (American Enterprise Institute Press, 1980); Michael Novak, *The Spirit of Democratic Capitalism* (New York: Simon & Schuster, 1982); Marvin Olasky, *The Tragedy of American Compassion* (New York: Regnery, 1994); Marvin Olasky, *Compassionate Conservatism: What It Is, What It Does, and How It Can Transform America* (New York: Free Press, 2000). For a worthy explanation of Olasky's arguments, see E. J. Dionne Jr., *Why the Right Went Wrong: Conservatism—From Goldwater to the Tea Party and Beyond* (New York: Simon & Schuster, 2016), 166–167. See also Karl Rove, interview with author, 6 August 2018. GWB quote in George W. Bush, *A Charge to Keep* (New York: William Morrow, 1999), 236.

8. GWB opponents quoted in Gerson, *Heroic Conservatism*, 43; Williams quoted in *Robin Williams: Comedy Genius*, DVD Collection, Time-Life, 2019.

9. Donald T. Critchlow, *The Conservative Ascendancy: How the Republican Right Rose to Power in Modern America*, 2nd ed., revised and expanded (Lawrence: University Press of Kansas, 2011), 258; Dan Balz, "Bush Shows a Shadow of Clintonism," *WP*, 7 October 1999; Dionne, *Why the Right Went Wrong*, 175.

10. "Bush Political Profile," C-SPAN, 25 January 1999, https://www.c-span.org/video/?119585-1/bush-political-profile. The story of the visit to Marlin is told in Hughes, *Ten Minutes from Normal*, 112–113.

11. George F. Will, "Government as Therapist," *WP*, 7 February 1999, B6.

12. James Mann, *Rise of the Vulcans: The History of Bush's War Cabinet* (New York: Viking Penguin, 2004), 250.

13. Condoleezza Rice, *No Higher Honor: A Memoir of My Time in Washington* (New York: Crown, 2011), 1–2; Mann, *Rise of the Vulcans*, 250.

14. For a useful introduction to the term, see Jack Donnelly, *Realism and International Relations* (Cambridge: Cambridge University Press, 2004), 6–11.

15. For a useful introduction to the term, see Irving Kristol, "The Neoconservative Persuasion," *Weekly Standard*, 25 August 2003.

16. Zalmay Khalilzad and Paul Wolfowitz, "Overthrow Him," *Weekly Standard*, 1 December 1997, 14.

17. Robert D. Novak, "Bush's Budding Brain Trust," *WP*, 22 February 1999.

18. Quoted in Baker, *Days of Fire*, 48–49.

19. Karl Rove, *Courage and Consequence: My Life as a Conservative in the Fight* (New York: Threshold Editions, 2010), 134; "Bush: 'Leave No One Out' as Nation Prospers," *NYT*, 20 June 1999; Jon Meacham, *Destiny and Power: The American Odyssey of George Herbert Walker Bush* (New York: Random House, 2015), 553; Mark K. Updegrove, *The Last Republicans: Inside the Extraordinary Relationship between George H. W. Bush and George W. Bush* (New York: HarperCollins, 2017), 275–276.

20. Baker, *Days of Fire*, 49.

21. Bush, *A Charge to Keep*, 184–186. Bush did not continue this motif in his second memoir. When speaking of his father in *Decision Points* (New York: Crown, 2010), Bush tended to concentrate on the personal dynamics of the father-son relationship rather than on a critique of his politics or his presidency (see, for example,

19–21). However, Bush returned to this line of criticism in his biography of his father, *41: A Portrait of My Father* (New York: Crown, 2014), where he suggested that after his father reversed himself on tax cuts, "The White House should have conducted a full-throated public relations campaign to explain the budget decision," and that in 1992 his father missed an opportunity to "consolidat[e] his base"—instead, he allowed Buchanan to attack and define him (see 219, 229). Hughes's recollections of writing *A Charge to Keep* can be found in *Ten Minutes from Normal*, 118–120.

22. Matthew Dowd, in *Electing the President, 2000: The Insider's View*, ed. Kathleen Hall Jamieson and Paul Waldman (Philadelphia: University of Pennsylvania Press, 2001), 17; Baker, *Days of Fire*, 47; Peter Schweizer and Rochelle Schweizer, *The Bushes: Portrait of a Dynasty* (New York: Doubleday, 2004), 459–460; Hughes, *Ten Minutes from Normal*, 117; Rove, *Courage and Consequence*, 136.

23. For Bush's speech at The Citadel, see http://www.citadel.edu/root/pres_bush.

24. All "Bushisms" found in Schweizer and Schweizer, *The Bushes*, 474. Hughes, *Ten Minutes from Normal*, 115–116; Rice, *No Higher Honor*, 7; Robert Draper, *Dead Certain: The Presidency of George W. Bush* (New York: Free Press, 2007), 10–11.

25. Richard L. Berke, "In a Fierce Debate, Bush Promises to Cut Taxes, Calling to Mind his Father," *NYT*, 7 January 2000.

26. Charles Wesley, "A Charge to Keep I Have" (1762). Lyrics taken from Leviticus 8:35 and Mark 13:33; Fitzgerald, *The Evangelicals*, 433–437, 458; Richard L. Berke, "Religion Center State in Presidential Race," *NYT*, 15 December 1999; Meacham, *Destiny and Power*, 553.

27. GWB to Mr. and Mrs. Gary Bauer, 21 July 1999, BGR, 2002/151-0365, General Counsel PIR Files, 2000, Elizabeth Cavendish, folder 5 of 6.

28. Quoted in Transcript, "Meet the Press," 22 November 1999, in Anthony Lewis Papers, LOC, Part II, box 722, folder 10.

29. Marisa Shea, "John McCain," in Greene, *The George W. Bush Years*, 93–95; Mann, *Rise of the Vulcans*, 259.

30. Quoted in Draper, *Dead Certain*, 16.

31. Bush, *Decision Points*, 72; Alberto Gonzales, *True Faith and Allegiance: A Story of Service and Sacrifice in War and Peace* (Nashville, TN: Nelson Books, 2006), 57; Rove, *Courage and Consequence*, 139.

32. Draper, *Dead Certain*, 18, 20; Hughes, *Ten Minutes from Normal*, 120; GHWB quoted in John Robert Greene, *The Presidency of George H. W. Bush*, 2nd ed., revised and expanded (Lawrence: University Press of Kansas, 2015), 249 (also quoted in Schweizer and Schweizer, *The Bushes*, 461, and Updegrove, *The Last Republicans*, 280); Rove, *Courage and Consequence*, 141.

33. Draper, *Dead Certain*, 26; Schweizer and Schweizer, *The Bushes*, 475.

34. Baker, *Days of Fire*, 53; Draper, *Dead Certain*, 26. Bush remembers that he told Josh Bolten to get the staff together and tell them that "they ought to hold their heads high because we're going to win this thing" (quoted in Bush, *Decision Points*, 73). Gerson, *Heroic Conservatism*, 53–55; Hughes, *Ten Minutes from Normal*, 128–129; Rove, *Courage and Consequence*, 142.

35. Baker, *Days of Fire*, 54; Bush, *Decision Points*, 72; Rove, *Courage and Consequence*, 142.

36. Matthew Dowd, in Jamieson and Waldman, *Electing the President, 2000*, 18; Rove, *Courage and Consequence*, 143.

37. Baker, *Days of Fire*, 54; Draper, *Dead Certain*, 66, Rove, *Courage and Consequence*, 144–145.

38. See Baker, *Days of Fire*, 54; Updegrove, *The Last Republicans*, 278; Hughes, *Ten Minutes from Normal*, 131; Rove, *Courage and Consequence*, 146.

39. Draper, *Dead Certain*, 65; Marc Lacey, "Five Senators Rebuke Bush for Criticism of McCain," *NYT*, 5 February 2000; John Kerry, *Every Day Is Extra* (New York: Simon & Schuster, 2018), 238–239.

40. Quoted in Draper, *Dead Certain*, 73.

41. Quoted in Rove, *Courage and Consequence*, 153. See also Updegrove, *The Last Republicans*, 278.

42. Rove, *Courage and Consequence*, 147, 149; Bush, *Decision Points*, 73; Hughes, *Ten Minutes from Normal*, 132; Matthew Dowd, in Jamieson and Waldman, eds., *Electing the President, 2000*, 47; Draper, *Dead Certain*, 71.

43. David Firestone and Alison Mitchell, "In Hot Debate, Bush and McCain Collide over Campaign's Tactics," *NYT*, 16 February 2000; Schweizer and Schweizer, *The Bushes*, 477; Updegrove, *The Last Republicans*, 279.

44. Rove, *Courage and Consequence*, 150; Draper, *Dead Certain*, 75.

45. Edward Walsh, "A Tight Race in Michigan," *WP*, 23 February 2000.

46. Frank Bruni, "McCain Backs Former Rival, Uniting G.O.P.," *NYT*, 10 May 2000; Draper, *Dead Certain*, 81.

47. Nina Serrianne, *America in the Nineties* (Syracuse, NY: Syracuse University Press, 2015), 102–103; Joe Klein, *The Natural: The Misunderstood Presidency of Bill Clinton* (New York: Broadway Books, 2002), 13; Baker, *Days of Fire*, 66.

48. Matthew Dowd, in Jamieson and Waldman, *Electing the President, 2000*, 25; Stanley Greenberg in Jamieson and Waldman, *Electing the President, 2000*, 91–92; Taylor Branch, *The Clinton Tapes: Wrestling History with the President* (New York: Simon & Schuster, 2009), 553–554, 622–624. Clinton hints that he disagreed with Gore's hands-off strategy in *My Life* (New York: Alfred A. Knopf, 2004), 873.

49. Carter Eskew, in Jamieson and Waldman, *Electing the President, 2000*, 67; typed notes (undated), Anthony Lewis Papers, LOC, Part II, box 713, folder 9.

50. Monique O. Madan, "New Supreme Court Nominee Kavanaugh Has Ties to Big Florida Moments," *Miami Herald*, 9 July 2018. Also working for the Bush campaign in Florida (working on litigation regarding absentee ballots in Martin County) was future Supreme Court justice Amy Comey Barrett (Beth Reinhard and Tom Hamburger, "How Amy Comey Barrett Played a Role in *Bush v. Gore*—and Helped the Republican Party Defend Mail Ballots," *WP*, 10 October 2020).

51. Matthew Dowd, in Jamieson and Waldman, *Electing the President, 2000*, 20.

52. "Lieberman on Lewinsky Affair: 'Embarrassing for All of Us as Americans,'" *NYT*, 8 August 2000.

53. Kathleen Frankovic, in Jamieson and Waldman, *Electing the President, 2000*, 123. The only candidate who exceeded Gore's postconvention bounce was George

H. W. Bush in 1988—who went from seventeen points behind to six points ahead. Robert Kaiser, "Political Scientists: Gore Is the Winner," *WP*, 31 August 2000.

54. Bush himself refers to this in *41*, 178.

55. Greene, *The Presidency of George H. W. Bush*, 310n49.

56. Dick Cheney, "Covert Operations: Who's in Charge?," *WSJ*, 3 May 1988.

57. Greene, *The Presidency of George H. W. Bush*, 68–69; James Mann, *The Great Rift: Dick Cheney, Colin Powell, and the Broken Friendship That Defined an Era* (New York: Henry Holt, 2020), 185; Bush, *Decision Points*, 68; Updegrove, *The Last Republicans*, 283. According to Baker, the elder Bush would later say that any claims that he had pushed for Cheney were "completely inaccurate" (quoted in Baker, *Days of Fire*, 58).

58. Dick Cheney, *In My Time: A Personal and Political Memoir* (New York: Threshold Editions, 2011), 305; Rove, *Courage and Consequence*, 168.

59. Baker, *Days of Fire*, 50; Barton Gellman, *Angler: The Cheney Vice Presidency* (New York: Penguin, 2008), 15; Updegrove, *The Last Republicans*, 281; Bush, *Decision Points*, 65; Cheney, *In My Time*, 254–255; Stephen F. Hayes, *Cheney: The Untold Story of America's Most Powerful and Controversial Vice President* (New York: HarperCollins, 2007), 277. The two-state requirement is found in the US Constitution, Article II, Sec. 1, Cl. 3.

60. Cheney, *In My Time*, 255; Baker, *Days of Fire*, 56; Hayes, *Cheney*, 278, 285.

61. Cheney, *In My Time*, 256; Gellman, *Angler*, 8; David Dubose and Jake Bernstein, *Vice: Dick Cheney and the Hijacking of the American Presidency* (New York: Random House, 2006), 141; Mann, *The Great Rift*, 202–203.

62. Rove, *Courage and Consequence*, 167; List in Baker, *Days of Fire*, 55. The story of Frank Keating and Lamar Alexander's inclusion on the short list—the questionnaires they had to answer and the material they had to provide—is found in Gellman, *Angler*, 1–30; Bush, *Decision Points*, 65.

63. Karl Rove, interview with author, 6 August 2018; Bush, *Decision Points*, 67–68. Baker, *Days of Fire*, 57.

64. Baker, *Days of Fire*, 57; Hughes, *Ten Minutes from Normal*, 142; Bush, *Decision Points*, 65, 68–69; Cheney, *In My Time*, 259.

65. Bush, *Decision Points*, 260; Cheney, *In My Time*, 260–262.

66. Rove, *Courage and Consequence*, 169–171; Cheney, *In My Time*, 264. Journalist Barton Gellman reports that at an unspecified time in the process, Cheney "told" Bush that he had been arrested twice for DUI. Gellman observed that "the nominee, with a DUI of his own, could hardly be expected to blanch" (*Angler*, 17–18). Neither Bush nor Cheney mentions this admission in his memoir, but in 2014 Cheney answered a question on the subject from interviewer James Rosen as follows: "I was driving at the time and I *had* been drinking . . . I didn't hit anything. There were no accidents involved. I was drinking and driving, and there was no question I was guilty" (quoted in James Rosen, *Cheney One on One: A Candid Conversation with America's Most Controversial Statesman* [New York: Regnery, 2015], 29 [emphasis in original]).

67. Rove, *Courage and Consequence*, 173–174; Baker, *Days of Fire*, 59; Cheney, *In My Time*, 264–265.

68. Bush, *Decision Points*, 70; Baker, *Days of Fire*, 60; Gellman, *Angler*, 23.

69. Andrew J. Card Jr., interview with author, 30 May 2019.

70. "Full Text of Bush's Acceptance Address," *NYT*, 4 August 2000.

71. Quoted in Baker, *Days of Fire*, 65–66.

72. Rove, *Courage and Consequence*, 163–165; Karl Rove, interview with author, 6 August 2018.

73. Cheney, *In My Time*, 271–272, 274; Hughes, *Ten Minutes from Normal*, 158, 160–161; Rove, *Courage and Consequence*, 179–181, 180.

74. Rove, *Courage and Consequence*, 180–181; Jamieson and Waldman, *Electing the President, 2000*, 7; Blahous, *Social Security*, 210.

75. Rove, *Courage and Consequence*, 182–183; Carter Eskew, in Jamieson and Waldman, *Electing the President, 2000*, 78; Stanley Greenberg, in Jamieson and Waldman, *Electing the President, 2000*, 88.

76. Karl Rove, interview with author, 6 August 2018; Rove, *Courage and Consequence*, 185–186; Baker, *Days of Fire*, 67.

77. Andrew J. Card Jr., interview with author, 30 May 2019; Bush quoted in *NYT*, 4 October 2000.

78. Cheney tells his side of the debate in *In My Time*, 277–284. Cheney is also the chief contributor to the assessment in Hayes, *Cheney*, 292–295.

79. Rove, *Courage and Consequence*, 187–188.

80. Andrew J. Card Jr., interview with author, 30 May 2018; Karl Rove, interview with author, 6 August 2018; Bush, *Decision Points*, 75; Baker, *Days of Fire*, 70; Rove, *Courage and Consequence*, 188.

81. Hughes, *Ten Minutes from Normal*, 165–166.

82. On Mrs. Bush's accident, see "Mrs. Bush Ran Stop Sign in Fatal Crash," *USA Today*, 3 May 2000. Mrs. Bush discussed the accident and its political ramifications in Laura Bush, *Spoken from the Heart* (New York: Scribner, 2010), 59–63, 156–157. The "young and irresponsible" comment is quoted by almost everyone. See Scott McClellan, *What Happened: Inside the Bush White House and Washington's Culture of Deception* (New York: Public Affairs, 2008), 47–48. In his memoir, McClellan writes of a conversation he overheard in which Bush said: "The media won't let go of these ridiculous cocaine rumors. You know, the truth is I honestly don't remember whether I tried it or not. We had some pretty wild parties back in the day, and I just don't remember" (McClellan, *What Happened*, 48–49). Karl Rove, in Jamieson and Waldman, *Electing the President, 2000*, 210; Gonzales, *True Faith and Allegiance*, 87–88; Hughes, *Ten Minutes from Normal*, 166; Rove, *Courage and Consequences*, 189–190.

83. Gonzales, *True Faith and Allegiance*, 87; Bush, *Decision Points*, 76; Hughes, *Ten Minutes from Normal*, 166.

84. Karl Rove, interview with author, 6 August 2018; Bush, *Decision Points*, 76.

85. Alison Mitchell, "Bush Acknowledges an Arrest for Drunken Driving in 1976," *NYT*, 3 November 2000; Rove, *Courage and Consequence*, 192–193.

86. Cheney, *In My Time*, 286; Schweizer and Schweizer, *The Bushes*, 487–488; Charles L. Zelden, *Bush v. Gore: Exposing the Hidden Crisis in American Democracy* (Lawrence: University Press of Kansas, 2010), 4–5.

87. Andrew J. Card Jr., interview with author, 30 May 2019.

## CHAPTER 4. NAMING A PRESIDENT

1. Jeffrey Toobin, *Too Close to Call: The Thirty-Six-Day Battle to Decide the 2000 Election* (New York: Random House, 2002), 18; Kathleen Frankovic, in *Electing the President, 2000: The Insider's View*, ed. Kathleen Hall Jamieson and Paul Waldman (Philadelphia: University of Pennsylvania Press, 2001), 131–132, 141–142; see also Karl Rove, *Courage and Consequence: My Life as a Conservative in the Fight* (New York: Threshold Editions, 2010), 197.

2. Frankovic, in Jamieson and Waldman, *Electing the President, 2000*, 129–132.

3. Frankovic, 132–136.

4. Quoted in George W. Bush, *Decision Points* (New York: Crown, 2010), 78; Karen Hughes, *Ten Minutes from Normal* (New York: Viking, 2004), 175.

5. Charles L. Zelden, *Bush v. Gore: Exposing the Hidden Crisis in American Democracy* (Lawrence: University Press of Kansas, 2010), 18.

6. Toobin, *Too Close to Call*, 24; Bush, *Decision Points*, 78; Hughes, *Ten Minutes from Normal*, 176; quotes from the phone conversation are from Zelden, *Bush v. Gore*, 18; James A. Baker III, *"Work Hard, Study, and Keep Out of Politics!": Adventures and Lessons from an Unexpected Public Life* (New York: G. P. Putnam's, 2006), 360.

7. Bush, *Decision Points*, 78; Toobin, *Too Close to Call*, 29.

8. Toobin, *Too Close to Call*, 13, 15, 33; Zelden, *Bush v. Gore*, 10.

9. Zelden, *Bush v. Gore*, 11–12; Toobin, *Too Close to Call*, 16.

10. Toobin, *Too Close to Call*, 9–11.

11. Bush, *Decision Points*, 79; Baker, "Work Hard," 364; Bush, *Decision Points*, 79; Peter Baker and Susan Glasser, *The Man Who Ran Washington: The Life and Times of James A. Baker III* (New York: Doubleday, 2020), 529–530, 533; Toobin, *Too Close to Call*, 41–42; Mark K. Updegrove, *The Last Republicans: Inside the Extraordinary Relationship between George H. W. Bush and George W. Bush* (New York: HarperCollins, 2017), 287–288.

12. Toobin, *Too Close to Call*, 33–34, 45–46, 52; Baker, "Work Hard," 365; Zelden, *Bush v. Gore*, 28–29.

13. Toobin, *Too Close to Call*, 36, 65–67; Baker, "Work Hard," 367.

14. Baker, "Work Hard," 363 (emphasis in original), 368–369; Toobin, *Too Close to Call*, 53; "Excerpts from Bush's Remarks about Election," *NYT*, 10 November 2000.

15. Toobin, *Too Close to Call*, 35, 49, 50; Baker, "Work Hard," 380; Evan Thomas, *First: Sandra Day O'Connor* (New York: Random House, 2019), 325.

16. Toobin reports that when Harris ran into Warren Christopher and Bill Daley at a Tallahassee restaurant, she went on about how she was going to make sure that Miami became the center of world commerce. Then she quipped to Daley: "Isn't it funny that here I do all this foreign trade, and you were secretary of commerce"; she then turned to Christopher and deadpanned, "And I'm a secretary of state, and you were a secretary of state!" (quoted in Toobin, *Too Close to Call*, 71).

17. Toobin, *Too Close to Call*, 69; Zelden, *Bush v. Gore*, 32, 49.

18. 3 U.S. Code § 5.

19. *Boardman v. Esteva*, 323 So. 2d 259 (1975).

20. Quoted in Zelden, *Bush v. Gore*, 30.

21. Zelden, 27.

22. Baker, "*Work Hard,*" 375.

23. Toobin, *Too Close to Call*, 73–76; Zelden, *Bush v. Gore*, 40.

24. Toobin, *Too Close to Call*, 88–91; Zelden, *Bush v. Gore*, 40–44.

25. Zelden, *Bush v. Gore*, 44–46.

26. Toobin, *Too Close to Call*, 99–101; Zelden, *Bush v. Gore*, 64–66.

27. Toobin, *Too Close to Call*, 103–109; Zelden, *Bush v. Gore*, 86–89.

28. Zelden, *Bush v. Gore*, 89.

29. Toobin, *Too Close to Call*, 127–128.

30. Toobin, 132–136.

31. Quoted in Zelden, *Bush v. Gore*, 98.

32. "Text of James Baker's response to Florida Supreme Court Opinion," *WSJ*, 22 November 2000.

33. Jeffrey Toobin, *The Nine: Inside the Secret World of the Supreme Court* (New York: Doubleday, 2007), 149; Baker, "*Work Hard,*" 379, 382.

34. Toobin, *Too Close to Call*, 144–145, 153.

35. Toobin, 155–158. Baker did not mention the riot in his memoir, arguing instead that it was the Democrats who were guilty of organizing protests to try to "delegitimize the Bush-Cheney victory" ("*Work Hard,*" 374).

36. Quoted in Toobin, *Too Close to Call*, 131.

37. Toobin, 176.

38. Frankfurter in *Colegrove v. Green*, 328 U.S. 556 (1946); Thomas, *First: Sandra Day O'Connor*, 322–323; Michael Isikoff, "The Truth behind the Pillars," *Newsweek*, 24 December 2000, Toobin, *Too Close to Call*, 249; Toobin, *The Nine*, 142–143.

39. John Paul Stevens, *The Making of a Justice: Reflections on My First 94 Years* (Boston: Little, Brown, 2019), 360–361; Toobin, *The Nine*, 151.

40. "Bush Says He Is 'Preparing to Serve,'" *NYT*, 27 November 2000.

41. Baker, "*Work Hard,*" 383; Toobin, *Too Close to Call*, 203; Zelden, *Bush v. Gore*, 117–118.

42. Toobin, *The Nine*, 153–154; Stevens, *The Making of a Justice*, 361.

43. *Gore v. Harris*, 772 So. 2d 1243 (2000).

44. Zelden, *Bush v. Gore*, 121.

45. *Bush v. Palm Beach Canvassing Board*, 531 U.S. 70 (2000), https://www.oyez.org/cases/2000/00-836.

46. *Gore v. Harris*, Supreme Court of Florida, No. SC00-2431, https://caselaw.findlaw.com/fl-supreme-court/1489363.html.

47. Toobin, *The Nine*, 160–161; Zelden, *Bush v. Gore*, 135; Toobin, *Too Close to Call*, 240–246.

48. Stevens, *The Making of a Justice*, 363.

49. Howard J. Graham, "The Conspiracy Theory of the Fourteenth Amendment," *Yale Law Journal* 47, no. 3 (January 1938): 371–403; Zelden, *Bush v. Gore*, 144.

50. Zelden, *Bush v. Gore*, 146–153 (emphasis in original).

51. Toobin, *Too Close to Call*, 257.

52. Audio tape of the oral argument can be found at https://www.c-span.org/video/?161185-1/bush-v-gore-oral-arguments. Summary of oral argument

in Stevens, *The Making of a Justice*, 366–367, and Toobin, *Too Close to Call*, 258–263. See also Rove, *Courage and Consequence*, 214.

53. Stevens, *The Making of a Justice*, 367.

54. Toobin, *Too Close to Call*, 263; Stevens, *The Making of a Justice*, 365, 367.

55. 531 U.S. 98 (2000).

56. Toobin, *The Nine*, 177; Stevens's recollection of the writing of that dissent is in his book *The Making of a Justice*, 372–374.

57. Toobin, *Too Close to Call*, 268; David Boies, *Courting Justice: From NY Yankees v. Major League Baseball to Bush v. Gore, 1997–2000* (New York: Miramax Books, 2004), 451.

58. Baker, "Work Hard," 361–362; Dick Cheney, *In My Time: A Personal and Political Memoir* (New York: Threshold Editions, 2011), 297; Bush, *Decision Points*, 81.

59. "Text of Gore's Concession Speech," *NYT*, 13 December 2000. For Bush's speech, see http://transcripts.cnn.com/TRANSCRIPTS/0012/13/bn.23.html.

60. The official general election results can be found at https://transition.fec.gov/pubrec/2000presgeresults.htm.

61. Matthew Dowd, in Jamieson and Waldman, *Electing the President, 2000*, 23; Carter Eskew, in Jamieson and Waldman, *Electing the President, 2000*, 56. Scholars have long disposed of the fiction that Nader, who polled 97,488 in Florida, somehow "cost" Gore the electoral votes in that state, and thus the election. For the most detailed evidence in this regard, see Michael C. Herron and Jeffrey B. Lewis, "Did Ralph Nader Spoil Al Gore's Presidential Bid? A Ballot-Level Study of Green and Reform Party Voters in the 2000 Presidential Election," *Quarterly Journal of Political Science* 2, no. 5 (2007): 205–226; Stanley Greenberg, in Jamieson and Waldman, *Electing the President, 2000*, 99–104.

62. Matthew Dowd, in Jamieson and Waldman, *Electing the President, 2000*, 23.

63. Greenberg, in Jamieson and Waldman, *Electing the President, 2000*, 99–104; Frances Fitzgerald, *The Evangelicals: The Struggle to Shape America* (New York: Simon & Schuster, 2017), 437; Donald T. Critchlow, *The Conservative Ascendancy: How the Republican Right Rose to Power in Modern America*, 2nd ed., revised and expanded (Lawrence: University Press of Kansas, 2011), 261.

## CHAPTER 5. TRANSITION

1. John P. Burke, *Becoming President: The Bush Transition, 2000–2003* (Boulder, CO: Lynne Rienner, 2004), 12–16.

2. Burke, *Becoming President*, 32n1, 37; Peter Baker, *Days of Fire: Bush and Cheney in the White House* (New York: Doubleday, 2013), 74.

3. Dick Cheney, *In My Time: A Personal and Political Memoir* (New York: Threshold Editions, 2011), 292–296; Burke, *Becoming President*, 25–26.

4. George W. Bush, *Decision Points* (New York: Crown, 2010), 81–82. Bush's assessment of Sununu's management style rings true; see John Robert Greene, *The Presidency of George H. W. Bush*, 2nd ed., revised and expanded (Lawrence: University Press of Kansas, 2015), 200–201.

5. Bush, *Decision Points*, 82; On Card's style of correspondence, see GWBPR, GWBL, White House Chief of Staff, Andrew (Andy) H. Card, Jr., Andrew H. Card, Jr. Correspondence, from FOIA 2014-0216-F[1].

6. Andrew J. Card Jr., interview with author, 30 May 2019; Bush, *Decision Points*, 82; Karen Hughes, *Ten Minutes from Normal* (New York: Viking, 2004), 184; Ron Suskind, "Mrs. Hughes Takes Her Leave," *Esquire*, July 2002.

7. Karl Rove, interview with author, 6 August 2018; Karl Rove, *Courage and Consequence: My Life as a Conservative in the Fight* (New York: Threshold Editions, 2010), 228; E. J. Dionne Jr., *Why the Right Went Wrong: Conservatism—from Goldwater to the Tea Party and Beyond* (New York: Simon & Schuster, 2016), 179.

8. Bush, *Decision Points*, 83; Burke, *Becoming President*, 43; Baker, *Days of Fire*, 80.

9. Bush, *Decision Points*, 83; Jane Perlez, "A Dual Path in Diplomacy," *NYT*, 18 December 2000; Ivo H. Daalder and I. M. Destler, *In the Shadow of the Oval Office: National Security Advisers and the Presidents They Served—from JFK to George W. Bush* (New York: Simon & Schuster, 2009), 255; Colin Powell, *It Worked for Me: In Life and Leadership* (New York: HarperCollins, 2012), 199.

10. Andrew J. Card Jr., interview with author, 30 May 2019. See also Bush, *Decision Points*, 83–84; Baker, *Days of Fire*, 81. In his memoir, Rumsfeld says that he suggested to Cheney that Bush appoint his vice president–elect as his secretary of defense, and Cheney responded, "The President-elect had the same idea" (quoted in Donald Rumsfeld, *Known and Unknown: A Memoir* [New York: Sentinel, 2011], 285).

11. Stephen Chapman, "Can Rumsfeld Add Another Line to a Strong Resume?," *Chicago Tribune*, 15 February 1987; James Mann, *Rise of the Vulcans: The History of Bush's War Cabinet* (New York: Viking Penguin, 2004), 166–167, 231.

12. Bush, *Decision Points*, 84; Andrew J. Card Jr., interview with author, 30 May 2019; Rumsfeld, *Known and Unknown*, 275; Rove, *Courage and Consequence*, 220.

13. James Mann, *The Great Rift: Dick Cheney, Colin Powell, and the Broken Friendship That Defines an Era* (New York: Henry Holt, 2020), 214; Rumsfeld, *Known and Unknown*, 279–285; Andrew J. Card Jr., interview with author, 30 May 2019; Cheney, *In My Time*, 299.

14. George W. Bush, *41: A Portrait of My Father* (New York: Crown, 2014), 119. The same point was made in Bush, *Decision Points*, 84.

15. Bush, *Decision Points*, 85; Cheney, *In My Time*, 298; Rove, *Courage and Consequence*, 219.

16. John Ashcroft, *Never Again: Securing America and Restoring Justice* (New York: Center Street, 2006), 40; Burke, *Becoming President*, 39; David Johnston and Neil Lewis, "Religious Right Made Big Push to Put Ashcroft in Justice Department," *NYT*, 7 January 2001.

17. Ashcroft, *Never Again*, 40; Burke, *Becoming President*, 39; Johnston and Lewis, "Religious Right Made Big Push."

18. Ashcroft, *Never Again*, pp 40–41.

19. Ashcroft, 43; Ben White, "Deepening Rift over Judge Vote," *WP*, 7 October 1999; Michael Grunwald, "Missouri Senate Race Is Heating Up Early," *WP*, 23 October 1999. On 7 November 2013, President Barack Obama nominated White for a

seat on the US District Court for the Eastern District of Missouri. He was confirmed by the Senate by a 53–44 vote. See also Tom Hamburger and Rachel Zimmerman, "Senate Panel Backs Ashcroft Despite Fund-Raising Issues," *WSJ*, 31 January 2001.

20. Tevi Troy, "My Boss the Fanatic," *New Republic*, 29 January 2001. Also Tevi Troy, interview with author, 14 June 2017.

21. Cheney, *In My Time*, 299.

22. Linda Chavez, *An Unlikely Conservative: The Transformation of an Ex-Liberal (or How I Became the Most Hated Hispanic in America* (New York: Basic Books, 2002), 1–22, 219–241. In 1993, Zoe Baird withdrew as Clinton's first appointee for attorney general when it was disclosed that she and her husband had hired illegal immigrants to serve as a chauffeur and nanny. One month later, the same fate met Clinton's second nominee, Kimba Wood, who had employed an illegal immigrant for childcare. The press dubbed the missteps "Nannygate."

23. Burke, *Becoming President*, 46.

24. Memorandum: Walter Mondale to Jimmy Carter, 9 December 1976, "The Role of the Vice President in the Carter Administration," http://www.mnhs.org/collections/upclose/Mondale-CarterMemo-Transcription.pdf. For an excellent survey of the development of the influence and power of the vice president, see Joel Goldstein, *The White House Vice Presidency: The Path to Significance, Mondale to Biden* (Lawrence: University Press of Kansas, 2017).

25. James Rosen, *Cheney One on One: A Candid Conversation with America's Most Controversial Statesman* (New York: Regnery, 2015), 222; Andrew J. Card Jr., interview with author, 30 May 2019; Rosen, *Cheney One on One*, 106, 118–119; Baker, *Days of Fire*, 80; Hughes, *Ten Minutes from Normal*, 204.

26. Daalder and Destler, *In the Shadow of the Oval Office*, 253; Cheney, *In My Time*, 314–315; Rosen, *Cheney One on One*, 112–113 (emphasis in original).

27. Quoted in Cheney, *One on One*, 124.

28. Baker, *Days of Fire*, 7.

29. Frank Bruni and David E. Sanger, "Bush, Taking Office, Calls for Civility, Compassion, and a 'Nation of Character," *NYT*, 21 January 2001; Bill Clinton, *My Life* (New York: Alfred A. Knopf, 2004), 953; Frank Bruni and David E. Sanger, "Bush, Taking Office, Calls for Civility, Compassion, and a 'Nation of Character," *NYT*, 21 January 2001; Cheney, *In My Time*, 303.

30. Laura Bush, *Spoken from the Heart* (New York: Scribner, 2010), 170–171; Bruni and Sanger, "Bush, Taking Office, Calls for Civility."

31. Bruni and Sanger, "Bush, Taking Office, Calls for Civility."

32. David McCullough, *John Adams* (New York: Simon & Schuster, 2001), 639.

33. GHWB to Sidey, 21 January 2001, in George H. W. Bush, *All the Best, George Bush: My Life in Letters and Other Writings*, updated edition (New York: Scribner, 2013), 639–644; Bush, *Decision Points*, 109; Baker, *Days of Fire*, 84; Greene, *The Presidency of George H. W. Bush*, 250; Jon Meacham, *Destiny and Power: The American Odyssey of George Herbert Walker Bush* (New York: Random House, 2015), 561–562; Timothy Naftali, *George H. W. Bush* (New York: Times Books, 2007), 167–168; Mark K. Updegrove, *The Last Republicans: Inside the Extraordinary Relationship between George H. W. Bush and George W. Bush* (New York: HarperCollins, 2017), 294–295.

## CHAPTER 6. "FULL SPEED AHEAD"

1. Dick Cheney, *In My Time: A Personal and Political Memoir* (New York: Threshold Editions, 2011), 298; Cheney quoted in Peter Baker, *Days of Fire: Bush and Cheney in the White House* (New York: Doubleday, 2013), 79–80.

2. Joshua Bolten, Interview II, GWBPOH.

3. Karen Hughes, *Ten Minutes from Normal* (New York: Viking, 2004), 213; Taylor Branch, *The Clinton Tapes: Wrestling History with the President* (New York: Simon & Schuster, 2009), 609; George W. Bush, *Decision Points* (New York: Crown, 2010), 442.

4. Joshua Bolten, Interview II, GWBPOH; Cheney, *In My Time*, 309.

5. Tom Daschle, *Like No Other Time: The Two Years That Changed America* (New York: Three Rivers Press, 2003), 66–67; James Jeffords, *An Independent Man: Adventures of a Public Servant* (New York: Simon & Schuster, 2007), 253, 256, 265–266; Karl Rove, *Courage and Consequence: My Life as a Conservative in the Fight* (New York: Threshold Editions, 2010), 230; Baker, *Days of Fire*, 104.

6. Daschle, *Like No Other Time*, 70. See also Jeffords, *An Independent Man*, 268–269.

7. Rove, *Courage and Consequence*, 230, 232; Baker, *Days of Fire*, 104; Cheney, *In My Time*, 310; David Frum, *The Right Man: An Inside Account of the Bush White House* (New York: Random House, 2003), 96; Hughes, *Ten Minutes from Normal*, 21.

8. Hughes, *Ten Minutes from Normal*, 212.

9. John D. Graham, *Bush on the Home Front: Domestic Policy Triumphs and Setbacks* (Bloomington: Indiana University Press, 2010), 35–38.

10. President George W. Bush, "No Child Left Behind," Foreword; White House Printing, GWBPR, GWBL, SMOF: White House Deputy Chief of Staff, Josh Bolten, box 26, Incoming Correspondence, January 2001 [2].

11. Baker, *Days of Fire*, 89; Bush, *Decision Points*, 272–273; Edward M. Kennedy, *True Compass: A Memoir* (New York: Twelve, 2009), 487–488; Edward M. Kennedy to GWB, February 2001 (handwritten), Letter on Display, GWBM; Frum, *The Right Man*, 54; Sandy Kress, interview with author, 7 August 2018.

12. Sandy Kress, interview with author, 7 August 2018. At that interview, Kress showed me a small, green spiral-bound notebook that he affectionately referred to as "The Little Green Book." This notebook—which Kress later made available to me—is entitled "A Draft Position for Governor George W. Bush on K-12 Education." It contains forty-two pages of closely handwritten prose that Kress claims—with much justification, given the content of the material—to be the basis for what would become No Child Left Behind. The notebook is inscribed: "To Sandy: The architect of a great policy. George Bush." See also President George W. Bush, "No Child Left Behind," 1; White House Printing, GWBPR, GWBL, SMOF: White House Deputy Chief of Staff, Josh Bolten, box 26, Incoming Correspondence, January 2001 [2]; Bush, *Decision Points*, 275; Patrick J. McGuinn, *No Child Left Behind and the Transformation of Federal Education Policy, 1965–2005* (Lawrence: University Press of Kansas, 2006), 168.

13. See Donald T. Critchlow, *The Conservative Ascendancy: How the Republican Right Rose to Power in Modern America*, 2nd ed., revised and expanded (Lawrence: University Press of Kansas, 2011), 264.

14. Sandy Kress, interview with author, 7 August 2018; Kennedy, *True Compass*, 489–490.

15. McGuinn, *No Child Left Behind*, 180.

16. Inscribed Photo, 21 December 2001, GWBPR, WHORM, Subject File, PP (Presidential Personal), Case 491326, from FOIA 2014-0215-F[1].

17. Executive Order 13199 of 29 January 2001; "Guidance to Faith-Based and Community Organizations on Partnering with the Federal Government," GWBPR, GWBL, SMOF: DPC, Jay Lefkowitz, box 8, Faith-Based folders [4]; Meeting with National Faith-Based and Philanthropic Organizations and Leaders, 29 January 2001, GWBPR, GWBL, WHORM, Subject Files, FG 001-07 (Briefing Papers), 01/29/2001 [460508], from FOIA 2014-0216-F[1].

18. Frances Fitzgerald, *The Evangelicals: The Struggle to Shape America* (New York: Simon & Schuster, 2017), 460–461; Frum, *The Right Man*, 101.

19. "The Jesus Factor," *Frontline*, PBS, originally broadcast 29 April 2004.

20. One enthusiastic supporter of Johnson's War on Poverty was paying close attention. In a note sent to Bush on 23 May 2001, she gushed: "Your generous reference to Lyndon and his launching the War on Poverty brought a rush of warmth into my heart. . . . But even more important was the hope your words brought to the whole country, and especially the less fortunate among us, with the decision to carry on that war." The note was signed Lady Bird Johnson (GWBPR, GWBL, WHORM: SP, Case 468476).

21. "Salvation Army Memo Cites Deal with Bush/Support on Faith-Based Funds for Rule Allowing Bias in Hiring," *WP*, 10 July 2001; Frum, *The Right Man*, 102, 104.

22. Quoted in Ron Suskind, "Why Are These Men Laughing?," *Esquire*, 1 January 2003, https://classic.esquire.com/article/2003/1/1/why-are-these-men-laughing. See also Fitzgerald, *The Evangelicals*, 470–474.

23. Executive Order 13210 of 2 May 2001; Charles Blahous, *Social Security: The Unfinished Work* (Stanford, CA: Hoover Institution Press, 2010), 203–204.

24. "President's Commission to Strengthen Social Security: Interim Report," August 2001, https://www.ssa.gov/history/reports/pcsss/Report-Final.pdf. An excellent view of the commission's work can be found in Blahous, *Social Security*, 210–224. See also Graham, *Bush on the Home Front*, 56–57.

25. Cheney, *In My Time*, 315.

26. "Excerpts from Overview of Task Force's Report on National Energy Policy," *NYT*, 17 May 2001.

27. Cheney, *In My Time*, 317; Linda Greenhouse, "Justices Hear Arguments in Energy Task Force Case," *NYT*, 28 April 2004. The case, *In re Cheney* (334 F.3d 1096), was decided on 24 June 2004; National Public Radio, 24 June 2004, https://www.pbs.org/newshour/politics/law-jan-june04-cheney_06-24.

28. Quoted in Edward Alden, *The Closing of the American Border: Terrorism, Immigration, and Security since 9/11* (New York: Harper Perennial, 2008), 76.

29. Donald Rumsfeld, *Known and Unknown: A Memoir* (New York: Sentinel, 2011), 419; Bush, *Decision Points*, 225–226.

30. Op-ed, "Air Strikes in Iraq," *NYT*, 17 February 2001.

31. Bush, *Decision Points*, 423; Robin Wright, "Trump Accepts North Korea's Audacious Invitation—But Then What?," *New Yorker*, 9 March 2018.

32. Condoleezza Rice, *No Higher Honor: A Memoir of My Time in Washington* (New York: Crown, 2011), 34–36, 158; Steven Mufson, "Bush to Pick Up Clinton Talks on North Korean Missiles," *WP*, 7 March 2001; Baker, *Days of Fire*, 95–95; James Mann, *The Great Rift: Dick Cheney, Colin Powell, and the Broken Friendship That Defines an Era* (New York: Henry Holt, 2020), 225–226.

33. Rice, *No Higher Honor*, 45; Rumsfeld, *Known and Unknown*, 312–313.

34. Rice, *No Higher Honor*, 48; Rumsfeld, *Known and Unknown*, 314; Baker, *Days of Fire*, 100; Reuters, "China: U.S. Crew Will Be Freed after 'Necessary Procedures,'" *NYT*, 11 April 2001; Bush, *Decision Points*, 426.

35. Douglas Jehl, "The 2000 Campaign: The Environment; On a Favorite Issue, Gore Finds Himself on a 2-Front Defense," *NYT*, 3 November 2000; David Sanger, "Bush Will Continue to Oppose Kyoto Pact on Global Warming," *NYT*, 12 June 2001.

36. Baker, *Days of Fire*, 97; Jacques Chirac, *My Life in Politics* (New York: Palgrave Macmillan, 2012), 248–249; Rice, *No Higher Honor*, 42.

37. Danforth to GWB, 23 May 2003, GWBPR, GWBL, White House Office of Chief of Staff, Card, Andrew H., Jr., Correspondence: Harriet Miers [2], from FOIA 2014-0216-F[1]. On 31 December 1999, Putin took over as acting president of Russia, following the resignation of Boris Yeltsin. On 26 March 2000, he was elected president of Russia.

38. Bush, *Decision Points*, 432.

39. Bush, 195–196; Rice, *No Higher Honor*, 62–63.

40. Cheney, *In My Time*, 326; GWB to Vladimir Putin (handwritten), 21 July 2001, GWBPR, GWBL, SMOF: NSC Records and Access Management—PRS Original Files, File 0105197.

41. Bush, *Decision Points*, 109.

42. Jay P. Lefkowitz, "Stem Cells and the President—An Inside Account," *Commentary*, January 2008; Bush, *Decision Points*, 110.

43. Text of the Dickey-Wicker Amendment, https://embryo.asu.edu/pages/dickey-wicker-amendment-1996; Lefkowitz, "Stem Cells and the President."

44. Sheryl Gay Stolberg, "Trying to Get Past Numbers on Stem Cells," *NYT*, 7 September 2001; Rove, *Courage and Consequence*, 244.

45. Jay Lefkowitz, interview with author, 23 April 2019; Bush, *Decision Points*, 111; Lefkowitz, "Stem Cells and the President"; Bush, *Decision Points*, 113.

46. Bush, *Decision Points*, 113–114, 116.

47. Bush, *Decision Points*, 112–113; GWB to Administrator of the United States Agency for International Development, 28 March 2001, GWBPR, GWBL, SMOF: DPC, Jay Lefkowitz, box 21, folder 5.

48. Jay Lefkowitz, interview with author, 23 April 2019; Lefkowitz, "Stem Cells and the President."

49. Referring to Tom DeLay (R-TX, House majority whip), Dick Armey (R-TX, House majority leader), and J. C. Watts (R-OK, chair, House Republican Conference), all conservative Republicans who held leadership positions in the House of Representatives.

50. Amo Houghton to Card (handwritten), undated, GWBPR, White House

Office of Chief of Staff, Andrew (Andy) H. Card, Jr., Correspondence, Karl Rove—Political Affairs [1], from FOIA 2014-0216-F[1] (emphasis in original).

51. Lefkowitz, "Stem Cells and the President"; Bush, *Decision Points*, 117; Rove, *Courage and Consequence*, 245–246.

52. "Thompson: Stem Cell Lines 'Viable for Research,'" CNN.com, 10 August 2001, http://www.cnn.com/2001/ALLPOLITICS/08/10/stemcell.decision/index.html.

53. Jay Lefkowitz, interview with author, 23 April 2019.

54. "Thompson: Stem Cell Lines 'Viable for Research'"; Lefkowitz, "Stem Cells and the President."

55. Sheryl Gay Stolberg, "Scientists Urge Bigger Supply of Stem Cells," *NYT*, 11 September 2001, A1.

56. Bush, *Decision Points*, 335; UNAIDS, "Report on the Global HIV/AIDS Epidemic," Joint United Nations Programme on HIV/AIDS, June 2000, http://data.Unaids.org/pub/report/2000/2000_gr_en.pdf.

57. Patty Stonesifer to GWB, 18 June 2001, GWBPR, GWBL, White House Office of Chief of Staff, Card, Andrew H. Jr., Correspondence: Harriet Miers [2], from FOIA 2014-0216-F[1]; Talking Points, Meeting with Congressional Leaders, 16 July 2003, GWBPR, GWBL, WHORM Subject File, FG 001-07 (Briefing Papers), from FOIA 2014-0067-1; Bush, *Decision Points*, 336–337; Chirac, *My Life in Politics*, 249; Jay P. Lefkowitz, "AIDS and the President—An Inside Account," *Commentary*, January 2009.

58. For background, see Dana Milbank, "White House Notebook: A Hard-Nosed Litigator Becomes Bush's Policy Point Man," *WP*, 20 April 2002; Lefkowitz, "AIDS and the President"; Bush, *Decision Points*, 337–338; Baker, *Days of Fire*, 234–236.

59. Bush, *Decision Points*, 338–339; Lefkowitz, "AIDS and the President."

60. Jay Lefkowitz, interview with author, 23 April 2019; Michael J. Gerson, *Heroic Conservatism: Why Republicans Need to Embrace America's Ideals (And Why They Deserve to Fail If They Don't)* (New York: Harper One, 2007), 144; Baker, *Days of Fire*, 235; Lefkowitz, "AIDS and the President."

61. White House website, "The President's Emergency Plan for AIDS Relief," copy in GWBPR, GWBL, SMOF: Domestic Policy Council, Jay Lefkowitz, box 41, folder 10; Helene Cooper, "Memo's Tone May Signal Retreat from Africa Aid," *NYT*, 14 January 2017.

62. Lefkowitz, "AIDS and the President."

63. Press Release, Health Gap (Global Access Project), 11 March 2019, https://healthgap.org/press/trump-budget-proposes-highest-ever-cuts-to-global-hiv-programs/.

## CHAPTER 7. "AMERICA IS UNDER ATTACK"

1. Some 13,310 Soviet soldiers were killed in the war, with 35,4789 wounded; between 500,000 and 2 million Afghans were killed. Figures in Robert M. Gates, *Ex-*

*ercise of Power: American Failures, Successes, and a New Path Forward in the Post–Cold War World* (New York: Alfred A. Knopf, 2020), 167–168.

2. The spelling of bin Laden's first name has led to confusion, as well as to varied theories as to why one has been chosen over the other by an organization. Of the two most often utilized spellings—Osama and Usama—there is no confirmation as to which is correct (see Robert K. Elder, "Usama, Osama? Tracking Suspects Spells Confusion," *Chicago Tribune*, 22 October 2001). I utilize "Usama" in the text of this work, largely because that is the most frequently utilized spelling in administration, intelligence, and law enforcement communications; indeed, the abbreviation "UBL" was utilized by the CIA to identify the terrorist (however, when documents are quoted directly, I have utilized the spelling extant to that document).

3. Steve Coll, *The bin Ladens: An Arabian Family in the American Century* (New York: Penguin, 2008), 142–152; Peter Bergen, *The Longest War: The Enduring Conflict between America and Al-Qaeda* (New York: Free Press, 2011), 14, 16.

4. As with bin Laden's surname, the organization known as Al-Qaida is often identified by different spellings, most commonly Al-Qaida and Al-Qa'eda. There is no official statement of proper spelling. In this case, I have chosen to utilize Al-Qaida in the text because it is the simplest spelling and the one most often used in government correspondence (however, when documents are quoted directly, I have utilized the spelling extant to that document).

5. Bergen, *The Longest War*, 16–18; Steve Coll, *Ghost Wars: The Secret History of the CIA, Afghanistan, and bin Laden, from the Soviet Invasion to September 10, 2001* (New York: Penguin, 2004), 203–204, 381–382; Lawrence Wright, *The Looming Tower: Al-Qaida and the Road to 9/11* (New York: Alfred A. Knopf, 2011), 143–144.

6. Bergen, *The Longest War*, 18–20; Coll, *Ghost Wars*, 268. For a full backgrounder on bin Laden, see Ernest R. May, *The 9/11 Commission Report with Related Documents* (New York: Bedford/St. Martin's, 2007), 55–62.

7. James D. Boys, *Clinton's War on Terror: Redefining U.S. Security Strategy, 1993–2001* (Boulder, CO: Lynne Rienner, 2018), 80. Pakistani forces captured Kansi and extradited him to the United States, where he was executed by lethal injection in 2002; Robert M. Gates, *Duty: Memoirs of a Secretary at War* (New York: Alfred A. Knopf, 2014), 171.

8. Coll, *Ghost Wars*, 9–10; May, *9/11 Commission Report*, 170.

9. Donald Rumsfeld, *Known and Unknown: A Memoir* (New York: Sentinel, 2011), 368. See also Wright, *The Looming Tower*, 230–231.

10. Dick Cheney, *In My Time: A Personal and Political Memoir* (New York: Threshold Editions, 2011), 333; Rumsfeld, *Known and Unknown*, 357; May, *9/11 Commission Report*, 62–63.

11. World Islamic Front Statement, "Jihad against Jews and Crusaders," 23 February 1998, www.fas.org/irp/world/para/docs/980223-fatwa.htm. Also in May, *9/11 Commission Report*, 171–172.

12. James Rosen, *Cheney One on One: A Candid Conversation with America's Most Controversial Statesman* (New York: Regnery, 2015), 100–101; John Robert Greene, *Syracuse University: The Eggers Years* (Syracuse, NY: Syracuse University Press, 1998), 237–247.

13. Boys, *Clinton's War on Terror*, 177–183, 244, 237.

14. Robert Mueller, Testimony Before the Senate Judiciary Committee, 20 May 2004, https://archives.fbi.gov/archives/news/stories/2004/may/thewall_052004.

15. May, *9/11 Commission Report*, 75, 78–79.

16. May, 65, 93–95.

17. Boys, *Clinton's War on Terror*, 186.

18. May, *9/11 Commission Report*, 25–87, 89–93.

19. May, 92.

20. May, 110, 112; Wright, *The Looming Tower*, 318–320.

21. Boys, *Clinton's War on Terror*, 237.

22. Bergen, *The Longest War*, 6–7.

23. Rumsfeld, *Known and Unknown*, 325–327; Rosen, *Cheney One on One*, 218–219.

24. Ivo H. Daalder and I. M. Destler, *In the Shadow of the Oval Office: National Security Advisers and the Presidents They Served—from JFK to George W. Bush* (New York: Simon & Schuster, 2009), 258, 260.

25. May, *9/11 Commission Report*, 115; Scott Shane, "'01 Memo to Rice Warned of Qaeda and Offered Plan," *NYT*, 12 February 2005; Condoleezza Rice, *No Higher Honor: A Memoir of My Time in Washington* (New York: Crown, 2011), 65.

26. May, *9/11 Commission Report*, 116–117, 126, 128–129; Rice, *No Higher Honor*, 66–67; Peter Baker, *Days of Fire: Bush and Cheney in the White House* (New York: Doubleday, 2013), 108; George W. Bush, *Decision Points* (New York: Crown, 2010), 135.

27. David Sanger, "Bush Was Warned Bin Laden Wanted to Hijack Planes," *NYT*, 16 May 2002; Bill Sanderson, "Bush Had Hijack Warning—Was Told before 9/11 Osama Goons Might Act," *New York Post*, 16 May 2002; President's Daily Brief, 6 August 2001 [declassified], https://nsarchive2.gwu.edu//NSAEBB/NSAEBB116/pdb8-6-2001.pdf.

28. Baker, *Days of Fire*, 115; May, *9/11 Commission Report*, 117.

29. May, *9/11 Commission Report*, 118, 131, 134.

30. May, 38–39.

31. May, 40–42.

32. May, 42–43.

33. May, 43–44; Mitchell Zuckoff, *Fall and Rise: The Story of 9/11* (New York: Harper, 2019), 14–16. For Rumsfeld's memory of this (he was inside his Pentagon office when the attack occurred), see Rumsfeld, *Known and Unknown*, 334–338.

34. May, *9/11 Commission Report*, 44–47; Peter Slevin, "Outside the Cockpit Door, a Fight to Save the Plane," *WP*, 24 July 2004.

35. Email, Eskew to Albert Hawkins, Mary Matalin, Claire Buchan, 11 September 2001, GWBPR, GWBL, from FOIA 2014-0039-F, Hawkins folder, Digital Library. Personally, I was walking across the Quad of Cazenovia College at about 9:00 a.m. One of my students stopped me and asked, "Hey, Doc, did you hear? A prop plane hit the World Trade Center."

36. Transcript at https://911timeline.s3.amazonaws.com/2001/abcnews091101.html.

37. Email, James R. Wilkinson to Staff, 11 September 2001, GWBPR, GWBL, from FOIA 2014-0039-F, Bolten folder, Digital Library (emphasis in original). For

Bush's notes for the remarks that were not delivered, see Speech at Emma Booker, 11 September 2001, GWBPR, GWBL, White House Office of the Staff Secretary, Harrier E. Miers, Presidential Remarks, 755754; Schedule of the President, 11 September 2001, GWBPR, GWBL, WHORM, Subject File, FG 001-07 (Briefing Papers), 9/11/2001 [460947], from FOIA 2014-0422-F.

38. Karl Rove, *Courage and Consequence: My Life as a Conservative in the Fight* (New York: Threshold Editions, 2010), 249; May, *9/11 Commission Report*, 48; Bush, *Decision Points*, 126–127; Sandy Kress, interview with author, 7 August 2018.

39. Bush, *Decision Points*, 127; Andrew J. Card Jr., interview with author, 30 May 2019.

40. Bush, *Decision Points*, 127; May, *9/11 Commission Report*, 49; Rove, *Courage and Consequence*, 251; Donovan Slack, "Newly Published Notes Recount 9/11 Aboard Air Force One: 'We're at War,'" *USA Today*, 10 September 2016.

41. In his biography of his father, Bush admitted that "the line stuck with me, at least subconsciously" (George W. Bush, *41: A Portrait of My Father* [New York: Crown, 2014], 200).

42. Bush, *Decision Points*, 129.

43. May, *9/11 Commission Report*, 50–51; Bush, *Decision Points*, 129; Rove, *Courage and Consequence*, 253.

44. May, *9/11 Commission Report*, 51; Bush, *Decision Points*, 129–130; Rove, *Courage and Consequence*, 254; Rice, *No Higher Honor*, 74; Rumsfeld, *Known and Unknown*, 339.

45. Rove, *Courage and Consequence*, 255.

46. Bergen, *The Longest War*, 51; Bush, *Decision Points*, 133; Rumsfeld, *Known and Unknown*, 341–342.

47. Sandy Kress, interview with author, 7 August 2018; Bush, *Decision Points*, 134; May, *9/11 Commission Report*, 139; Karen Hughes, *Ten Minutes from Normal* (New York: Viking, 2004), 241–242; Rove, *Courage and Consequence*, 261–262. Of all the phrases used by Bush administration alumni to describe their service, the term "fog of war"—referring to the chaos of the first hours after the terrorist attacks—is the most ubiquitous. Every major player uses the phrase to describe some measure of their experience during those chaotic hours. Along with Bush, see Cheney, *In My Time*, 329; Rice, *No Higher Honor*, 82; Rove, *Courage and Consequence*, 262–263. Cheney also uses the phrase when responding to an interviewer's question in Rosen, *Cheney One on One*, 207.

48. Bush, *Decision Points*, 137; Rove, *Courage and Consequence*, 263.

49. Hughes, *Ten Minutes from Normal*, 245. For more detail on this speech and its delivery, see John Robert Greene, "Crusade: The Rhetorical Presidency of George Bush," in *The Second Term of George W. Bush: Prospects and Perils*, ed. Robert Maranto, Douglas M. Brattebo, and Tom Lansford (New York: Palgrave Macmillan, 2006), 106. Speechwriter David Frum takes credit for the "make no distinction" line (*The Right Man: An Inside Account of the Bush White House* [New York: Random House, 2003], 142).

50. Presidential Daily Diary (handwritten), 11 September 2001, GWBPR, GWBL, White House Office of Appointments and Scheduling, Presidential Daily Diary Backup, dated folder.

51. Bush, *Decision Points*, 138–139; Laura Bush, *Spoken from the Heart* (New York: Scribner, 2010), 205; Rice, *No Higher Honor*, 77–78.

52. The full text of the North Atlantic Treaty, signed on 4 April 1949, is accessible at https://www.nato.int/cps/en/natolive/official_texts_17120.htm; Jacques Chirac, *My Life in Politics* (New York: Palgrave Macmillan, 2012), 250; "Factbox: Saddam Hussein in His Own Words," Reuters, 21 January 2007, https://www.re uters.com/article/us-iraq-saddam-quotes/factbox-saddam-hussein-in-his-own -words-idUSPAR96305520061230.

53. Daily Diary, 12 September 2001, GWBPR, GWBL, WHORM, FG 001-07 (Briefing Papers), 09/12/2001 [509154], from FOIA 2014-0077-F; Bush, *Decision Points*, 140–142; Rice, *No Higher Honor*, 79–80; Tom Daschle, *Like No Other Time: The Two Years That Changed America* (New York: Three Rivers Press, 2003), 121–123; Rove, *Courage and Consequence*, 271; Byrd quoted in Hughes, *Ten Minutes from Normal*, 247 (Byrd does not mention the exchange in his *Losing America: Confronting a Reckless and Arrogant Presidency* [New York: W. W. Norton, 2004]).

54. Daily Diary, 12 September 2001, GWBPR, GWBL, WHORM, FG 001-07 (Briefing Papers), 09/12/2001 [509154], from FOIA 2014-0077-F; Bush's remarks to military leadership quoted in Hughes, *Ten Minutes from Normal*, 248.

55. Bush, *Decision Points*, 142–143; Rumsfeld, *Known and Unknown*, 351; Transcript of Conversation, Bush, Pataki, and Giuliani, 13 September 2001, https:// www.presidency.ucsb.edu/documents/remarks-telephone-conversation-with -new-york-city-mayor-rudolph-w-giuliani-and-new-york; Talking Points, 13 September 2001, GWBPR, GWBL, White House Office of the Staff Secretary, Harriet Miers Records, Presidential Talking Points: Dated folder; Baker, *Days of Fire*, 136–137.

56. May, *9/11 Commission Report*, 143; Black quoted in Bergen, *The Longest War*, 53. Baker (*Days of Fire*, 136) says that this occurred at a morning intelligence briefing with Cheney. However, the President's Daily Diary has Black at the afternoon NSC meeting, but not at the morning briefing (see Daily Diary, 13 September 2001, GWBPR, GWBL, WHORM, FG 001-07 [Briefing Papers], 09/12/2001 [1], from FOIA 2014-0077-F).

57. Bush, *Decision Points*, 143–144; Baker, *Days of Fire*, 138; Andrew J. Card Jr., interview with author, 30 May 2019; Hughes, *Ten Minutes from Normal*, 250–251.

58. Bush, *Decision Points*, 144.

59. Rove, *Courage and Consequence*, 269; Bush, *41*, 266. The speech went through six drafts. See Draft of Speech (draft 6), National Cathedral Service, 14 September 2001, GWBPR, GWBL, SMOF, White House Office of Speechwriting, Anne Campbell Papers, National Cathedral Service folder 1, from FOIA 2014-0041-F. See also Program, National Day of Prayer and Remembrance, 14 September 2001, GWBPR, GWBL, White House Office of Speechwriting, Anne Campbell Papers, National Cathedral Service 9/14/01 [1], from FOIA 2014-0040-F.

60. Rudolph W. Giuliani, *Leadership* (New York: Hyperion, 2002). 354; Bush, *Decision Points*, 148.

61. Bush, *Decision Points*, 148.

62. Bush, 150; Rove, *Courage and Consequence*, 277–283. Howard's badge is on display at the GWBM. On 30 May 2002, Bush wrote himself a note: "Somber day[.]

Removed last piece of debris from Ground Zero[.] . . . Thanks from our nation to all those who worked hard[.] Pray for those who still suffer" (Handwritten Note to Himself, 30 May 2002, GWBPR, GWBL, WHORM, Presidential Personal, 527103).

63. S. J. Res. 23 (14 September 2001), at 155 Stat. 224.

64. Bush, *Decision Points*, 154.

65. Gustav Niebuhr, "U.S. 'Secular' Groups Set Tone for Terror Attacks, Falwell Says," *NYT*, 14 September 2001. On Robertson's television show *700 Club*, Falwell said: "I really believe that the pagans, and the abortionists, and the feminists, and the gays and the lesbians . . . the ACLU, People for the American Way, all of them have tried to secularize America. I point the finger in their face and say, 'You helped this to happen.'" Robertson's response: "Well, I entirely concur" (quoted in Frances Fitzgerald, *The Evangelicals: The Struggle to Shape America* [New York: Simon & Schuster, 2017], 466). Limbaugh and Hannity quoted in Boys, *Clinton's War on Terror*, 2.

66. Robert Draper, *To Start a War: How the Bush Administration Took America into Iraq* (New York: Penguin, 2020), 25. Both Rice and Laura Bush cautioned Bush not to use such language, but he was unrepentant—as he would later quip, "They understood me in Midland" (Rice, *No Higher Honor*, 146; Jon Meacham, *Destiny and Power: The American Odyssey of George Herbert Walker Bush* [New York: Random House, 2015], 591).

67. Daily Diary, 15 September 2001, GWBPR, GWBL, White House Office of Appointments and Scheduling, Presidential Daily Diary Backup, 09/15/2001, from FOIA 2014-0077-F.

Detailed descriptions of this meeting are found in the memoir of every major participant. See John Ashcroft, *Never Again: Securing America and Restoring Justice* (New York: Center Street, 2006), 141–142; Bush, *Decision Points*, 185–190; Cheney, *In My Time*, 331–334; Alberto Gonzales, *True Faith and Allegiance: A Story of Service and Sacrifice in War and Peace* (Nashville, TN: Nelson Books, 2006), 133–140; General Richard B. Myers, *Eyes on the Horizon: Serving on the Front Lines of National Security* (New York: Threshold Editions, 2009), 165–168; Rumsfeld, *Known and Unknown*, 358–360; Rice, *No Higher Honor*, 83–89; General Hugh Shelton, *Without Hesitation: The Odyssey of an American Warrior* (New York: St. Martin's Press, 2010), 443–444; George Tenet, *At the Center of the Storm: My Years at the CIA* (New York: HarperCollins, 2007), 177–179. For the first reporting of this meeting, see Bob Woodward, *Bush at War* (New York: Simon & Schuster, 2002), 74–92.

68. Bush, *Decision Points*, 187; Rumsfeld, *Known and Unknown*, 373.

69. Gonzales, *True Faith and Allegiance*, 136; Bush, *Decision Points*, 188–189; Rumsfeld, *Known and Unknown*, 358–359, 386.

70. Bush, *Decision Points*, 189–190; Gonzales, *True Faith and Allegiance*, 137–138; Bergen, *The Longest War*, 56; Baker, *Days of Fire*, 144; Mark K. Updegrove, *The Last Republicans: Inside the Extraordinary Relationship between George H. W. Bush and George W. Bush* (New York: HarperCollins, 2017), 311; Rice, *No Higher Honor*, 86; Andrew J. Card Jr., interview with author, 30 May 2019.

71. Quoted in Michael Morell, *The Great War of Our Time: The CIA's Fight against Terrorism—from al Qa'ida to ISIS* (New York: Twelve, 2015), 63.

72. Bush, *Decision Points*, 190; Draper, *To Start a War*, 22.

73. Mullah Omar quoted in Bergen, *The Longest War*, 9.

74. On the writing of the address to Congress, see Hughes, *Ten Minutes from Normal*, 256–261. See also Greene, "Crusade," 107–108.

75. Bush, *Decision Points*, 194; Cheney, *In My Time*, 336–337; Rumsfeld, *Known and Unknown*, 370–371; Baker, *Days of Fire*, 160.

76. Bush, *Decision Points*, 196–197.

77. Bush, 197.

78. Bush, 198. See also Gonzales, *True Faith and Allegiance*, 145.

79. Baker, *Days of Fire*, 167–168; Cheney, *In My Time*, 34; Rumsfeld, *Known and Unknown*, 395; Bush, *Decision Points*, 199.

80. R. W. Apple, "A Military Quagmire Remembered: Afghanistan as Vietnam," *NYT*, 31 October 2001; Rumsfeld, *Known and Unknown*, 378; Cheney, *In My Time*, 345.

81. Bush, *Decision Points*, 200.

82. Steve Coll, *Directorate S: The CIA and America's Secret Wars in Afghanistan and Pakistan* (New York: Penguin, 2018), 95, 100–101; Bush, *Decision Points*, 202.

83. Bush, *Decision Points*, 202; Rumsfeld, *Known and Unknown*, 402; Barton Gellman and Thomas Ricks, "U.S. Concludes That Bin Laden Escaped at Tora Bora Fight," *WP*, 17 April 2002; Bergen, *The Longest War*, 80–81.

84. Bush, *Decision Points*, 202; Rumsfeld, *Known and Unknown*, 559.

85. Bergen, *The Longest War*, 250–251.

## CHAPTER 8. "DON'T EVER LET THIS HAPPEN AGAIN"

1. George W. Bush, *Decision Points* (New York: Crown, 2010), 144.

2. Bush, 151.

3. Dick Cheney, *In My Time: A Personal and Political Memoir* (New York: Threshold Editions, 2011), 334–335.

4. John Ashcroft, *Never Again: Securing America and Restoring Justice* (New York: Center Street, 2006), 124 (emphasis in original); Bush, *Decision Points*, 157; Peter Baker, *Days of Fire: Bush and Cheney in the White House* (New York: Doubleday, 2013), 167. For but one example of mail screened for anthrax, see GWBPR, GWBL, WHORM, SP, box 1, Case 516263.

5. Bush, *Decision Points*, 152–153; Cheney, *In My Time*, 341–343; Condoleezza Rice, *No Higher Honor: A Memoir of My Time in Washington* (New York: Crown, 2011), 101–102; Baker, *Days of Fire*, 168–169.

6. Laura Bush, *Spoken from the Heart* (New York: Scribner, 2010), 227; Baker, *Days of Fire*, 169; 178; Bush, *Decision Points*, 159–160.

7. Peter Bergen, *The Longest War: The Enduring Conflict between America and Al-Qaeda* (New York: Free Press, 2011), 121–122.

8. George Tenet, *At the Center of the Storm: My Years at the CIA* (New York: HarperCollins, 2007), xxx; Ron Suskind, *The One Percent Doctrine: Deep Inside America's Pursuit of Its Enemies since 9/11* (New York: Simon & Schuster, 2007), 65.

9. Bush, *Decision Points*, 154.

10. Speech, John A. Rizzo, Cazenovia Forum (Cazenovia, NY), 10 September

2015; Jack Goldsmith, *The Terror Presidency: Law and Judgement inside the Bush Administration* (New York: W. W. Norton, 2007), 66, 81.

11. Yoo to Flanagan, 25 September 2001, in *TTP*, 3; quoted in Goldsmith, *The Terror Presidency*, 97–98.

12. John F. Freie, *The Making of the Postmodern Presidency from Ronald Reagan to Barack Obama* (Boulder, CO: Paradigm, 2011), 124–125; Robert J. Spitzer, "The Commander in Chief: Power and Constitutional Invention in the Bush Administration," in *The Presidency and the Challenge of Democracy*, ed. Michael A. Genovese and Lori Cox Han (New York: Palgrave Macmillan, 2006).

13. Joel Brinkley and Stephen Engelberg, eds., *Report of the Congressional Committees Investigating the Iran Contra Affair, with the Minority Views* (New York: Times Books, 1988), 401.

14. James Rosen, *Cheney One on One: A Candid Conversation with America's Most Controversial Statesman* (New York: Regnery, 2015), 81–82.

15. Michael J. Berry, "Controversially Executing the Law: George W. Bush and the Constitutional Signing Statement," *Congress and the Presidency* 36 (2009): 245–246.

16. Quoted in Berry, "Controversially Executing the Law," 251. See also Philip J. Cooper, *By the Order of the President: The Use and Abuse of Executive Action* (Lawrence: University Press of Kansas, 2002), 199–230; "Correction: For the Record," *Boston Globe*, 4 May 2006; Ashley Moraguez, "Does Bipartisanship Pay? Executive Manipulation of Legislative Coalitions during the George W. Bush Presidency," *Congress and the Presidency* 47, no. 1 (2020): 62–91. All of Bush's signing statements can be accessed at https://www.presidency.ucsb.edu/documents/presidential-docu ments-archive-guidebook/presidential-signing-statements-hoover-1929-obama.

17. Eric Lichtblau, *Bush's Law: The Remaking of American Justice* (New York: Pantheon Books, 2008), 58; Ashcroft, *Never Again*, 125, 127. In 2017, many of these former prisoners prepared to sue the federal government over their detainment. See Eric Lichtblau, "Justices Consider Lawsuit over Post-9/11 Detentions," *NYT*, 19 January 2017.

18. Ernest R. May, *The 9/11 Commission Report with Related Documents* (New York: Bedford/St. Martin's, 2007), 141; Executive Order 13228.

19. Pub. L. No. 107-56, https://www.hsdl.org/?abstract&did=537.

20. For the view of the American Library Association, see http://www.ala.org /advocacy/advleg/federallegislation/theusapatriotact; Ashcroft, *Never Again*, 159.

21. Bush, *Decision Points*, 162–164; Alberto Gonzales, *True Faith and Allegiance: A Story of Service and Sacrifice in War and Peace* (Nashville, TN: Nelson Books, 2006), 282 (emphasis in original); Americo R. Cinquegrana, "The Walls (and Wires) Have Ears: The Background and First Ten Years of the Foreign Intelligence Surveillance Act of 1978," *University of Pennsylvania Law Review* 137, no. 3 (January 1989): 793–828; "The Foreign Intelligence Surveillance Court," *WP*, 7 June 2013; Cheney, *In My Time*, 348–349; Rosen, *Cheney One on One*, 119–120; Baker, *Days of Fire*, 164.

22. Bush, *Decision Points*, 164; Baker, *Days of Fire*, 164.

23. Rice, *No Higher Honor*, 115; Baker, *Days of Fire*, 164; Cheney, *In My Time*, 350.

24. *Ex Parte Quirin*, 317 U.S. 1 (1942). For a short but useful history of military

commissions in the United States, see https://www.mc.mil/ABOUTUS/Military CommissionsHistory.aspx.

25. Military Order of 13 November 2001, *Federal Register* 66, no. 222 (16 November 2001): 57833–57836 (also in *TTP*, 25–28, and at https://www.esd.whs.mil /Portals/54/Documents/FOID/Reading%20Room/Detainne_Related/10 -F-0341_Doc_1.pdf). See also Gonzales, *True Faith and Allegiance*, 170; Rice, *No Higher Honor*, 105–106; Baker, *Days of Fire*, 174–175; James Mann, *The Great Rift: Dick Cheney, Colin Powell, and the Broken Friendship That Defined an Era* (New York: Henry Holt, 2020), 248; Donald Rumsfeld, *Known and Unknown: A Memoir* (New York: Sentinel, 2011), 590; and Bush, *Decision Points*, 167. The advisory group consisted of Lloyd Cutler, White House counsel under Carter and Clinton; William Coleman, Ford's secretary of transportation; Bernard Meltzer, a prosecutor at the Nuremburg War Trials; Griffin Bell, attorney general under Carter; Newton Minow, former chairman of the Federal Communications Commission; Martin Hoffman, former secretary of the army; Terrence O'Donnell, a Washington attorney; William Webster, former director of the CIA and FBI; and Ruth Wedgewood, a former federal prosecutor (Rumsfeld, *Known and Unknown*, 589).

26. 339 U.S. 763.

27. Patrick F. Philbin and John C. Yoo to William J. Haynes III, 28 December 2001, *TTP*, 29.

28. 542 U.S. 507 (2004).

29. On 9 October 2004, Hamdi was released without being charged and was deported to Saudi Arabia.

30. 542 U.S. 466 (2004).

31. Bush, *Decision Points*, 166.

32. Rumsfeld, *Known and Unknown*, 536, 566; Gonzales, *True Faith and Allegiance*, 157.

33. Rumsfeld, *Known and Unknown*, 566; Baker, *Days of Fire*, 184.

34. On 3 March 2002, the OLC's Jay S. Bybee answered a query from William J. Haynes III, the general counsel for the Department of Defense: "We conclude that the President has plenary constitutional authority, as Commander in Chief, to transfer such individuals who are captured and held outside the United States to the control of another country" (Jay S. Bybee to William J. Haynes II, 13 March 2002, GWBPR, White House Counsel's Office, General File—Confidential File, Detainees Interrogation Issues [Folder 1, 2], from FOIA 2014-0078-F[1]); Memorandum of Notification for Members of the National Security Council, 17 September 2001, quoted in *SSCI*, 11.

35. Bush, *Decision Points*, 165.

36. See "Geneva Convention Relative to the Treatment of Prisoners of War," 12 August 1949, https://www.un.org/en/genocideprevention/documents/atroci ty-crimes/Doc.32_GC-III-EN.pdf.

37. Rumsfeld, *Known and Unknown*, 562; *SSCI*, 20. There is no record as to whether Tenet's letter was actually sent to GWB.

38. John C. Yoo and Robert J. Delahunty to Gonzales, 30 November 2001, GWBPR, White House Counsel's Office, Timothy Flanagan Files, Detainees Folder [3], from FOIA 2014-0078-F[1]; Jay S. Bybee to Gonzales and William J. Haynes III,

22 January 2002, GWBPR, White House Counsel's Office, Timothy Flanagan Files, Detainees Folder [4], from FOIA 2014-0078-F[1] (also in *TTP*, 81–117).

39. Gonzales to GWB, 25 January 2002, *TTP*, 118; Rumsfeld to Chairman of the Joint Chiefs of Staff, 19 January 2002, GWBPR, GWBL, White House Counsel's Office, Jamil Jaffer Files, Public DOD Memo Regarding Interrogation Binder, from FOIA 2014-0078-F[1]; Rumsfeld, *Known and Unknown*, 558.

40. Gonzales to GWB, 25 January 2002, *TTP*, 118; Powell to Gonzales, 26 January 2002, GWBPR, GWBL, White House Counsel's Office, Jamil Jaffer Files, Public DOD Memo Regarding Interrogation Binder, from FOIA 2014-0078-F[1] (also in *TTP*, 122–123); William H. Taft IV to Gonzales, 2 February 2002, GWBPR, GWBL, White House Counsel's Office, Jamil Jaffer Files, Public DOD Memo Regarding Interrogation Binder, from FOIA 2014-0078-F[1] (also in *TTP*, 129); Gonzales to GWB, 25 January 2002, *TTP*, 118; Ashcroft to Bush, 1 February 2002, *TTP*, 127.

41. Memo, GWB to Vice President, Secretary of State, Secretary of Defense, Attorney General, Chief of Staff to the President, Director of Central Intelligence, Assistant to the President for National Security Affairs, and Chairman Joint Chiefs of Staff, 7 February 2002, GWBPR, White House Counsel's Office, Garth Baer Files, Binder-Materials for 01/03/2005 Session [Binder on Detainees] folder, from FOIA 2014-0078-F[1] (also in *TTP*, 134–135). An opinion from Jay Bybee, arguing that the Taliban was not entitled to prisoner of war status under the Geneva Convention, reached Gonzales on 7 February, the day Bush announced his executive order. It is not known if Bush took this opinion into consideration before he released his order, but the order effectively mooted Bybee's argument. Jay S. Bybee to Gonzales, 7 February 2002, GWBPR, White House Counsel's Office, Timothy Flanagan Files, Detainees folder [6], from FOIA 2014-0078-F[1] (also in *TTP*, 136).

42. UNCAT is accessible at https://www.ohchr.org/EN/ProfessionalInterest/Pages/CAT.aspx.

43. 18 U.S.C. 2340A.

44. Bush, *Decision Points*, 168; Rice, *No Higher Honor*, 116; Bergen, *The Longest War*, 109.

45. *SSCI*, 23, 25, 47. This was the prison operated by Gina Haspel, who in 2018 would be nominated by President Donald Trump and confirmed as the director of the Central Intelligence Agency. While Haspel was not at Detention Site Green when Abu Zubaydah was being interrogated, she was there for subsequent interrogations. Adam Goldman, "Gina Haspel, Trump's Choice for C.I.A., Played Role in Torture Program," *NYT*, 13 March 2018; Annabelle Timsit, "What Happened at the Thailand 'Black Site' Run by Trump's CIA Pick," *The Atlantic*, 14 March 2018; Julian E. Barnes and Scott Shane, "Cables Detail CIA Waterboarding at Secret Prison Run by Gina Haspel," *NYT*, 10 August 2018); Ali Soufan, *The Black Banners Declassified: How Torture Derailed the War on Terror after 9/11* (New York: W. W. Norton, 2020), 373–392; Bergen, *The Longest War*, 110.

46. CIA email, 1 April 2002, quoted in *SSCI*, 26–28; Steve Coll, *Directorate S: The CIA and America's Secret Wars in Afghanistan and Pakistan* (New York: Penguin, 2018), 173–175.

47. *SSCI*, 29. According to the Senate intelligence report, the CIA would later

argue that this information resulted in the thwarting of Jose Padilla's planned attack. However, the *SSCI* reported that "the chief of the Abu Zubaydah task force stated that 'AZ's info alone would never have allowed us to find them,' while another CIA officer stated that the CIA was already 'alert' to the threat posed by Padilla, and that the CIA's 'suspicion' was only 'enhanced during the debriefings of Abu Zubaydah" (CIA email, 22 July 2002, quoted in *SSCI*, 29–30).

48. CIA document, 3 July 2002, quoted in *SSCI*, 32–33.

49. *SSCI*, 33. There is no record of the letter actually being delivered to Ashcroft.

50. *SSCI*, 33–34.

51. John Yoo to John Rizzo, 13 July 2002, https://www.hsdl.org/?abstract&did=741695.

52. *SSCI*, 34; Gonzales, *True Faith and Allegiance*, 190.

53. *SSCI*, 36–37; Memorandum for the Record from John Moseman, Chief of Staff, re: NSC Weekly Meeting, 31 July 2002; quoted in *SSCI*, 38.

54. Jay S. Bybee to Gonzales, 1 August 2002, GWBPR, White House Counsel's Office, Garth Baer Files, Binder-Materials for 01/03/2005 Session [Binder on Detainees], from FOIA 2014-0078-F[1] (also in *TTP*, 213–214).

55. John Yoo to Gonzales, 1 August 2002, *TTP*, 218–222. In a 2004 op-ed piece in the *Los Angeles Times*, Yoo attempted to distance himself from the controversy caused by the release of this memo: "The memo did not advocate or recommend torture; indeed, it did not discuss the pros and cons of any interrogation tactic. Rather, the memo sought to answer a discrete question: What is the meaning of 'torture' under the federal criminal laws. What the law permits and what policymakers chose to do are entirely different things. Second, there was nothing wrong and everything right with analyzing a law that establishes boundaries on interrogation in the war on terrorism. . . . precedent and history support the idea that the president, as commander-in-chief, may have to take measures in extreme wartime situations that might run counter to Congress' wishes" (John C. Yoo, "A Crucial Look at Torture Law," *Los Angeles Times*, 6 July 2004).

56. Jay Bybee to John Rizzo, 1 August 2002, https://www.hsdl.org/?abstracts&did=37518; also in David Cole, *The Torture Memos: Rationalizing the Unthinkable* (New York: New Press, 2009), 106–127.

57. Bush, *Decision Points*, 169; Paul Kramer, "The Water Cure," *New Yorker*, 25 February 2008. The cover of *Life* magazine for 22 May 1902 depicts an American soldier practicing what then was known as the "water cure" on a Philippine rebel.

58. *SSCI*, 41–45.

59. *SSCI*, 61–62, 68–69, 96.

60. Bergen, *The Longest War*, 253; *SSCI*, 81.

61. *SSCI*, 82–93.

62. Bergen, *The Longest War*, 113; Matthew Rosenberg and Nicholas Fandos, "Gina Haspel, Nominee for C.I.A., Says Era of Torture is Over," *NYT*, 9 May 2018; Adam Goldman, "Gina Haspel, Trump's Choice for C.I.A., Played Role in Torture Program," *NYT*, 13 March 2018; Amy Davidson Sorkin, "Gina Haspel and the Enduring Questions About Torture," *The New Yorker*, 10 May 2018.

63. Bush, *Decision Points*, 171.

## CHAPTER 9. PREVENTATIVE WAR

1. Hussein is not Saddam Hussein's surname; as one observer put it, "Calling him 'Mr. Hussein' is like calling George W. Bush 'Mr. W.'" Most analysts refer to him as "Saddam"—perhaps because that given name comes from the Arabic word meaning "he who confronts"—and this book adopts that format (Brian Whitaker, "Saddam Who?," *The Guardian*, 22 September 2000).

2. Brent Scowcroft, interview with author, 11 June 1997, quoted in John Robert Greene, *The Presidency of George H. W. Bush*, 2nd ed., revised and expanded (Lawrence: University Press of Kansas, 2015), 174.

3. The Bush White House collected dozens of testimonials, both from interviews with victims and others published in the press, and posted them to the White House website. These are available as "Tales of Saddam's Brutality," https:// georgewbush-whitehouse.archives.gov/news/releases/2003/09/20030929-14 .html. Rumsfeld remembered being given a video, recovered by American forces in the days following the fall of Saddam in 2003. Produced as a warning to Saddam's enemies, it showed, in graphic detail, many of the types of torture and murder that Saddam's security forces employed (Donald Rumsfeld, *Known and Unknown: A Memoir* [New York: Sentinel, 2011], 417n); US Department of State, Archive, "Saddam's Chemical Weapons Campaign: Halabja, March 16, 1988," https://2001-2009 .state.gov/r/pa/ei/rls/18714.htm. See also Greene, *The Presidency of George H. W. Bush*, 140, 175.

4. United Nations Resolution 687, 3 April 1991, https://peacemaker.un.org /sites/peacemaker.un.org/files/IQ%20KW_910403_SCR687%281991%29_0.pdf.

5. S. J. Res. 54 (Pub. L. No. 105-235); Pub. L. No. 105-338, 112 Stat, https:// www.govinfo.gov/content/pkg/PLAW-105pub1338/html/PLAW-105pub1338 .htm; Presidential Determination No. 2000-05 of 29 October 1999, GWBPR, GWBL, NSC-Records and Access Management, PRS Chronological File, 0109338; Robert M. Gates, *Exercise of Power: American Failures, Successes, and a New Path Forward in the Post–Cold War World* (New York: Alfred A. Knopf, 2020), 204; James D. Boys, *Clinton's War on Terror: Redefining U.S. Security Strategy, 1993–2001* (Boulder, CO: Lynne Rienner, 2018), 140; "Clinton's Statement: 'We Are Delivering a Powerful Message to Saddam,'" *NYT*, 17 December 1988.

6. Michael R. Gordon and General Bernard E. Trainor, *Cobra II: The Inside Story of the Invasion and Occupation of Iraq* (New York: Pantheon Books, 2006), 118–121; Peter Bergen, *The Longest War: The Enduring Conflict between America and Al-Qaeda* (New York: Free Press, 2011), 150.

7. Robert Draper, *To Start a War: How the Bush Administration Took America into Iraq* (New York: Penguin, 2020), 172; George Packer, *The Assassins' Gate: America in Iraq* (New York: Farrar, Straus and Giroux, 2005), 45; George W. Bush, *Decision Points* (New York: Crown, 2010), 226.

8. Paul Wolfowitz, "Victory Came Too Easily: Review of Rick Atkinson, *Crusade: The Untold Story of the Gulf War*," *National Interest*, no. 35 (April 1994): 87–92; Peter Baker, *Days of Fire: Bush and Cheney in the White House* (New York: Doubleday, 2013), 90–91; Bush, *Decision Points*, 228.

9. Gordon and Trainor, *Cobra II*, xxxi.

10. Dick Cheney, *In My Time: A Personal and Political Memoir* (New York: Threshold Editions, 2011), 369.

11. Ernest R. May, ed., *The 9/11 Commission Report with Related Documents* (New York: Bedford/St. Martin's, 2007), 145; Baker, *Days of Fire*, 135; Bergen, *The Longest War*, 52.

12. *Meet the Press*, 16 September 2001; Baker, *Days of Fire*, 148.

13. May, *9/11 Commission Report*, 145; Murray Waas, "Key Bush Intelligence Briefing Kept from Hill Panel," *National Journal*, 22 November 2005; Bergen, *The Longest War*, 137–140.

14. Patrick E. Tyler with John Tagliabue, "Czechs Confirm Iraqi Agent Met with Terror Ringleader," *NYT*, 27 October 2001; *Meet the Press*, 9 December 2001; James Risen, "How Politics and Rivalries Fed Suspicions of a Meeting," *NYT*, 21 October 2002. A spokesman for the Czech government would later deny that the call had been made, but he reiterated that there was no evidence of the Prague meeting.

15. 108th Congress, *Report of the Senate Select Committee on Intelligence on the Intelligence Community's Prewar Intelligence Assessments on Iraq*, 9 July 2004, 36–37.

16. Bush, *Decision Points*, 234–235; Rumsfeld, *Known and Unknown*, 425, 429–432; Bob Woodward, *Plan of Attack* (New York: Simon & Schuster, 2004), 30; Cheney, *In My Time*, 369–370.

17. Speech Drafts, West Point Address, 1 June 2002, GWBPR, GWBL, WHORM, Subject Files—FG 001-07 (Briefing Papers), Case 460845, from FOIA 2014-0555-F.

18. "National Security Strategy, September, 2002," https://georgewbush-whitehouse.archives.gov/nsc/nss/2002/. On the writing of the document, see Condoleezza Rice, *No Higher Honor: A Memoir of My Time in Washington* (New York: Crown, 2011), 152–156.

19. Michael W. Doyle, *Striking First: Preemption and Prevention in International Conflict* (Princeton, NJ: Princeton University Press, 2008), 5.

20. John Locke, *Treatise of Civil Government and a Letter Concerning Toleration* (New York: Appleton-Century-Crofts, 1937), 14–15.

21. Quoted in Packer, *The Assassins' Gate*, 45.

22. Rice, *No Higher Honor*, 135–136; Michael F. Cairo, *The Gulf: The Bush Presidencies and the Middle East* (Lexington: University Press of Kentucky, 2012), 122–124; Bush, *Decision Points*, 400–401.

23. Baker, *Days of Fire*, 196–197.

24. Bush, *Decision Points*, 402–403.

25. "The Secret Downing Street Memo," *Sunday Times* (London), 1 May 2005. Minutes of this meeting were recorded by a foreign policy aide and addressed to David Manning, British ambassador to the United States, on 23 May 2002. The existence of this document, known as the "Downing Street Memo," or the "Downing Street Minutes," would not be made public until 2005. See also Draper, *To Start a War*, 185.

26. Draper, *To Start a War*, 176; Brent Scowcroft, "Don't Attack Saddam," *WSJ*, 15 August 2002.

27. Mark K. Updegrove, *The Last Republicans: Inside the Extraordinary Relationship between George H. W. Bush and George W. Bush* (New York: HarperCollins, 2017),

325; Bush, *Decision Points*, 238. Journalist Bob Woodward wrote that Scowcroft had sent the senior Bush an advance copy of the article; according to Woodward, Scowcroft "received no reaction. That meant it was okay" (Woodward, *Plan of Attack*, 160). Jean Becker, the senior Bush's chief of staff, recalled for a biographer that "President Bush's view was that Brent had a right to speak out" (quoted in Jon Meacham, *Destiny and Power: The American Odyssey of George Herbert Walker Bush* [New York: Random House, 2015], 570); Maureen Dowd, "Junior Gets a Spanking," *NYT*, 18 August 2002; Bartholomew Sparrow, *The Strategist: Brent Scowcroft and the Call of National Security* (New York: Public Affairs, 2015), 523.

28. Rice, *No Higher Honor*, 179.

29. James A. Baker III, "The Right Way to Change a Regime," *NYT*, 25 August 2002.

30. Bush, *Decision Points*, 237–238; Colin Powell, *It Worked for Me: In Life and Leadership* (New York: HarperCollins, 2012), 209–211. Also on this meeting: Draper, *To Start a War*, 167–168; Gordon and Trainor, *Cobra II*, 71; and James Mann, *The Great Rift: Dick Cheney, Colin Powell, and the Broken Friendship That Defined an Era* (New York: Henry Holt, 2020), 286.

31. Alberto Gonzales, *True Faith and Allegiance: A Story of Service and Sacrifice in War and Peace* (Nashville, TN: Nelson Books, 2006), 241–242; Baker, *Days of Fire*, 214; Cheney, *In My Time*, 389; Alastair Campbell, *The Blair Years: The Alastair Campbell Diaries* (New York: Alfred A. Knopf, 2007), 635. Bush claims that he made the quip in Spanish: "Your man has got cojones" (Bush, *Decision Points*, 239).

32. Jacques Chirac, *My Life in Politics* (New York: Palgrave Macmillan, 2012), 268.

33. Gordon and Trainor, *Cobra II*, 127–128; National Intelligence Estimate, "Iraq's Continuing Programs for Weapons of Mass Destruction," https://www.scribd.com/doc/259216899/Iraq-October-2002-NIE-on-WMDs-unedacted-version?ad_group=35871X943606Xa75dbc7de9c928d4f42d9879c73c5cb6&campaign=SkimbitLtd&keyword=660149026&medium=affiliate&source=hp_affiliate. In response to a FOIA request, the CIA released the NIE in 2004, but in a highly redacted form. A lesser redacted copy was released in March 2015, in response to another FOIA request (Jason Leopold, "The CIA Just Declassified the Document That Supposedly Justified the Iraq Invasion," *Vice News*, 19 March 2015, https://news.vice.com/en_us/article/9kve3z/the-cia-just-declassified-the-document-that-supposedly-justified-the-iraq-invasion); Powell, *It Worked for Me*, 218; Baker, *Days of Fire*, 223; Murray Waas, "What Bush Was Told about Iraq," *National Journal*, 2 March 2006.

34. George Tenet, *At the Center of the Storm: My Years at the CIA* (New York: HarperCollins, 2007), 323, 375–379; Bob Drogin and John Goetz, "How U.S. Fell under the Spell of 'Curveball,'" *LAT*, 20 November 2005; Baker, *Days of Fire*, 223; Michael McConnell, interview with author, 29 April 2017; Bob Drogin and Greg Miller, "'Curveball' Debacle Reignites CIA Feud," *LAT*, 2 April 2005; Sam Roberts, "Obituary: Tyler Drumheller, 63, Ex-C.I.A. Official Who Disputed Bush," *NYT*, 10 August 2015.

35. Baker, *Days of Fire*, 223.

36. The force resolution is H. J. Res. 114 (Pub. L. No. 107-243); Bush, *Decision*

*Points*, 241; Cheney, *In My Time*, 393; Karl Rove, *Courage and Consequence: My Life as a Conservative in the Fight* (New York: Threshold Editions, 2010), 303; Michael J. Gerson, *Heroic Conservatism: Why Republicans Need to Embrace America's Ideals (And Why They Deserve to Fail If They Don't* (New York: Harper One, 2007), 138.

37. The "Daisy Girl" ad can be viewed at https://www.youtube.com/watch?v=2cwqHB6QeUw.

38. Donald T. Critchlow, *The Conservative Ascendancy: How the Republican Right Rose to Power in Modern America*, 2nd ed., revised and expanded (Lawrence: University Press of Kansas, 2011), 267; Terry Nelson, interview with author, 15 June 2017; Garance Franke-Ruta, "The GOP Deploys," *American Prospect*, 15 January 2004.

39. The twenty-two agencies that were folded into the Department of Homeland Security were US Customs Service; Immigration and Naturalization Service; Federal Protective Service; Transportation Security Administration; Federal Law Enforcement Training Center; Animal and Plant Health Inspection Service; Federal Emergency Management Agency; Strategic National Stockpile; National Disaster Medical System; Nuclear Incident Response Team; Domestic Energy Support Team; Center for Domestic Preparedness; Chemical, Biological, Radiological and Nuclear (CBRN) Countermeasures Programs; Environmental Measurements Laboratory; National Biological Warfare Defense Analysis Center; Plum Island Animal Disease Center; Federal Computer Incident Response Center; National Communications System; National Infrastructure Protection Center; Energy Security and Assurance Program; US Coast Guard; and US Secret Service.

40. Critchlow, *The Conservative Ascendancy*, 268; Bill Sammon, *Misunderestimated: The President Battles Terrorism, John Kerry, and the Bush Haters* (New York: Regan Books, 2004), 97; Matthew Cooper, "A Big Night for Bush," *Time*, 6 November 2002.

41. The advertisement is accessible at https://www.youtube.com/watch?v=tKFYpd0q9nE. Max Cleland, *Heart of a Patriot: How I Found the Courage to Survive Vietnam, Walter Reed, and Karl Rove* (New York: Simon & Schuster, 2009), 187–199; Rove, *Courage and Consequence*, 311–313.

42. Bush, *Decision Points*, 85; Cheney, *In My Time*, 395.

43. Bush, *Decision Points*, 241; Rumsfeld, *Known and Unknown*, 440–442; Baker, *Days of Fire*, 232–233.

44. Bush, *Decision Points*, 242; Cheney, *In My Time*, 394; Baker, *Days of Fire*, 239.

45. Bush, *Decision Points*, 242; James Rosen, *Cheney One on One: A Candid Conversation with America's Most Controversial Statesman* (New York: Regnery, 2015), 263; Tenet, *At the Center of the Storm*, 361; Cheney, *In My Time*, 395; Woodward, *Plan of Attack*, 247–250; Mann, *The Great Rift*, 293.

46. Among these observers, the best-known reporting is that of Bob Woodward. See Woodward, *Plan of Attack*, 247–250; Bush, *Decision Points*, 242; Tenet, *At the Center of the Storm*, 362. Agreeing with this assessment is John McLaughlin, interview with author, 27 June 2018.

47. On 8 February Team Bravo conducted the first search of Curveball's work site at Djerf al Nadaf. There, they found evidence that those involved with Curveball had lied (Drogin and Goetz, "How U.S. Fell under the Spell of 'Curveball'"); Bergen, *The Longest War*, 146.

48. Powell, *It Worked for Me*, 217–218.

49. Powell, 219–220. The initial reporting on the writing of this speech can be found in Bryan Burrough, Evgenia Peretz, David Rose, and David Wise, "The Path to War," *Vanity Fair*, May 2004.

50. A transcript of the speech is available at https://www.washingtonpost .com/wp-srv/nation/transcripts/powelltext_020503.html.

51. Tenet, *At the Center of the Storm*, 373; Drogin and Goetz, "How U.S. Fell under the Spell of 'Curveball,'"; Bush, *Decision Points*, 245; Rumsfeld, *Known and Unknown*, 449.

52. The crew included Rick D. Husband (commander), William C. McCool (pilot), Michael P. Anderson (payload commander), Ilan Ramon (payload specialist), Kalpana Chawla (mission specialist), David M. Brown (mission specialist), and Laurel Blair Saulton Clark (mission specialist).

53. Powell, *It Worked for Me*, 7. See also Chirac, *My Life in Politics*, 281.

54. This meeting is mentioned briefly in Bush, *Decision Points*, 244–245. David Manning's memo on this meeting, revealed on the February 2, 2006, broadcast of Britain's Channel 4 News, went into greater detail, claiming that Bush made it clear that he was ready to employ any one of three ways of provoking Saddam into making the first move: flying a U-2 plane over Iraq, painted in UN colors, and hope that the Iraqis would shoot at it; having an Iraqi turncoat give a public presentation on Iraqi WMDs; and assassinating Saddam Hussein. They also discussed postwar Iraq—Bush said he doubted there would be much civil warfare after Hussein's fall, and Rice said there had been a "great deal of work" done at the Defense Department to prepare for postwar Iraq (Gary Gibbon, "The White House Memo," Channel 4 News, http://www.channel4.com/news/articles/pol itics/the+white+house+memo/161410.html). See also Tony Blair, *A Journey: My Political Life* (New York: Alfred A. Knopf, 2010), 413–437; Bush, *Decision Points*, 253.

55. Quoted in Bush, *Decision Points*, 253.

56. Bush, 223. Rumsfeld already possessed the execute order, in the form of an undated memorandum: "Attached is a copy of the Execute Order for Operation Plan 1003-V that directs Commander, U.S. Central Command, to execute Operation Iraqi Freedom. I am prepared to order its execution, when so directed by you." The memorandum was signed by Rumsfeld; below his signature was written: "Plan approved for execution when I so direct. George W. Bush" (Rumsfeld to Bush, undated, GWBPR, GWBL, NSC, David Travers Records, Iraqi Freedom Folder). See also Gonzales, *True Faith and Allegiance*, 276–277; Rice, *No Higher Honor*, 205.

57. Quoted in Bush, *Decision Points*, 224–225, and in George W. Bush, *41: A Portrait of My Father* (New York: Crown, 2014), 209. Also quoted in Meacham, *Destiny and Power*, 573–574; Updegrove, *The Last Republicans*, 335.

## CHAPTER 10. "CATASTROPHIC SUCCESS"

1. Donald Rumsfeld, *Known and Unknown: A Memoir* (New York: Sentinel, 2011), 459–460; for detail on the raid, see Michael R. Gordon and General Bernard E. Trainor, *Cobra II: The Inside Story of the Invasion and Occupation of Iraq* (New York:

Pantheon Books, 2006), 164–181. At the time of the invasion, the Multi-National Force ("coalition") was led by the United States, Great Britain, Australia, Spain, and Poland. Before 2011, some thirty-five nations sent individual small numbers of troops to join the coalition effort. In addition, NATO sent a small number of advisers.

2. Colin Powell, *It Worked for Me: In Life and Leadership* (New York: Harper-Collins, 2012), 126; Condoleezza Rice, *No Higher Honor: A Memoir of My Time in Washington* (New York: Crown, 2011), 206–207; Peter Baker, *Days of Fire: Bush and Cheney in the White House* (New York: Doubleday, 2013), 261; Gordon and Trainor, *Cobra II*, 178.

3. Gordon and Trainor, *Cobra II*, 184.

4. Gordon and Trainor, 205–207.

5. Rumsfeld, *Known and Unknown*, 464–465.

6. John Robert Greene, *The Presidency of George H. W. Bush*, 2nd ed., revised and expanded (Lawrence: University Press of Kansas, 2015), 124–125; George W. Bush, *Decision Points* (New York: Crown, 2010), 256–257.

7. Rumsfeld, *Known and Unknown*, 479.

8. Saad Eskander, "The Tale of Iraq's 'Cemetery of Books,'" *Information Today* 21, no. 11 (December 2004): 1–54; George Packer, *The Assassins' Gate: America in Iraq* (New York: Farrar, Straus and Giroux, 2005), 139; Bush, *Decision Points*, 258; Rumsfeld, *Known and Unknown*, 475–477.

9. Packer, *The Assassins' Gate*, 294–297; Jessica Stern and J. M. Berger, *ISIS: The State of Terror* (New York: HarperCollins, 2015), 13–17.

10. Packer, *The Assassins' Gate*, 133.

11. National Security Presidential Directive 24, 20 January 2003 (Secret), Declassified 17 January 2013, https://fas.org/irp/offdocs/nspd/nspd-24.pdf. See also Bush, *Decision Points*, 249.

12. Packer, *The Assassins' Gate*, 122.

13. "L. Paul Bremer," in *Presidential Profiles: The George W. Bush Years*, ed. John Robert Greene (New York: Facts on File, 2011), 19–20.

14. L. Paul Bremer, telephone interview with author, 4 June 2019; Baker, *Days of Fire*, 270.

15. Bush, *Decision Points*, 259, Packer, *The Assassins' Gate*, 145; L. Paul Bremer III, telephone interview with author, 4 June 2019; Rumsfeld, *Known and Unknown*, 506.

16. Packer, *The Assassins' Gate*, 192; Powell, *It Worked for Me*, 214; Rice, *No Higher Honor*, 194; Baker, *Days of Fire*, 250.

17. Stern and Berger, *ISIS*, 18, 21.

18. William J. Broad, "U.S., in Assessment, Terms Trailers Germ Laboratories," *NYT*, 29 May 2003; George Tenet, *At the Center of the Storm: My Years at the CIA* (New York: HarperCollins, 2007), 403; Dick Cheney, *In My Time: A Personal and Political Memoir* (New York: Threshold Editions, 2011), 412.

19. James Risen and Judith Miller, "No Illicit Arms Found in Iraq, U.S. Inspector Tells Congress," *NYT*, 2 October 2003.

20. Bob Drogin and John Goetz, "How U.S. Fell under the Spell of 'Curveball,'" *LAT*, 20 November 2005; Baker, *Days of Fire*, 307–308.

21. Bush, *Decision Points*, 262.

22. Nicholas D. Kristof, "Missing in Action: Truth," *NYT*, May 6, 2003.

23. Cheney, *In My Time*, 403; Massimo Calabresi, "When They Knew," *Time*, 8 August 2005; Nicholas Kristof, "White House in Denial," *NYT*, 13 June 2004.

24. Indictment, *United States of America v. I. Lewis Libby*, Grand Jury Sworn in on 31 October 2003, in Murray Waas, ed., *The United States v. I. Lewis Libby* (New York: Union Square Press, 2007), 13, 45, 55–56, 62, 397, 404, 413–414, 570–571; Baker, *Days of Fire*, 280; Jim VanderHei and Carol Leonnig, "Woodward Was Told of Plame More Than Two Years Ago," *WP*, 16 November 2005; Jeffrey Smith, "Ex-Colleague Says Armitage Was Source of CIA Leak," *WP*, 29 August 2006; Don Van Natta Jr., Adam Liptak, and Clifford J. Levy, "The Miller Case: A Notebook, a Cause, a Jail Cell, and a Deal," *NYT*, 12 October 2005; Pub. L. No. 97-200; 50 U.S.C. §§ 421–426.

25. Joseph C. Wilson IV, "What I Didn't Find in Africa," *NYT*, 6 July 2003; Baker, *Days of Fire*, 278.

26. Press Gaggle with Ari Fleischer, 7 July 2003, https://georgewbush-white house.archives.gov/news/releases/2003/07/20030707-5.html.

27. Karl Rove, *Courage and Consequence: My Life as a Conservative in the Fight* (New York: Threshold Editions, 2010), 328, 347; Frances Townsend, interview with author, 22 April 2019; Matthew Cooper, "What I Told the Grand Jury," *Time*, 25 July 2005. In his memoir, Rove says that "to this day I have no recollection" of the phone call, "but I wrote an e-mail after the call confirming it, and Cooper wrote a longer e-mail a few days later to his colleagues about the same call" (Rove, *Courage and Consequence*, 330); Walter Pincus, "Anonymous Sources: Their Use in a Time of Prosecutorial Interest," *Nieman Reports*, Summer 2005.

28. Robert D. Novak, "Mission to Niger," *WP*, 14 July 2005; Mike Allen and Dana Priest, "Bush Administration Is Focus of Inquiry," *WP*, 28 September 2003. It would later be reported that the source for the story was State Department official Marc Grossman (Jason Leopold, "Libby Filing: A Denial and a Mystery," truthout .org, 14 April 2006).

29. Baker, *Days of Fire*, 329, 336–337.

30. Baker, 555–556.

31. Quoted in Bush, *Decision Points*, 356; Rumsfeld, *Known and Unknown*, 667.

32. Bush, *Decision Points*, 264–266; Rice, *No Higher Honor*, 246–248.

33. Bush, *Decision Points*, 267; Cheney, *In My Time*, 411; Rice, *No Higher Honor*, 251–252; Will Bardenwerper, *The Prisoner in His Palace: Saddam Hussein, His American Guards, and What History Leaves Unsaid* (New York: Scribner, 2017), 43–45; Rumsfeld, *Known and Unknown*, 530; L. Paul Bremer III, telephone interview with author, 4 June 2019.

34. Quoted in James Rosen, *Cheney One on One: A Candid Conversation with America's Most Controversial Statesman* (New York: Regnery, 2015), 129; Rumsfeld, *Known and Unknown*, 630; Rice, *No Higher Honor*, 249–251.

35. Cheney, *In My Time*, 350; Alberto Gonzales, *True Faith and Allegiance: A Story of Service and Sacrifice in War and Peace* (Nashville, TN: Nelson Books, 2006), 291; Baker, *Days of Fire*, 314.

36. Gonzales, *True Faith and Allegiance*, 293–294; Baker, *Days of Fire*, 315.

37. Baker, *Days of Fire*, 315; James Comey, *A Higher Loyalty: Truth, Lies, and Leadership* (New York: Flatiron Books, 2018), 85–87.

38. Baker, *Days of Fire*, 315–316; Cheney, *In My Time*, 351; Gonzales, *True Faith and Allegiance*, 310–313.

39. For the wildly diverging tales of the hospital visit, see Baker, *Days of Fire*, 316–317; Comey, *A Higher Loyalty*, 87–92; Gonzales, *True Faith and Allegiance*, 314–322. In his memoir *The Terror Presidency: Law and Judgement inside the Bush Administration* (New York: W. W. Norton, 2007), Jack Goldsmith offers an abbreviated narrative of events that does not include the hospital visit; in 2007 he fleshed out his participation in that event for Jeffrey Rosen, "Conscience of a Conservative," *New York Times Magazine*, 9 September 2007. See also Andrew Card, interview with author, 30 May 2019.

40. Journalist Peter Baker reports that Addington retyped the reauthorization order to leave out the attorney general's signature, substituting instead the signature of the White House counsel (*Days of Fire*, 317–318).

41. Bush, *Decision Points*, 173.

42. Bush, 173–174; Baker, *Days of Fire*, 318

43. James Dao, "Private Guards Take Big Risks, for the Right Price," *NYT*, 2 April 2004. The contractors were Wesley Batalona, Scott Helveston, Mike Teague, and Jerry Zovko; Rumsfeld, *Known and Unknown*, 533.

44. Baker, *Days of Fire*, 322.

45. Rumsfeld, *Known and Unknown*, 537; L. Paul Bremer III, telephone interview with author, 4 June 2019.

46. Bush, *Decision Points*, 357; "Zarqawi Beheaded U.S. Man in Iraq," BBC News, 13 May 2004, http://news.bbc.co.uk/2/hi/middle_east/3712421.stm.

47. Bush, *Decision Points*, 359; Rice, *No Higher Honor*, 278; Baker, *Days of Fire*, 337. The note from Rice is on display at GWBM.

48. Baker, *Days of Fire*, 343; "Iraq Index: Tracking Variables of Reconstruction and Security in Post-Saddam Iraq," Brookings Institution, updated 20 September 2004, 4, 13, https://www.brookings.edu/wp-content/uploads/2017/11/index20040920.pdf.


## CHAPTER 11. REELECTING A PRESIDENT

1. Gallup, "Presidential Approval Ratings—George W. Bush,"https://news.gallup.com/poll/116500/presidential-approval-ratings-george-bush.aspx; Jonathan Chait, "Mad about You," *New Republic*, 29 September 2003.

2. Dan Rather, *Rather Outspoken* (New York: Grand Central Publishing, 2013), 7.

3. Rather, 18. These photographs can be accessed at https://www.cbsnews.com/pictures/abuse-photos-ii/.

4. Rather, *Rather Outspoken*, 23–24; Seymour Hersh, "Torture at Abu Ghraib," *New Yorker*, 10 May 2004. Hersh expands upon his stories in *Chain of Command: The Road from 9/11 to Abu Ghraib* (New York: HarperCollins, 2004), and discusses his Abu Ghraib reporting in *Reporter: A Memoir* (New York: Alfred A. Knopf, 2018), 308–313.

5. Rather, *Rather Outspoken*, 27; George W. Bush, *Decision Points* (New York: Crown, 2010), 88–89; Dick Cheney, *In My Time: A Personal and Political Memoir* (New York: Threshold Editions, 2011), 420; Colin Powell, *It Worked for Me: In Life and Leadership* (New York: HarperCollins, 2012), 122–123.

6. Peter Baker, *Days of Fire: Bush and Cheney in the White House* (New York: Doubleday, 2013), 328.

7. Rumsfeld to Bush (handwritten), 5 May 2004, GWBPR, GWBL, White House Office of the Staff Secretary, Raul Yanes, Subject Files, Rumsfeld Resignation Letters, from FOIA 2014-0216-F[1]; Bush, *Decision Points*, 89; Cheney, *In My Time*, 420–421; Donald Rumsfeld, *Known and Unknown: A Memoir* (New York: Sentinel, 2011), 550–551, 547–548; Baker, *Days of Fire*, 327–330 Rather, *Rather Outspoken*, 29. Bush's presidential papers contain an envelope labeled "Abu Ghraib Rumsfeld Resignation Letter" and dated 9 May 2004—but the letter is not in the envelope (GWBPR, GWBL, White House Office of the Staff Secretary, Raul Yanes, Subject Files, Rumsfeld Resignation Letters, from FOIA 2014-0216-F[1].

8. Michael Allen, *Blinking Red: Crisis and Compromise in American Intelligence after 9/11* (New York: Potomac Books, 2013), 7, 23.

9. Ernest R. May, ed., *The 9/11 Commission Report with Related Documents* (New York: Bedford/St. Martin's, 2007), 6; Allen, *Blinking Red*, 33.

10. May, *9/11 Commission Report*, 6; Allen, *Blinking Red*, 33. The rest of the commission consisted of four Republicans (Washington attorney Fred Fielding; three-term senator from Washington State Slade Gorton; former secretary of the navy John Lehman; and former Illinois governor James Thompson) and four Democrats (former head of the Watergate task force and Clinton lawyer Richard Ben-Veniste; former deputy attorney general Jamie Gorelick; former congressman from Indiana Timothy Roemer; and former Nebraska senator Bob Kerrey, who replaced former Georgia senator Max Cleland, who resigned from the commission to take a job at the Import-Export Bank).

11. "First Interim Report of the National Commission on Terrorist Attacks upon the United States," 8 July 2003, GWBPR, GWBL, SMOF, Domestic Policy Council, Jay Lefkowitz, folder 2.

12. "First Interim Report of the National Commission on Terrorist Attacks upon the United States," 8 July 2003, GWBPR, GWBL, SMOF, Domestic Policy Council, Jay Lefkowitz, folder 2; May, *9/11 Commission Report*, 10–11.

13. May, *9/11 Commission Report*, 13; National Commission on Terrorist Attacks upon the United States," Eighth Public Hearing, 24 March 2004, https://govinfo .library.unt.edu/911/archive/hearing8/9-11Commission_Hearing_2004-03-24 .htm#clarke; Alberto Gonzales, *True Faith and Allegiance: A Story of Service and Sacrifice in War and Peace* (Nashville, TN: Nelson Books, 2006), 337–339; Condoleezza Rice, *No Higher Honor: A Memoir of My Time in Washington* (New York: Crown, 2011), 260–264.

14. When the report of the committee was made public, twenty-eight pages of it were redacted. The families of those killed in the attack, as well as journalists and historians, demanded that the pages be made public, particularly when it was rumored that they dealt with Saudi Arabian involvement in the attacks (fifteen of the nineteen hijackers were Saudis). When the pages were declassified in 2016, they

showed that several of the 9/11 hijackers had received financial help from members of the Saudi government. These pages are accessible at https://web.archive .org/web/20160715183528/http://intelligence.house.gov/sites/intelligence .house.gov/files/documents/declasspart4.pdf; May, *9/11 Commission Report*, 165.

15. Bush, *Decision Points*, 281.

16. Bush, 283.

17. Baker, *Days of Fire*, 293–295.

18. Karl Rove, *Courage and Consequence: My Life as a Conservative in the Fight* (New York: Threshold Editions, 2010), 368; transcript, John Kerry Testimony Before Senate Committee, 22 April 1971, https://www.npr.org/templates/story/story .php?storyId=3875422; Kathleen Hall Jamieson, ed., *Electing the President, 2004: The Insiders' View* (Philadelphia: University of Pennsylvania Press, 2006), 34.

19. John Kerry, *Every Day Is Extra* (New York: Simon & Schuster, 2018), 262.

20. Bush, *Decision Points*, 287; Jamieson, *Electing the President, 2004*, 39; Rove, *Courage and Consequence*, 369.

21. Thomas Frank, *What's the Matter with Kansas? How Conservatives Won the Heart of America* (New York: Picador, 2004), 1, 5–6.

22. 539 U.S. 558 (2003).

23. 478 U.S. 186 (1986).

24. 798 N.E. 2d 941 (Mass. 2003).

25. *Roe v. Wade*, 410 U. S. 113 (1975); Sheryl Gay Stolberg, "Senate Approves Ban on Abortion Procedure," *NYT*, 21 January 2003.

26. In 2007, the Supreme Court upheld the law (*Gonzales v. Carhart*, 550 U.S. 124 (2007)).

27. Rachel Gordon, "The Battle over Same-Sex Marriage/Uncharted Territory/Bush's Stance Led Newsom to Take Action," *San Francisco Chronicle*, 15 February 2004; Baker, *Days of Fire*, 310.

28. Baker, *Days of Fire*, 312; Garance Franke-Ruta, "George W. Bush's Forgotten Gay-Rights History," *The Atlantic*, 8 July 2013.

29. Bush, *Decision Points*, 288; Baker, *Days of Fire*, 319.

30. Cheney, *In My Time*, 417–418; Karl Rove, interview with author, 6 August 2018; Bush, *Decision Points*, 86–87.

31. Kerry, *Every Day Is Extra*, 279.

32. "Barack Obama's Remarks to the Democratic National Convention," *NYT*, 27 July 2004. See also Barack Obama, *A Promised Land* (New York: Crown, 2020), 50–52.

33. Kerry, *Every Day Is Extra*, 272–275.

34. Kerry, 280.

35. The ad is accessible at https://www.youtube.com/watch?v=phqOuEhg9yE.

36. Rove, *Courage and Consequence*, 390. Along with prohibiting the use of "soft money" donations to the national political parties and banning foreign corporations or foreign nations from participating in campaign spending decisions, McCain-Feingold banned the use of issue advocacy ads (Pub. L. No. 107-155). Most of the law was upheld in *McConnell v. FEC*, 540 U.S. 93 (2003), but seven years later the Court struck down the ban on issue advocacy ads as part of its decision in *Citizens United v. FEC*, 558 U.S. 310 (2010). See also Jamieson, *Electing the President,*

*2004*, 56, 69; Kerry, *Every Day Is Extra*, 305. These numbers represent the average of fourteen national polls, found at Real Clear Politics: https://www.realclearpol itics.com/epolls/2004/president/us/general_election_bush_vs_kerry-939.html.

37. Baker, *Days of Fire*, 343.

38. Mary Mapes, *Truth and Duty: The Press, the President, and the Privilege of Power* (New York: St. Martin's Press, 2005), 1–3.

39. Rather, *Rather Outspoken*, 32–47.

40. Jim Rutemberg and Kate Zernike, "CBS Apologizes for Report on Bush Guard Service," *NYT*, 21 September 2004.

41. These numbers represent the average of fourteen national polls, found at Real Clear Politics: https://www.realclearpolitics.com/epolls/2004/president /us/general_election_bush_vs_kerry-939.html.

42. Kerry, *Every Day Is Extra*, 314; Rove, *Courage and Consequence*, 392–393; Bush, *Decision Points*, 293. These numbers represent the average of fourteen national polls, found at Real Clear Politics: https://www.realclearpolitics.com /epolls/2004/president/us/general_election_bush_vs_kerry-939.html.

43. Kerry, *Every Day Is Extra*, 317.

44. Cheney, *In My Time*, 424–425; Baker, *Days of Fire*, 349–351.

45. Quoted in Jamieson, *Electing the President, 2004*, 131–137. For his part, Kerry breezes by this moment in his memoir: "It was a strange exclamation point on the politics of division" (*Every Day Is Extra*, 319).

46. These numbers represent the average of fourteen national polls, found at Real Clear Politics: https://www.realclearpolitics.com/epolls/2004/president /us/general_election_bush_vs_kerry-939.html; Gonzales, *True Faith and Allegiance*, 332–333.

47. Bin Laden speech, videotaped, released 1 November 2004, transcript available at http://www.aljazeera.com/archive/2004/11/200849163336457223.html.

48. Richard W. Stevenson and Jodi Wilgoren, "Candidates Give Tough Response to al Qaeda Tape," *NYT*, 30 October 2004.

49. These numbers represent the average of fourteen national polls, found at Real Clear Politics: https://www.realclearpolitics.com/epolls/2004/president /us/general_election_bush_vs_kerry-939.html.

50. Rove, *Courage and Consequence*, 397–400; Bush, *Decision Points*, 296.

51. James A. Baker III *"Work Hard, Study, and Keep Out of Politics!": Adventures and Lessons from an Unexpected Public Life* (New York: G. P. Putnam's, 2006), 393–394.

52. Frances Fitzgerald, *The Evangelicals: The Struggle to Shape America* (New York: Simon & Schuster, 2017), 437–438, 501–506.

53. Email, Addington to Alberto Gonzales, David Leitch, Reginald Brown, Dabney Friederich, and Jennifer Newstead, 3 November 2004, GWBPR, GWBL, Electronic Material, from FOIA 2014-0049-F.

## CHAPTER 12. STORMS

1. Robert Draper, *Dead Certain: The Presidency of George W. Bush* (New York: Free Press, 2007), x; Bob Woodward, *Plan of Attack* (New York: Simon & Schuster, 2004), 421.

2. David Frum, *The Right Man: An Inside Account of the Bush White House* (New York: Random House, 2003), 13; Robert Draper, *To Start a War: How the Bush Administration Took America into Iraq* (New York: Penguin, 2020), 29; Peter Baker, *Days of Fire: Bush and Cheney in the White House* (New York: Doubleday, 2013), 86; on Bush's impatience, see Karen Hughes, *Ten Minutes from Normal* (New York: Viking, 2004), 193; Robert M. Gates, *Duty: Memoirs of a Secretary at War* (New York: Alfred A. Knopf, 2014), 94; George W. Bush, *A Charge to Keep* (New York: William Morrow, 1999), 27.

3. Hughes, *Ten Minutes from Normal*, 81, 85; Draper, *Dead Certain*; Bush, *A Charge to Keep*, 103; Karl Rove, *Courage and Consequence: My Life as a Conservative in the Fight* (New York: Threshold Editions, 2010), 171; Karl Rove, interview with author, 6 August 2018.

4. Keith Hennessey, "George Bush Is Smarter Than You," Keithhennessey .com, 24 April 2013, http://keithhennessey.com/2013/04/24/smarter/?tid=a_inl.

5. Jonathan Chait, "Yes, George W. Bush Was a Terrible President, and No, He Wasn't Smart," *New York*, 25 April 2013.

6. John Robert Greene, *The Presidency of Gerald R. Ford* (Lawrence: University Press of Kansas, 1995), 6; Frances Townsend, interview with author, 22 April 2019; Karl Rove, interview with author, 6 August 2018.

7. Baker, *Days of Fire*, 147; Tevi Troy, *What Jefferson Read, Ike Watched, and Obama Tweeted: 200 Years of Popular Culture in the White House* (Washington, DC: Regnery, 2013), 203–204; George W. Bush, *Decision Points* (New York: Crown, 2010), 52; Karl Rove, "Bush Is a Book Lover," *WSJ*, 26 December 2008; Frances Townsend, interview with author, 22 April 2019; Matthew Mosk, "George W. Bush in 2005: 'If We Wait for a Pandemic to Appear, It Will Be Too Late to Prepare,'" ABC News, 5 April 2020.

8. Troy, *What Jefferson Read*, 45. See also Baker, *Days of Fire*, 479–480.

9. Speech Notes, 18 September 2001, GWBPR, GWBL, White House Office of Speechwriting, Jeanette Reilly Papers, Speech Files, Meeting with Flight 93 Families, from FOIA 2014-0077–1; Frum, *The Right Man*, 169; GWBPR, GWBL, SMOF: Domestic Policy Council Jay Lefkowitz, box 51, folders 7–13; Bush to [NAME REDACTED], 25 September 2008, GWBPR, WHORM, FG 015-01 (Marine Corps), Case 766309, from FOIA 2014-0106-F.

10. Bush, *Decision Points*, 1. Bush uses the term "habitual personality" twice in *Decision Points* (pp. 1, 34) to describe himself. Indeed, it is telling that Bush described his decision to quit in the phraseology of addiction—"Not drinking became a habit of its own—one I was glad to keep" (*Decision Points*, 3).

11. Bush, 200–201; Laura Bush, *Spoken from the Heart* (New York: Scribner, 2010), 237–238; Hughes, *Ten Minutes from Normal*, 275–276.

12. Susan Page, *The Matriarch: Barbara Bush and the Making of an American Dynasty* (New York: Twelve, 2019), 344; Baker, *Days of Fire*, 54, 527.

13. The speech is accessible at https://americanrhetoric.com/speeches/laura bushwhitehousecorrespondentsdinner2005.htm. See also Laura Bush, *Spoken from the Heart*, 325–327.

14. Email, Scott McClellan to Brian Montgomery, 4 November 2004, GWBPR, GWBL, Electronic Material, from FOIA 2014-0049-F.

15. James Mann, *The Great Rift: Dick Cheney, Colin Powell, and the Broken Friendship That Defined an Era* (New York: Henry Holt, 2020), 261–272; Colin Powell, *It Worked for Me: In Life and Leadership* (New York: HarperCollins, 2012), 36; Dick Cheney, *In My Time: A Personal and Political Memoir* (New York: Threshold Editions, 2011), 425.

16. Bush, *Decision Points*, 90; Andrew J. Card Jr., interview with author, 30 May 2019; Baker, *Days of Fire*, 363–366; Condoleezza Rice, *No Higher Honor: A Memoir of My Time in Washington* (New York: Crown, 2011), 291–292; Baker, *Days of Fire*, 365–366. The best summary of the drama surrounding Powell's resignation can be found in Mann, *The Great Rift*, 322–326. Powell would later protest that "President Bush and I parted on good terms" (Powell, *It Worked for Me*, 36).

17. Patrick Leahy to Gonzales, 3 December 2004, GWBPR, GWBL, White House Counsel's Office, Alberto R. Gonzales, Subject Files, Nomination: Follow-Up Questions from Senate: ARG [Alberto R. Gonzales] Supporters: Organization [1], from FOIA 2014-0216-F[1]. Gonzales offers little information on his confirmation hearings in *True Faith and Allegiance: A Story of Service and Sacrifice in War and Peace* (Nashville, TN: Nelson Books, 2006), 345.

18. Baker, *Days of Fire*, 368–369.

19. Bush, *Decision Points*, 91–92.

20. Elliot Abrams Interview, GWBPOH; Natan Sharansky, *The Case for Democracy: The Power of Freedom to Overcome Tyranny and Terror* (New York: Public Affairs, 2004); Troy, *What Jefferson Read*, 205; Bush to Shevardnadze, 30 November 2003, GWBPR, GWBL, WHORM, Subject Files, C0063 (Georgia), SS 1489, from FOIA 2014-0216-F[1]; Powell, *It Worked for Me*, 126–127. In 2008, with the support of the United States, both Georgia and the Ukraine would apply for membership in NATO. Opposition within the organization was so strong that the best that Bush could get was a promise of future membership for the two nations (Bush, *Decision Points*, 430–431).

21. Bush, *Decision Points*, 396–398; Baker, *Days of Fire*, 360, 370–375.

22. Bartholomew Sparrow, *The Strategist: Brent Scowcroft and the Call of National Security* (New York: Public Affairs, 2015), 526–527.

23. Elliot Abrams Interview, GWBPOH; Donald Rumsfeld, *Known and Unknown: A Memoir* (New York: Sentinel, 2011), 498.

24. Dexter Filkins, "Defying Threats, Millions of Iraqis Flock to Polls," *NYT*, 31 January 2005; David E. Sanger, "Bush Hails Iraqi Vote, but Warns of More Fighting Ahead," *NYT*, 31 January 2005.

25. Charles Blahous, *Social Security: The Unfinished Work* (Stanford, CA: Hoover Institution Press, 2010), 233–235; Rove, *Courage and Consequence*, 408; John D. Graham, *Bush on the Home Front: Domestic Policy Triumphs and Setbacks* (Bloomington: Indiana University Press, 2010), 59.

26. William A. Galston, "Why the 2005 Social Security Initiative Failed, and What It Means for the Future," Report, Brookings Institution, 21 September 2007; Bush, *Decision Points*, 299.

27. Graham, *Bush on the Home Front*, 59–60. The three Democrats who refused to sign were Kent Conrad of North Dakota, Blanche Lincoln of Arkansas, and Ben Nelson of Nebraska.

28. Bush, *Decision Points*, 302, 304.

29. Rice, *No Higher Honor*, 568; Rove, *Courage and Consequence*, 409; Karl Rove, interview with author, 6 August 2018; Baker, *Days of Fire*, 381.

30. 539 U.S. 558 (2003).

31. 478 U.S. 186 (1986).

32. *McConnell v. Federal Election Commission*, 540 U.S. 93.

33. David Cole, "The Liberal Legacy of *Bush v. Gore*," *Georgetown Law Journal* 94 (2006), 1427–1428; Jeffrey Toobin, *The Nine: Inside the Secret World of the Supreme Court* (New York: Doubleday, 2007), 205–208; Linda Greenhouse, "The Year Rehnquist May Have Lost His Court," *NYT*, 5 July 2004.

34. Miers to GWB, 4 July 2005, GWBPR, GWBL, White House Office of the Staff Secretary, Raul Yanes, Binder: Supreme Court Potential Nominees [1], from FOIA 2014-0108-F[1]; Bush, *Decision Points*, 97; Cheney, *In My Time*, 322; Gonzales, *True Faith and Allegiance*, 108–109, 342–344.

35. John Robert Greene, *The Presidency of George H. W. Bush*, 2nd ed., revised and expanded (Lawrence: University Press of Kansas, 2015), 80–83; Bush, *Decision Points*, 96–97.

36. Joan Biskupic, *The Chief: The Life and Turbulent Times of Chief Justice John Roberts* (New York: Basic Books, 2019), 144, 146–147; Jan Crawford Greenberg, *Supreme Conflict: The Inside Story of the Struggle for Control of the United States Supreme Court* (New York: Penguin, 2007), 190.

37. Bush, *Decision Points*, 97; Evan Thomas, *First: Sandra Day O'Connor* (New York: Random House, 2019), 369, 372, 376–377; Jeffrey Toobin, *The Oath: The Obama White House and the Supreme Court* (New York: Random House, 2012), 209; Greenberg, *Supreme Conflict*, 19.

38. Andrew J. Card Jr., interview with author, 30 May 2019; Cheney, *In My Time*, 323. In her memoir, Mrs. Bush professed surprise at the fuss over the remark—"as if I were pointedly instructing George and drawing a line in the sand" (Laura Bush, *Spoken from the Heart*, 352).

39. Gonzales, *True Faith and Allegiance*, 113, 116–117, 355–356; Kate O'Beirne, "High Society," *National Review*, 20 April 2001; Greenberg, *Supreme Conflict*, 188–189, 225–227, 246; Baker, *Days of Fire*, 398.

40. Bush, *Decision Points*, 98; Biskupic, *The Chief*, 156; Greenberg, *Supreme Conflict*, 185–211, 213.

41. Briefing Book, undated, "The Honorable John G. Roberts," GWBPR, GWBL, White House Counsel's Office, Dabney Langhorne Friederich Papers, General Supreme Court Files: John Roberts Floor Binder folder, from FOIA 2014-0108-F[1]; Biskupic, *The Chief*, 161.

42. Thomas, *First: Sandra Day O'Connor*, 384n; Andrew J. Card Jr., interview with author, 30 May 2019; Baker, *Days of Fire*, 417; Greenburg, *Supreme Conflict*, 245.

43. Andrew J. Card Jr., interview with author, 30 May 2019.

44. Bush, *Decision Points*, 100–101; Andrew J. Card Jr., interview with author, 30 May 2019. Card refused to identify the justice.

45. Cheney, *In My Time*, 324; Rove, *Courage and Consequence*, 421; Gonzales, *True Faith and Allegiance*, 359; Briefing Book, undated, GWBPR, GWBL, White House Counsel's Office, Dabney Langhorne Friederich, Miers Talking Points folder, from

FOIA 2014-0123-F[1]; Questionnaire, United States Senate Committee on the Judiciary, Nominee for Supreme Court of the United States, GWBPR, GWBL, SMOF, White House Counsel, Dabney Langhorne Friedrich, Miers Materials folder, from FOIA 2014-0123-F[1].

46. See GWBPR, GWBL, SMOF: White House Counsel's Office, Dabney Langhorne Friederich, Miers Material-Bar Suspensions, from FOIA 2014-0123-F; Arlen Specter and Patrick Leahy to Harriet Miers, 19 October 2005, GWBPR, GWBL, SMOF: White House Counsel, Dabney Langhorne Friederich, Miers Material Folder, from FOIA 2014-0123-F[1].

47. Baker, *Days of Fire*, 423; Harriet Miers to GWB, 27 October 2005, GWBPR, GWBL, SMOF, White House Counsel, Dabney Langhorne Friedrich, Miers Materials Folder, from FOIA 2014-0123-F[1].

48. Dana Priest, "CIA Holds Terror Suspects in Secret Prisons," *WP*, 2 November 2005.

49. Neil A. Lewis, "An Intense Experience for Family Members, Too," *NYT*, 12 January 2006.

50. Peter Wallsten and Edwin Chen, "Bush Defends U.S. Response to Disaster," *LAT*, 30 December 2004; Mark K. Updegrove, *The Last Republicans: Inside the Extraordinary Relationship between George H. W. Bush and George W. Bush* (New York: HarperCollins, 2017), 355–356; GHWB to Hugh Sidey, 22 February 2005, in Bush, *All the Best*, 673–680; Greene, *The Presidency of George H. W. Bush*, 254.

51. Bush, *Decision Points*, 312–314; Jeb Bush to Card, 24 August 2004, GWBPR, GWBL, WHORM: FG 006-03A (Chief of Staff, Office Files), Case 633497, from FOIA 2015-0122-F; Shaila K. Dewan, "Hurricane Rips Path of Damage across Florida," *NYT*, 14 August 2004 (the four hurricanes were Hurricane Charley, Frances, Ivan, and Jeanne); Bush to Michael D. Brown, 29 August 2005, GWBPR, GWBL, WHORM, DI-002, Case 673539; Cheney, *In My Time*, 429; Saffir-Simpson Hurricane Wind Scale, National Oceanic and Atmospheric Administration, https://www.nhc.noaa.gov/aboutsshws.php.

52. Bush, *Decision Points*, 315–316; Baker, *Days of Fire*, 407–408.

53. Rove, *Courage and Consequence*, 445; Baker, *Days of Fire*, 408.

54. Bush, *Decision Points*, 317.

55. Baker, *Days of Fire*, 409; Cheney, *In My Time*, 429; C. Morgan Babst, *The Floating World* (Chapel Hill, NC: Algonquin Books, 2018).

56. Bush, *Decision Points*, 317; Rove, *Courage and Consequence*, 457; Kenneth T. Walsh, "The Undoing of George W. Bush," *U.S. News & World Report*, 28 August 2015; Page, *The Matriarch*, 282.

57. 18 U.S.C. § 1385.

58. Andrew J. Card Jr., interview with author, 30 May 2019; Rumsfeld, *Known and Unknown*, 619; Bush, *Decision Points*, 320–321; Baker, *Days of Fire*, 410.

59. Bush, *Decision Points*, 321–322.

60. Rove, *Courage and Consequence*, 451; Bush, *Decision Points*, 308–309; Baker, *Days of Fire*, 410–414.

61. Bush, *Decision Points*, 323, 331.

62. Campbell Robertson, "Survey Finds Racially Disparate Views of New Orleans's Recovery after Hurricane," *NYT*, 25 August 2015; Bush, *Decision Points*, 325.

63. Rick Jervis, "Hurricane Katrina Ten Years Later," *USA Today*, 28 August 2015; Josh Bolten to GWB, and GWB to Dennis Hastert, 1 September 2005, GWBPR, GWBL, WHORM, DI 002, Case 672772; Bill Frist, Rick Santorum, Kay Bailey Hutchinson, Mitch McConnell, Jon Kyl, and Elizabeth Dole to GWB, 13 September 2005, GWBPR, GWBL, WHORM, DI-002, Case 674223; Conrad Burns to GWB, 20 September 2005, GWBPR, GWBL, WHORM, DI-002, Case 674372; Jack Reed [senator, Rhode Island] to GWB, 13 September 2005, GWBPR, WHORM, DI 002, Case 673183; Edward M. Kennedy to GWB, 13 September 2005, GWBPR, GWBL, WHORM, DI 002, Case 673299; Obama to GWB, 8 September 2005, GWBPR, GWBL, WHORM, Subject File Katrina, Case 673801, from FOIA 2014-0073-F, Digital Library.

64. Bush, *Decision Points*, 310; Rick Jervis, "Bush Returns to the City That Once Vilified Him," *USA Today*, 28 August 2015.

## CHAPTER 13. SURGES

1. Sabrina Tavernese, "Data Shows Rising Toll of Iraqis from Insurgency," *NYT*, 14 July 2005.

2. George W. Bush, *Decision Points* (New York: Crown, 2010), 210; Robert M. Gates, *Duty: Memoirs of a Secretary at War* (New York: Alfred A. Knopf, 2014), 198.

3. Gates, *Duty*, 199.

4. Peter Baker, *Days of Fire: Bush and Cheney in the White House* (New York: Doubleday, 2013), 394.

5. Richard W. Stevenson, "Mother Takes Protest to Bush's Ranch," *NYT*, 7 August 2005; Kathleen Sullivan, Chris Heredia, Janine DeFao, and Todd Wallack, "Thousands Protest the Iraq War," *San Francisco Chronicle*, 24 September 2005.

6. Dick Cheney, *In My Time: A Personal and Political Memoir* (New York: Threshold Editions, 2011), 359.

7. Baker, *Days of Fire*, 428.

8. Charlie Savage, "Bush Could Bypass New Torture Ban," *Boston Globe*, 4 January 2006; Erin Louise Palmer, "Reinterpreting Torture: Presidential Signing Statements and the Circumvention of U.S. and International Law," *Human Rights Brief* 14, no. 1 (2006): 21–24. All of Bush's signing statements can be accessed at https://www.presidency.ucsb.edu/documents/presidential-documents-archive-guidebook/presidential-signing-statements-hoover-1929-obama.

9. Dana Priest, "CIA Holds Terror Suspects in Secret Prisons," *WP*, 2 November 2005; *SSCI*, 151–152; Baker, *Days of Fire*, 428–429; Condoleezza Rice, *No Higher Honor: A Memoir of My Time in Washington* (New York: Crown, 2011), 501–502.

10. Bush, *Decision Points*, 176; Baker, *Days of Fire*, 433–434; James Risen and Eric Lichtblau, "Bush Lets U.S. Spy on Callers without Courts," *NYT*, 15 December 2005; James Risen, "The Biggest Secret: My Life as a *New York Times* Reporter in the Shadow of the War on Terror," *The Intercept*, 3 January 2018; Alberto Gonzales, *True Faith and Allegiance: A Story of Service and Sacrifice in War and Peace* (Nashville, TN: Nelson Books, 2006), 333.

11. Gallup, "Presidential Approval Ratings—George W. Bush," https://news.gallup.com/poll/116500/presidential-approval-ratings-george-bush.aspx.

12. Bush, *Decision Points*, 361; Rice, *No Higher Honor*, 431–432. Quotation from Baker, *Days of Fire*, 447.

13. No Heading, undated, GWBPR, GWBL, WHORM, PP (Presidential Personal), Case 688621, from FOIA 2014-0106-F[1].

14. Bush, *Decision Points*, 95.

15. Bush, 95.

16. In explaining this decision regarding Rove, Bolten would later tell an audience that a president's decisions that "involve life and death for the people in uniform [should not be] tainted by any political decisions." Quoted in Glenn Thrush and Maggie Haberman, "Bannon Is Given Security Role Usually Held for Generals," *NYT*, 29 January 2017. See also Bush, *Decision Points*, 96.

17. Joshua Bolten Interview IV, GWBPOH; Andrew Ross Sorkin, *Too Big to Fail: The Inside Story of How Wall Street and Washington Fought to Save the Financial Crisis—and Themselves* (New York: Viking, 2009), 43–47.

18. Baker, *Days of Fire*, 452–454.

19. Bush, *Decision Points*, 361–362; Rice, *No Higher* Honor, 453–449; Baker, *Days of Fire*, 463; James Rosen, *Cheney One on One: A Candid Conversation with America's Most Controversial Statesman* (New York: Regnery, 2015), 151.

20. Bush, *Decision Points*, 365; Cheney, *In My Time*, 436; Donald Rumsfeld, *Known and Unknown: A Memoir* (New York: Sentinel, 2011), 693–694; John F. Burns, "U.S. Strike Hits Insurgent at Safehouse," *NYT*, 8 June 2006.

21. Bush, *Decision Points*, 367, 371; "U.S. Casualties in Operation Enduring Freedom," https://www.GlobalSecurity.org.

22. 548 U.S. 557 (2006).

23. Bush, *Decision Points*, 178; Rice, *No Higher Honor*, 501; Rumsfeld to Secretaries of the Military Departments, et al., 7 July 2006, GWBPR, GWBL, White House Counsel's Office, Harriet Miers Files, Hamdan v. Rumsfeld folder, from FOIA 2014-0224-F; Baker, *Days of Fire*, 486; "Human Intelligence Collector Operations" (Army Field Manual 2-22.3), released 6 September 2006, copy in GWBPR, GWBL, White House Counsel's Office, Harriet Miers Files, Interrogation/War Crimes Issues, folder 1, from FOIA 2014-0078-F[1].

24. Bush, *Decision Points*, 210, 212.

25. Bush, 364; Ivo H. Daalder and I. M. Destler, *In the Shadow of the Oval Office: National Security Advisers and the Presidents They Served—from JFK to George W. Bush* (New York: Simon & Schuster, 2009), 297–298.

26. Bush, *Decision Points*, 365.

27. Bush, 355; Baker, *Days of Fire*, 487.

28. Peter Baker and Susan Glasser, *The Man Who Ran Washington: The Life and Times of James A. Baker III* (New York: Doubleday, 2020), 564–565; Jon Meacham, *Destiny and Power: The American Odyssey of George Herbert Walker Bush* (New York: Random House, 2015), 585; Bush, *Decision Points*, 93.

29. Gates, *Duty*, 4.

30. Cheney, *In My Time*, 442–443; Rosen, *Cheney One on One*, 130–131; Bush, *Decision Points*, 93; Baker, *Days of Fire*, 498.

31. Gates, *Duty*, 7; Bush, *Decision Points*, 94; Cheney, *In My Time*, 443–444; Rumsfeld, *Known and Unknown*, 706.

32. The blue-ribbon panel consisted of Sandra Day O'Connor, Leon Panetta, Vernon Jordan, Richard Gates, Rudolph Giuliani, William J. Perry, Charles Robb, and Alan Simpson. When he was nominated as secretary of defense, Gates stepped down and was replaced by Lawrence Eagleburger; Giuliani stepped down to run for the 2008 Republican nomination for president; he was replaced by Edwin Meese III. James A. Baker III and Lee H. Hamilton, cochairs, *Iraq Study Group Report* (New York: Vintage Books, 2006), xiii, xvi; Cheney, *In My Time*, 447 (emphasis in original).

33. Baker, *Days of Fire*, 515–516. See also Cheney, *In My Time*, 448–449; Rice, *No Higher Honor*, 538–545.

34. Bush, *Decision Points*, 376; Cheney, *In My Time*, 451–453; Baker, *Days of Fire*, 519–520; Gates, *Duty*, 39.

35. Baker, *Days of Fire*, 521.

36. Will Bardenwerper, *The Prisoner in His Palace: Saddam Hussein, His American Guards, and What History Leaves Unsaid* (New York: Scribner, 2017), 175–186; Baker, *Days of Fire*, 523.

37. Gates, *Duty*, 48.

38. Bush, *Decision Points*, 380. See also Cheney, *In My Time*, 461.

39. Bush, *Decision Points*, 380; Gates, *Duty*, 52; Baker, *Days of Fire*, 542.

40. Baker, *Days of Fire*, 532.

41. Gates, *Duty*, 51, 70, 227; Bush, *Decision Points*, 383, 385.

42. Jessica Stern and J. M. Berger, *ISIS: The State of Terror* (New York: HarperCollins, 2015), xvi; Baker, *Days of Fire*, 601, 619–620; Bush, *Decision Points*, 389–390; Peter Bergen, *The Longest War: The Enduring Conflict between America and Al-Qaeda* (New York: Free Press, 2011), 293–294; Rice, *No Higher Honor*, 694–696.

## CHAPTER 14. BAILOUTS

1. "Fired U.S. Attorneys," *WP*, 6 March 2007.

2. Gonzales remembered that Ryan and Chiara were asked to leave because of mismanagement; Lam (misspelled in the memoir) was removed because of concerns over the low number of gun prosecutions in her district; Charlton was removed because of decisions surrounding a death penalty case and immigration policy; McKay was dismissed because of a difference of opinion with a deputy attorney general over an information-sharing program; and Iglesias and Bogden had run afoul of the senators from their respective states (Alberto Gonzales, *True Faith and Allegiance: A Story of Service and Sacrifice in War and Peace* [Nashville, TN: Nelson Books, 2006], 398); "Fired U.S. Attorneys"; Adam Zagorin, "Why Were These U.S. Attorneys Fired?," *Time*, 7 March 2007.

3. Gonzales, *True Faith and Allegiance*, 401; Ari Shapiro, "Timeline: Behind the Firing of Eight U.S. Attorneys," National Public Radio, 15 April 2007, https://www.northcountrypublicradio.org/news/npr/8901997/timeline-behind-the-firing-of-eight-u-s-attorneys; Peter Baker, *Days of Fire: Bush and Cheney in the White House* (New York: Doubleday, 2013), 542–543.

4. Paul Clement to GWB, 27 June 2007; Fred Fielding to George T. Manning, 28 June 2007; Manning to Conyers, 11 July 2007; Conyers to Manning, 11 July 2007;

Conyers to Manning, 13 July 2007; Conyers to Fielding, 17 July 2007; Michael Mukasey to Nancy Pelosi, 29 February 2008; Robert D. Luskin to Conyers, 29 April 2008; Conyers to Luskin, 1 May 2008; email, Tony Fratto to Edward W. Gillespie et al., 2 May 2008, GWBPR, White House Counsel's Office, Fred Fielding, General Files, Miers/Bolten/Addington [1], from FOIA 2014-0216-F[1]. In August 2009, email and interview transcripts were released by the House Judiciary Committee which its chairman, John Conyers, claimed showed that Rove had played an active role in the firings. Rove claimed that those documents exonerated him (Tom Hamburger and David G. Savage, "Rove Role Is Seen in Firing," *LAT*, 12 August 2009). Gonzales spends the last four chapters of his memoir discussing the road to his separation from the administration (*True Faith and Allegiance*, chaps. 35–38).

5. Anne Hull and Dana Priest, "Soldiers Face Neglect, Frustration at Army's Top Medical Facility," *WP*, 18 February 2007.

6. David S. Cloud, "Army Secretary Is Ousted in Furor over Hospital Care," *NYT*, 3 March 2007; Robert M. Gates, *Duty: Memoirs of a Secretary at War* (New York: Alfred A. Knopf, 2014), 110–114.

7. "The Six Party Talks at a Glance," Arms Control Association, https://www.armscontrol.org/factsheets/6partytalks.

8. George W. Bush, *Decision Points* (New York: Crown, 2010), 423–424; "Chronology of U.S.–North Korean Nuclear Missile Diplomacy," Arms Control Association, https://www.armscontrol.org/factsheets/dprkchron.

9. Bush, *Decision Points*, 424–425.

10. Bush, *Decision Points*, 425; James Rosen, *Cheney One on One: A Candid Conversation with America's Most Controversial Statesman* (New York: Regnery, 2015), 4; Baker, *Days of Fire*, 529, 535–536; Dick Cheney, *In My Time: A Personal and Political Memoir* (New York: Threshold Editions, 2011), 474–475.

11. Cheney, *In My Time*, 466; Rosen, *Cheney One on One*, 1–23, 125; Bush, *Decision Points*, 420–421.

12. Rosen, *Cheney One on One*, 21; Cheney, *In My Time*, 470–471; Baker, *Days of Fire*, 551; Michael McConnell, interview with author, 29 April 2017.

13. Rosen, *Cheney One on One*, 5, 127; Cheney, *In My Time*, 471; Gates, *Duty*, 172, 176; Bush, *Decision Points*, 421–422; Baker, *Days of Fire*, 558. In other sources, the strike was known as Operation Silent Melody and Operation Orchard. See Toi Staff, "MK's Warned about Syria's Nuke Plans Years before Reactor Strike," *Times of Israel*, 6 June 2018.

14. Gates, *Duty*, 197–223.

15. Ben S. Bernanke, Timothy F. Geithner, and Henry M. Paulson Jr., *Firefighting: The Financial Crisis and Its Lessons* (New York: Penguin, 2019), 29; Bush, *Decision Points*, 448; John D. Graham, *Bush on the Home Front: Domestic Policy Triumphs and Setbacks* (Bloomington: Indiana University Press, 2010), 273.

16. Quoted in Jo Becker, Sheryl Gay Stolberg, and Stephen Labaton, "White House Philosophy Stoked Mortgage Bonfire," *NYT*, 20 December 2008; Bernanke, Geithner, and Paulson, *Firefighting*, 28.

17. Bernanke, Geithner, and Paulson, *Firefighting*, 33–35.

18. Bernanke, Geithner, and Paulson, 31–35, 40.

19. Graham, *Bush on the Home Front*, 274; Ryan Dezember, "My 10-Year Odys-

sey through the Housing Crisis," *WSJ*, 27–28 January 2018; Marcy Kaptur to GWB, 8 December 2008, GWBPR, GWBL, WHORM, Subject File, Case 775785, from FOIA 2014-0222-F.

20. Bush, *Decision Points*, 453; Bernanke, Geithner, and Paulson, *Firefighting*, 48.

21. Bush, *Decision Points*, 453; Baker, *Days of Fire*, 582.

22. Statement of Henry Paulson, 5 September 2008, U.S. Department of the Treasury, https://www.treasury.gov/press-center/press-releases/Pages/hp1129.aspx.

23. Quoted in Baker, *Days of Fire*, 568.

24. Baker, 605.

25. Laurence M. Ball, *The Fed and Lehman Brothers: Setting the Record Straight on a Financial Disaster* (New York: Cambridge University Press, 2018), ix; Bush, *Decision Points*, 456.

26. Email, cosjbb [for Chief of Staff Joshua B. Bolten] to Jared Weinstein and Blake Gottesman, 12 September 2008, GWBPR, GWBL, WHORM, Subject File, PP (Presidential Personal) folder 768190, from FOIA 2014-0048-F.

27. Bush, *Decision Points*, 458; Sebastian Mallaby, "The Cult of the Expert—and How It Collapsed," *The Guardian*, 20 October 2016.

28. "Troubled Assets Relief Program, Section 115 Plan to Exercise Authority," 12 January 2009, GWBPR, GWBL, SMOF: White House Counsel's Office, Heath Tarbert, President's TARP Certification folder, from FOIA 2014-0222-F; Bush, *Decision Points*, 458; Cheney, *In My Time*, 507.

29. Speech Draft, 24 September 2008, GWBPR, GWBL, SMOF: White House Office of the Staff Secretary, Raul Yanes, Address to the Nation, 24 September 2008, folder 2, from FOIA 2014-0222-F (emphasis in original).

30. Bush, *Decision Points*, 461.

31. Bush, 462; GWB to Pelosi, undated, GWBPR, GWBL, SMOF: White House Counsel's Office, Heath Tarbert, President's TARP Certification folder, from FOIA 2014-0222-F; Bush, *Decision Points*, 461–462; Baker, *Days of Fire*, 613–615; Cheney, *In My Time*, 508–509; John Heilemann and Mark Halperin, *Game Change* (New York: HarperCollins, 2010), 386–390; Barack Obama, *A Promised Land* (New York: Crown, 2020), 185–190.

32. Gary C. Jacobson, "George W. Bush, the Iraq War, and the Election of Barack Obama," *Presidential Studies Quarterly* 40, no. 2 (June 2010): 224; "2008: Ten Years after the Crash, We Are Still Living in the World It Brutally Remade," *New York Magazine*, 13 August 2018, http://nymag.com/intelligencer/2018/08/america-10-years-after-the-financial-crisis.html.

33. Bush, *Decision Points*, 459.

34. Robert Barnes, Dan Eggen, and Anne E. Kornblut, "Preparing for the Obama Era," *WP*, 9 November 2008. Speech quoted in Robert M. Gates, *Exercise of Power: American Failures, Successes, and a New Path Forward in the Post–Cold War World* (New York: Alfred A. Knopf, 2020), 32.

35. Graham, *Bush on the Home Front*, 286–289; Bush, *Decision Points*, 469; Baker, *Days of Fire*, 620–621.

36. Steven Lee Meyers and Alyssa J. Rubin, "Iraq Journalist Hurls Shoes at Bush and Denounces Him on TV as a 'Dog,'" *NYT*, 14 December 2008.

37. William Bennett et al. to GWB, 2 July 2007, GWBPR, GWBL, WHSMOF, Office of the Staff Secretary, Raul Yates Records, January 2007–December 2007, folder 4, from FOIA 2014-0073-F; letters are found in GWBPR, GWBL, White House Counsel's Office, William Burck Files, Libby Matter folder, from FOIA 2014-0127-F.

38. Bush, *Decision Points*, 104–105. Cheney has the comment as "You are leaving a good man wounded on the field of battle" (*In My Time*, 410).

39. Cheney, *In My Time*, 517.

40. Bush, *Decision Points*, 474.

41. Ana Campoy, "E-Mail Trove Is Big Job for Bush Library," *Dow Jones Industrial News*, 24 April 2013; Jon Marcus, "A Library Fit for a President," *Times Higher Education*, 19 June 2014.

42. Quoted in Ashley Parker and Maggie Haberman, "Bush Brothers Swipe at Trump," *NYT*, 16 February 2016; Bush, *Decision Points*, 476; George W. Bush, *41: A Portrait of My Father* (New York: Crown, 2014); Mark K. Updegrove, *The Last Republicans: Inside the Extraordinary Relationship between George H. W. Bush and George W. Bush* (New York: HarperCollins, 2017), 5.

43. George W. Bush, *Portraits of Courage: A Commander in Chief's Tribute to America's Warriors* (New York: Crown, 2017), 12–14; Winston S. Churchill, *Painting as a Pastime* (London: Unicorn Publishing Group, 2013), 19.

44. Stockwell to Bush (handwritten), undated; Bush to Stockwell, 23 April 2008, both on display at GWBL; Bush, *Portraits of Courage*, 150–153. For the author's assessment of Bush's books, see the bibliographical essay.

45. Quoted in Mark Landler, "Bush-Obama Rapport Recalls a Lost Virtue: Political Civility," *NYT*, 26 September 2016.

46. Parker and Haberman, "Bush Brothers Swipe at Trump"; Scott Wong, "Bush World Goes for Clinton, but Will a Former President?," *The Hill*, 29 June 2016. See also Seema Mehta, "George W. Bush's Iraq War Architect Says He Will Likely Vote for Clinton," *LAT*, 26 August 2016.

47. Yashar Ali, "What George W. Bush Really Thought of Donald Trump's Inauguration," *New York*, 29 March 2017; George W. Bush, "PEPFAR Saves Millions of Lives in Africa. Keep It Funded," *WP*, 7 April 2017; Cleve R. Wootson Jr., "Both Bush Presidents Just Spoke Out on Charlottesville—and Sound Nothing Like Trump," *WP*, 16 August 2018; Justin Wise, "Trump Rips George W. Bush after He Calls for Unity amid Coronavirus Outbreak," *The Hill*, 3 May 2020; Jonathan Martin, "Vote for Trump? These Republican Leaders Aren't on the Bandwagon," *NYT*, 6 June 2020.

## CHAPTER 15. CONCLUSIONS

1. George W. Bush, *Fox News Sunday*, 10 February 2008.

2. Robert S. McElvaine, "Historians vs. George Bush," History News Network, 5 December 2005, https://hnn.us/articles/5019.html; Robert S. McElvaine, "HNN Poll: 61% of Historians Rate the Bush Presidency Worst," "History News Network," undated, https://historynewsnetwork.org/article/48916; "Rushmore Plus One," Siena Research Institute, 1 July 2010; Results of C-SPAN poll at

https://www.c-span.org/presidentsurvey2017/; Brandon Rottinghaus, "Measuring Obama against the Great Presidents," Brookings Institution, 13 February 2015; Brandon Rottinghaus and Justin S. Vaughan, "How Does Trump Stack Up against the Best—and Worst—Presidents?," *NYT*, 19 February 2018. The present author participated in several of these polls.

3. Jean Edward Smith, *Bush* (New York: Simon & Schuster, 2016), xv; Sean Wilentz, "George W. Bush: The Worst President in History?," *Rolling Stone*, 4 May 2006.

4. Thomas Jefferson, "First Inaugural Address," 4 March 1801, in *The Portable Thomas Jefferson*, ed. Merrill Peterson (New York: Penguin Books, 1975), 294.

5. Peter Baker, *Days of Fire: Bush and Cheney in the White House* (New York: Doubleday, 2013), 261.

6. The best collection of available interviews has been done by the Miller Center at the University of Virginia, which at the time of this writing has released forty-six interviews dealing with the presidency of George W. Bush. They can be accessed at https://millercenter.org/the-presidency/presidential-oral-histories/george-w-bush.

7. George W. Bush, *Decision Points* (New York: Crown, 2010), 129.

8. Bush, 181.

9. Alberto Gonzales, *True Faith and Allegiance: A Story of Service and Sacrifice in War and Peace* (Nashville, TN: Nelson Books, 2006), 289; Dick Cheney, *In My Time: A Personal and Political Memoir* (New York: Threshold Editions, 2011), 353; McConnell quoted in Karl Rove, *Courage and Consequence: My Life as a Conservative in the Fight* (New York: Threshold Editions, 2010), 299.

10. "Excerpts from the Oval Office Interview," *Jerusalem Post*, 12 May 2008.

# BIBLIOGRAPHICAL ESSAY

The archival record of presidencies after 1980 is governed by the Presidential Records Act of 1978 (PRA; 44 U.S.C. §§2201–2207). Under that act, documents prepared by employees of the executive office in the performance of their daily duties remain the property of the federal government, under the supervision of the Archivist of the United States. Those records are turned over to the National Archives for processing at a presidential library. However, in the processing of that material, the archivists are required under the PRA to keep closed certain documents for a period of twelve years following the end of that administration. Even after that twelfth year, material no longer covered by the PRA may continue to be closed to public scrutiny under the terms of the Freedom of Information Act (FOIA; 1966, 5 U.S.C. §552), which closes material for the reasons listed under the PRA as well as for other reasons. On 1 November 2001, President George W. Bush (hereafter GWB) issued Executive Order 132336, which gave the incumbent president, former presidents, and former vice presidents much broader authority, under the doctrine of executive privilege, to deny the opening of material past the twelve-year limit; there was no time limit placed on how often an incumbent president could challenge the review process. However, on 21 January 2009, during his first full day in office, President Barack Obama issued Executive Order 134589,* which revoked Bush's Executive Office 132336; now only the incumbent president had the right to assert constitutional privileges to withhold presidential records. In November 2014, Congress passed the Presidential and Federal Records Act Amendments of 2014 (H. R. 1233), codifying Obama's executive order and creating ground rules for

*See E.O. 13233 (1 November 2001) and E.O. 13489 (21 January 2009) For an excellent summary of this issue, see Wendy Ginsberg, "The Presidential Records Act: Background and Recent Issues for Congress," Congressional Research Service (7-5700, R0238, 30 May 2014), and David J. Mengel, "Access to United States Government Records at the U.S. National Archives and Records Administration" (paper presented at the Japan-U.S. Archives Seminar, May 2007), https://www.archivists.org/publications/proceedings/accesstoarchives/07_David_MENGEL.pdf, accessed August 2014.

gaining access to those records. Once the Archivist of the United States announces that new presidential records will be made available to the public, both the sitting president and any affected former presidents have sixty days to review the records; should they disagree, there is only one option available to them, and that is to extend the review period for another thirty days.

The essential archival sources used for this book are housed in the George W. Bush Presidential Records (George W. Bush Presidential Library, Dallas, Texas; hereafter GWBPR). At the present time, the most productive way to utilize that material is by consulting processed and opened Freedom of Information Act (FOIA) requests. Materials opened as a result of the following FOIA requests were of particular help in this book:

- FOIA 2014-0041-F Drafts of President GWB's Remarks at the National Day of Prayer and Remembrance on September 14, 2001.
- FOIA 2014-0043-F Drafts of the Beginnings of the Iraq War Speeches.
- FOIA 2014-0047-F E-Mails Sent or Received by Karl Rove That Mention John Kerry, January 1, 2004–November 4, 2004.
- FOIA 2014-0048-F Records on Lehman Brothers from September 11, 2008–September 15, 2008.
- FOIA 2014-0049-F E-Mails Sent or Received by Commissioned Officers on November 3 and 4, 2001.
- FOIA 2014-0072-F Correspondence between President GWB and His Pastors and Spiritual Advisors.
- FOIA 2014-0073-F Communications between President GWB and Barack Obama or Their Representatives, 2001–2009.
- FOIA 2014-0077-F Audio and Video Recordings of Meetings with President GWB and Transcripts of Such Meetings from September 11, 2001–September 20, 2001.
- FOIA 2014-0086-F Records on Communication from Secretary Rumsfeld to President GWB on November 21, 2001.
- FOIA 2014-0098-F Select Dates of the Presidential Daily Diary.
- FOIA 2014-0106-F[1] Correspondence Sent to President GWB Related to the War in Iraq, between October 8, 2002, and January 19, 2009.
- FOIA 2014-0108-F[1] Correspondence to the President on Vacancies on the Federal District Courts, Federal Courts of Appeal, and the United States Supreme Court.
- FOIA 2014-0123-F[1] All Records Related to Harriet E. Miers's Nomination and Withdrawal to the United States Supreme Court.
- FOIA 2014-0130-F All Records Related to Valerie Wilson, also known as Valerie Plame, or to Her Husband, Joseph Wilson, and a List of Folder Titles Related to Unauthorized Disclosures of Classified Information.
- FOIA 2014-0157-F Records on the Skull and Bones Society.
- FOIA 2014-0158 Records for GWB, Laura Bush, Joshua Bolten, Andrew Card, Ari Fleischer, Karl Rove, Karen Hughes, Joe Hagin, and Condoleezza Rice from 11 September 2001.
- FOIA 2014-0206-F[1] Records Pertaining to Valerie Plame (Plamegate).

- FOIA 2014-0215-F[1] Records Sent by or Received by President GWB Regarding al Qaida and Osama bin Laden.
- FOIA 2014-0222-F Records Sent to, Sent by, or Received by President GWB between January 2007 and January 2009 Regarding the Financial Crisis.
- FOIA 2014-0224-F Records Sent to, Sent by, or Received by President GWB on *Hamdan v. Rumsfeld,* January 2002–December 2006.
- FOIA 2014-0234-F Records Sent to, Sent by, or Received by President GWB Regarding Scooter Libby, Valerie Plame et al. between January 2001 and December 2007.
- FOIA 2014-0243-F Correspondence between President GWB and William F. Buckley.
- FOIA 2014-0349-F Records Created by or Sent to Henry Paulson Jr., Secretary of the Treasury, Related to Securities Regulation, the SEC, and Market Regulation.
- FOIA 2014-0390-F Final Copies of Unclassified HSPDs (Homeland Security Presidential Directives) and NSPDs (National Security Presidential Directives).
- FOIA 2014-0457-F Records on Iraq within the Condoleezza Rice Files between January 2001 and March 2003.
- FOIA 2014-0555-F Drafts of President GWB's Remarks at United States Military Academy at West Point on 1 June 2002.
- FOIA 2015-0121-F Any and All Documents, Correspondence, and E-Mails Exchanged between John Ellis ("Jeb") Bush and President GWB between January 1, 2003, and January 1, 2004.
- FOIA 2015-0122-F Any and All Documents, Correspondence, and E-Mails Exchanged between John Ellis ("Jeb") Bush and President GWB between January 1, 2004, and January 1, 2005.
- FOIA 2015-0175-F Records of White House Evacuation on 11 September 2001.
- FOIA 2014-0216-F[1] Records Sent to, Sent by, or Received by President GWB Concerning Certain Cabinet Members.
- FOIA 2016-0131-F Records Pertaining to a Lunch President GWB Had with Rush Limbaugh on 13 January 2009.

The White House Staff Members Office Files (SMOF) also yielded several collections of value: the records of Susan Buckland; Joshua B. Bolten; Jessica Headley; Jay Lefkowitz; Diana Schacht; Robert (Tony) Snow; H. James (Jim) Towey III; and Thomas (Tommy) von der Heydt. Also useful were several sections of the White House Office of Records Management (WHORM). Of particular interest were DI[-saster] 002—Natural Disasters (Katrina-related material) and SP[eeches].

A great deal of the available material at the Bush Library comes in the form of email records, stored in the Automated Records Management System (ARMS). Much of it is still classified, much of what is open is daily email chaff, and there is an enormous amount of duplication. Yet there are several helpful series, particularly ARMS: B. Alexander "Sandy" Kress, which contains singular e-mail traffic relating to the planning of No Child Left Behind.

Other archival collections consulted include James A. Baker III Papers (Seeley G. Mudd Manuscripts Library, Princeton University); Gubernatorial Records of George W. Bush (Texas State Library and Archives Commission); Anthony Lewis Papers (Library of Congress); and the Daniel Schorr Papers (Library of Congress).

The Miller Center, located at the University of Virginia, interviewed dozens of alumni of the Bush administration. At the time of the publication of this work, transcripts of thirty-nine of these interviews are available at https://millercen ter.org/the-presidency/presidential-oral-histories/george-w-bush. One reference work is John Robert Greene, ed., *Presidential Profiles: The George W. Bush Years* (New York: Facts on File, 2011).

George W. Bush has written two volumes of memoirs, a biography that may well serve as a third memoir of sorts, and a fourth book that gives insight into the work of his postpresidency. *A Charge to Keep* (New York: William Morrow, 1999) was written and published as a campaign biography. In it, Bush speaks to his faith ("I could not be governor if I did not believe in a divine plan that supersedes all human plans" [6]), hammers at what he did in Texas on education reform, and includes a lengthy section devoted to establishing Laura Bush's bona fides as a potential First Lady. The book goes soft and easy on Bush's youth—it is best known for its omission of any reference of his 1976 DUI. Bush's postpresidential memoir, *Decision Points* (New York: Crown, 2010), offers an interesting structural choice; rather than deal with his presidency chronologically, Bush looks at several of his major decisions in a topical fashion, hoping to convey his belief that "I've never been afraid to make a decision" (27). In many places, the book is very closely argued—almost as if the author were making a case for himself in court. Bush is not above admitting that he was wrong on certain things (on Hurricane Katrina, for example, he emphasizes that he took too long to decide on a course of action, and he did not adequately convey his concern for the victims of the storm (310). Several years later, Bush wrote *41: A Portrait of My Father* (New York: Crown, 2014). There are many glimpses of the writer in here—some of which are not included in the first two volumes of Bush's memoirs. For example, *41* includes the very best description available of the tortuous last days of Bush's sister Robin (53–58) and a lengthy section on how his decision to invade Iraq was not about "getting even" for his father's refusal to topple Saddam in 1991 (206–211). In 2017, Bush published a collection of ninety-eight of his own portraits of veterans of the War on Terror. The paintings are stark and affecting; the captions and introductory material in *Portraits of Courage: A Commander in Chief's Tribute to America's Warriors* (New York: Crown, 2017) establish the kinship that Bush had come to feel with those veterans.

To date, there are only two full biographies of George W. Bush. James Mann, *George W. Bush* (New York: Times Books, 2015), is brief and based largely on secondary sources, but insightful. Jean Edward Smith, *Bush* (New York: Simon & Schuster, 2016), is more detailed, while being unremittingly hostile toward its subject. Other studies of Bush's life attempt to place him in the context of his family. The most balanced of these treatments is Bill Minutaglio, *First Son: George W. Bush and the Bush Family Dynasty* (New York: Times Books, 1999). Elizabeth Mitchell, *W: The Revenge of the Bush Dynasty* (New York: Berkeley Books, 2003), is less about the Bush dynasty than it is an attempt at psychohistory that stretches the available evidence. Even less helpful were Robert Bryce, *Cronies: Oil, the Bushes, and the Rise of Texas, America's Superstate* (New York: Public Affairs, 2004); Kevin Phillips, *American Dynasty: Aristocracy, Fortune, and the Politics of Deceit in the House of Bush* (New York: Viking, 2004); and Peter Schweizer and Rochelle Schweizer, *The Bushes: Portrait of a Dynasty* (New York: Doubleday, 2004). Both Justin A. Frank, MD, *Bush on the Couch: Inside the Mind of the President* (New York: Regan Books, 2004), and Jacob Weisberg, *The Bush Tragedy* (New York: Random House, 2008), attempt armchair psychology on the forty-third president, both with middling success.

Dick Cheney, *In My Time: A Personal and Political Memoir* (New York: Threshold Editions, 2011), is one of the more compact memoirs written by a Bush cabinet member. But more so than the others, Cheney tells his reader what he *thinks* about things in a much more direct—often confrontational—tone than is found in the memoir of any of the administration principals. His second memoir, Dick Cheney and Jonathan Reiner, *Heart: An American Medical Odyssey* (New York: Scribner, 2013), looks at the author's vice presidency through the prism of Cheney's health. Less helpful is Dick Cheney and Liz Cheney, *Exceptional: Why the World Needs a Powerful America* (New York: Simon & Schuster, 2015). James Rosen, *Cheney One on One: A Candid Conversation with America's Most Controversial Statesman* (New York: Regnery, 2015), is both unique—the entire book is made up of the transcripts of several days of interviews between Rosen and Cheney—and useful. Stephen F. Hayes, *Cheney: The Untold Story of America's Most Powerful and Controversial Vice President* (New York: HarperCollins, 2007), is an authorized biography that largely takes the author's interviews with its subject at face value.

Colin Powell has yet to write a comprehensive memoir of his life and career. For the period of his service as Bush's secretary of state, consult his *It Worked for Me: In Life and Leadership* (New York: HarperCollins, 2012). Featuring the language and structure of a self-help book, Powell uses a chapter on his 5 February 2003 speech to the United Nations to settle some scores, most notably with the intelligence community as well as with the Washington "big egos" who took the nation into Iraq (p. 163). Also useful is Robert Draper, "Colin Powell Still Wants Answers," *New York Times Magazine*, 19 July 2020. Condoleezza Rice, who first served as Bush's national security adviser and then as Powell's successor at State, is a more prolific writer than Powell. Her *No Higher Honor: A Memoir of My Time in Washington* (New York: Crown, 2011) is essentially two books in one. For her time in the 2000 Bush campaign and as his national security adviser, Rice is thoughtful and analytical; for her time as secretary of state, however, *No Higher Honor* becomes pedantic, as the author offers deep detail about every foreign trip she made from 2005 through 2009. Rice's second memoir, *Extraordinary, Ordinary People: A Memoir of My Family* (New York: Crown, 2010), offers new insight into her early years but is repetitive of *No Higher Honor* in its brief treatment of her service in the Bush administration. Her *Democracy: Stories from the Long Road to Freedom* (New York: Twelve, 2017) is an introspective look at the stories of several nations that were attempting to develop a democratic form of government; it includes several vignettes that apply to the Bush years. James Mann, *The Great Rift: Dick Cheney, Colin Powell, and the Broken*

*Friendship That Defined an Era* (New York: Henry Holt, 2020), is a fast-paced dual biography that is pro-Powell (who was interviewed for the book) and less favorable to Cheney (who was not interviewed).

For all its heft and detail, Donald Rumsfeld, *Known and Unknown: A Memoir* (New York: Sentinel, 2011), is engagingly written. It is heavily footnoted—unique for a memoir—and the author is dependent on a cache of his papers that he hand-picked and placed online; those papers are available at http://papers.rumsfeld.com/. Bradley Graham, *By His Own Rules: The Ambitions, Successes, and Ultimate Failures of Donald Rumsfeld* (New York: Public Affairs, 2009), is critical of its subject. *The Unknown Known* (Participant Media, 2013) is a useful documentary on Rumsfeld's career. Rumsfeld's successor at Defense, Robert Gates, wrote two strong memoirs. His *Duty: Memoirs of a Secretary at War* (New York: Alfred A. Knopf, 2014) offers a strong look at the move to a counterinsurgency strategy through the surge and the national security policies of the last two years of the administration. It is also the best firsthand look yet available on the transition to the Obama presidency. Gates's *Exercise of Power: American Failures, Successes, and a New Path Forward in the Post–Cold War World* (New York: Alfred A. Knopf, 2020) spares no postwar president—including George W. Bush and Barack Obama, both of whom he served at Defense—as he assesses the limitations of the use of American power throughout the world. Gates's *A Passion for Leadership: Lessons on Change and Reform from Fifty Years of Public Service* (New York: Alfred A. Knopf, 2016) sheds little light on the Bush presidency.

John Ashcroft, *Never Again: Securing America and Restoring Justice* (New York: Center Street, 2006), speaks to the role played by the Justice Department after 11 September but is marred by its omission of any mention of the hospital-bed-side-Stellar-Wind-reauthorization drama. Ashcroft's deputy James Comey tells his side of that melodrama in *A Higher Loyalty: Truth, Lies, and Leadership* (New York: Flatiron Books, 2018). See also Nancy V. Baker, *General Ashcroft: Attorney at War* (Lawrence: University Press of Kansas, 2006), and Tevi Troy, "My Boss the Fanatic," *New Republic*, 29 January 2001. Ashcroft's successor at Justice, Alberto Gonzales, in *True Faith and Allegiance: A Story of Service and Sacrifice in War and Peace* (Nashville, TN: Nelson Books, 2006), offers a chapter on the ramp-up to war in Iraq that includes a day-by-day account of meetings found nowhere else.

Ron Suskind, *The Price of Loyalty: George W. Bush, the White House, and the Education of Paul O'Neill* (New York: Simon & Schuster, 2004), clearly shows why Paul O'Neill was a dysfunctional choice as Bush's first secretary of the Treasury. Ben S. Bernanke, Timothy F. Geithner, and Henry M. Paulson Jr., *Firefighting: The Financial Crisis and Its Lessons* (New York: Penguin, 2019), is a joint memoir written by three of the major players in the 2008 financial crisis. It is metaphor-happy and repetitive but nevertheless offers both a worthy survey of the facts surrounding the crisis and a succinct presentation of the authors' postmortems. Using this relatively brief book negates the need to slog through the lengthy memoirs of these three individuals: Ben S. Bernanke, *The Courage to Act: A Memoir of a Crisis and Its Aftermath* (New York: W. W. Norton, 2015); Timothy F. Geithner, *Stress Test: Reflections on Financial Crises* (New York: Crown, 2014); and Henry M. Paulson Jr., *On the Brink: Inside the Race to Stop the Collapse of the Global Financial System* (New York: Business Plus, 2010).

For observations on the development of the Department of Homeland Security, see the memoirs both of its first secretary, Tom Ridge, *The Test of Our Times: America under Siege . . . And How We Can Be Safe Again* (New York: Thomas Dunne Books, 2009), and of his successor, Michael Chertoff, *Homeland Security: Assessing the First Five Years* (Philadelphia: University of Pennsylvania Press, 2009).

Linda Chavez, *An Unlikely Conservative: The Transformation of an Ex-Liberal (or How I Became the Most Hated Hispanic in America* (New York: Basic Books, 2002), tells her side of the story of her ill-fated nomination as secretary of labor.

The memoir of Bush's first director of the Central Intelligence Agency, George Tenet, *At the Center of the Storm: My Years at the CIA* (New York: HarperCollins, 2007), is largely a defense of the author's actions at the CIA and an explanation of why he believes the agency was set up to take the fall for the decision to invade Iraq. John Rizzo, the acting general counsel of the CIA, explains his role in the crafting of the "torture memos" as well as the destruction of the "torture tapes" in *Company Man: Thirty Years of Controversy and Crisis in the CIA* (New York: Scribner, 2014). The memoir of Bush's final head of the CIA, Michael V. Hayden, *Playing to the Edge: American Intelligence in the Age of Terror* (New York: Penguin, 2016), is most useful for its view of the author's service as the head of the National Security Agency. See also the memoir of Michael Morell, *The Great War of Our Time: The CIA's Fight against Terrorism—from al Qa'ida to ISIS* (New York: Twelve, 2015).

Memoirs of diplomats who served in the Bush administration include Elliott Abrams, *Tested by Zion: The Bush Administration and the Israeli-Palestinian Conflict* (Cambridge: Cambridge University Press, 2013); John Bolton, *Surrender Is Not an Option: Defending America at the United Nations and Abroad* (New York: Threshold Editions, 2007); L. Paul Bremer, *My Year in Iraq: The Struggle to Build a Future of Hope* (New York: Threshold Editions, 2006); Paul Cellucci, *Unquiet Diplomacy* (Toronto: Key Porter Books, 2005); Zalmay Khalilzad, *The Envoy: From Kabul to the White House, My Journey through a Turbulent World* (New York: St. Martin's Press, 2016); and Michael McFaul, *From Cold War to Hot Peace: An American Ambassador in Putin's Russia* (Boston: Houghton Mifflin Harcourt, 2018).

Of Bush's many congressional critics, three standout attacks on the administration are Robert C. Byrd, *Losing America: Confronting a Reckless and Arrogant Presidency* (New York: W. W. Norton, 2004); Max Cleland, *Heart of a Patriot: How I Found the Courage to Survive Vietnam, Walter Reed, and Karl Rove* (New York: Simon & Schuster, 2009); and Tom Daschle, *Like No Other Time: The Two Years That Changed America* (New York: Three Rivers Press, 2003).

Three of Bush's closest staff aides have written memoirs. Michael J. Gerson, *Heroic Conservatism: Why Republicans Need to Embrace America's Ideals (And Why They Deserve to Fail If They Don't* (New York: Harper One, 2007), is at once a thoughtful and nuanced memoir with an excellent analysis of Bush the man, and a pro-Christian polemic that does not shy away from preaching to its reader. Karen Hughes, *Ten Minutes from Normal* (New York: Viking, 2004), is hardly the traditional Washington memoir, in that Hughes writes in as much depth about her family as she does about her White House job. See also Ron Suskind, "Mrs. Hughes Takes Her Leave," *Esquire*, July 2002. Often funny, eminently quotable, and always readable, Karl Rove, *Courage and Consequence: My Life as a Conservative in the Fight* (New York: Threshold Editions, 2010), settles scores with "Democrats," who the author blames as a group for *everything*. Rove has earned one biography, James Moore and Wayne Slater, *Bush's Brain: How Karl Rove Made George W. Bush Presidential* (New York: John Wiley, 2003), one that is virulently negative toward its subject ("traitor" [6]) and swings well beyond the evidence ("co-president" [12]). Harriet Miers has written no memoir, and to date her role is served by only one prepresidential piece by Joyce Saenz Harris, "Harriet Miers: Reflections of a Lawyer-Politician," *Dallas Morning News*, 28 July 1991. On the national security side, James Mann, *Rise of the Vulcans: The History of Bush's War Cabinet* (New York: Viking Penguin, 2004), offers an excellent starting point for the background of Bush's closest foreign policy advisers.

Memoirs of other staffers largely exist either to inflate their position at the White House (including Richard A. Clarke, *Against All Enemies: Inside America's War on Terror* [New York: Free Press, 2004]; David Frum, *The Right Man: An Inside Account of the Bush White House* [New York: Random House, 2003]; and Matt Latimer, *Speech-Less: Tales of a White House Survivor* [New York: Crown, 2009]); to criticize the administration (including David Kuo, *Tempting Faith: An Inside Story of Political Seduction* [New York: Free Press, 2006]; and Scott McClellan, *What Happened: Inside the Bush White House and Washington's Culture of Deception* [New York: Public Affairs, 2008]); or to criticize the critics of the administration (including Ari Fleischer, *Taking Heat: The President, the Press, and My Years in the White House* [New York: William Morrow, 2005]; and Timothy S. Goeglein, *Man in the Middle: An Inside Account of Faith and Politics in the George W. Bush Era* [Nashville, TN: B & H Publishing Group, 2011]).

The jabs at the Bush family, particularly Barbara, in Laura Bush, *Spoken from the Heart* (New York: Scribner, 2010), made press when the book came out, as did her discussion of her 1963 automobile accident. She is also not afraid to criticize her husband (e.g., on how he managed the DUI incident). However, the First Lady portion of the book turns into an "everyday diary" of events. To date, there has been no scholarly biography of the First Lady. Those biographies available— including Christopher P. Andersen, *George and Laura: Portrait of an American Marriage* (New York: William Morrow, 2002); Antonia Felix, *Laura: America's First Lady, First Mother* (Avon, MA: Adams Media Corporation, 2002); Ann Gerhardt, *The Perfect Wife: The Life and Choices of Laura Bush* (New York: Simon & Schuster, 2004)—are lightly researched hagiographies. Rounding out the memoirs of the First Family is Jenna Bush Hager and Barbara Pierce Bush, *Sisters First: Stories from a Wild and Wonderful Life* (New York: Grand Central Publishing, 2017).

Other useful memoirs include James A. Baker, III, *"Work Hard, Study, and Keep Out of Politics!": Adventures and Lessons from an Unexpected Public Life* (New York: G. P. Putnam's, 2006); Douglas J. Feith, *War and Decision: Inside the Pentagon at the Dawn of the War on Terrorism* (New York: Harper, 2008); Barack Obama, *A Promised Land* (New York: Crown, 2020); and Rudolph W. Giuliani, *Leadership* (New York: Hyperion, 2002). Memoirs that were less helpful include Stewart Baker, *Skating on*

*Stilts: Why We Aren't Stopping Tomorrow's Terrorism* (Stanford, CA: Hoover Institution Press, 2010); and April Ryan, *The Presidency in Black and White: My Up-Close View of Three Presidents and Race in America* (Lanham, MD: Rowman and Littlefield, 2015).

Begin a serious study of the relationship between Bush the elder and Bush the younger with the unusually candid correspondence found in George H. W. Bush, *All the Best, George Bush: My Life in Letters and Other Writings,* updated edition (New York: Scribner, 2013). Jon Meacham, *Destiny and Power: The American Odyssey of George Herbert Walker Bush* (New York: Random House, 2015), is rich on the relationship between father and son; quotes from interviews with both men make this book indispensable. The first stab at a comparative biography of the two Bush presidents is Mark K. Updegrove, *The Last Republicans: Inside the Extraordinary Relationship between George H. W. Bush and George W. Bush* (New York: HarperCollins, 2017), which offers a worthy survey of the secondary sources. Add to this John Robert Greene, *The Presidency of George H. W. Bush,* 2nd ed., revised and expanded (Lawrence: University Press of Kansas, 2015); Timothy Naftali, *George H. W. Bush* (New York: Times Books, 2007); and Todd Purdum, "43+41=84," *Vanity Fair,* September 2006.

Also useful on the background of Bush the younger are Doro Bush Koch, *My Father, My President: A Personal Account of the Life of George H. W. Bush* (New York: Grand Central Publishing, 2006); Warren Goldstein, *William Sloane Coffin, Jr.: A Holy Impatience* (New Haven, CT: Yale University Press, 2004); Myra G. Gutin, *Barbara Bush: Presidential Matriarch* (Lawrence: University Press of Kansas, 2008); and Susan Page, *The Matriarch: Barbara Bush and the Making of an American Dynasty* (New York: Twelve, 2019).

Bush's two terms as Texas governor deserve a serious scholarly study. Molly Ivins and Lou Dubose, *Shrub: The Short but Happy Political Life of George W. Bush* (New York: Vintage Books, 2000), is a nasty book that is full of unsubstantiated insults. Yet the book was influential toward substantiating a negative opinion of Bush as governor, largely because Ivins was eminently quotable. On the 1994 gubernatorial campaign of Ann Richards, see Patricia Kilday Hart, "Little Did We Know," *Texas Monthly,* November 2004. For a worthy summary of the 1998 Gary Mauro campaign, see Helen Thorpe, "Less Is Mauro," *Texas Monthly,* August 1998. While virulently anti-Bush, Ben Barnes, *Barn Burning, Barn Building: Tales of a Political Life, from LBJ through George W. Bush and Beyond* (Albany, TX: Bright Sky Press, 2006), is an important source toward an understanding of Bush's service in the Air National Guard. See also Dave McNeely and Jim Henderson, *Bob Bullock: God Bless Texas* (Austin: University of Texas Press, 2008).

To get a proper perspective on the presidential election of 2000, two excellent books should be read in tandem. Jeffrey Toobin, *Too Close to Call: The Thirty-Six-Day Battle to Decide the 2000 Election* (New York: Random House, 2002), does not have the benefit of scholarly distance, but because the author had access to all the principals involved and was on the ground in Florida himself during the crisis over the recount, it offers both original reporting and grace of writing. To the extent that Toobin offers a thesis, it is that he blames the Democrats'—and Gore's—lack of a killer political instinct for much of their loss. Charles L. Zelden, *Bush v. Gore: Expos-*

*ing the Hidden Crisis in American Democracy* (Lawrence: University Press of Kansas, 2010), is also engagingly written but with a depth of scholarly research that Toobin cannot match. Zelden wants his reader to concentrate less on the result of either the case or the election and more on the fact that in his view, the entire American electoral system is broken, with *Bush v. Gore* but a symptom of that dysfunction.

Al Gore has yet to write a memoir. For Bill Clinton's thoughts on the Gore campaign, see Taylor Branch, *The Clinton Tapes: Wrestling History with the President* (New York: Simon & Schuster, 2009). Clinton's *My Life* (New York: Alfred A. Knopf, 2004), is less than helpful. John McCain's campaign autobiography, *Faith of My Fathers: A Family Memoir* (New York: Random House, 1999), is both moving in its telling of McCain's captivity in North Vietnam and politically motivated in its use of that tale to show he has the personal qualifications and strengths to assume the presidency. McCain's *The Restless Wave: Good Times, Just Causes, Great Fights, and Other Appreciations* (New York: Simon & Schuster, 2018), has little on the election of 2000 but is stronger on 2008. Ralph Nader, *Crashing the Party: Taking on the Corporate Government in an Age of Surrender* (New York: Thomas Dunne Books, 2002), is a polemic of marginal value. More helpful is Ralph Nader, "My Untold Story," *Brill's Content*, February 2001, 100–103, which bemoans the lack of media coverage given the Green Party's candidate and documents his campaign's unsuccessful attempts to get that coverage. See also Michael C. Herron and Jeffrey B. Lewis, "Did Ralph Nader Spoil Al Gore's Presidential Bid? A Ballot-Level Study of Green and Reform Party Voters in the 2000 Presidential Election," *Quarterly Journal of Political Science*. 2, no. 5 (2007): 205–226.

Katherine Harris, *Center of the Storm: Practicing Principled Leadership in Times of Crisis* (Nashville, TN: Wind Books, 2002), is a combination memoir and self-help tome. David Boies, *Courting Justice: From NY Yankees v. Major League Baseball to Bush v. Gore, 1997–2000* (New York: Miramax Books, 2004), is useful. Less useful is Stuart Stevens, *The Big Enchilada: Campaign Adventures from the Cockeyed Optimists from Texas Who Won the Biggest Prize in Politics* (New York: Free Press, 2001). The reminiscences of journalists who covered the campaign include Frank Bruni, *Ambling into History: The Unlikely Odyssey of George W. Bush* (New York: HarperCollins, 2002), and Joe Klein, *Politics Lost: How American Democracy Was Trivialized by People Who Think You're Stupid* (New York: Doubleday, 2006). Useful for this subject, as well as several others, is Peter Baker and Susan Glasser, *The Man Who Ran Washington: The Life and Times of James A. Baker III* (New York: Doubleday, 2020).

Kathleen Hall Jamieson and Paul Waldman, eds., *Electing the President, 2000: The Insiders' View* (Philadelphia: University of Pennsylvania Press, 2001), offers the edited transcripts of a ten-hour seminar held at the Annenberg School for Communication at the University of Pennsylvania on 10 February 2001. Overall, the discussion, which featured political operatives from both the Bush and the Gore campaign, is very revealing. John Harwood and Gerald F. Seib, *Pennsylvania Avenue: Profiles in Backroom Power* (New York: Random House, 2008), includes sketches of many of the key political operatives on both sides of the campaign. The best single statement of Bush's foreign policy goals in 2000 can be found in Condoleezza Rice, "Campaign 2000: Promoting the National Interest," *Foreign Affairs* 79, no.

1 (January/February 2000): 45–62. On financing the election, Charles Lewis, *The Buying of the President 2000* (New York: Avon Books, 2000), is indispensable.

E. J. Dionne and William Kristol, eds., *BUSH V. GORE: The Court Cases and the Commentary* (Washington, DC: Brookings Institution Press, 2001), offers a handy compendium of all the relevant court decisions, as well as a strong, reasonably balanced taste of the relevant press commentary. Jeffrey Toobin is harsher on the Supreme Court's role in the election in *The Nine: Inside the Secret World of the Supreme Court* (New York: Doubleday, 2007) than he is in *Too Close to Call* (above). Richard A. Posner, *Breaking the Deadlock: The 2000 Election, the Constitution, and the Courts* (Princeton, NJ: Princeton University Press, 2001), is highly statistical and burdened with technical prose. See also John Paul Stevens, *The Making of a Justice: Reflections on My First 94 Years* (Boston: Little, Brown, 2019).

While offering useful demographic data, Gerald M. Pomper, "The 2000 Presidential Election: Why Gore Lost," *Political Science Quarterly* 116, no. 2 (2001), is indicative of the anger felt by most of academe at the election of Bush ("The presidential election of 2000 stands at best as a paradox, at worst as a scandal, of American democracy. . . . The final decision was made not by 105 million voters, but by a 5–4 majority of the unelected U.S. Supreme Court, issuing a tainted and partisan verdict"). Less useful polemics are Alan Dershowitz, *Supreme Injustice: How the High Court Hijacked Election 2000* (New York: Oxford University Press, 2001); and Bill Sammon, *At Any Cost: How Al Gore Tried to Steal the Election* (Washington, DC: Regnery, 2001).

The best book on the transition from the Clinton to the Bush presidency is John P. Burke, *Becoming President: The Bush Transition, 2000–2003* (Boulder, CO: Lynne Rienner, 2004). As its title suggests, the book is not just on the transition but is also the first, and to date the only, scholarly look at the management of the first-term Bush White House.

To date, there are few surveys of the presidency of George W. Bush, and none that make use of the vast amount of archival material at the George W. Bush Presidential Library. The researcher has had to make do with instant histories, the works of journalists, and anti-Bush screeds. The first journalist to tackle a survey of the achievements of the administration was Ronald Kessler, *A Matter of Character: Inside the White House of George W. Bush* (New York: Sentinel, 2004), which is a pro-Bush hagiography. Next was Robert Draper, *Dead Certain: The Presidency of George W. Bush* (New York: Free Press, 2007). Draper employs a familiar, chatty, often hyperbolic tone that all too often takes stabs at pop psychology. Kessler's and Draper's works were supplanted by Peter Baker, *Days of Fire: Bush and Cheney in the White House* (New York: Doubleday, 2013), an indispensable starting point written by a journalist who covered the Bush White House. Its title can be misleading—this is more a straight survey of the Bush administration, with an occasional detour into the influence of Cheney. Fred Barnes, *Rebel in Chief: Inside the Bold and Controversial Presidency of George W. Bush* (New York: Crown Forum, 2006), offers the provocative thesis that Bush was a renegade who "operat[ed] in Washington like the head of a small occupying army of insurgents" (14). Lou Cannon and Carl M. Cannon, *Reagan's Disciple: George W. Bush's Troubled Quest for a*

*Presidential Legacy* (New York: Public Affairs, 2008), argues that Bush deliberately modeled his presidency after that of Ronald Reagan. *Washington Post* journalist Bob Woodward's four volumes on the inner workings of the Bush presidency are in a category of their own. Published in real time (often mirroring his reporting in the *Post*), Woodward's books are both strengthened by and burdened by the endless details of meetings that show the author's inside access. The first, *Bush at War* (New York: Simon and Schuster, 2002), is full of praise for Bush as a strong leader; the second, *Plan of Attack* (New York, Simon & Schuster, 2004), is more nuanced in its assessment. But by the third, *State of Denial: Bush at War, Part III* (New York: Simon & Schuster, 2008), and the fourth, *The War Within: A Secret White House History, 2006–2008* (New York: Simon & Schuster, 2008), the author treats Bush in a much more critical light. Eric Draper, *Front Row Seat: A Photographic Portrait of the Presidency of George W. Bush* (Austin: University of Texas Press, 2013), is also quite useful as a survey.

Of the few scholarly surveys of the Bush tenure, the most provocative is Stephen F. Knott, *Rush to Judgment: George W. Bush, the War on Terror, and His Critics* (Lawrence: University Press of Kansas, 2012), which serves as a spirited defense of Bush and his administration based almost exclusively on a synthesis of secondary sources. Gary C. Jacobson, *A Divider, Not a Uniter: George W. Bush and the American People* (New York: Pearson-Longman, 2008), is a highly statistical but intriguing study of the partisan divide, which the author argues was ushered in by Bush. Also thoughtful but concentrating on a specific area of foreign policy is Michael F. Cairo, *The Gulf: The Bush Presidencies and the Middle East* (Lexington: University Press of Kentucky, 2012). The early—and predominately negative—observations of academics can be found in several edited collections: Jon Kraus, Kevin J. McMahon, and David Rankin, eds., *Transformed by Crisis: The Presidency of George W. Bush and American Politics* (New York: Palgrave Macmillan, 2004); Steven E. Schier, ed., *High Risk and Big Ambition: The Presidency of George W. Bush* (Pittsburgh: University of Pittsburgh Press, 2004); Robert Maranto, Douglas M. Brattebo, and Tom Lansford, eds., *The Second Term of George W. Bush: Prospects and Perils* (New York: Palgrave Macmillan, 2006); George C. Edwards III, ed., *The Polarized Presidency of George W. Bush* (New York: Oxford University Press, 2007); Robert Maranto, Tom Lansford, and Jeremy Johnson, eds., *Judging Bush* (Stanford, CA: Stanford University Press, 2009); and Steven E. Schier, ed., *Ambition and Division: Legacies of the George W. Bush Presidency* (Pittsburgh: University of Pittsburgh Press, 2009).

Of the many journalistic pokes at Bush and his presidency, the funniest are Maureen Dowd, *Bushworld: Enter at Your Own Risk* (New York: G. P. Putnam's, 2004); Molly Ivins and Lou Dubose, *Bushwhacked: Life in George W. Bush's America* (New York: Vintage, 2004); and Al Franken, *Lies and the Lying Liars Who Tell Them: A Fair and Balanced Look at the Right* (New York: Dutton, 2003). Anti-Bush screeds include David Corn, *The Lies of George W. Bush: Mastering the Politics of Deception* (New York: Crown, 2003); John W. Dean, *Worse Than Watergate: The Secret Presidency of George W. Bush* (New York: Little, Brown, 2004); J. H. Hatfield, *Fortunate Son: George W. Bush and the Making of an American President* (Brooklyn, NY: Soft Skull Press, 2002); Mark Crispin Miller, *Cruel and Unusual: Bush/Cheney's New World Order* (New York: W. W. Norton, 2004); and Paul Waldman, *Fraud: The Strategy be-*

*hind the Bush Lies and Why the Media Didn't Tell You* (Naperville, IL: Sourcebooks, 2004).

The indisputable and controversial influence of Dick Cheney in the Bush White House has led to a number of books that survey the Bush presidency from the point of view of the Cheney vice presidency. After consulting Baker, *Days of Fire*, one should consult the work of journalist Barton Gellman, *Angler: The Cheney Vice Presidency* (New York: Penguin, 2008), a book that is reasonably subtle in its assessments. Less so is Shirley Anne Warshaw, *The Co-presidency of Bush and Cheney* (Stanford, CA: Stanford University Press, 2009), whose thesis is in its title and is unremittingly critical of both its subjects. Less helpful is the shrill and condescending David Dubose and Jake Bernstein, *Vice: Dick Cheney and the Hijacking of the American Presidency* (New York: Random House, 2006).

There is also room for a scholarly study of the Bush administrative presidency. The closest available is found in Burke, *Becoming President* (above), as well as the material dealing with Bush in Ivo H. Daalder and I. M. Destler, *In the Shadow of the Oval Office: National Security Advisers and the Presidents They Served—from JFK to George W. Bush* (New York: Simon & Schuster, 2009).

To fully understand the conservatism of the Bush era, one can do no better than to read three outstanding studies in tandem: Donald T. Critchlow, *The Conservative Ascendancy: How the Republican Right Rose to Power in Modern America*, 2nd ed., revised and expanded (Lawrence: University Press of Kansas, 2011); E. J. Dionne Jr., *Why the Right Went Wrong: Conservatism—from Goldwater to the Tea Party and Beyond* (New York: Simon & Schuster, 2016); and Frances Fitzgerald, *The Evangelicals: The Struggle to Shape America* (New York: Simon & Schuster, 2017). Less helpful is John Micklethwait, *The Right Nation: Conservative Power in America* (New York: Penguin, 2004).

Bush refined his theory of "compassionate conservativism" after reading the works of Michael Novak (*Democracy and Mediating Structures: A Theological Inquiry* [Washington, DC: American Enterprise Institute Press, 1980] and *The Spirit of Democratic Capitalism* [New York: Simon & Schuster, 1982]) and Marvin Olasky (*The Tragedy of American Compassion* [New York: Regnery, 1994] and *Compassionate Conservatism: What It Is, What It Does, and How It Can Transform America* [New York: Free Press, 2000]). On the question of whether or not Bush was a conservative in the tradition of Ronald Reagan, see Cannon and Cannon, *Reagan's Disciple* (above), and Bill Keller, "Reagan's Son: The Radical Presidency of George W. Bush," *New York Times Magazine*, 26 January 2003.

The best survey of Bush's domestic policies is John D. Graham, *Bush on the Home Front: Domestic Policy Triumphs and Setbacks* (Bloomington: Indiana University Press, 2010). Although Graham served in the Office of Management and Budget from 2001 to 2006, this is neither a memoir nor a full-throated defense of Bush's policy—it is well researched and judicious in its tone. James Jeffords, *An Independent Man: Adventures of a Public Servant* (New York: Simon & Schuster, 2007), speaks to the first tax cut and how it played a role in his switch to the Democratic Party. The faith-based initiative is addressed in "The Jesus Factor," *Frontline* (PBS), originally broadcast 29 April 2004. Jay P. Lefkowitz, "Stem Cells and the President—An Inside Account," *Commentary*, January 2008, offers excellent detail on the president's decision-making process. The best study of Bush's education reforms is Patrick J. McGuinn, *No Child Left Behind and the Transformation of Federal Education Policy, 1965–2005* (Lawrence: University Press of Kansas, 2006). Edward M. Kennedy, *True Compass: A Memoir* (New York: Twelve, 2009), is also useful on the genesis of No Child Left Behind. Charles Blahous served as the executive director of the President's Commission to Strengthen Social Security; his *Social Security: The Unfinished Work* (Stanford, CA: Hoover Institution Press, 2010) offers a strong survey of the administration's reform initiative. Jay P. Lefkowitz, "AIDS and the President—An Inside Account," *Commentary*, January 2009, is indispensable for tracing the presidential decision-making that led to the President's Emergency Plan for AIDS Relief (PEPFAR).

The best survey of America's coming to grips with post–World War II terrorism is Timothy Naftali, *Blindspot: The Secret History of American Counterterrorism* (New York: Basic Books, 2005). The best place to begin a study of the origins of Al-Qaida is Lawrence Wright's brilliant and readable *The Looming Tower: Al-Qaida and the Road to 9/11* (New York: Alfred A. Knopf, 2011). James D. Boys, *Clinton's War on Terror: Redefining U.S. Security Strategy, 1993–2001* (Boulder, CO: Lynne Rienner, 2018), establishes the methods employed by Bush's predecessor to deal with domestic and foreign terrorism. See also Steve Coll, *The bin Ladens: An Arabian Family in the American Century* (New York: Penguin, 2008). *The Report of the Joint Congressional Inquiry into Intelligence Community Activities before and after the Terrorist Attacks of September 11, 2001* (107th Cong., 2d Sess., S. Rep. No. 107-351; H.R. Rep. No. 107-792) can be found online at https://www.intelligence.senate.gov/sites/default/files/documents/CRPT-107srpt351-5.pdf. The twenty-eight pages of the report that were originally redacted upon its release, and which address possible Saudi complicity in the attacks, are now available at https://web.archive.org/web/20190503002405/https://28pagesdotorg.files.wordpress.com/2016/08/declasspart4.pdf. The complete report of the National Commission on Terrorist Attacks upon the United States ("the 9/11 Commission") is available in print (New York: W. W. Norton, 2004) and online at http://www.9-11commission.gov/report/911Report.pdf. An abbreviated version of the report, *The 9/11 Commission Report with Related Documents* (New York: Bedford/St. Martin's, 2007), edited by historian Ernest R. May, who was also a member of the commission's staff, is an invaluable source. The memoir of the two chairs of the commission, Tom Kean and Lee Hamilton, *Without Precedent: The Inside Story of the 9/11 Commission* (New York: Alfred A. Knopf, 2006), is largely the story of what the authors viewed as White House intransigence toward their efforts. Michael Allen, *Blinking Red: Crisis and Compromise in American Intelligence after 9/11* (New York: Potomac Books, 2013), is an enhanced memoir (the author worked on the Intelligence Reform and Terrorism Prevention Act (IRTPA) as a White House legislative aide) and clearly tells the story of the creation of the legislation in response to *The 9/11 Commission Report*.

The best popular history of the events of 11 September 2001 is Mitchell Zuckoff, *Fall and Rise: The Story of 9/11* (New York: Harper, 2019). Other helpful views into the human suffering of that day include Jim Dwyer and Kevin Flynn, *102 Minutes: The Untold Story of the Fight to Survive Inside the Twin Towers* (New York: Times Books, 2005), and William Langewiesche, *American Ground: Unbuilding the*

*World Trade Center* (New York: North Point Press, 2002). Kate Andersen Brower, *The Residence: Inside the Private World of the White House* (New York: HarperCollins, 2016), includes a fascinating section on the reaction of the White House staff to the attacks. Rudolph Giuliani, *Leadership* (above), gives insight into the response to the attacks in New York City.

The best general survey of the War on Terror in both Afghanistan and Iraq is by journalist Peter Bergen, *The Longest War: The Enduring Conflict between America and Al-Qaeda* (New York: Free Press, 2011). Other surveys of the War on Terror tend to underreport the war in Afghanistan. They are represented by Terry H. Anderson, whose book *Bush's Wars* (New York: Oxford University Press, 2011) purports to study all of the conflicts that occurred during the Bush administration, but has only a few pages on Afghanistan. The best study of the war in Afghanistan is Seth G. Jones, *In the Graveyard of Empires: America's War in Afghanistan* (New York: W. W. Norton, 2009). The works of Steve Coll on the role of the CIA in Afghanistan—*Ghost Wars: The Secret History of the CIA, Afghanistan, and bin Laden, from the Soviet Invasion to September 10, 2001* (New York: Penguin, 2004), and *Directorate S: The CIA and America's Secret Wars in Afghanistan and Pakistan* (New York: Penguin, 2018)—are indispensable. Also useful is Joshua Partlow, *A Kingdom of Their Own: The Family Karzai and the Afghan Disaster* (New York: Alfred A. Knopf, 2016). For the point of view of the American ambassador to Afghanistan (2005–2007), see Ronald E. Neumann, *The Other War: Winning and Losing in Afghanistan* (Washington, DC: Potomac Press, 2009), and his *Three Embassies, Four Wars: A Personal Memoir* (Xlibris.com, 2017). For the reminiscences of the commander of the CIA-led incursion into Afghanistan (Operation Jawbreaker), see Gary S. Schroen, *First In: An Insider's Account of How the CIA Spearheaded the War in Afghanistan* (New York: Ballantine Books, 2005). Flattering views of the role played by the intelligence community in the War on Terror include Ronald Kessler, *The CIA at War: Inside the Secret Campaign against Terror* (New York: St. Martin's Press, 2003). More critical views include James Bamford, *A Pretext for War: 9/11, Iraq, and the Abuse of America's Intelligence Agencies* (New York: Doubleday, 2004).

No scholarly survey of the war in Iraq has yet been written. Those most useful are contemporary works. The best available study continues to be the two volumes by Michael R. Gordon and General Bernard E. Trainor: *Cobra II: The Inside Story of the Invasion and Occupation of Iraq* (New York: Pantheon Books, 2006) and *The Endgame: The Inside Story of the Struggle for Iraq, from George W. Bush to Barack Obama* (New York: Pantheon Books, 2012). George Packer, *The Assassins' Gate: America in Iraq* (New York: Farrar, Straus and Giroux, 2005), is a thoughtful and accessible work of reporting. Thomas E. Ricks, *Fiasco: The American Military Adventure in Iraq* (New York: Penguin, 2006), is less a balanced treatment and more of an indictment of the Bush administration's actions. The best available study of the administration's ramp-up to war is Robert Draper, *To Start a War: How the Bush Administration Took America into Iraq* (New York: Penguin, 2020). See also Ron Suskind, *The One Percent Doctrine: Deep Inside America's Pursuit of Its Enemies since 9/11* (New York: Simon & Schuster, 2007).

Along with the memoirs of virtually every member of the Bush administration listed above, the student of the War on Terror should consult a significant subgenre of works: the memoirs of Bush's commanding generals, most of which were written to explain their side of either their dismissal or their demotion. They include Daniel P. Bolger, *Why We Lost: A General's Inside Account of the Iraq and Afghanistan Wars* (New York: Houghton Mifflin Harcourt, 2014); General Tommy Franks, *American Soldier* (New York: Regan Books, 2004); Gen. Stanley McChrystal, *My Share of the Task: A Memoir* (New York: Portfolio, 2014); General Richard B. Myers, *Eyes on the Horizon: Serving on the Front Lines of National Security* (New York: Threshold Editions, 2009); Lt. Gen. Ricardo S. Sanchez, *Wiser in Battle: A Soldier's Story* (New York: HarperCollins, 2008); and General Hugh Shelton, *Without Hesitation: The Odyssey of an American Warrior* (New York: St. Martin's Press, 2010).

For a generally positive perspective on the coalition with Great Britain, see Tony Blair, *A Journey: My Political Life* (New York: Alfred A. Knopf, 2010). For a useful counterpoint to Blair's view, see Alastair Campbell, *The Blair Years: The Alastair Campbell Diaries* (New York: Alfred A. Knopf, 2007). For a less than charitable assessment of the US role in Iraq from the point of view of the French, see Jacques Chirac, *My Life in Politics* (New York: Palgrave Macmillan, 2012).

Begin a study of the constitutional and legal justifications for the administration's actions in the War on Terror with two excellent studies, both of which are highly critical of the Bush administration: historian Karen J. Greenberg, *Rogue Justice: The Making of the Security State* (New York: Broadway Books, 2016), and journalist Eric Lichtblau, *Bush's Law: The Remaking of American Justice* (New York: Pantheon Books, 2008). John Yoo, *War by Any Other Means: An Insider's Account of the War on Terror* (New York: Atlantic Monthly Press, 2006), is much less a traditional memoir than it is a defense of the author's actions while in the Office of Legal Counsel. Less helpful was John Yoo, *The Powers of War and Peace: The Constitution and Foreign Affairs after 9/11* (Chicago: University of Chicago Press, 2005). Jack Goldsmith, *The Terror Presidency: Law and Judgement inside the Bush Administration* (New York: W. W. Norton, 2007), is less a full memoir than an exegesis on the May 2004 imbroglio on the reauthorization of Stellar Wind. For this, see also Jeffrey Rosen, "Conscience of a Conservative," *New York Times Magazine*, 9 September 2007. Also of value was Howard Ball, *Bush, the Detainees, and the Constitution* (Lawrence: University Press of Kansas, 2007). Less helpful was Harold H. Bruff, *Bad Advice: Bush's Lawyers in the War on Terror* (Lawrence: University Press of Kansas, 2009). On the issue of detention, see Karen Greenberg, *The Least Worst Place: Guantanamo's First 100 Days* (New York: Oxford University Press, 2009), for a prescient study of the transformation of "Camp X-Ray" to "Gitmo."

Critical to understanding the creation, maintenance, and evolution of the enhanced interrogation program is *Report of the Senate Select Committee on Intelligence. Committee Study of the Central Intelligence Agency's Detention and Interrogation Program. Together with Foreword by Chairman Weinstein and Additional and Minority Views* (113th Cong., 2d Sess., 9 December 2014; cited as *SSCI* in notes in this book). A careful reading of this report must be joined with Bill Harlow, ed., *Rebuttal: The CIA Responds to the Senate Intelligence Committee's Study of Its Detention and Interrogation Program* (Annapolis, MD: Naval Institute Press, 2015). What have become known as the "torture memos"—the correspondence between the president, the

White House Counsel's Office, the Department of Defense and its legal counsel, and members of the uniformed military dealing with the creation, maintenance, and evolution of the Enhanced Interrogation Program—are well preserved on the internet, but without guidance from a site or a collection, the researcher would have to know the particulars of the memo they wish to consult, that is, the name of correspondents and date of creation. The researcher is not helped by the fact that there is no single source—published or online—that contains all of the extant "torture memos." The most comprehensive published source is Karen J. Greenberg and Joshua L. Dratel, *The Torture Papers: The Road to Abu Ghraib* (New York: Cambridge University Press, 2005; cited as *TTP* in notes in this book). It includes twenty-eight relevant memos, as well as nine relevant reports from various investigations and committees. Care must be taken with this collection, however—strictly speaking, several of the memos deal not with the issue of enhanced interrogation but with other issues that some scholars might find to be related to that issue, such as the expansion of the presidential war-making power, the application of the Geneva Accords in general, and the habeas corpus protection of detainees. David Cole, *The Torture Memos: Rationalizing the Unthinkable* (New York: New Press, 2009), includes only seven memos (three of which—memos for the CIA's John Rizzo—are not in *TTP*). "The Interrogation Documents: Debating U.S. Policy and Methods," National Security Archive, https://nsarchive2.gwu.edu/NSAEBB/NSAEBB127/, is useful as a searchable online source. Less inclusive than *TTP*, it nevertheless holds three memos from the Department of Defense that are not found in *TTP*. It is also searchable, and it includes a more up-to-date summary of events. Less helpful (more difficult to navigate) is "The Torture Database," American Civil Liberties Union, http://www.thetorturedatabase.org/search/apachesolr_search. Andrew Cohen, "The Torture Memos, Ten Years Later," *The Atlantic*, 6 February 2012, offers a useful reconstruction of several of the memos.

On Operation Stellar Wind, see James Risen, *State of War: The Secret History of the CIA and the Bush Administration* (New York: Free Press, 2006).

Robert G. Kaufman, *In Defense of the Bush Doctrine* (Lexington: University Press of Kentucky, 2007), is an articulate defense of the policy of preventative war. Arthur M. Schlesinger Jr., *War and the American Presidency* (New York: W. W. Norton, 2004), is an equally thoughtful essay in opposition. Michael W. Doyle, *Striking First: Preemption and Prevention in International Conflict* (Princeton, NJ: Princeton University Press, 2008), is a series of lectures dealing with the subtleties of the two disparate theories.

For a look at the neoconservative belief that Saddam Hussein needed to be neutralized, see Paul Wolfowitz, "Victory Came Too Easily: Review of Rick Atkinson, *Crusade: The Untold Story of the Gulf War*," *National Interest*, no. 35 (April 1994): 87–92. Other books that supported the overthrow of Saddam include Lawrence F. Kaplan and William Kristol, *The War over Iraq: Saddam's Tyranny and America's Mission* (San Francisco: Encounter Books, 2003), and Kenneth M. Pollack, *The Threatening Storm: The Case for Invading Iraq* (New York: Random House, 2002).

Of the many criticisms of the administration's "message" on the war, see Michael Isikoff and David Corn, *Hubris: The Inside Story of Spin, Scandal, and the Selling of the Iraq War* (New York: Three Rivers Press, 2007), and Frank Rich, *The Greatest Story Ever Sold: The Decline and Fall of Truth from 9/11 to Katrina* (New York: Penguin, 2006), a book that is distinguished by its outstanding appendix/timeline.

A study of postinvasion Iraq and the rise of the insurgency should begin with Gordon W. Rudd, *Reconstructing Iraq: Regime Change, Jay Garner, and the ORHA Story* (Lawrence: University Press of Kansas, 2011). Then turn to L. Paul Bremer, *My Year in Iraq* (above), and Greg Muttit, *Fuel on the Fire: Oil and Politics in Occupied Iraq* (New York: New Press, 2012). Useful books on the insurgency include Ahmed S. Hashim, *Insurgency and Counter-insurgency in Iraq* (Ithaca, NY: Cornell University Press, 2006); Mark Etherington, *Revolt on the Tigris: The Al Sadr Uprising and the Governing of Iraq* (Ithaca, NY: Cornell University Press, 2005); and Bard O'Neill, *Insurgency and Terrorism: Inside Modern Revolutionary Warfare* (Washington, DC: Brassey's, 1990). Jessica Stern and J. M. Berger, *ISIS: The State of Terror* (New York: HarperCollins, 2015), offers a useful background on Zarqawi. See also Will Bardenwerper, *The Prisoner in His Palace: Saddam Hussein, His American Guards, and What History Leaves Unsaid* (New York: Scribner, 2017).

On the opposition to the War in Iraq by the Republican Realists, see Bartholomew Sparrow, *The Strategist: Brent Scowcroft and the Call of National Security* (New York: Public Affairs, 2015) which offers useful background on Scowcroft's 15 August 2002 *Wall Street Journal* opinion piece. The findings of James A. Baker III and Lee H. Hamilton, cochairs, *Iraq Study Group Report* (New York: Vintage Books, 2006), sent the Bush administration into fits of apoplexy.

For firsthand observations on the Valerie Plame Wilson affair, see Judith Miller, *The Story: A Reporter's Journey* (New York: Simon & Schuster, 2015); Joseph Wilson, *The Politics of Truth: Inside the Lies That Led to War and Betrayed My Wife's CIA Identity* (New York: Carroll and Graf, 2004); and Valerie Plame Wilson, *Fair Game: My Life as a Spy, My Betrayal by the White House* (New York: Simon & Schuster, 2007). Also helpful is Murray Waas, ed., *The United States v. I. Lewis Libby* (New York: Union Square Press, 2007).

The role played by CBS News in reporting the story of Abu Ghraib is found in Mary Mapes, *Truth and Duty: The Press, the President, and the Privilege of Power* (New York: St. Martin's Press, 2005), and Dan Rather, *Rather Outspoken* (New York: Grand Central Publishing, 2013). Seymour Hersh's series of stories in the *New Yorker*, beginning with "Torture at Abu Ghraib (10 May 2004), as well as his *Chain of Command: The Road from 9/11 to Abu Ghraib* (New York: HarperCollins, 2004), are indispensable. His memory of his reporting of the story, found in *Reporter: A Memoir* (New York: Alfred A. Knopf, 2018), is less revealing.

There are countless books on the soldier's experience in Iraq and Afghanistan. Of those consulted for this book, see Rick Atkinson, *In the Company of Soldiers: A Chronicle of Combat* (New York: Henry Holt, 2004); Dexter Filkins, *The Forever War* (New York: Alfred A, Knopf, 2008); and Bing West, *The Wrong War: Grit, Strategy and the Way Out of Afghanistan* (New York: Random House, 2011).

For a decidedly critical view of Bush's view of presidential power, see Charlie Savage, *Takeover: The Return of the Imperial Presidency and the Subversion of American Democracy* (New York: Little, Brown, 2007). See also Michael J. Berry, "Controversially Executing the Law: George W. Bush and the Constitutional Signing

Statement," *Congress and the Presidency* 36 (2009): 244–271; Philip J. Cooper, *By the Order of the President: The Use and Abuse of Executive Action* (Lawrence: University Press of Kansas, 2002); Brett M. Kavanaugh, "Separation of Powers during the Forty-Fourth Presidency and Beyond," *Minnesota Law Review* 103, no. 5 (2009: 1454–1486; and Jeremy M. Sharp, "Congressional Action on Iraq, 1990–2002: A Compilation of Legislation" (Congressional Research Service, 2002). One of the first statements of the unitary theory of the executive can be found in the minority report (issued under then representative Dick Cheney's name) of the Iran-Contra Report—see Joel Brinkley and Stephen Engelberg, eds., *Report of the Congressional Committees Investigating the Iran Contra Affair, with the Minority Views* (New York: Times Books, 1988). Also see John F. Freie, *The Making of the Postmodern Presidency from Ronald Reagan to Barack Obama* (Boulder, CO: Paradigm, 2011), 124–125; Andrew Rudalevige, "Executive Branch Management and Presidential Unilateralism: Centralization and the Issuance of Executive Orders," *Congress and the Presidency* 42 (2015): 342–365; and Robert J. Spitzer, "The Commander in Chief: Power and Constitutional Invention in the Bush Administration," in *The Presidency and the Challenge of Democracy*, ed. Michael A. Genovese and Lori Cox Han (New York: Palgrave Macmillan, 2006).

Any study of the Supreme Court during Bush's tenure should begin with the literature on *Bush v. Gore*, discussed above. David Cole, "The Liberal Legacy of *Bush v. Gore*," *Georgetown Law Journal* 94 (2006): 1427–1474, offers a provocative assessment of the liberalization of the Court after 2001. Jan Crawford Greenberg, *Supreme Conflict: The Inside Story of the Struggle for Control of the United States Supreme Court* (New York: Penguin, 2007), offers the best view on the drama surrounding the nominations of John Roberts, Harriet Miers, and Samuel Alito. Jeffrey Toobin, *The Nine* (above) offers insider information on Bush's 2005 court picks. Allen A. Ryan, *The 9/11 Terror Cases: Constitutional Challenges in the War against Al Qaida* (Lawrence: University Press of Kansas, 2015), is the standard book on its subject. From inside the Court, John Paul Stevens, *The Making of a Justice: Reflections on My First 94 Years* (Boston: Little, Brown, 2019), was useful. Less revealing was Stephen Breyer, *The Court and the World: American Law and the New Global Realities* (New York: Alfred A. Knopf, 2015). Helpful biographies and studies on the justices include Joan Biskupic, *The Chief: The Life and Turbulent Times of Chief Justice John Roberts* (New York: Basic Books, 2019); Frank J. Colucci, *Justice Kennedy's Jurisprudence: The Full and Necessary Meaning of Liberty* (Lawrence: University Press of Kansas, 2009); and Evan Thomas, *First: Sandra Day O'Connor* (New York: Random House, 2019). Less useful was Jane Sherron De Hart, *Ruth Bader Ginsberg: A Life* (New York: Alfred A. Knopf, 2018).

As was the case with the 2000 election, the Annenberg School for Communication at the University of Pennsylvania held a two-day symposium at the end of the presidential election of 2004, featuring the key players from the campaign staffs on both sides. These proceedings, published as Kathleen Hall Jamieson, ed., *Electing the President, 2004: The Insiders' View* (Philadelphia: University of Pennsylvania Press, 2006), are a key primary source. *A Call to Service: My Vision for a Better America* (New York: Viking, 2003) is John Kerry's campaign autobiography; his second volume of memoirs, *Every Day is Extra* (New York: Simon & Schuster, 2018), offers insight into his campaign. Ed Gillespie, Republican operative and chairman of the Republican National Committee, offers far less insight into the campaign in his *Winning Right: Campaign Politics and Conservative Policies* (New York: Threshold Editions, 2006).

There is as yet no scholarly survey of the presidential election of 2004. The standard work on the financing of the election is Charles Lewis, *The Buying of the Presidency, 2004* (New York: Perennial, 2004). George C. Edwards III, *Governing by Campaigning: The Politics of the Bush Presidency* (New York: Pearson-Longman, 2007), offers a look at the Bush administration's embracing of the "constant campaign." Joe Klein, *Politics Lost* (above), offers the close observation of a journalist who covered the campaign. Key to understanding Rove's strategy of getting people to vote their values instead of their pocketbook is Thomas Frank, *What's the Matter with Kansas? How Conservatives Won the Heart of America* (New York: Picador, 2004). On the National Guard story, the role played by CBS News is told in Mapes, *Truth and Duty* (above), and Rather, *Rather Outspoken* (above). For her view on the "Mary Cheney Bump," see Mary Cheney, *Now It's My Turn: A Daughter's Chronicle of Political Life* (New York: Threshold, 2006).

The best analysis of the disaster brought by Hurricane Katrina is Douglas Brinkley, *The Great Deluge: Hurricane Katrina, New Orleans, and the Mississippi Gulf Coast* (New York: William Morrow, 2006). See also C. Morgan Babst, *The Floating World* (Chapel Hill, NC: Algonquin Books, 2018). Michael D. Brown, *Deadly Indifference: The Perfect (Political) Storm: Hurricane Katrina, the Bush White House, and Beyond* (Lanham, MD: Taylor Trade Publishing, 2011), is a largely unsuccessful exercise in reputation rehabilitation. The best personal memoir of the Katrina crisis is Sarah M. Brown, *The Yellow House* (New York: Grove Press, 2019).

The memoirs of Ben Bernanke, Timothy Geithner, and Henry Paulson (above) address the issue of the financial crisis of 2008–2009. They also address it in their interesting and compact joint memoir *Firefighting: The Financial Crisis and Its Lessons* (above), which not only apologizes for their missing the warning signs of the meltdown but also points fingers at others they deem more blameworthy. They are not helped by the Yoda of the Federal Reserve Board; in his book *The Age of Turbulence: Adventures in a New World* (New York: Penguin, 2008), Alan Greenspan strains to avoid the topic. For a more objective view of the genesis and development of the crisis, see *The Financial Crisis Inquiry Report: Final Report of the National Commission on the Causes of the Financial and Economic Crisis in the United States* (New York: Public Affairs, 2011). Andrew Ross Sorkin, *Too Big to Fail: The Inside Story of How Wall Street and Washington Fought to Save the Financial Crisis—and Themselves* (New York: Viking, 2009), is the standard work on the fall of Lehman; also useful is Laurence M. Ball, *The Fed and Lehman Brothers: Setting the Record Straight on a Financial Disaster* (New York: Cambridge University Press, 2018). Adam Tooze, *Crashed: How a Decade of Financial Crises Changed the World* (New York: Viking, 2018), is excellent on the international implications of the crisis. In the what-goes-around-comes-around department, see "2008: Ten Years after the Crash, We Are Still Living in the World It Brutally Remade," *New York Magazine*, 13 August 2018.

There is no scholarly survey yet available on the presidential election of 2008. Most of the available literature concentrates, with good reason, on the campaign of Barack Obama. The role of the Bush administration in the campaign is largely ignored—save in the literature on the financial crisis (above). The exception is John McCain, *The Restless Wave* (above), which candidly explores the relationship between his campaign and the Bush White House. John Heilemann and Mark Halperin, *Game Change* (New York: HarperCollins, 2010), although best known for its insiders' look at the choice of Sarah Palin as McCain's running mate, also serves as a worthy survey of the entire election.

# INDEX

*All references to George H. W. Bush have been abbreviated as GHWB. All references to George W. Bush have been abbreviated as GWB.*

Bush, George Walker (GWB) (*continued*)
religious conversion of, 17; and
Condoleezza Rice, 37–38, 39, 135, 256;
and John Roberts, 264–265; and "Rose
Revolution" (2003), 258; and Karl
Rove, 22, 253; and Donald Rumsfeld,
96, 233–234, 257, 283–285; and Russia,
118–119; and Brent Scowcroft, 201–202;
and shootdown order for commercial
airliners on 9/11, 141–142; and Social
Security reform, 13, 34–35, 48, 259–261,
283, 309; on David Souter, 262; and
Spectrum 7, 15–16; and Stem Cell
Research Controversy, 119–123; and
US Supreme Court, 261–267; and tax
reform, 27–28, 33, 41, 43, 106–109;
as teenager, 5–6; and George Tenet,
209, 345n37; and terrorism before
9/11, 135–138, 309–310; and terrorist
attacks of 11 September 2001, 110,
120, 140–145, 168, 340n41; and Texas
Rangers (baseball team), 18–19; and
tort reform (as Texas Governor), 26;
and transition team for GHWB, 18; and
Troubled Asset Relief Program (TARP),
299; and Donald Trump, 305–306; and
Karla Faye Tucker, 28–30; and the
Unitary Executive, 173–174, 309; and
United Nations. 123, 202–204; and use
of military commissions, 177–178; and
Vietnam War, 7–8, 318n18; and visit to
New York City (14 September 2001),
146, 147–149, 253; and the "Vulcans,"
40; and Walter Reed Medical Center
scandal, 291; on "waterboarding,"
188; and Paul Wolfowitz, 150–151; and
Bob Woodward, 196; and World Series
(2001), 170–171; and Yale University,
6–7, 9, 11, 252, 318n16; on Abu Musab
al-Zarqawi, 280; on Abu Zubaydah, 183
Bush, George W., and Iraq War, 224,
288, 310; and attack on Dora Farms,
214–215; attempt to introduce
democracy into Iraq, 257–259; and
congressional force resolution against
Iraq, 204–206; on execute order for
War in Iraq, 352n56; and Saddam
Hussein, 115–116, 194–195, 225–226;
on increasing violence in Iraq, 217,
219–220; on Iraqi Insurgency, 229; letter
to GHWB on commencement of war

in Iraq, 212; and meeting of National
Security Team (15 September 2001,
Camp David), 149–151, 195; and search
for Weapons of mass destruction (Iraq),
220–221, 310; and surge of American
troops in Iraq (2006–2008), 281–282,
285–288, 294, 302, 311; and transfer
of sovereignty in Iraq (30 June 2004),
229–230; and visits to troops in Iraq,
224–225, 253, 302
Bush, George W., speeches, press
conferences, statements, and television
appearances: 25 January 1999
(interview with C-SPAN), 36; July
1999 (Indianapolis), 35; 23 September
1999 (The Citadel), 42; 16 May 2000
(Rancho Cucamonga, California, on
Social Security), 34–35, 114; 3 August
2000 (Acceptance Address, Republican
National Convention, 59; 20 January
2001, First Inaugural Address),
103–104; 20 May 2001 (Commencement
Address, University of Notre Dame),
112–113; 11 September 2001 (from
Emma E. Booker Elementary School,
Sarasota, Florida), 141; 11 September
2001 (Oval Office Address to the
Nation), 144, 151; 14 September
2001 (National Day of Prayer and
Remembrance Service, National
Cathedral), 147, 148; 14 September
2001 (New York City/"Ground Zero,"
148; 17 September 2001 (Statement at
Islamic Center of Washington, 149;
20 September 2001 (Joint Session of
Congress), 151–152; 5 October 2001
(Oval Office Address announcing
beginning of war in Afghanistan),
153; 29 January 2002 (State of the
Union Address), 197, 292; 4 April
2002 (statement, White House Rose
Garden, on Middle East), 200; 1 June
2002 (Commencement address as
US Military Academy), 197–198,
310; 12 September 2002 (speech to
United Nations General Assembly
on Iraq), 203–204; 7 October 2002
(Cincinnati, OH, on Congressional
resolution supporting use of force
in Iraq), 205; 28 January 2003 (State
of the Union Address), 125, 221,